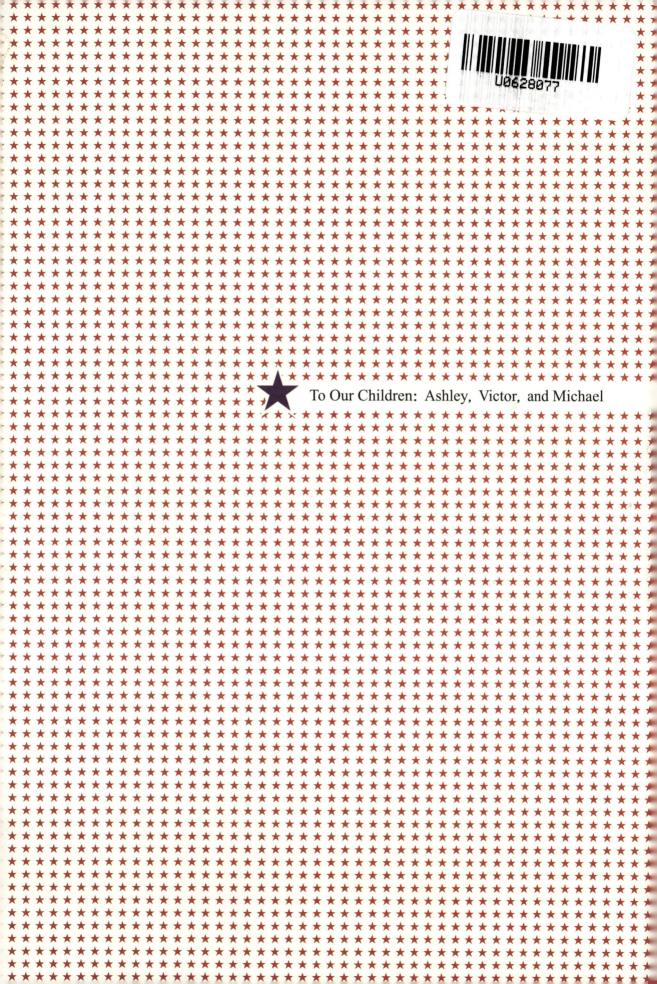

To Our Children: Ashley, Victor, and Michael

每个学英语的人必读，每个赴美国留学、旅游者必阅

美国语言文化知识必备
Essentials of American English and Culture

主　编　伍毅强

副主编　任　彤

湖南师范大学出版社

Preface   序言

Learning English does not merely entail acquiring pronunciation, memorizing vocabulary, and familiarizing oneself with grammar. To be able to speak authentic English and understand English accurately involves acquiring the background of the English language, all aspects of the country and its people and English usages in the appropriate academic, cultural, political, religious, customary, and legal context. Because language is shaped by the interaction between people and society in which language is used, it is important to learn it in the social context. Essentials of American English and Culture was written with the purpose of helping readers deepen their English knowledge and enhance their ability to use the language in practical settings. This guide is a must-have for those learning English, especially if they plan on studying abroad or traveling to the United States or any other English-speaking countries. The book features six chapters that cover culture and customs, schools and studies, vocabulary usages, entertainment, idioms and slants, and daily life.

学习英语不仅仅是学学发音，背背单词和句子，熟悉语法就成了。要学会说地道的英语，准确无误的理解英语，你必须了解英语语言的背景，及使用英语为母语的国家和人的方方面面，这包括文化、政治、宗教、习俗、法律等方面的知识。因为语言是由人和社会之间的互动所决定的，所以在社会环境中学习语言是非常重要的。本《美国语言文化知识必备》一书就是以帮助读者扩大英语知识，增强英语的实用能力为宗旨而编写的。对于学习英语，特别是打算留学美国的学生或出国进修、参观、访问、旅游的人士来说是一本必备的指南。它包括文化风俗篇、学校学习篇、词汇用法篇、文艺娱乐篇、习惯用语篇和生活常识篇等六个部分。

Based on the authors' forty years of experience teaching English in both China and the United States, the book focuses on the difficulties Chinese learners encounter in learning English with question and answer format.This book displays responses to more than 300 questions with strategies for improving reading comprehension, writing, and vocabulary. As known all, the key to learn English efficiently is to master the most commonly used words and phrases so in this book idioms, collocations and usages associated with many commonly used words are selected.

The concept of idioms in English is quite different from those in Chinese,which consists of four characters. English idioms are made up of conventionally used phrases, which are made up of numerous noun phrases, phrasal verbs, adjunctive phrases, and prepositional phrases. These include proverbs, sayings, and expressions used in daily life. English learners searching the dictionary to study these idioms may become overwhelmed due to not knowing which ones are obsolete and there being so many idioms. After all, it is not uncommon for even native English speakers to be unfamiliar with some idioms, such as "New broom sweeps clean."(New officer shows his power 新官上任三把火). Therefore, to make learning idioms and proverbs reasonable, this book narrows them down to about 100 most common proverbs and about 400 most commonly used idioms and usages. Additionally, for many of the responses to the questions,web pages on the given topic are provided for further study.

根据作者在中国和美国四十年从事英语教育的经历，针对中国学生学英语的现状，以问答的形式，着重解答了学习英语中遇到的难点。在三百多个问题的答案中介绍了许多有关如何增强阅读理解、写作、词汇能力的策略，有助于读者提高学习的效率。众所周知，有效学习英语的关键是掌握最常用的单词和短语，因此在本书中选择了许多常用单词相关的习语，搭配和用法。

英语中成语的概念与中文中由四个字组成的成语形式大不相同。英语的成语是由约定俗成的短语构成，如名词短语、短语动词、形容词短语、介词短语等，而且数量众多，日常用语中随时可见。英语中的谚语、习惯用语也不少。但是拿起一本成语、谚语或是习惯用语辞典，往往会让人忘而生畏，无从下手，而且很多成语、谚语和习惯用语早已过时，连现代的英美人都听不懂。如谚语：New broom sweeps clean. (新官上任三把火)。为了使读者学则有用，本书收录了一百个左右最常用的成语和使用的范例，还包括了一百个左右最常用的谚语和习惯用语以及四百多最常用的日常用语。在许多问题的解答中，为读者提供了与问题有关的网页，以便进一步的学习。

While studying in the Foreign Languages Department of Hunan Normal College in the 1970s I was fortunate enough to have received valuable guidance from renowned English professors. My sincere gratitude goes out to Professor Zhou Dingzhi, my first English teacher, Professor Liao Shiqiao, Professor Zhao Zhentao, Professor Liu Zhongde, Professor Zhang Wenting, Professor Ni Peilin, Professor Shen Enrongas well as Professor Tu Rongying, my mother from Hunan University. Their academic excellence and language knowledge have tremendously benefited not only my career but also my personal life.

I also extend my gratitude to Associate Professor Liu Huying from Hunan International Economics University, who made a constructive suggestions and proofreading, and Professor Peng Jinding from Central South University, who offered valuable feedback, during the preparation of this book.

Yiqiang Wu, Ph.D.
2018 in New Jersey, the United States

1970 年代在湖南师范学院外语系学习期间，我很幸运地得到了多位名师的宝贵指教。衷心感谢我的启蒙老师周定之教授，及廖世翘教授，赵甄陶教授，刘重德教授，张文庭教授，倪培霖教授，徐立吾教授、申恩荣教授以及我的母亲湖南大学外语系的涂荣英教授。他们的学术成就和语言知识使我的职业生涯和人生受益匪浅。

本书的编写过程中，湖南涉外经济学院的刘胡英副教授对书提出了宝贵的建议和参加了校对工作，中南大学外语学院彭金定教授提供了很多宝贵的建议，在此表示感谢。

伍毅强博士
2018 年于美国新泽西

五十个州的州名
Names of 50 States

Alabama 阿拉巴马

Alaska 阿拉斯加

Arizona 亚利桑那

Arkansas 阿肯色

California 加利福尼亚

Colorado 科罗拉多

Connecticut 康涅狄格

Delaware 特拉华

Florida 佛罗里达

Georgia 佐治亚

Hawaii 夏威夷

Idaho 爱达荷州

Illinois 伊利诺伊

Indiana 印第安纳

Iowa 爱荷华

Kansas 堪萨斯

Kentucky 肯塔基

Louisiana 路易斯安那

Maine 缅因

Maryland 马里兰

Massachusetts 马萨诸塞

Michigan 密歇根

Minnesota 明尼苏达

Mississippi 密西西比

Missouri 密苏里

Montana 蒙大拿

Nebraska 内布拉斯加

Nevada 内华达

New Hampshire 新罕布什尔

New Jersey 新泽西

New Mexico 新墨西哥

New York 纽约

North Carolina 北卡罗来纳

North Dakota 北达科达

Ohio 俄亥俄

Oklahoma 俄克拉荷马

Oregon 俄勒冈

Pennsylvania 宾夕法尼亚

Rhode Island 罗得岛

South Carolina 南卡罗来纳

South Dakota 南达科达

Tennessee 田纳西

Texas 德克萨斯

Utah 犹他州

Vermont 佛蒙特

Virginia 弗吉尼亚

Washington 华盛顿

West Virginia 西弗吉尼

Wisconsin 威斯康星

Wyoming 怀俄明

CONTENTS
目 录

Culture & Customs
文化风俗篇

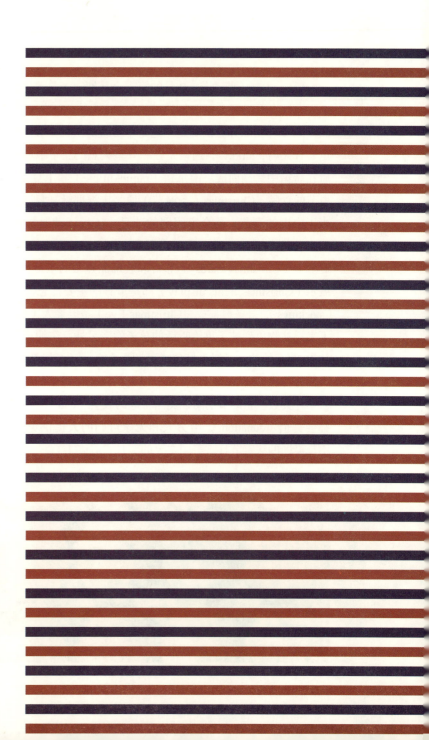

1. Which of the following is not a national holiday of USA?

A. Labor Day

B. Easter

C. Thanksgiving Day

D. Christmas

问题：以下哪个不是美国的法定节日？

答案：B.复活节

    Labor Day（劳动节，9月的第一个星期一）是美国的法定节日，庆祝美国劳工运动和工人在社会及经济方面取得的成就。Thanksgiving Day（感恩节）是在11月的第四个星期四，1941年由联邦立法确定。这是个传统的庆祝丰收之年的节日。感恩节餐桌上的食品一定要有火鸡（turkey），通常是在一只整火鸡的肚子中填充混合食品（stuffing/dressing），然后在烤箱中烤制而成。南瓜饼（pumpkin pie）和土豆泥（mashed potatoes）也是常见的感恩节的食品。Christmas（圣诞节）原是庆祝耶稣基督诞生的节日，是美国最长的假日，相当于中国的春节，是全家团圆的节日。庆祝活动通常在12月25日举行。圣诞节期间美国到处都在播放圣诞音乐和唱颂歌（Christmas Carols）。人们都互相送礼品（gifts）和圣诞贺卡（Christmas Cards）。彩灯和装饰品点缀的圣诞树（Christmas tree）和住宅外的灯火展示（Christmas lights display）都是节日的主要标志。在美国家庭的壁炉旁会挂着长袜子（stockings），等圣诞前夜（Christmas Eve）圣诞老人（Santa Clause）从烟囱（chimney）中下来把礼物放到袜子里给听话的孩子们。另外，纽约市洛克菲勒中心（Rockefeller Center）从1933开始的圣诞树点灯仪式可谓最有名。圣诞树都是每年在全美精心挑选运来纽约的，大部分都在70英尺（21米34）以上。仪式在每年的11月底或12月初举行，前往观赏的人不计其数。圣诞节期间，美国各地的教会（churches）和慈善机构（charity organizations）都会募捐（donation），给穷人和无家可归的人提供免费食品和圣诞餐。Easter（复活节）不是美国的法定节日。美国主要的节日参看表1-1。

表 1-1　美国主要的节日（Major national holidays in the U.S.）

1 January （1 月 1 日）	New Year's Day* （新年）	Welcome the new year with parties starting on New Year's Eve（从除夕晚上开始的迎新年的晚会活动）
3rd Monday in January （1 月第 3 个星期一）	Martin Luther King, Jr. Day* （马丁·路德·金日）	Commemorate the birthday of the African-American civil rights leader Martin Luther King, Jr., who won the Nobel Peace Prize in 1964.（纪念 1964 年获得诺贝尔和平奖的非裔美国人民权利领袖马丁·路德·金的生日。）
14 February （2 月 14 日）	Valentine's Day （情人节）	Celebrate love and romance by exchanging tokens of love（usually cards, candy or gifts）.（通过交换爱的信物——通常是卡片、糖果或礼物来庆祝爱情和营造浪漫氛围。）
3rd Monday of February （2 月第 3 个星期一）	President's Day* （总统节）	Honor past American presidents like George Washington（the nation's first President）and Abraham Lincoln（Civil War hero who helped abolish slavery）.（敬仰美国总统如乔治·华盛顿（美国第一任总统）和亚伯拉罕·林肯（帮助废除了奴隶制的内战英雄）。）
17 March （3 月 17 日）	Saint Patrick's Day （圣帕特里克节）	Celebrate the patron saint of Ireland with parades and parties decorated in Irish green.（以爱尔兰绿色装饰的游行和派对来庆祝爱尔兰守护神。）
1 April （4 月 1 日）	April Fool's Day （愚人节）	Play a clever（but harmless）trick or tell a joke to someone with a good sense of humor.（玩一个聪明但无害的恶作剧，或者以幽默方式给人开一个玩笑。）
Last Monday of May （5 月最后 1 个星期一）	Memorial Day* （阵亡将士纪念日）	Remember the men and women who died while serving in the U.S. Armed Forces.（纪念在美军服务期间死亡的男女将士。）
4 July （7 月 4 日）	Independence Day* （国庆节/独立日）	View public displays of fireworks as Americans mark the date when thirteen U.S. states declared their independence from England on July 4, 1776.（观看美国人庆祝 1776 年 7 月 4 日十三个州宣布从英国独立的烟花表演。）
1st Monday in September （9 月第 1 个星期一）	Labor Day* （劳动节）	Honor the contributions and efforts of hard workers throughout the country.（尊重全国辛勤劳动者的贡献和努力。）
2nd Monday in October （10 月第 2 个星期一）	Columbus Day* （哥伦布日）	Pay tribute to Christopher Columbus, who is traditionally thought of as the discoverer of the Americas in 1492.（向克里斯托弗·哥伦布致敬，传统上认为他在 1492 年发现了美洲。）
11 November （11 月 11 日）	Veterans Day* （退伍军人节）	The Veterans Day is to honor and thank all who served in the United States Armed Forces.（退伍军人节是感谢所有在美国武装部队里服役过的人。）
Last Thursday in November （11 月最后 1 个星期四）	Thanksgiving Day* 感恩节	Feast on a traditional meal that commemorates the dinner shared by the Pilgrims, first settlers of the thirteen colonies, and the Native Americans.（为纪念香客即十三个殖民地的第一批定居者和美洲原住民分享的晚餐而举办的传统美食盛宴。）
25 December （12 月 25 日）	Christmas Day* （圣诞节）	Celebrate the birth of Christ, leader of the Christian faith, by exchanging gifts with family and friends.（通过与家人和朋友交换礼物来庆祝基督信仰的领袖——基督的诞生。）

*美国法定的十个节日（Federal Holidays）

2. What is the national flower of the United States?

A. Tulip

B. Plum Blossom

C. Carnation

D. Sugar Maple

问题：美国的国花是什么？
答案：C. 康乃馨

　　世界上很多国家都以自己国土上某一种有代表性的动物或植物作为国家的一个标志。有些国家有国花（floral emblem），有些地区有本地的象征物，一般是由政府确定或是由民意而定的。在美国几乎每个州都有州花。美国的国花是玫瑰（rose），由里根总统于1986年写入宪法。那为什么本题的答案是carnation（康乃馨）呢？这是个脑筋急转弯的题，因为美国是个汽车的王国（car nation），而康乃馨的英文正好是"car+nation"，即汽车的国家，所以也就成了当之无愧的国花了。其他一些国家的国花是：Australia（澳大利亚）——golden wattle（金荆树）；Japan（日本）——cherry blossom/flowering cherry（樱花）；Turkey（土耳其）——tulip（郁金香）；Ukraine（乌克兰）——sunflower（向日葵）；Spain（西班牙）——carnation（康乃馨）；Bulgaria（保加利亚）——rose（玫瑰）；Russia（俄罗斯）——camomile（甘菊）；South Korea（韩国）——hibiscus syriacus（金荆/木槿）；Canada（加拿大）——sugar maple（糖槭，一种枫树）。中国没有确定国花，通常认为是peony（牡丹）或plum blossom（梅花）。中国其他常见的花有：chrysanthemum（菊花）、osmanthus（桂花）、daffodils（水仙花）、orchids（兰花）等。其他与花有关的用语：florist（花商）、florist's（花店）、flowerbed（花坛）、flowerpot（花盆）。请注意flour（面粉）的发音与flower一样。

3. Which of the following pairs is different from others?

A. Bill-William

B. Sue-Susan

C. Beth-Elizabeth

D. Vicky-Victor

问题：以下答案中哪组的搭配与其他的不同？

答案：D. Vicky-Victor

英美人的名字分为姓（surname/family name/last name）、中间名（middle name/initial）和名（first name/given name）。名在前，姓在后，与中国的姓名顺序相反。当女性结婚后，她原来的姓改为其丈夫的姓。如 Miss Amy Brown 女士与 Mr. Bryan Green 先生结婚后，成了 Mrs. Amy Green 太太。Official name 是在公文中使用的正式名字。英美人的名字往往有昵称（nick name），昵称大部分来自名字的一个部分。有的源自姓名的前部分，常见的有：Al—Alan、Deb—Debra、Chris—Christine/Christopher、Tom—Thomas、Dan—Daniel、Dave—David、Ben—Benjamin、Chuck—Charles、Ed—Edward、Frank—Francisco、Jenny/Jen—Jennifer、Joe/Joey—Joseph、Kathy/Kate—Katherine、Ken—Kenneth、Larry—Lawrence、Pat—Patrick/Patricia、Sue/Susie—Susan。有的取自名字的后一部分，常见的有：Tony—Anthony、Becky—Rebecca、Gina—Regina、Bert—Albert、Beth/Lisa—Elizabeth、Lynn—Carolyn、Trisha—Patricia。但有个别的昵称与名字完全不一样，如：Bill—William/Robert、Peggy—Margaret、Dick—Richard、Bob—Robert、Chuck—Charles、Stacy—Anastasia。在美国，常要求在填写表格时和在文件上用 initials（草签）即用名和姓的第一个字母签名。Please sign your initials at the highlighted places in the document.（请在文件中标注的地方草签上你的名字。）Please sign your full name here.（请在这儿签上你的全名。）

4. When you want someone to leave your room or office, you say politely:

A. Get out of here.

B. Show him the door.

C. Leave me alone.

D. Sorry, I have a meeting to attend very soon.

问题：当你用客气的口吻请某人离开你的房间或办公室时，你可以说：

答案：D. 对不起，我马上要去开会了。

用客气的口吻请某人离开时，常用的英语表达有：It's late. Let's talk tomorrow.（时间不早啦，我们明天再谈吧。）I have a meeting to attend very soon. Talk to you later.（我就要开会去了，以后再谈。）Sorry, I have to go. Catch you later.（对不起，我有事得走啦，下次见面再聊。）Sorry, I have a class this afternoon. I am running late.（真抱歉，我下午有课。我要迟到了。）Sorry, gotta rush.（对不起，来不及了。）Sorry, I have a doctor's appointment.（对不起，我有预约去看医生。）如你不想有人再烦你，可以说：Leave me alone.（别烦/吵我啦。）Don't bother me again.（别再打扰我好吗！）不客气地叫人出去，你可以用：show him/her/them the door. 很气愤的说法是：Get out of here！ Period. 或 Get out of my room.（滚蛋）。但是，如是与朋友交谈时用 Get out of here！其含义就完全不同了，是 You're joking! 或 You are kidding（me）! Are you kidding? You must be kidding.（你在开玩笑吧。）的意思，表明对刚才对方说的话很吃惊。如果在与人交谈或开会时，想暂时离开一会，去上卫生间、喝杯水/咖啡什么的，通常可以说 Excuse me. I need to use the bathroom/have a cup of coffee.（对不起，我要用一下洗手间/喝杯咖啡。）I will be back shortly.（一会就回来。）I will be little quick.（去一下就来。）

5. What is the lucky number of most Americans?

A. 8

B. 4

C. 13

D. 7

问题：对大部分美国人而言，幸运数字是哪个？

答案：D. 7

在中国，8 是个吉祥的数字，因为 8 字与"发财"的"发"字的元音相同。中国人最讨厌的数字是 4，因为它与"死"字同音，是个不吉祥的数字。美国人也对数字有选择，最吉利的数字是 7。他们都喜欢带数字 7 的车号、电话号码和门牌号。赌场中获奖的号码也是 777 或 7777。美国一家有名的连锁便利店就带有 7 字，叫作 7-Eleven。当然这里 7 的含义是一周 7 天每天从 7 点开到 11 点营业。24-7 是指提供 24 小时服务的意思。如美国的911 呼救电话以及不少 1-800 打头的商业电话都是全天服务的。美国有名的电影主角 James Bond 的秘密代号 007 中就有 7 字。7 为什么是最吉祥的数字？其原因不详。可能来自古代世界七大奇观（the Seven Wonders of the Ancient World）或是因为古埃及（Ancient Egypt）曾认为 7 是上帝的数字（God number）的原因吧——上帝定下每周为 7 天（seven days of the week）。大家知道 13 是他们最忌讳的数字。每个月的 13 号都是不好的日子，如果碰上星期五就更糟糕,成了黑色星期五(Black Friday)啦。有人说这与名画《最后的晚餐》(*The Last Supper*)有关,耶稣(Jesus)和十二门徒(disciples)共 13 人围着桌子就餐,门徒之一的犹大(Judas)出卖了耶稣,这是不幸的。不过,感恩节后的黑色星期五却是一年中最廉价的购物日。各个商店都出奇招大降价吸引顾客,甚至通宵营业。紧接着的下一个星期一是 Cyber Monday,即网上疯狂购物的一天,在美国,商店通常在该星期一列出大折扣(discount)的商品,发布在网上来吸引顾客。

6. Which city holds the best Thanksgiving Parade in the U.S.?

A. Los Angeles

B. New York City

C. Chicago

D. San Francisco

问题:美国哪个城市举行的感恩节游行活动最好?

答案:B. 纽约市

　　美国最大的感恩节游行是在纽约市举行的 Macy 感恩节大游行(Macy's Thanksgiving Day Parade)。它由美国有名的高档连锁商店 Macy 赞助,始于 1924 年,有 90 多年的历史了。感恩节的游行在上午 9 点从第 77 街和中央公园西交接处开始到 34 街,最后右转到纽约市的第七大道的 Macy 商店大楼前结束。游行中有歌舞和中学的乐队(school band)的表演,各种彩车(floats),巨型的气球(giant balloons)等,十分壮观。芝加哥市(Chicago)举办的是麦当劳感恩节大游行(The McDonald's Thanksgiving Parade)。其最出名的是巨大的充气字符气球(giant inflatable character balloons)。该游行是全国转播的三大游行之一。美国最古老的感恩节游行属宾夕法尼亚州费城举办的 ABC IKEA Thanksgiving Day Parade 的感恩节大游行,可以追溯到 1910 年,通常由 ABC 广播公司第六频道举办。玫瑰游行(The Rose Parade)的正式名称是大学足球比赛玫瑰游行(the Tournament of Roses Parade),是美国的新年庆祝活动之一。玫瑰游行在加州(California)洛杉矶(Los Angeles)的帕萨迪纳市(Pasadena)举行。游行中有众多鲜花覆盖的花车(flower-covered floats),步操乐队(marching bands),马术表演(horse show)和玫瑰碗大学足球赛。旧金山(San Francisco)每年在唐人街(China town)举办中国新年即春节(Spring Festival)游行。

7. What does "sleep over" mean?

A. Overslept

B. Stay over night at a friend's house

C. Lazy bones

D. Sleepy

问题："Sleep over" 的意思是什么？

答案：B. 在朋友家过夜

　　在美国，周末孩子们喜欢互相串门（visiting friends），玩得开心了就不想回家，带上个睡袋（sleeping bag）就在同学或朋友家过夜（stay over night at a friend's house），即 sleep over。所以答案是B。Overslept是睡过头了。She overslept yesterday and missed the school bus.（她昨天睡过头了，没搭上校车）。I felt very sleepy all afternoon.（我觉得下午昏昏欲睡。）Jack is a lazy bone.（Jack很懒惰。）与睡眠有关的表达还有：stay up late（熬夜）或be up all night（昼夜无眠）。睡得不好的英文表达是：I did not sleep well last night.（我昨夜睡得不好。）Mike did not get enough sleep.（Mike的睡眠不足。）He is suffering from insomnia（could not get to sleep）.（他患了失眠症。）It's time to go to sleep.（该睡觉啦。）Go to sleep./Go to bed./Time for sleep.（睡觉去。）其他短语还有：sleepwalk（梦游）、sleep together/sleep with（同居）、sleeping around（随便跟别人上床）、wake up early（醒得早）、snoring（打鼾）、sound asleep/sleep like a log/rock（呼呼大睡）、take a nap（午休/打盹）。

8. What do you call your brother's daughter?

A. Niece

B. Nephew

C. Cousin

D. Step-sister

问题：你怎么称呼你兄弟的女儿？

答案：A. 侄女

　　你兄弟的女儿即侄女，英文叫niece。按中国的传统文化，一个家庭常常几代人都住在一起，三、四代同堂。而美国人的家庭成员（family members）的概念是直系亲属（immediate family members），只包括spouse（配偶：丈夫/husband或妻子/wife）及children

（子女：儿子和女儿/son and daughter）。所以通常只有两代人住一起。其他的亲属都是扩大的家庭成员（extended family members），包括great-grandfather和great-grandmother（曾祖父母），grandparents：grandfather/grandmother（爷爷奶奶），grandchildren：grandson and granddaughter（孙子孙女），great-grandchild（重孙）。家庭成员的称呼包括：parents：father、mother（父母）、stepfather（继父）、stepmother（继母）；brother、sister、siblings、twins（兄弟姊妹），不同父母的兄弟姊妹称为stepbrother、stepsister或half-brother、half-sister。其他相关的单词还有：adopted children：adopted son and daughter（领养儿女：养子和养女）；foster family（寄养家庭）：foster parents：foster father and mother（养父母：养父和养母），foster children：foster son and daughter（领养儿女：养子和养女）；relatives（亲戚）：uncle（叔叔）、aunt（婶婶）；nephew（侄子）、niece（侄女）；cousin：first cousin、second cousin（堂兄弟姐妹或表兄弟姐妹）；close relatives（近亲），distant relatives（远亲）；my relatives/my folks/my kin（亲戚）；relatives by marriage（联姻亲戚）：in-laws（亲家）、father-in-law（岳父）、mother-in-law（岳母）、son-in-law（女婿）、daughter-in-law（媳妇）、brother-in-law（姐夫、妹夫、小舅子、大舅子、连襟）、sister-in-law（姑嫂、妯娌）。

9. What do kids usually say during the Halloween night?

A. Would you give me some candies?

B. Happy Halloween.

C. Trick-or-treat!

D. I'd like some candies.

问题：在万圣节晚上孩子们通常会说什么？
答案：C.不款待就捣乱！给钱还是给吃的？

　　Halloween（万圣节）是每年10月31日庆祝的基督教节日。万圣节虽不是法定节日，却是孩子们最喜爱的节日之一。许多学者认为万圣节最初是西欧的丰收节，基督教的盛宴。万圣节的标志之一是用南瓜雕刻成的灯笼（a Jack-o-lantern）。Trick-or-treating是万圣节中最典型的活动，但来源已很难考证。从节日的傍晚开始，孩子们化妆成各种人物，有天使（angels）、鬼怪（ghosts）、巫婆（witches）、动物（animals）、电影中的人物（movie characters）等，然后喊着Trick-or-treat成群结队地挨门挨户讨糖。各家各户都得准备好很多的糖果（candies）发给讨糖的孩子们，有的还在自己家门口装点上人工蜘蛛网（web）、塑料人骨架（skeleton）、稻草人（scarecrow）和南瓜灯笼（pumpkin lantern）等。其他活动还包括参加化装聚会（costume parties），参观闹鬼的景点（visiting haunted attractions），玩恶作剧（play pranks），讲恐怖故事（scary story telling）和看恐怖片（horror movie）等。

10. What is the symbol of the Republican Party in the U.S.?

A. Elephant

B. Panda

C. Eagle

D. Donkey

问题：美国共和党的标志是什么？

答案：A. 大象

　　美国当代有两大政党：the Republican Party（共和党）和the Democratic Party（民主党）。共和党成立于1854年，党的传统吉祥物是大象（elephant），出了18位总统（president）。美国的第一任总统是George Washington（乔治·华盛顿，1732~1799），他不属于哪个政党。Abraham Lincoln（亚伯拉罕·林肯，1861~1865）是第一任共和党总统（第16位总统），以赢得南北战争和解放黑人而享有极高的声誉。民主党在1800年选举中上台，党的传统吉祥物是驴子（Donkey）。自20世纪30年代以来，民主党推动了社会自由和进步，可能是世界上历史最悠久的政党。Andrew Jackson（安德鲁·杰克逊）通常被认为是美国民主党的第一任美国民主党总统。Barack Obama（奥巴马）是第44位总统，也是第一位黑人总统（2009~2017）。其他有名的美国民主党总统有John F. Kennedy（JFK，肯尼迪，第35位总统，1961~1963），Ronald Reagan（里根，第40位总统，1981~1989）和Bill Clinton（克林顿，第42位总统，1993~2001）。总统之下是副总统（Vice-President），the Speaker of the United States House of Representatives 或Speaker of the House（美国众议院议长），Majority leader（多数党领袖）和Minority leader（少数党领袖）。The US Congress（美国国会）由众议院也称作下议院（Lower House of US Congress）和参议院（The United States Senate 或Upper House of US Congress）组成。众议院有议员435位，按每州人口比例的人数定额，任期为两年。众议院有几个专属权力：启动税收法案，弹劾官员，在选举人团（Electoral College）的总统选票达不到多数时选举美国总统。参议院一共有100位议员，每个州有两位，任期6年。参议院有几个不授予众议院的专属权力，其中包括批准并同意条约或确认内阁部长、联邦法官、其他联邦行政官员、军官、大使等的任命，及对被弹劾（impeached）的联邦众议院官员进行审判。

11. When a blue balloon is hanging over your neighbor's mailbox, it means:

A. There will be a party in the house.

B. The family just had a baby boy.

C. There is going to be a yard sale.

D. It is a holiday.

问题：邻居家的邮箱上挂个了蓝色气球是表示什么意思？

答案：B.你的邻居刚刚生了一个男婴。

美国的家庭诞生了新生婴儿的时候，会在自家的邮箱上挂个气球以示喜庆。蓝色气球（blue balloon）表示是男孩，粉红的（pink balloon）表示是女孩。气球在美国人的生活中是常见的装饰品。过生日时，会买气球。新商店开张或节庆时，常发气球给孩子们。如果你看到街边和住宅草坪上挂有黄色气球的小牌子时，那是出售房子的广告。过节时，有的家庭会在门前做一些装饰。美国国庆节（National Day，7月4号）时，很多家庭在门口挂国旗（national flag）。在万圣节(Halloween)时，挂南瓜灯（Jack-o-Lantern）和布满蜘蛛网（spider webs）。圣诞节时，在门上挂用松枝编成的花环（Christmas garland），在院子的树上、屋顶、屋檐、窗户上挂彩灯等。其他答案的含义是：There will be a party in the house.（邻居家里会开一个派对。）There is going to be a yard sale.（邻居家会在庭院摆摊售卖。）每年秋天的周末，美国很多家庭都在各自的前院摆摊，出售家中不用的物品，价格非常低廉。这种摆摊称作a yard sale，很受欢迎。另一种方式是在跳蚤市场（flea market）上自家摆摊。周末在很多小镇里，附近的农夫在临时设立的农贸市场（farm market）出售新鲜的蔬菜、水果等农产品，价格较贵，尤其是有机的水果和蔬菜（organic fruit and vegetables）。

12. Which is not one of the three branches of the U.S. government?

A. President

B. Supreme Court

C. Congress

D. U.S.Department of State

问题：哪个不是美国政府的三个部门？

答案：D.国务院

美国国家的权力分布于政府的三个分支（the three branches）：即the Executive（行政部门）—President（总统）拥有日常管理的最高权威（任期为四年，最多两届）；the Legislative（立法部门）—由国会（Congress）的House of Representatives（众议院，议员任期为两年）和US Senate（参议院，议员任期为六年）组成，其责任是立法；the Judicial（司法部门）—Supreme Court（最高法院），其责任是执法。在美国政治中，常使用"铁三角（iron triangle）"这个术语来形容国会委员会（congressional committees）在做决策时，与the bureaucracy（官僚）、executive（行政）或政府机构（government agencies）和利益集团（interest groups）之间的关系。美国的行政官员有：Secretary of State（国务卿/总理）、Secretary（部长），如教育部长是Secretary of Education，Senate（参议院）、Representative（众议院）、Governor（州长）、Commissioner（专员），市长和镇长都叫Mayer。州长任期为四年，一般最长为两届。副州长是Lieutenant Governor。州最高法院叫State Supreme Court。每个州都设有自己的立法部门：众议院（House of Representatives/Delegates）或State（General）Assembly和参议院（State Senate）其职责是制定本州的法律和法规。因此，每个州的法律，如开车容许的酒精含量、可以开车的年龄要求、高速公路的限速、教师证书的要求都不一样。

13. When you are married for 25 years in the U.S., the name of your anniversary is:

A. Diamond.

B. Crystal.

C. Silver.

D. Gold.

问题：在美国,当你结婚25周年的时候，结婚纪念日的名字叫什么?
答案：C. 银婚。

在美国,每个结婚周年（wedding anniversary）都有一个名称。25周年是Silver（银婚）。根据国际英文百科全书有关结婚周年的表达是：结婚一周年为纸婚（Paper wedding）、两年为Cotton（棉花婚）、3年为Leather（皮革婚）、4年为Linen（亚麻婚）、5年为Wood（木婚）、6年为Iron（铁婚）、7年为Wool/Copper（羊毛/铜婚）、8年为Bronze（青铜婚）、9年为Pottery（陶器婚）、10年为Tin/Aluminium（锡/铝婚）、11年为Steel（钢婚）、12年为Silk（丝绸婚）、13年为Lace（蕾丝婚）、14年为Ivory（象牙婚）、15年为Crystal（水晶婚）、20年为China（瓷器婚）、25年为Silver（银婚）、30年为Pearl（珍珠婚）、35年为Coral/Jade（珊瑚/玉石婚）、40年为Ruby（红宝石婚）、45年为Sapphire（蓝宝石婚）、50年为Gold（金婚）、55年为Emerald（翡翠婚）、60年以上都是Diamond/Yellow（钻石婚）。与结婚有关的词语还有：新郎（bridegroom/groom）、新娘（bride）、bridesmaid（伴娘）、彩礼（bride gifts）、洞房（bridal chamber）、婚戒（ring）、订婚（engagement）、蜜月（honey moon）、求婚（propose a marriage）。Their marriage took place in a church. （他们的婚礼在教堂举行。）They have been unhappy in their arranged marriage. （他们的包办婚姻过得不美满。）The marriage certificate confirms their union. （结婚证书确认他们的婚姻关系。）Will you marry me? （你愿意嫁给我吗？）After only a year they needed marriage counselling. （他们结婚才一年，就需要婚姻咨询服务了。）She was engaged last week. （她上礼拜订了婚。）

14. **"Do you know Mary who is dating John?"**
"I'm sorry, <u>it doesn't ring a bell.</u>"
The underlined phrase means:

A. Call for service.

B. A bell rings.

C. The bell strikes hourly.

D. I don't recall.

问题："你认识那个和约翰约会的玛丽吗？"
　　　"很抱歉，<u>我记不得了</u>。"
　　　画线短语的意思是什么？
答案：D. 我没有印象（想不起来）。

　　在美国的服务机构或部门里，接待处常设有按铃。来访人若没有人接待，就可以按铃通知，表示需要服务（Call for service）。在美国，你要进入中小学校，必须在大门口先按通报门铃，在得到同意后，门才会解锁，让你进入。进入后，必须在主办公室登记，贴上来访者标签。在美国的学校里，上下课与中国一样打铃（ring a bell）。而在本问题中 It doesn't ring a bell. 不是没有打铃，而是记不起来，没有印象（not recall/recognize something）的意思。A bell rings 是铃响了。在美国，大部分的大学与教堂一样建有钟楼，而且都在主楼上，每个小时都报时间（The bell strikes hourly）。宾夕法尼亚州的费城是美国独立宣言（the Declaration of Independence）的诞生地，那儿有一座自由钟（Liberty Bell），是美国独立的一个标志性象征物，最初放置在宾夕法尼亚州议会大厦的尖顶上，现改名为独立厅（Independence Hall）。自由钟现在放在位于市中心市场街与第 5 和第 6 街交界的一座展览馆内，全年对游人开放。1752 年该钟上刻上了以下字句：Proclaim LIBERTY throughout all the land unto all the inhabitants thereof（向大地上的所有居民宣告自由）。

15. Which of the following is the most popular magazine in the U.S.?

A. *Reader Digest*

B. *National Geography*

C. *Economist*

D. *Times Magazine*

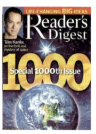

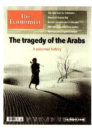

问题：下列哪个杂志是美国最流行的？

答案：A.《读者文摘》。

　　许多美国人都喜爱看报纸杂志，最有名的当属为普遍家庭而出版的《读者文摘》（*Reader's Digest*）。它的总部在纽约市，始建于1922年，是美国最畅销的消费类杂志（best-selling consumer magazine）之一。它的发行量比《财富》（*Fortune*），《华尔街日报》（*The Wall Street Journal*），《商业周刊》（*Business Week*）的总和还多。《读者文摘》有49个版本，以21种语言在70多个国家出版，发行量（circulation）达1050万，是世界上发行量最大的杂志。文摘的语言通俗、题材广泛，是极好的英语阅读材料。《国家地理》（*National Geography*）是美国国家地理学会（National Geography Association-NGS）的官方月刊（Monthly）杂志，从1888年第一期出版以来从没有间断过。它主要包含了地理、历史、世界文化的文章，是扩展知识、提高英语阅读能力的读物。该杂志以36种语言版本在全世界流通，发行量为400多万册。《经济学人》（*Economist*）是经济类的英文周报，总部在伦敦，1843年9月开始发行，平均发行量为150万，其中一半在美国售出。它的读者是受过高等教育的管理人员和政策制定者等专业人士。《时代杂志》（*Times Magazine*）是在纽约市出版的美国新闻周刊（American weekly news magazine），主要报道世界的政治、经济、文化等方面的消息和评论，第一期于1923年3月3日出版。《时代杂志》是世界上最大的新闻周刊，读者达300多万。喜爱运动的人们一定会看《体育画报》（*Sports Illustrated*），它有350万用户，每星期有2300万成年男女阅读。它是赢得国家杂志奖的第一个发行量超过100万的杂志。2015年的民意调查中，《滚石》（*Rolling Stone*）被评为最好的杂志。它1967年成立于美国旧金山，是个半月刊（Biweekly），专注于流行文化。该杂志以其覆盖广泛的音乐吸引对电视节目、电影演员和流行音乐感兴趣的年轻读者。

　　其他的各类流行杂志还有：《时尚》（Vogue）、《男子健康》（Man's Health）、《育儿》（Parenting）、《电视指南》（TV Guide）、《十七杂志》（Seventeen Magazine）、ESPN杂志（ESPN the Magazine）、《人物》（People）、《娱乐周刊》（Entertainment Weekly）、《好管家》（Good Housekeeping）、《食谱大全》（All Recipes）、《医生谈健康》（WebMD)等。

16. The rules one should follow while in public in the U.S., include all except:

A. Do not yawn, sneeze or cough without covering your mouth.

B. Do not drink in public.

C. Do not spit in public.

D. No littering.

问题：除了下列一条之外其他都是我们在美国应该遵守的公共条例。

答案：B.不在公众场合喝酒。

在美国，社会协议（social protocol）相当放松，很少有禁忌（taboo）。美国人对环境和公共卫生很重视，不容许随地吐痰（Do not spit in public.）。任何地方都不能乱丢垃圾（No littering.）。不能在公众场所吸烟。（Don't smoke in public.）有些公共道德规则不会强制执行，但是美国人都自觉遵循，比如：打哈欠、打喷嚏或咳嗽时应捂住嘴。（Do not yawn, sneeze or cough without covering your mouth.）他们认为没有捂住嘴打喷嚏或咳嗽是不卫生的，会传播病菌。在公共场合，如餐馆、候机室、飞机上，不大声喧哗或打嗝。（Do not speak or belch loudly in public.）不要在公众面前剔牙齿或抠鼻子。（Do not pick your teeth or nose in public.）不要老盯着人看。（Do not stare continuously at someone.）美国人爱喝酒，可以在很多公众场合喝酒（电影院、剧场、体育场等例外），但是绝对禁止酒后开车。小孩和未满 21 岁年轻人是不容许喝酒的，如果你让他们喝了酒，或卖酒给他们都是违法的，会遭到起诉。另外，法律规定商店礼拜天上午不可以卖酒。

17. Which is the tallest building in the U.S.?

A. The Twin Towers

B. The Willis Tower

C. One World Trade Center

D. Empire State Building

问题：美国最高的建筑是哪一个？

答案：C.世界贸易中心

美国是摩天大楼（skyscrapers）的故乡。从1890年到1998年，世界第一高楼都是在美国。1885年建于芝加哥高10层的家庭保险大楼被认为是世界第一座摩天大楼。位于芝加哥的威利斯大厦（the Willis Tower，也叫Sears Tower）曾是美国最高的大楼。在纽约市2001年9月11日被撞毁的世界贸易中心双子塔（the Twin Towers of the World Trade Center）曾是美国第二和第三高的大楼，2013年落成的世界贸易中心（One World Trade Center）是在世界贸易中心双子塔的原址上重建的，并在附近建了一个"9·11"纪念馆（"9·11"Memorial & Museum）。新的世界贸易中心超过了威利斯大厦成为美国最高的摩天大楼。其建筑高度加天线塔（antenna）为1776英尺（541米），象征当年美国独立宣言上签字的年份（1776年）。据说芝加哥市区在计划盖一个高达2000英尺（610米），120层的双子塔。很多摩天大楼都带有观景台（observation platform/floor）或旋转餐厅（revolving restaurant），让游人一览城市风光。Empire State Building（帝国大厦）位于纽约市，该大楼的观景台和餐厅是世界闻名的情人约会的地方。目前世界第一高楼是迪拜的哈里发塔(Burj Khalifa)，高828米。

18. A mother could call a baby girl the following, except:

A. adorable

B. charming

C. sweetie

D. cute

问题：妈妈不会用以下哪个字称呼小女孩？
答案：B. 迷人的

美国人称呼小孩有许多常用的词语。母亲对自己的女孩子称honey或sweetie。男人也用它来称呼自己的爱人或情人。而赞赏别人的小女孩时说adorable或cute。称赞小孩时说，Good boy/girl（好孩子），Smart boy/girl（聪明的孩子）。描绘美女时用She is beautiful（漂亮），pretty（秀丽），charming（迷人），attractive（很有魅力）；对男生多用handsome（英俊）或是good-looking（长得标志）、robust（健壮）等。美国社会安全局2014年的数据显示，男孩名字前三十名的是：1. Noah，2. Liam，3. Jacob，4. Mason，5. William，6. Ethan，7. Michael，8. Alexander，9. Jayden，10. Daniel，11. Elijah，12. Aiden，13. James，14. Benjamin，15. Matthew，16. Jackson，17. Logan，18. David，19. Anthony，20. Joseph，21. Joshua，22. Andrew，23. Lucas，24. Gabriel，25. Samuel，26. Christopher，27. John，28. Dylan，29. Isaac，30. Ryan。女孩名字前三十名的是：1. Sophia，2. Emma，3. Olivia，4. Isabella，5. Ava，6. Mia，7. Emily，8. Abigail，9. Madison，10. Elizabeth，11. Charlotte，12.

Avery，13. Sofia，14. Chloe，15. Ella，16. Harper，17. Amelia，18. Aubrey，19. Addison，20. Evelyn，21. Natalie，22. Grace，23. Hannah，24. Zoey，25. Victoria，26. Lillian，27. Lily，28. Brooklyn，29. Samantha，30. Layla。参见家庭教育网页（Read more on Family Education：http://baby-names.familyeducation.com/popular-names/girls/#ixzz3TiP7mwFo）。

19. What is the nickname of New Jersey?

A. Sunshine State

B. Peach State

C. Garden State

D. First State

问题：新泽西州的昵称是什么？

答案：C. 花园州

　　美国的每个州都有昵称，一些州有多个昵称，常以州的某些特色而命名，很多州的汽车牌照上都有州的昵称。新泽西州的人喜爱在庭前院后种植花卉而闻名，所以有花园州的美称。纽约是美国的象征，称之为帝国州（Empire State）毫不过分，帝国大厦（Empire State Building）很早就闻名于天下。加州在 1848 发现有金矿后，引起了 Gold Rush（淘金热），而成为 Golden State（金州）。Golden Bridge（金门大桥）也举世闻名。Florida（佛罗里达州）有漫长的海岸线，到处是享受阳光的最理想的沙滩，享有阳光州（Sunshine State）的美誉。Delaware（特拉华州）是原宪法批准的 13 个州中的第一个州 "The First State"，该州的绰号由此而来，也有诸如 The Diamond State（钻石州），Small Wonder（小奇迹），Blue Hen State（蓝母国）等昵称。夏威夷州（Hawaii）被视为 "阿罗哈州（The Aloha State）"，阿罗哈是夏威夷原住民的一种问候语，相当于 "你好" 或 "再见"。大峡谷（the Grand Canyon）是 Arizona（亚利桑那州）最著名的国家公园，约翰·韦斯利·鲍威尔（John Wesley Powell）在 1870 年代探索科罗拉多河（the Colorado River）期间创造了 "大峡谷" 一词。从而亚利桑那州有了 The Grand Canyon State（大峡谷州）之称。佐治亚州（Georgia）因盛产高质量味道鲜美的桃子而享有 The Peach State（桃子州）的美称。其他州的昵称参见 18 页的各州昵称表。

表 1-2　美国各州的别名（Nicknames of the 50 States）*

Alabama/Yellow Hammer State 阿拉巴马州 / 黄锤子州	Montana/Treasure State 蒙大拿州 / 宝藏国
Alaska/Last Frontier 阿拉斯加 / 最后的边疆	Nebraska/Cornhusker State 内布拉斯加州 / 玉米穗州
Arizona/Grand Canyon State 亚利桑那州 / 大峡谷州	Nevada/Silver State 内华达州 / 银州
Arkansas/Natural State 阿肯色州 / 自然州	New Hampshire/Granite State 新罕布尔州 / 花岗岩州
California/Golden State 加州 / 金州	New Jersey/Garden State 新泽西州 / 花园州
Colorado/Centennial State 科罗拉多州 / 百年纪念州	New Mexico/Land of Enchantment 新墨西哥 / 附魔之地
Connecticut/Constitution State 康涅狄格州 / 宪法州	New York/Empire State 纽约 / 帝国州
Delaware/First State 特拉华州 / 第一州	North Carolina/Tar Heel State 北卡罗来纳 / 焦油州
Florida/Sunshine State 佛罗里达州 / 阳光州	North Dakota/Peace Garden State 北达科他州 / 和平花园州
Georgia/Peach State 格鲁吉亚 / 桃子州	Ohio/Buckeye State 俄亥俄州 / 七叶树州
Hawaii/Aloha State 夏威夷 / 阿罗哈州	Oklahoma/Sooner State 俄克拉荷马州 / 抢先者州
Idaho/Gem State 爱达荷州 / 宝石州	Oregon/Beaver State 俄勒冈州 / 海狸州
Illinois/Land of Lincoln 伊利诺伊州 / 林肯之地	Pennsylvania/Keystone State 宾夕法尼亚州 / 拱心石州
Indiana/Hoosier State 印第安纳州 / 印第安人州	Rhode Island/Ocean State 罗德岛 / 海洋州
Iowa/Hawkeye State 爱荷华州 / 鹰眼州	South Carolina/Palmetto State 南卡罗来纳 / 帕尔梅托州
Kansas/Sunflower State 堪萨斯州 / 向日葵州	South Dakota/Mount Rushmore State 南达科他州 / 拉什莫尔山州
Kentucky/Bluegrass State 肯塔基州 / 蓝草州	Tennessee/Volunteer State 田纳西州 / 志愿州
Louisiana/Pelican State 路易斯安那州 / 鹈鹕州	Texas/Lone Star State 德州 / 孤星州
Maine/Pine Tree State 缅因州 / 松树州	Utah/Beehive State 犹他州 / 蜂巢州
Maryland/Old Line State 马里兰州 / 旧线州	Vermont/Green Mountain State 佛蒙特州 / 绿山州
Massachusetts/Bay State 马萨诸塞州 / 湾州	Virginia/Old Dominion 弗吉尼亚州 / 旧多米尼加
Michigan/Wolverine State 密歇根州 / 金刚狼州	Washington/Evergreen State 华盛顿州 / 长青州
Minnesota/The North Star State 明尼苏达州 / 北星州	West Virginia/Mountain State 西弗吉尼亚州 / 山地州
Mississippi/The Magnolia State 密西西比州 / 玉兰州	Wisconsin/Badger State 威斯康星州 / 獾州
Missouri/The Show-Me State 密苏里州 /Show-Me 州	Wyoming/Equality State 怀俄明州 / 平等州

* Adopted from Wikipedia.

20. In the States, you can drink alcohol when you reach the age of _____.

A. 20

B. 21

C. 19

D. 18

问题：在美国，当你满_____岁时，就可以饮酒了。

答案：B. 21

　　在美国，21 岁以下的人购买，甚至企图购买或藏有酒精或其他醉人的物质（intoxicating substances）都是非法的。因此不能出售酒精饮料给 21 岁年龄以下的任何人。学生必须出示两种带照片的有效身份证(valid photo identification-ID)才能买酒。学生及未成年人(minor)如提供虚假身份（ false/fake ID ）以获取酒将会受到纪律处分（ disciplinary sanction ）。在家庭聚会时，如有未成年人喝了酒，其家长要负法律责任。与酒有关的词汇有：grape wine（葡萄酒）、red wine（红葡萄酒）、white wine（白葡萄酒）、whisky（威士忌）、Vodka（伏特加）、Sake（清酒）、champagne（香槟）、brandy（白兰地）、cocktail（鸡尾酒）、alcohol（酒精）、spirit（酒精）。在美国常见的啤酒有：Heineken、Budweiser、Coors Light、Miller Lite、But Light 等。生啤酒叫 draft。非酒精饮料（ non-alcoholic drinks/soft drink ）有：Coca Cola、Diet Coke、Pepsi、Mt Drew、Sprite、Dr. Pepper 等。常见的表达有：Take a drink.（喝一杯吧。）Don't drink and drive.（不要酒驾。）They drank to their victory.（他们为了胜利而干杯。）Let's go to the bar and get a drink.（我们去酒吧喝一杯吧。）Let's go for a drink this evening.（我们今晚去喝酒。）Yesterday I was drunk.（我昨天喝醉了。）Let's get out of the hot sun and enjoy a nice cool drink indoors.（让我们走出烈日，在室内享受不错的清凉饮料。）与饮酒的制度一样，美国抽烟的制度也是很严格的。在美国的公众场所，包括餐厅，都是禁止吸烟的。要吸烟只能在某些指定的区域和地点。禁止的毒品(drugs)有：opium（鸦片）、marijuana（大麻）、heroin（海洛因）、morphine（吗啡）、cocaine（可卡因）、amphetamines（安非他命）、ecstasy（摇头丸）、methamphetamine（冰毒）等。

近来来，美国不少州通过法律容许作为医用或娱乐出售大麻。

21. What is the proper distance between speakers during a conversation for Americans?

A. 5 inches

B. 10 inches

C. 18 inches

D. 20 inches

问题：美国人在交谈中，说话人之间合适的空间距离是多少？
答案：C. 18 英寸

每个民族都有自己的谈话空间距离（ distance between speakers ）。美国人喜欢保持自己的空间，他们与说话人之间保持约 18 英寸（ 46 厘米）的距离。这个个人空间是非常重要的，如果隔得太近或太远都会就会令人感到不舒服（ uncomfortable ）。就女性而言，在平时随意交谈时，是面对面（ face to face ）的，而男性之间闲聊（ chat ）时往往是侧面相对（ side by side ）。在通常情况下，美国人不会在说问候语时拥抱（ hug/embrace ）或亲吻（ kiss ）熟人，而是握手（shake hands）或点头（nod their heads）。在交谈时也不会触碰对方，虽然在手臂或肩膀简短的接触（touch）可能表示同情或关心（sympathy or concern）对方。关系很好的人之间，会在久别重逢与告别时拥抱。在毕业典礼上教授也会拥抱毕业生以示祝贺。另外，在西方人的交流中，目光交流（eye contact）是很重要的。在与美国人交谈时，不要低头或四处张望，眼睛一定要看着对方，这是一种礼貌，表示尊重。上课时也应与老师目光交流。说话时不要太大声，不然对方会认为你在对他/她吼叫发火（yell at him/her）。在与警察交流时更要注意，绝对不要提高嗓门（raise your voice）。见到可爱的小孩，千万不要去抚摸（touch）他们的头、脸或其他部位。触碰小孩是很不礼貌的，甚至会被人误认为有虐待儿童（child abuse）之嫌。

22. What is NOT a proper dining manner in the U.S.?

A. pick at your teeth

B. ask others to pass you the salt

C. talk while eating

D. ask for more food

问题：在美国哪种饮食举止不合适？
答案：A. 剔牙。

　　美国各地的饮食方式（the dining manner）都不同。去做客时，最好的方法是听主人的指点或跟随其他美国客人行事。It is not polite to pick up the plate from which you are eating.（拿起你吃饭的盘子是不礼貌的。）Food is generally eaten in small bites.（一般来说食品要一小口一小口地吃。）Do not slurp soup or beverages.（不要啜食汤或饮料。）It is polite to converse during a meal unless you are attending a lecture or a toast is being made.（用餐时交谈是礼貌的，但不能太大声，也不能在有人发言或有人正在敬酒的时候交谈。）Always chew with your mouth closed.（嚼的时候都要闭上嘴。）Wait until everybody is seated at the table before you start eating.（等到大家都在桌子边坐好后你再开始吃。）Don't pick your teeth.（不要剔牙。）Ask others to pass you other food away from you.（请别人将远离你的其他食物传给你，而不是自己起身去拿。）Please pass me the salt/sugar.（请把盐/糖递给我。）Ask for more food is polite.（要更多的食物是有礼貌的。）Don't force guests to eat any food, dishes, or drink.（不要强迫客人吃任何食品、菜或饮料。）Don't put any food on to the plates of your guests.（不要给客人夹菜。）Would you like to try some of this?（你想尝尝这个吗？）Try some more.（多来点。）Don't you care for a drink?（想来点饮料吗？）I'm good, thank you.（我够了，谢谢。）

No，thanks.（不用啦，谢谢。）I'm stuffed. I'm quite full.（我吃得太多啦。）很多美国人对一些食品过敏（allergic to food），如花生（peanuts）、海鲜（seafood）等。请客时，一定要问客人对食品是否过敏并注明食品所用的材料。

23. What is not a typical American value?

A. Individualism

B. Privacy

C. Work ethic

D. Selfless

问题：下面哪个不是美国人典型的价值观？
答案：D. 无私

    大多数美国人都说不上他们具体的价值观是什么。这本身就说明他们相信每一个人都有自己独特的价值观。华盛顿国际中心执行董事 L. Robert Kohls 认为美国人的价值观大概有以下一些方面供参考：1. Personal control over the environment（个人控制环境：不相信所谓的"宿命 power of fate"，认为人应该控制自然）；2. Change（变化：变化是好的，与开发、改进、进步、成长密切相关）；3. Time and its control（时间及控制时间：时间就是价值，至关重要）；4. Equality/egalitarianism（平等、平均主义）；5. Individual and privacy（个人和隐私）；6. Self-help control（自助控制）；7. Competition and free enterprise（竞争和自由企业）；8. Future orientation（注重未来）；9. Action/work orientation（实干精神）；10. Informality（不拘小节）；11. Directness，openness and honesty（直接、公开和诚实）；12. Practicality and efficiency（实用性和有效性）；13. Materialism/acquisitiveness（唯物主义/利欲）。Selfless（unselfish）无私似乎不是美国人的价值观，可是他们对 selfless 的行动，对社会无私的奉献及慈善事业（charity）给予极高的评价。学校从小就鼓励学生做社会义工（community volunteer service），为贫困的人捐献食品衣物（donation to the poor and needy），大部分的消防队员（firefighters）都是自愿者（volunteers），教会处处助人为乐。想要更深入地了解美国人的这些价值观，请参阅原文：http://www.claremontmckenna.edu/pages/faculty/alee/extra/American_values.html。

24. "Mind your P's and Q's." means:

A. To behave with manners and to be polite.

B. Mind your own business.

C. Keep in mind.

D. I don't mind.

问题：短语"注意你的P和Q"的意思是：

答案：A.行为与举止要有礼貌。

　　Mind your P's and Q's的意思是 mind your manners（注意你的礼貌），mind your language（说话要有礼貌），be on your best behavior（展示你最好的行为）等。与To behave with manners and to be polite（行为与举止要有礼貌）的含义一样。短语中，P's和Q's的另一种解释认为，是Please（请）和Thank you（谢谢你）的简称，后者包含了类似字母"Q"字的发音。还有一种说法是"Q"字是Excuse me（对不起）的简称。美国的父母常用这句话来教育自己的孩子不要忘记在与人讲话时使用这些客气话。Mind your own business.（管好你自己的事/少管闲事。）Keep in mind：you have a test next week.（下周有个考试，要记得啊。）I don't mind.（我不介意。）与mind一词有关的用法还有很多，如：absent mind（心不在焉）、a beautiful mind（美好心灵）、lost your mind（你糊涂了吧）、She changed her mind.（她改变了注意。）I will remain open minded about that topic.（我对那个话题不会持偏见。）The young man was mindful of his responsibilities.（这个年轻人很有责任感。）Remind me to buy a gift for her birthday.（记得提醒我给她买个生日礼物。）Mind your step when go downstairs.（下楼时注意你的脚下。）Do you mind if I smoke?（你介意我抽烟吗？）

25. Which of the sentences does not describe punctuality?

A. To attend the meeting on time.

B. Mary got home around 11pm.

C. Compete the project on schedule.

D. Hand in the assignment on due date.

问题：哪个句子不是表达准时?

答案：B.玛丽大概是在晚上11点回家的。

　　英语中，准时的表达是on time，in time是及时。Get the job done on time.（按时完成任务。）The fire fighters just arrived in time and saved the house.（消防人员及时赶到，挽救

了房子。）To attend the meeting on time.（准时出席会议。）Complete the project on schedule.（按计划完成项目。）Hand in the assignment on due date.（按时交作业。）在美国，人们高度重视对时间的安排和做事的正点性。大多数上班族都有一个记事本，现在多用电脑和手机安排日程（daily schedule）。对时间的安排，尤其是与人见面都要事先预约好（make an appointment）。准时赴约是对将见面的人表示尊重的标志。私人聚会（private parties）和休闲活动（casual events）的正点性较灵活。但如果你会迟到或必须取消的话，一定要通知晚宴或正式场合的主人。学生去上课或约见导师，也应如此。如果你迟到多次或失约，你的成绩可能会受到影响。在美国，去朋友和同事家串门一定要事先联系好。不然的话不仅会吃闭门羹，而且还可能被误认为私闯民宅（trespassing），未经主人许可进入土地或房产（entry to a person's land or property without their permission）是很危险的。

26. **Which of the words has nothing to do with American Indians?**

A. Native Americans

B. Reservations

C. Indian Americans

D. Indigenous peoples

问题：以下哪个词与美国印第安人无关？

答案：C. 美国印度人

Indian Americans（美国印度人）是指移民美国的印度人。American Indians（美洲印第安人）是美洲原住民（Native Americans）之一。哥伦布（Columbus）发现美洲时，误以为是到了亚洲的印度，而将美洲原住民称为印度人。美洲原住民还包括其他土著民族（indigenous peoples of the Americas），如阿拉斯加（Alaska）和夏威夷（Hawaii）的原住民。人口总计有5220,579（2010年人口普查局 Census Bureau 的数据）。他们一共有562个联邦政府认可的不同部落（distinct tribes）。Navajo是最大的一个全血缘（full-blood）的部落，有286,000人。Cherokee部落的人最多有819,000人，但只有284,000是全血缘的。在15世纪开始的殖民主义政策的围剿之下，美洲印第安人被迫离开家园，最后被赶到了多处印第安人保留地（Indian reservations）。自20世纪60年代以来，努力倡导和保护土著语言的运动促进土著美国人文化的发展。他们办起了独立的报纸和网络媒体，包括FNX，即美国本土人的第一个电视频道，建立了美国本土的研究项目、部落学校和大学、博物馆和语言课程。然而美洲印第安人的权益并没有逐渐扩大。当前，他们面临很多问题，如保留地内的生活贫困、医疗和各种健康问题，社区里酗酒的比例很高。与其他所有的美国人相比，本土美国人死于糖尿病（diabetes）、酒精中毒（alcoholism）、结核病（tuberculosis）、自杀（suicide）的比率很高。

很多年轻人都离开部落到城市里去谋生。其他表达有：It was an Indian summer.（小阳春天气。小阳春是指一段异常温暖，干燥的天气，有时出现于北半球的秋季。美国国家气象局的定义是 9 月下旬到 11 月中旬阳光明媚，气温高于常年的天气。）Indian corn is very colorful.（印第安玉米色彩丰富。）The company has too many chiefs and not enough Indians.（公司拥有太多的首领却没有足够的印第安人——当官的多，做事的少）。

27. Which of the following states has the acronym MI?

A. Michigan

B. Minnesota

C. Mississippi

D. Missouri

问题：MI 是以下哪个州的缩写？

答案：A. 密歇根州

美国共有 50 个州，每个州都有缩写，常用在信封的地址和文件上。19 个州的缩写是州名的前两个字母，如：Alabama–AL、Arkansas–AR、California–CA、Colorado–CO、Delaware–DE、Florida–FL、Idaho–ID、Illinois–IL、Indiana–IN、Massachusetts–MA、Michigan–MI、Nebraska–NE、Ohio–OH、Oklahoma–OK、Oregon–OR、Utah–UT、Washington–WA、Wisconsin–WI、Wyoming–WY。12 个州的缩写是由州名的第一个和最后一个字母组成：Connecticut–CT、Georgia–GA、Hawaii–HI、Iowa–IA、Kansas–KS、Kentucky–KY、Louisiana –LA、Maine–ME, Maryland–MD、Pennsylvania–PA、Vermont–VT、Virginia–VA。由州名的第一个字母和第二个音节的第一个字母组成的有 9 个州：Minnesota–MN、Mississippi–MS、Nevada–NV、Tennessee–TN、Texas–TX、Alaska–AK、Arizona–AZ、Missouri–MO、Montana–MT。10 个州名由两个字组成，其缩写为字头字母：New Hampshire –NH、New Jersey–NJ、New Mexico–NM、New York–NY、North Carolina–NC、North Dakota–ND、Rhode Island–RI、South Carolina–SC、South Dakota–SD、West Virginia–WV。另外波多黎各（The Commonwealth of Puerto Rico）是美国在加勒比海地区的一个自由邦（境外领土），人口三百七十多万，首府为圣胡安。居民享有美国公民的同等待遇。2012 年 11 月 6 日，61% 的波多黎各人在公投中赞成成为美国第 51 州，但尚需美国国会通过才能真正成为美国的一个州。美属维尔京群岛（Virgin Islands of the United States），也称为 United States Virgin Islands，或简称为 USVI。该群岛原属丹麦，1916 年被美国买下，由 50 多个大小岛和珊瑚礁组成，面积达 344 平方公里。根据美国 2000 年人口普查数据，该群岛共有居民 108,612 人，享有美国公民的同等待遇。

28. Where is it unlikely for American kids to have their birthday party?

A. At home

B. In a recreation center

C. In school

D. At ice-skating rink

问题：美国的孩子不太可能在哪里过自己的生日派对？

答案：C. 在学校

　　在美国除了幼儿园之外，读书的孩子很少在学校里过生日。和中国的孩子一样他们常在自己的家里（at home）开生日派对（birthday party），邀请同学来参加。过生日的孩子家会准备好生日蛋糕（birthday cake）和一些饮料和小吃（figure food/snack）。通常还会订几盒比萨饼（order pizzas）。过生日的孩子也喜欢邀请同学一起到一些娱乐场所（a recreation center）过生日，如溜冰场（at ice-skating rink）、攀岩俱乐部（climbing club），有时还一道去看电影或去快餐店（fast food restaurant）等。一般来说，参加和举办生日派对都送礼物（birthday gifts）。过生日的孩子，在活动结束时，会给参加生日派对的孩子们各发一小袋礼物（a small bag of gifts）。与生日有关的常用英语有：Happy Birthday!（生日快乐！）Many happy returns of the day!（生日快乐另一种较正式的说法）。此外，还有 Birthday Song（生日快乐歌）、Birthday Invitation（生日派对邀请信）、Birthday gifts（生日礼物）、Birthday Card（生日卡）、candle（蜡烛）。The little boy is on the beach in his birthday suit（totally naked）.（小男孩光着身子在沙滩上晒太阳。）

29. What do the signs alongside the road in the picture mean?

A. House for Sale

B. Ads

C. Election campaign

D. Celebration

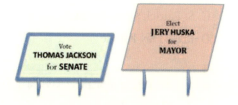

问题：道路两边的小牌子是做什么用的？

答案：C. 竞选活动用的

　　美国是个民主的国家，上至总统下至大学的系主任都是由选举（election）产生的。选举的程序严谨公正，确保获选人是多数选民的意愿。常见的政府官员竞选活动（election campaign）的方式之一是在选区的主要道路边树立小的牌子。通常上面都写上竞选人的全名和竞选的职位。如：Vote Thomas Jackson for Senate（选Thomas Jackson为议员），Lin Zhang for School Board（选Lin Zhang为学区委员会委员），Elect Jeff Huska for Mayer（选Jeff Huska为市长）。18岁以上的公民才能参加选举，选民需要登记才能投票选举政府官员。美国的大选不仅仅是选总统，而且同时还选议员、州长等官员、并对州政府的重要议案投票。路边的这种小牌子还有其他的用途，在出售住宅的前庭草地上，常可以看到"For Sale"和"For Sale by Owner"（房屋自售）的牌子，上面有电话号码，想买房子的人可以打电话与房主或地产经纪人（restate agent）联系。周末，地产经纪人会树立一个"Open House"（开放参观）的牌子，购房者可以自由参观出售的住宅。房子卖出后，牌子便换成了"Sold"（已售）。有的住宅会在门前草地上插上"ADT"的牌子，示意该住宅安装了由安达泰公司提供的电子安全系统（home electronic security system）。美国的大学经常设有"Open House"（开放日），让有意向报考的学生和家长参观和了解学校。周末，"Yard Sale"和"Garage Sale"的牌子四处可见，是美国人在自家的院子里出售不用的物品，价格非常便宜。其他的牌子还有：Private Property（私人住地）No Trespassing!（不容许擅入！）No Soliciting!（不要打扰！）Pesticide application, Keep off!（施用农药，勿入！）商店和公司的门口挂的牌子有：Open（营业），We are open.（营业中），Closed（关门了）。75% Off（打75折）。On Sale!（大减价！）还有：Help wanted. We're hiring. Now Hiring.雇人这些广告通常也出现在报刊的广告栏中。注意Most Wanted. 是通缉罪犯的意思。

30. Which parade is not organized by a single ethnic group?

A. Puerto Rican Parade

B. Chinese New Year Parade

C. St Patrick's Day Parade

D. Pixar Play Parade

问题：哪个游行不是由一个族裔举办的?

答案：D. 皮克斯影剧游行

　　Pixar Play Parade（皮克斯影剧游行）是在迪斯尼的加利福尼亚冒险乐园（Disneyland's California Adventure）举行的游行，它不是由一个族裔举办的。游行中的花车（floats）和人物（characters）都展现迪斯尼的皮克斯电影公司制作的影片中怪兽、超人和玩具的故事。迪斯尼乐园还举办多种表演游行，如，圣诞幻想游行（Christmas Fantasy Parade）。在美国，每年许多少数族裔都举办庆祝自己节日的大游行。如，美裔波多黎各人的Puerto Rican Parade（波多黎各游行）。Puerto Rico 是美国在加勒比海（Caribbean）东北部的一个领地（territory）。波多黎各人享有美国永久居民的待遇。美裔爱尔兰人（Irish）每年三月十七日在纽约市举办圣帕特里克节游行（St. Patrick's Day Parade）。它是世界上规模最大的圣帕特里克节游行，也是最古老的市民游行。Chinese New Year Parade 是华裔在中国城举办的庆祝中国新年的游行。

31. How many stripes are on the National Flag of USA?

A. 15

B. 20

C. 50

D. 13

问题：美国的国旗上有多少条带？

答案：D.13

　　美国的全称是美利坚合众国（United States of America），她由 50 个州组成，因而在国旗上（Flag of America/Flag of the United States of America）有 50 颗五角星象征这 50 个州。人们也称国旗为 the Star-Spangled Banner。在国旗上有 13 条蓝白相间的横条（stripes）象征从英国殖民地（British colony）中最早宣布独立而成为联邦（the Union）的 13 个州。他们分别是 Delaware（特拉华）、Pennsylvania（宾夕法尼亚）、New Jersey（新泽西）、Georgia（佐治亚）、Connecticut（康涅狄格）、Massachusetts（马萨诸塞）、Maryland（马里兰）、South Carolina（南卡罗来纳）、New Hampshire（新罕布什尔）、Virginia（弗吉尼亚）、New York（纽约）、North Carolina（北卡罗来纳）和 Rhode Island（罗得岛）。美国的各个州都有自己的法院和法律。每个州的驾照（drive license）、教师证书（teaching license）、购物税率（sale's tax）、死刑（death penalty）、最低工资（minimum wage）等都有自己的规定。最后加入美国的州是：47. New Mexico（新墨西哥），1912；48. Arizona（亚利桑那），1912；49. Alaska（阿拉斯加），1959；50. Hawaii（夏威夷），1959。

32. On which occasion do people need to sing the national anthem?

A. At the court

B. At official sports games

C. In school classroom

D. At graduation

问题：在哪种场合要唱国歌？

答案：B. 在举办正式的体育比赛时

通常，美国的国歌是在重大文体活动前演唱（at major games）。在毕业典礼（at graduation）、法庭（at the court）和课堂上（in classroom）是不唱国歌的。美国的国歌是"星条旗"（The Star Spangled Banner）。1916 年，伍德罗总统（Woodrow Wilson）命令在陆军和海军的仪式上演奏该歌曲，但直到 1931 年国会才通过法案定其为国歌。歌词（lyrics）是由弗兰西斯史科特·克伊（Francis Scott Key）在 1814 写的，歌曲用的是当时流行的旋律，"To Anacreon in Heaven"（在天堂的人）。国歌由四节组成。但是几乎在每种场合，都只唱第一节。歌词如下（译文来自互联网，作者不明）：

The Star Spangled Banner

（星条旗，永不落）

Oh, say can you see by the dawn's early light

（啊！在晨曦初现时，你可看见）

What so proudly we hailed at the twilight's last gleaming?

（是什么让我们如此骄傲地在黄昏的最后闪光中欢呼？）

Whose broad stripes and bright stars thru the perilous fight, O'er the ramparts we watched were so gallantly streaming?

（我们看到是谁的星条旗帜在激战中，在要塞上那样英勇飘扬？）

And the rockets' red glare, the bombs bursting in air, Gave proof through the night that our flag was still there.

（熊熊的烈火，天空中炮弹的闪光，证实在整夜里我们的旗帜依然耸立。）

Oh, say does that star-spangled banner yet wave, O'er the land of the free and the home of the brave?

（哦，你看星条旗不是还在，自由的土地上和勇者的家园上飞扬？）

33. Which is not a required duty for a US citizen?

A. Pay Income Tax

B. Serve a Jury Duty

C. Service in the Army

D. Vote for President

问题：哪个选项不是美国公民必须尽的义务？

答案：D. 选举总统

在美国，每个公民都有其应尽的义务（compulsory duty）。但参加投票选举总统（presidential election）是自愿的，而且要提前注册为选民（registered voter）才能投票（vote）。在大选投票时，选民还要对州和地区的各种重大议案（motion）和提案（proposal）投票。公民也必须服兵役。但是有年龄的限制，而且只有在战争期间才有义务兵役制（compulsory military service）。公民都要缴纳所得税（pay income tax）。纳税的多少是根据本人或家庭的收入而定，收入越高，税率越高。每年的 4 月 15 日是报税（Tax Return）的截止日。不缴税、偷税或漏税（Tax evasion）是会被罚款（fine）或坐牢（imprisonment）的。任陪审员（Jury Duty）也是公民的重要义务。任何案件（suit）的嫌疑人（suspects）是否有罪由陪审团来做决定，而法官（lawyer）只是按陪审团的决定依据法律定徒刑（sentence/imprisonment）或免罪、免刑（exempt from punishment）。你所在州的法院（court）会在本州的居民中抽选出陪审员参加各种案件的陪审团。如你被抽上（called for jury duty），就会收到法院寄来的陪审团传票（a jury summons）。你必须在指定的日期去法院报到（report to court），否则无视陪审团传票会受到重罚（strict penalties）：罚款或入狱（jail time）。陪审的时间根据案子而定，可能是 a trial（一天）也可能是几周。如果你因病或其他重要原因不能出席的话，你必须在陪审团传票收到五天或规定的期限内在指定网页上告知法院。一般来说，做了一次陪审员（juror）后，三年内不会再被抽上。

34. Which of the ethnic groups in the States is not considered a language minority?

A. American Indians

B. African Americans

C. Asian Americans

D. Hispanics

问题：哪个族裔不是少数语言族裔?

答案：B. 非裔

　　虽然 African Americans（非裔）即美国黑人（Black Americans）的语言不是标准的英语，但仍是英语。通常称为 Ebonics/black English 或 black vernacular，即非洲裔美国人所讲的英语方言。在 1996 年，加州奥克伦学区（Oakland School District）曾因将 Ebonics 定为非洲语言而引发了全国的争议。其他种族是少数语言族裔。据美国 2013 年美国人口普查局（United States Census Bureau）的数据，American Indians（美国印第安人）和阿拉斯加原住民有大约 520 万，占美国总人口的 2% 左右，Asian Americans（亚裔美国人）占美国总人口的 5.6%。亚裔中最大的族群分别是中国人（452 万），菲律宾人（365 万），印度人（346 万），越南人（191 万），韩国人（177 万）和日本人（143 万）。Hispanics（西班牙语裔）是美国最大的少数语言族裔，共有 5530 万人，占美国总人口的 17.4%。现在加利福尼亚州和佛罗里达州西班牙语裔人数已经超过半数成了该两州的多数族裔。按美国人口普查局的数据，2016 年 9 月 5 日 5 点 45 分，美国的总人口约为 3.24 亿人。根据联邦 2010 年的数据，美国的少数语言族裔占全国人口的 36.3%。据估算，到 2020 年 52% 的儿童是少数族裔，到 2044 年少数族裔将超过白人成为美国人数最多的族裔（majority）。

35. Which state has the greatest Chinese population?

A. New York

B. California

C. New Jersey

D. Texas

问题：美国哪个州华人最多?

答案：B. 加利福尼亚州

　　根据美国 2010 年的人口普查，美籍华人（Chinese Americans）有 450 万，华人最多的州是加利福尼亚州（1253100，3.4%），其次是纽约州（577000，3.0%），德州（157000，

0.6％），新泽西州（134500，1.5％），马萨诸塞州（123000，1.9％），伊利诺伊州（104200，0.8％），华盛顿州（94200，1.4％），宾夕法尼亚州（85000，0.7％），马里兰州（69400，1.2％），弗吉尼亚州（59800，0.7％），和俄亥俄州（51033，0.5％）。夏威夷州的美籍华人有55000人，密度最高，达4.0％。在以下三个大都市区中的华人最多：大纽约区为735019人，圣荷西—旧金山—奥克兰联合统计区有629243人，大洛杉矶联合统计区约566968人。纽约市的华人最多，有522619。根据美国政府的记录，第一个中国移民1820来到美国。随后，中国人从广东到加州从事淘金（Gold Rush），苦力（coolies）劳动的人数剧增，从1852年的25000到1880年的105465人，达到当时加州人口的十分之一。几乎所有的早期移民都是来自广东省的教育水平低的年轻男性。在19世纪60年代，ALS太平洋铁路公司招收了大量的中国劳力团，为建造部分横贯大陆的铁路提供了主要劳力，华人为铁路建成立下丰功。然而，1882年开始至1942年的排华法案(the Chinese Exclusion Act)禁止了中国人移民。从20世纪中叶开始，不少台湾、香港的中国学生和学者赴美国留学。从80年代初至今的大陆留学潮中，数十万学生到美国留学，其中很大一部分毕业后在美工作，因此从根本上改变了美籍华人的学历和经济水平。根据2010年的人口普查，美籍华人中有本科学历的占51.8％，超过美籍日本人的47.4％和白人的29.5％。美籍华人中26.6％有硕士或博士学历，美籍华人家庭的平均收入$65273高过白人的$52480。

36. Which of the following abbreviations means "Reply is needed"?

A. VIP

B. ASAP

C. RSVP

D. SOS

问题：下面哪个缩写的意思是"需要回复"？

答案：C. RSVP

　　RSVP或R.S.V.P.来自法语短语répondez s'il vous plaît，意思是please respond（请答复），通常是写在一个邀请信上。如果你不回复，将被视为接受邀请。如果你不接受时才需要回复。不能接受而回复时，较流行的用语是 Regrets（遗憾）或是 Regrets only（谨请告知）等短语。SOS是国际莫尔斯电码求救信号（the international Morse code distress signal）常用的电码。第二届国际无线电报公约于1906年11月3日签署，1908年7月1日起生效，SOS成为全球标准的海上无线电求救信号。1999年，全球海上遇险安全系统（the Global Maritime Distress Safety System）替代了SOS，但SOS仍然是公认的一个求救信号。人们常把SOS作为save our ship（拯救我们的船）和save our soul（拯救我们的灵魂）等短语的缩写。VIP 是最重要的人物或客人（the very important person）的缩写。ASAP（as soon as possible）是越快越好的缩写。其他常见的缩写还有：P.S. 或 PS 是 post script 的缩写，用在信件（附笔）和电邮结尾处来表示添加额外的信息（又及）。还有一些常用的缩写：ETA（estimated time of arrival）预计到达的时间，ETD（estimated time of departure）预计出发的时间，B.Y.O.B.（bring your own beverage/drinks）自备饮料。

37. Which American President abolished slavery and emancipated the black slaves?

A. George Washington

B. Abraham Lincoln

C. Thomas Jefferson

D. Benjamin Franklin

问题：废除奴隶制度和解放黑奴的是哪位美国总统？

答案：B. 亚伯拉罕·林肯

　　Abraham Lincoln（亚伯拉罕·林肯，1809 年 2 月 12 日至 1865 年 4 月 15 日）是美国第十六任总统。1861 年 3 月任职，在 1865 年 4 月遇刺（assassination）。林肯领导美国通过了最血腥的内战、最大的道德宪政（moral constitutional）和政治危机（political crisis）。他保留了联盟，废除了奴隶制（abolished slavery），加强了联邦政府和现代化经济。George Washington（乔治·华盛顿，1732 年 2 月 22 日至 1799 年 12 月 14 日）是美国的第一任总统（1789 年至 1797 年），美国独立战争期间（the American Revolutionary War）为大陆军的总司令（Commander-in-Chief），是美国的开国元勋之一（one of the founding fathers of the United States）。他主持起草了现行的美国宪法（United States Constitution），被称为"国父"（the father of his country）。Thomas Jefferson（托马斯·杰斐逊，1743 年 4 月 13 日至 1826 年 7 月 4 日）是美国国父，1776 年《独立宣言》（*the Declaration of Independence*）的主要作者，他 1800 年当选为美国第三任总统（1801 年至 1809 年）。Benjamin Franklin（本杰明·富兰克林，1706 年 1 月 17 日至 1790 年 4 月 17 日）是美国的开国元勋之一和著名的博学家（renowned polymath）。富兰克林是独立宣言的主要作者、印刷商（printer）、政治理论家（political theorist）、政治家（politician）、邮政局长（postmaster）、科学家（scientist）、发明家（inventor）、公民活动家（civic activist）和外交家（diplomat）。他是美国启蒙运动（the American Enlightenment）的重要人物（a major figure）。他发明了闻名的避雷针（the lightning rod）、双光眼镜（bifocals）和富兰克林炉子（Franklin Stove）等。他还创建了宾夕法尼亚大学（the University of Pennsylvania）。

38. Which of the following is a real question and needs an answer?

A. Hi, how are you?

B. How is it going?

C. Hello.

D. What's up?

问题：下列哪句是真正的问题，需要回答的?

答案：D. 有什么事吗?

　　What's up?（有什么事吗？）这句话是需要回答的。美国人打招呼（greeting）往往会说，Hi, how are you?（嗨，你好吗？），Hi Mark?（马克，你好！）或 How is it going?（你怎么样？）这些都是问好的表达，是另一版本的 hello（你好），并不是一个问题，通常不需要回答。你可以也用问好回复：I am good. How about you？或 Fine. Thank you. And you? 其他的表达还有：Long time no see. How's everything?（好久不见了。一切都好吗？）Hello 一词从古德语的 Hallo 和 Holo 演变而来，1833 第一次在出版物中使用。Hello 作为电话中的问候语（a telephone greeting）归功于发明家爱迪生（Thomas Edison）。1877 爱迪生给匹兹堡电报公司的总裁写信，建议用 Hello 取代最初使用的电话问候语 Ahoy（船上用语）。他说："I do not think we shall need a call bell as Hello! can be heard 10 to 20 feet away."（我认为我们不需要打电话的电话铃！ Hello 的声音在 10 到 20 英尺的距离都可以听到。）在中国，路上遇到熟人，打招呼时喜欢说，"Where are you going? / Where are you heading?"（你上哪儿去？）或是 "What are you going to do?"（你干嘛去？）这种问句在西方会被认为是不礼貌的，有干涉他人私事之嫌。人们会回应说 "Mind your own business!"（不关你的事！）

39. "Four scores and seven years ago…" is the beginning words of _____ by an American president.

A. The Declaration of Independence

B. The Gettysburg Address

C. The State of the Union address

D. Graduation Speech

问题："Four score and seven years ago..." 是美国总统哪个讲演的开场白?

答案：B. 葛底斯堡演说

The Gettysburg Address（葛底斯堡演说）是美国历史上最著名的一个演说。由美国总统亚伯拉罕•林肯（Abraham Lincoln）在美国内战（the Civil War）期间，于 1863 年 11 月 19 日星期四下午，在宾夕法尼亚州的葛底斯堡的国家战士公墓（the Soldiers' National Cemetery）做的演讲。四个月前联盟军队（the Union armies）在葛底斯堡战役中打败了邦联（the Confederacy）。林肯的演说是对国家的目标作出的一个最有影响力的陈述。在短短两分钟的演讲中，林肯重申了人类平等与《独立宣言》的原则，支持并宣布联盟内战会以"自由的新生（a new birth of freedom）"，给它所有的公民带来真正的平等。林肯还对内战重新下了定义：它不只是一个联盟的斗争，也是为争取人类平等的原则作的斗争。《独立宣言》是于 1776 年 7 月 4 日在美国宾夕法尼亚州的费城（Philadelphia）第二届大陆会议上通过的。它宣布十三个美国殖民地（the thirteen American colonies）为新独立的主权国家——美利坚合众国，不再是大英帝国（the British Empire）的一部分。约翰•亚当斯（John Adams）是独立的倡导者。The State of the Union Address 是由美国总统每年向美国国会联合会议发表的讲演即"国情咨文"。总统不仅报告了国家的状况，也阐述他的立法议程和国家优先事项。美国宪法要求总统定期给国会提供"国情咨文"信息、建议和必要而适当的措施。在大多数国家里，总统只是给国会提交书面政府工作报告。Graduation Speech 是毕业演说。

40. You don't need to "Wait Behind the Yellow Line" when you are _____.

A. at a Customers service

B. at a bus stop

C. at a flea market

D. at the casher

问题：在以下哪个地方你不需要在黄线后排队？

答案：C. 在跳蚤市场

排队（wait in line/stand in line）是美国人自行遵守的公共准则和礼节。在很多公共场所，如车站、机场、影院、球赛的售票处（ticket office）、商店收银柜台（checkout counter/at the cashier）、海关（customers service）、银行、机场检票处（check in）、旅馆服务台（service desk）等的窗口和柜台前都划有黄线（waiting line）。让人们在线后排队（wait Behind the Yellow Line）。即使你就是想问个问题，也要排队。另外，你是不能进入以上工作人员的工作区域的。当排到你时，一般也要等到对方示意（叫你或目光接触）后，才能前往窗口或服务台。除了黄线之外很多的地方还设有支柱障碍（stanchions barriers）或可伸缩的支柱栏杆（retractable belt stanchions）。在美国，插队（cut in line/jump the queue）和不排队的现象很少。在跳蚤市场（at a flea market）是不用排队的。排队（get in line），在票房前排队（queue up at the box office）。keep right（靠右）是个公共准则，在机场、车站、地铁（subway）、商场的扶梯（escalator）上，如随电梯行进或慢行时，不要并排，应该靠右，这样不会阻碍快速行走的人。上公车、上火车、进电梯（elevator）、大楼和大门时，也要靠右站排队，遵照先下后上，先出后入的次序进出。在街道和商场等场合不要并排以免造成通道堵塞（block passage）。开车时除了超车之外，也要靠右 keeping to the right。

41. Caucasian is sometimes used to refer to all except:

A. White people

B. White American

C. Hispanic whites

D. Non- Hispanic whites

问题：除了_____之外，Caucasian 常用来表示以下各项。

答案：C. 拉美裔白人

Caucasian "白种人" 这个术语是由德国哲学家克里斯托夫•迈纳斯（Christoph Meiners）在他 1785 年的《人类现代史纲要》（*The Outline of History of Mankind*）一书中创造的。布鲁门巴赫（Blumenbach）在《人类的自然分类》（*On the Natural Variety of Mankind*）一书中，根据颜色加上科学的术语、颅测量（cranial measurements）和五官的特征（facial features）为佐证，给人的五个种族下了定义。他建立了 Caucasian 白色的 "白种人"（White race）, Mongoloid（蒙古人种）的 "黄种人"（Yellow race）, Malayan（马来亚）的 "棕色人种"（Brown race）, Ethiopian（埃塞俄比亚）的 "黑色人种"（Black race）, 以及美国的 "红色人种"（Red race）的定义。在美国，Caucasian 泛指白人（white people）。称白人的其他用语有：White Americans, Whites, Non- Hispanic whites。而 Hispanic whites 是指来自南美洲（拉丁美洲）的移民。美国是个移民国家，常被称为大熔炉（melting pot）。现在流行的称呼是 salad bowl（沙拉碗），既融合又保留各自民族特色的国家。虽然种族隔离（racial segregation）早已消除，然而种族歧视（racial discrimination）仍然存在。执法机构（law enforcement agencies）以种族貌相（racial profiling）作为依据，来怀疑人是否犯法的事例常有发生。

42. Which of the following is not part of the U.S. Presidential election?

A. Red state and blue state

B. Electoral college

C. Election campaign

D. Town hall meeting

问题：下列哪个词语不是美国总统选举的一个部分？

答案：A. 红色州和蓝色州。

美国的总统和副总统的选举是间接投票（indirect vote），由公民投票选举美国选举团成员，再由选举团成员投票（cast ballots/vote）选举总统和副总统。如果大多数选民不投票选总统候选人，则由众议院选择总统；如果大多数选民不投票给副总统候选人，则由参议院表决选择副总统。自 1845 年以来总统选举日定在 11 月的第一个星期二。与其他各州的大选，以及本地选举恰逢。2016 年美国总统选举定于 11 月 8 日。每个州的选举团成员的数量与该州的参议员和众议员在美国国会的数量相同。美国的总统候选人基本来自共和党（Republican）和民主党（Democratic）两大党。也可以以非党派（non partisan）人士参加。每个候选人都进行竞选募捐（election campaign fund raising）和参加在各地的竞选活动。如在市政厅会议（town hall meeting）由媒体举办的全国辩论会（national debates）上向选民阐述自己的政见。他们首先要在本党的竞选中获得提名（presidential nomination），然后参加全国大选。提名过程包括初选（the primary elections），预选（caucuses）和提名大会（the nominating conventions）。全国投票日各个电视台都会现场直播，常在美国地图上用 red state（共和党）和 blue state（民主党）来显示各党候选人在各州的得票数。不确定的州以紫色州（purple state）表示。总统任期是在就职日（Inauguration Day），1 月 20 日正式开始。就职典礼（inaugural ceremony）在国会大厦前举行。如果 20 日是个星期天，那么就职典礼就在 21 日举行。

43. Which is not part of the Chinese communities?

A. Chinese schools

B. Chinese TV stations

C. Chinese universities

D. Chinese newspaper

问题：哪个部分不属于美籍华人社区？

答案：C. 中文大学

　　随着在美华人人数的日益增长，华人社区（Chinese communities）也在不断增多。从 1848 年旧金山建立全美第一个唐人街（China Town）后，洛杉矶、纽约、芝加哥等大城市里的唐人街日益扩大，东西海岸的城市几乎都有了唐人街。在大小城镇里和近郊形成了一个个华人社区，建立了各种为华人服务的机构，如：菜市场、商店、药店、餐厅、书局、娱乐场所、健身、文体活动团体等。华人家长们自办的中文学校遍及全国的社区，促进了华人儿童学习中文，了解和发扬中华文化。在大纽约地区，仅华夏中文学校就有十几个分校 7000 多学生。中文学校一般都是在周末上课，家长们也聚合在一起，开展各种比赛，如篮球、排球（volleyball）、羽毛球（badminton）、足球（soccer）等球类和田径（Track and Field）等，还有绘画（painting）、书法（calligrapher）、舞蹈（dance）、健美操（aerobics）、太极拳（tai chi）、围棋（Go）、象棋（chess）、纸牌（playing cards）等文娱活动。全美还设有好几家中文电视台，中文报刊也愈来愈多。如世界日报和中文月刊。每年一到中国的传统节日，如中秋节（Middle Autumn Festival）和中国新年（Chinese New Year），社区都会举办各种庆祝活动，常有狮子舞（Lion Dance）表演。近年来，在不少华人多的学区，公立学校开始设立中文课，有的在中国新年还放假一天。

44. "Jesus Christ! I left my key in the car!"
The speaker＿＿.

A. is a Christian

B. is a priest

C. has a Christian name

D. is unpleasantly surprised

问题："我的天啊！我把钥匙落在车上了！"说话人＿＿？

答案：D. 表示不愉快的惊讶

Jesus Christ通常是指耶稣基督，但在这个句子中，说话人不是在教堂（church）做礼拜时称呼耶稣基督，而是表示惊讶的意思：我的天呀！我把钥匙忘在车上了！不能认定说话人是一个基督徒（a Christian）或是一名牧师（a priest），但与有没有基督徒的教名（a Christian name）无关。当表示惊讶、恐惧或非常不愉快的时候，美国人的用语中常带有宗教词语，如，My God!（我的天啦！）Oh God!（天啊！）Oh my God!（哦，我的上帝！）Holy Cow!/Holy smoke!（天呐！）Holy shit! The whole house is flooded!（天啊！整个房子被水淹了！）还有 Oh my Gosh!（我的天啊！）等。大部分美国人都信宗教（believe in religion），礼拜天上午都会上教堂（go to church）作祈祷（make/utter/say a prayer）。就餐前，教徒也需要作祈祷。Lord, please help me find courage.（上帝，赐给我勇气吧。）美国信天主教（Catholic）和基督教（Christianity）的人较多，还有犹太人（Jewish）信仰的犹太教（Judaism），回教徒的伊斯兰教（Islam）等。佛教的英文是Buddhism，佛教徒为Buddhist。与宗教有关的词语还有：Christian holiday（基督教节日）：Easter（复活节），Christmas（圣诞节），Bible（圣经），God（上帝），Godfather（教父）。God knows! 天知道。当你打喷嚏时，美国人就一定会说：God bless you!（上帝保佑你！）I swear to God（I swear），I did not do it.（我发誓，这不是我干的。）For God's sake, stop arguing. I can't hear myself think!（看在老天爷的份上，别吵啦。吵死我了/我没办法思考啦！）

45. Which word of color in the sentences below means a true color?

A. His hair turned grey over the matter of a sex scandal.

B. Forgive him. It's just a white lie.

C. White-collar workers usually get paid more than blue-collar workers.

D. You can find his address and phone number in the yellow book.

问题：哪个句子中颜色的词表示真正的颜色？

答案：C. 通常白领工人的工资比蓝领工人的高。

在英语中，颜色的词在使用时经常并不一定是表示该词的颜色。His hair turned grey over the matter of sex scandal.（由于性绯闻的烦恼，他的头发都花白了。）英语中表示头发变白不是用white，而是用grey（灰色）。There is a grey area between bribery and political deal - making.（贿赂与政治交易之间存在着一个灰色的地带。）又如，句子 Forgive him. It's just a white lie.（原谅他吧。这只是一个善意的谎言，不是"白色"的谎言）。white elephant 是指大而无用之物：The new office building cost a fortune and became a white elephant.（这座新办公大楼耗资昂贵却成了华而不实的摆设。）A white-collar worker usually gets paid more than a blue-collar worker.（一个白领的收入通常会高过一个蓝领工人。）blue 还可用来表示

不高兴、悲伤（sad）、郁闷（depressed）：Jennett has been very blue since her divorce.（Jennett 离婚后一直很郁闷。）yellow book 在美国不是黄色书籍（Pornographic books）的意思，而是电话簿（telephone book），上面有很多黄页的广告。You can find his address and phone number in the yellow book.（你可以在电话簿上找到他的地址和电话号码。）其他表示颜色的常用词语有：black and white（黑白/一目了然）、color blind（色盲）。

46. When you praise a child for something very well done, you usually say the following except:

A. Way to go!

B. Good job!

C. Give me a high five!

D. Congratulations!

问题：当你因为一个小孩做得很好而表扬他的时候，
你不会说下面哪一个词语？

答案：D. 祝贺！

　　对某人做的事表示赞赏的英语可以有多种表达。就小孩而言，大人可说 Way to go!（做得好，继续努力！）或是来个 Give me a high five!（击个掌）。Great job! Keep it up.（做得好极了！继续努力。）Good/Nice job! 和 Well done!（干得好！）这两个句子可以用于各种年纪的人。在比较正式的场合，对取得了很显著成绩的人说 Congratulations! 或 Congrats! 以示恭喜和祝贺！ Congratulations on your new job/achievements/promotion.（恭喜你找到新工作/获得成就/晋升。）对生日和节日的祝贺：Happy birthday/reunion/gathering/holiday!（祝你生日/团聚/聚会/节日快乐！）Have a nice weekend!（周末愉快！）Enjoy your vacation.（假期快乐。）Pleasant journey.（旅途快乐。）Smooth trip.（一路顺风。）Tom, I heard the big news that you're engaged! How wonderful!（汤姆，听说了你订婚的大新闻！恭喜！）Ashley, your father told me that you got full scores on SAT. Congratulations!（Ashley，你爸爸告诉我你的 SAT 得了满分。祝贺你！）Laura, I just saw your Facebook post. I am so excited to hear that you're having a baby!（罗拉，我刚在你的脸书上看到你要生孩子了，我太兴奋了！）Marcus, we just heard the great news that you were promoted to senior manager. Hats off!（马库斯，我们刚听说你被提升为高级经理的好消息。向你致敬！）The graduates wearing the cap and gown, are tossing hats in the air in celebration.（身着毕业礼服戴着帽子的毕业生把帽子抛向天空以示庆祝。）

47. Which of the following words is not coined in the U.S.?

A. Catch 22

B. Baby boomer

C. Indian summer

D. Tea

问题：下列哪个词不是在美国创造的？

答案：D. 茶

    Catch 22（第二十二条军规）：一个企图逃跑但又不可能逃脱的悖论。（A paradox in which the attempt to escape makes escape impossible.）这个词来自美国著名小说《第二十二条军规》。从它派生出了a no-win situation 及 a double bind（"一个没有双赢的局面"或"双重约束"）的词语，表示处于一种困境（dilemma），即 Damned if you do and damned if you don't.（做也不是，不做也不是）的恶性循环（the vicious circle）。Baby boomer（婴儿潮）是指在1946年和1964年之间出生的人口，即第二次世界大战后的宝宝热潮。1970年在《华盛顿邮报》（*Washington Post*）的一篇文章中，首次使用"婴儿潮一代"这个词。许多人都试图确定在历史影响下，这一代人文化的相似性，因而这个词得到了广泛的流行。Indian summer（晚春/小阳春），指一个在深秋时，经过一段时间的寒冷天气或霜冻后反常的温暖、干燥、无风的天气。一位来自法国的美国农夫 J. H. St. John de Crèvecoeur 在1778年写的信中第一次用到这一词。当时美国的土族人被误认为是印度大陆人，所以很多新词都有 Indian 一字。Tea 茶一词可能起源于中国，16世纪时茶作为药用饮料被葡萄牙教士和商人首次从中国引入欧洲。17世纪饮茶在英国走红，以福建话"茶"的发音称之为 tea。美国快餐店用的番茄酱（Ketchup/catchup）也是来源于中国。在17世纪，中国混合调制好的酸菜鱼和香料，厦门方言称之为 Kôe-chiap，意思是酸菜鱼盐水酱。18世纪早期，英国探险家发现了传到马来西亚和新加坡的 kecap（印尼马来话）。这个词后来演变成英语单词 katchup（番茄酱），被英国殖民者带到了美洲殖民地。英语中还有不少借自中文的外来语（loan words），如 silk（丝）、Confucius（孔夫子）、Taoism（道教）、typhoon（台风）、coolie（苦力）、ginseng（人参）、kung-fu（功夫）、Mandarin（官话/国语）等。参见 http://www.phrases.org.uk/meanings/american-phrases-and-sayings.html。

48. Which is NOT one of the rights from the First Ten Amnedaments of the U.S. Constitution?

A. Freedom of speech

B. Assembly

C. Freedom of repeal

D. Petition the government

问题：下面哪个不是美国宪法第一修正案中的权利？

答案：C. 上诉的自由

美国宪法中共有 27 个修正案（Amendaments）。其中最有影响的是第一到第十的修正案，也称之为《人权法案》（*the Bill of Rights*）。它包括言论自由（the freedom of speech）、宗教自由（the freedom of religion）、聚会结社自由（the right of the people of peaceably to assembly）、出版自由（the freedom of press）和人民有向政府请愿的自由（the right of the people to petition the government）。在美国建国的独立宣言中，美国宪法的主要作用有三个：建立政府体系（sets up the government）、建立政府规范（defines the government）和保障美国人的基本权利（protests basic rights of Americans）。答案中 C. freedom of repeal（上诉的自由）是法律的一个部分，而不是宪法中修正案的部分。

49. The abbreviation for afternoon is:

A. AD

B. BC

C. am

D. pm

问题：下午的缩写形式是什么？

答案：D. pm

英语中不少缩写来自拉丁语。如 AD/A.D.（公元）是拉丁文 Anno Domini 的缩写，意思为 Since the birth of Christ（从耶稣诞生开始）。西方的日历是以耶稣诞生年开始的，称为公元或阳历年。在此之前的年代称为 BC/B.C.，即公元前，是英语 Before Christ（耶稣诞生之前）的缩写，不是来自拉丁语。公元前 48 年是 48 BC，公元 2014 年的英文是 AD 2014。AD 和 BC 表示时代的开始，没有零年，所以公元 1 年紧跟在公元前 1 年之后。中国是以阴历年（Lunar Year）来计时的。西方的日历将每一天划分成两个周期：a.m. 是拉丁文 ante meridiem 的缩写，即 before midday（午前），p.m. 是 post meridiem 的缩写，即 after midday（午后）。12 小时时钟的使用可以追溯到公元前 1500 年的美索不达米亚（Mesopotamia）和古埃及。罗马人也用一天分为两个 12 小时的时钟。24 小时的机械模拟表盘和时间系统建于 14 世纪，而 12 小时的模拟表盘和时间系统是在 15 世纪和 16 世纪之间，由于更简单方便而逐渐成为北欧的标准计时。24 小时的计时制则用于更专业的应用，如天文时钟和计时器。使用 12 小时的计时要特别注意：12pm 是上午 12 点而不是晚上 12 点（12am）。其他常见的缩写：Etc.（Et cetera），是一个拉丁短语，意思是"和其他东西，等"。We prepared a lot of food, drink, fruit, etc.（我们准备了大量的食物、饮料、水果等）。e.g. 来自拉丁文 examli gratia 读成 for example。Don't eat sweet foods, e.g. cake, ice scream, chocolate.（不要吃甜食，例如蛋糕、冰淇淋、巧克力。）Et al. 来自拉丁文 et alii 意思是 and others（以及其他），常用于论文作者人数较多时。vice versa 或 versa vice，是 the other way around（反过来/反之亦然）的意思。versus（vs）or（v.）意思是 against（相对、与某某比赛）。via 的意思是 by way of（通过、途径），而 by means of 的意思是以某种方式，借助于。

50. When you say "You bet!" you mean all except:

A. Yes.

B. Sure.

C. No problem!

D. Fine.

问题：当你说"You bet！"时，下面哪个不是你要表达的意思？

答案：D. 好的。

You bet! 是一般交谈中的顺意用语，通常表示 Yes，Sure，或 You are welcome. 等含义。并不是"打赌"的意思。如，Tim：Are you going to Rick's birthday party? Jennifer：You bet!（蒂姆：你会参加里克的生日派对吗？珍妮弗：是的！）Nick：Thank you. Jessica：You bet.（尼克：谢谢。杰西卡：不用谢。）Charlie：May I borrow your iPhone? Mary：You bet!（查理：我可以借你的 iPhone？玛丽：可以！）回答对方的谢意，也可以说 No problem! 而通常 fine 用来回答对方的问好。如，How's going? I'm fine. Thank you!（你怎么样？我很好，谢谢！）如对某事很确定，也可以用 bet 构成的短语来表达：I'll bet my bottom dollar that she won't be at the party tonight.（我打赌她今晚不会参加聚会。）在美国，赌博是容许的，但只能在法定的赌场进行，很多州都建有赌场，如内华达州（Nevada）的赌城拉斯维加斯（Las Vegas）和新泽西州的大西洋赌城（Atlantic City）。人们也容许参加赛马场（horse race）的赌马，买彩票（buy lottery tickets）等。

51. What is a nickel worth?

A. $0.05

B. $0.1

C. $0.01

D. $0.25

问题：美国的一个镍币值多少钱？

答案：A. 5 分

　　美国的货币是美元：dollar, U.S. dollar（USD）, American dollar。它分为硬币（coins）和纸币（note/bill）两种。硬币有 1 分（cent/penny），正面是第 16 任总统林肯（Abraham Lincoln）的头像，反面是（Union Shield）联盟之盾；nickel/five cents（5 分），正面是第 3 任总统托马斯·杰斐逊（Tomas Jefferson）的头像，反面是杰斐逊在弗吉尼亚州中部夏洛茨维尔的家；Dime/ten cents（1 角），钱币上面是第 32 任总统罗斯福（Franklin Delano Roosevelt）的头像，反面是橄榄枝（olive branch），火炬（torch），橡树枝（oak branch）；Quarter/25 cents（25 分），钱币正面是第 1 任总统华盛顿（George Washington）的头像，反面的图案每年都有五种不同的。50 cents/half-dollar（50 分），钱币正面是第 35 任总统肯尼迪（John F. Kennedy）的头像，反面是总统印章（Presidential Seal），50 分的很少流行；one dollar（1 元）钱币的正面是第 34 任总统艾森豪威尔（Dwight D. Eisenhower）的头像，反面是在飞翔的秃头鹰（bald eagle）。硬币上都印有 LIBERTY（自由）和 IN GOD WE TRUST（我们相信上帝的字样）。美元的纸币（note/bill）有 $1，图案是华盛顿/美国国徽（Great Seal of US）；$2，图案是杰斐逊/特朗布尔画的独立宣言（Trumbull's Declaration of Independence）；$5，图案是林肯/林肯纪念堂（Lincoln Memorial）；$10 图案是第一任财政部长哈密顿（Alexander Hamito）/美国财政部（U.S. Treasury）；$20 图案是第 7 任总统杰克逊（Andrew Jackson）/白宫（White House）；$50，图案是 18 任总统格兰特（Ulysses S. Grant）/国会大厦（US Capitol）；$100 图案是富兰克林/独立大厅（Independent Hall）等。美元的昵称有：buck（s），意为 $1 或几块美元；grand（s），意为 $1000 或几千美元；k 也用来说一千美元，如 10k 即 $10000。

52. Which of the following is different from the others?

A. Ladies First

B. Ladybugs

C. The Lady of the house

D. First Lady

问题：下面哪个答案与其他的不同？

答案：B. 瓢虫。

Ladies First（女士优先/先走）是西方一种礼貌的表现。First Lady 是对总统夫人的一种敬称。lady of the house（家庭中做主的女主人）。I have to ask the lady of the house to let you stay, as she's the one who makes decisions in here.（我要问房子的老太太是否同意让你留下来，因为家里她做主。）ladybugs 是瓢虫的英文名。first 一词有许多的搭配用法，如 first things first（首要的事情），另一种说法是：first and foremost. Although running for the U.S. president, Donald Trump remains first and foremost a businessman, not a politician.（唐纳德·特朗普虽然在竞选美国总统，但他首先仍然是一个商人，而不是一个政治家。）First Come First Serve（先到先得），常用于餐厅、商店等服务场合。At first glance, the problem appeared quite simple. But it is a very complex one.（乍一看，这个问题似乎很简单，但是问题非常复杂。）Jack and Betty fell in love at the first glance.（杰克和贝蒂一见钟情。）

53. What does Turnpike mean?

A. Highway

B. Freeway

C. A toll road

D. Parkway

问题：Turnpike 是什么？

答案：C. 收费公路

美国的公路四通八达，直通每家每户。公路分成各种级别，有州际公路（interstate highway）即横贯多州的公路、州内公路（state highway）、地方公路（local road）等。许多公路在接近城市的时候分成商业道（business）和本地路（local）。Parkway 是有绿化、风景优美的公路，用于与公园连接的道路，通常卡车和其他重型车辆不能在上面行驶。许多parkway最初为景区，休闲驾驶的parkway现已演变成了城市之间和上下班的主要道路。高速公路在美国称作freeway或是expressway，它提供一条畅通无阻，没有交通信号灯和交叉路口（intersections）的道路，是对所有的流量和出入口管制的道路（a controlled-access highway）。其他的公路、铁路（railways）或人行道（pedestrian paths）是在高速公路上的天桥（overpasses）和地下通道（underpasses）中与高速公路相交。Highway则是任何公共道路的统称，与高速公路相对，如Route 1、Route 22等。Turnpike是收费公路（a toll road）。进入前要在收费站取票（ticket），保管好票，在出高速公路时交票付费。有的parkway和expressway也要收费。通常在进入收费公路前几英里会有明显的告示牌。大部分收费站设有E-ZPass（快速通道），预付钱后不用在收费站停下付钱。要特别注意的是，在个别的收费公路上有些地段是无人收费站，设有投币的网，所以你一定事先准备好硬币（coins），不然就麻烦了。

54. What things do you not have to pay taxes in the U.S.?

A. Food and food ingredients

B. Cars

C. Houses

D. Home property

问题：在美国什么东西不要交税？

答案：A.食品和食品配料

　　在美国，每个工作的人都要交税。税的种类很多，首先是所得税（income tax）。每年在4月15日之前，都要填好税表（file tax return form）寄到国税局（Internal Revenue Service, IRS）。通常联邦税（Federal income tax）和州税（state tax）都已在发工资前就扣除了。税表上要注明工资外的收入，如银行的利息（interests）和股票收入（stock income）等。交税的比率是按个人或家庭的总收入的多少而定。家庭人口的多少也是交税比率的因素之一。国税局会根据税表计算出应交的税额，多退少补。除了联邦税和州税之外，有房产的人要交地税（home property tax）。地税的多少按房和地的价值而定，地域和学区好的地方税就高。另外，在购物方面，大部分商品都要交购物税（sale tax），但是每个州的税法不一样。如纽约市的税是8.875%，新泽西的是7%，而加州是7.5%。注意加州除了州税之外还有市政、区税等，所以税的总额很高。以下四个州没有购物税：Delaware（特拉华），New Hampshire（新罕布什尔），Oregon（俄勒冈）和Montana（蒙大拿）。这些州附近的居民常去无税州购物，尤其是买贵重物件可省钱不少。还有人在网上购物后将物件寄到无税州的亲戚和朋友家省钱。食品（grocery items）通常都不用交购物税，但是熟食（prepared grocery food）和饮料（beverage）常要交税。药不论是需要处方（prescription）的或不用处方的（over the counter）都不用交税。

55. Baby shower means:

A. A baby takes a shower.
B. Name a baby.
C. A party for the expectant mother.
D. Bridal Shower.

问题："婴儿沐浴"是什么意思？
答案：C. 准妈妈的派对

　　Baby shower 不是"婴儿沐浴"（a baby takes a shower/bath）的意思，也不是给婴儿取名（name a baby）。生活中最精彩的一件事就是准备迎接一个新婴儿的诞生（welcome a new baby）。baby shower 就是给准妈妈（the expectant mom）开派对送礼物以示祝贺。礼品多为婴儿用品。在美国最有名的婴儿用品连锁店叫 Babies Rus。儿童用品店是 Toys Rus。准妈妈派对和中国传统的婴儿满月的庆祝相似。Every life is worth celebrating!（每一个生命都是值得庆贺！）Bridal shower（新娘沐浴）是一个准新娘（a bride-to-be）在她举行婚礼前办的送礼聚会。该习俗起源于 19 世纪 90 年代，当今在美国、加拿大、澳大利亚（Australia）和新西兰（New Zealand）最为常见。准新郎（a bridegroom-to-be）也有相对的聚会，叫 bachelor parties（单身聚会）。单身聚会上喝大量的酒，雇用脱衣舞女，未婚妻是不能参加的。赌城拉斯维加斯（Las Vegas）既是办婚礼的热门也是单身派对的一个热门地点。近年来,越来越多的"单身聚会"选择加拿大的蒙特利尔（Montreal）、魁北克（Quebec）和墨西哥（Mexico）。

56. What does 20/20 mean in measuring vision in the U.S.?

A. 1.2
B. 0.8
C. 1.0
D. 2.0

问题：在美国做视力检查时，20/20 是什么意思？
答案：C. 1.0。

在做视力测试时，最常用的视力表（Eye Chart）有 Snellen 和 Tumbling E Chart 两种。Snellen 视力表上有各种字母，而 Tumbling 视力表上是不同方向的 E 字母。方便让不知道字母怎么发音的小孩子使用。另外也分 far vision（远距离测试）和 near vision（近距离测试），也叫 Jaeger Eye Chart 的视力表。在美国做视力测试时，视力程度的表达方式不一样。20/20 是指正常人的视力，相当于中国的 5.0 或国际标准的 1.0 视力。即你站在 20 尺（6 米）的地方，能看到正常人站在 20 尺能看到的视力表范围。如果你站在 20 尺的地方，只能看到最上面的 E 字母，那么你的视力就是 20/200，是普通人站在 200 尺的地方看到的范围，所以你的视力是 0.1，需要戴较深度的眼镜啦！以下是美国，国际和中国视力记录法及相应的眼镜度数对照表：

国际	2.0	1.5	1.2	1.0	0.8	0.6	0.5	0.4	0.3	0.2	0.1
中国	5.3	5.2	5.1	5.0	4.9	4.8	4.7	4.6	4.5	4.3	4.0
美国	20/10	20/13	20/15	20/20	20/25	20/30	20/40	20/50	20/70	20/100	20/200
眼镜度数					100	150	200	250	300-350	450	650

另外 color blindness test（色盲测试）的方式是让孩子在一些图案中，找出数字或图像来，在美国常用的测试方法是 Ishihara 38 Plates CVD Test。与眼睛有关的词语有：青光眼（glaucoma）、白内障（cataract）、老花眼镜（presbyopic glasses）、散光（astigmatism）、眼科医生（ophthalmologists）、验光师（optometrists）。

57. In an American family, who is likely taking care of young children?

A. Nanny

B. Mother

C. Grand parents

D. Father

问题：在美国，谁在家带小孩？

答案：B. 母亲

　　在美国，带小孩的方式与中国很不一样。大多数的工薪族母亲，生了孩子之后，就辞职专门在家带孩子（full time mother）。有几种考虑,其一是如你的工资不高,请保姆（nanny）在费用上省不了几个钱，其二是不放心保姆，因常有保姆虐待儿童的事件发生。另外孩子的爷爷奶奶是根本不会给你带孩子的。孩子几岁后就送幼儿园（kindergarten），自己再重新工作。有的等小孩上小学后才去上班。孩子的幼年得到了较好的照看和教育。美国没有计划生育（birth control），生几个孩子完全由家庭自己做决定。很多州堕胎（abortion）是违法的（illegal）。另外，生孩子时，父亲一定得在产房里（delivery room）协助产妇。如是顺产，产妇只能在医院里住三天就得出院。西方没有坐月子（confinement）和月嫂（confinement nurse）的概念，英语中这两个词的翻译加上解释还不一定让美国人听明白。很多身体状况良好的母亲产后几天便带着新生婴儿逛街了。医生要求产后天天洗淋浴（take showers）并进行适当的活动，以促进身体的恢复。孩子出生后，如母亲的奶不够，可以喂婴儿配方奶粉（baby formula），大一点可以喂营养丰富、品种很多的婴儿食品（baby food）。常用的词汇有：妇产科医生（obstetrician）、孕妇（pregnant women）、破水（water broke）、顺产（natural labor）、剖宫产（caesarean section）、急诊室（emergency room）、救护车（ambulance）、保姆（housemaid/babysitter）、奶瓶（baby bottle）、儿科医生（pediatrician）、验血（blood test）、奶嘴/奶头（nipples）、假奶嘴（pacifier）、奶瓶（milk bottle）、喂母奶（breast feeding）、围兜和打嗝布（bibs & burp cloths）、尿片（diapers）、换尿片（change diapers）、更换垫（changing pad）、澡盆（bathtub）、婴儿（toddler/infant/new born baby）、婴儿床（cribs）、童车（bassinet）、摇篮（cradle）、婴儿座椅（car seat）、婴儿推车（baby stroller）、婴儿玩具（toddler toys）等。

58. At what age do most Americans retire?

A. 55

B. 62

C. 67

D. 50

问题：大多数美国人在什么年龄退休？

答案：C. 67 岁

　　美国人什么时候想退休或能退休，什么时候适合退休，很大程度上取决于什么时候能拿到全额退休金（pension）。每个公民的收入都要缴纳所得税，其中联邦税（federal tax）是充公了，而社会安全税（society security tax）其实就是存你自己的退休金。根据美国社会安全局（Society Security Bureau）的规定，在 1943~1954 年出生的人，可以在 66 岁领取全额退休福利金，1960 年或以后出生的要在 67 岁才能领取全额退休福利金。可以提前申请取退休福利金的最早年龄是 62 岁，但退休福利金的全额会每月减少大约 5%。退休福利金额的多少同你缴纳的税有关。另外，很多较好的企业、单位或政府机构包括公立学校等都有很好的退休计划（retirement plan）。如 401 之类的退休计划，即每月从工资的 3%~5% 扣下来，加上单位配上 3%~5%，一起存入一定机构的退休金计划里，不用交税，等到退休时使用。有的人工作年限长，收入较好，到了 62 岁，他的退休福利金加上单位退休金很可能与他的工资不相上下。这时候，工作和不工作收入一样，当然绝大部分人就会选择提前退休（early retirement）。退休后，可以继续工作；但是提前退休时，收入超过一定数额的话（一年 15120 美元），超过的部分，每 2 美元要从退休福利金扣除 1 美元。到了 67 岁后，无论你收入多少都不会从退休福利金中扣除任何钱。

59. Which of the following is allowed to bring to the U.S.?

A. Vegetables and fruits

B. Meat

C. Cash

D. Gifts

问题：以下哪个物品可以带入美国？

答案：C. 现金

乘飞机进入美国之前，空姐（air hostess）或乘务员（crew members）都会给旅客发海关申报表格（Customs Declaration Form）。一家只填一份。填写的内容如下：1. Family Name（姓），First（Given）Name（名），Middle Name（中间名）、2. Birth date（出生日）：Day 日 /Month 月 /Year 年；3. Number of Family members traveling with you（同机旅行的家庭人数）；4. US Street Address 在美国的地址（Hotel name/destination 旅馆名称或目的地）City（城市），State（州）；5. Passport issued by country（颁发护照的国家）；6. Passport number（护照号码）；7. Country of Residence（国籍）；8. Countries visited on this trip prior to U.S. arrival（到达美国之前去过那些国家）；9. Airline/Flight No. or Vessel Name（航空公司/航班或船只的名称）；从 10 到 14 项的填写都是 Yes（是）或 NO（不是），一般情况下都是填 No：10. The primary purpose of this trip is business（本次旅行的主要目的是商务）；11. I am（We are）bring in（我/我们带有以下物品）；12. I（We）have been in close proximity of（such as touching or handling）livestock（我/我们接近过/如接触和处理牲口）；13. I am（We are）carrying currency or monetary investments over $10,000 US dollars or foreign equivalent（我/我们带有超过一万美元现金或外币）；14. I（We）have commercial merchandise:（我/我们带有商品）；15. Residents—the total value of all goods（美国居民所带物品的总价值）最高限量 800 美元，Visitors—the total value of all goods（访问者所带物品的总价值），最高限量 100 美元，不包括自用的。去美旅行，切记不能带肉类（meat）、家禽（poultry）、水果（fruits）、种子（seeds）等，不然会被没收（confiscate）或罚款（fine）。参见 http://www.cbp.gov/travel/us-citizens/sample-declaration-form。

60. Which is the official language of the United States?

A. English

B. Spanish

C. Chinese

D. None of the above

问题：美国的官方语言是什么？

答案：D. 以上都不是

大家都知道美国人是说英语的，官方语言（official language）当然是英语，不可能是西班牙语（Spanish）或中文。实际上，就美国的法律而言，英语的确不是美国的官方语言。根据美国政府文件，美国没有官方语言（There is no official language of the U.S.）。美国是多种族、多语言的国家，在美国，人们说 300 多种语言。语言用得最多的前五位是英语、西班牙语、中文、法语（French）和德语（German）。虽然官方的文件（government documents）都使用英文，学校教学的语言（language of instruction）除了外语和特殊教育（special education）的手语（sign language）之外，也基本只有英文，但是在法律中没有规定任何一种语言为官方语言。近几十年来，在English-only movement运动的影响下，许多州通过投票将英文定为官方语言，目前18个州仍然没有规定官方语言。阿拉斯加州除英语之外，土著语言都是官方语言。在夏威夷，英语和夏威夷语都是官方语言。另一方面，由于新移民在某些地区不断增加，当地政府为满足需要而在官方文件中附加移民的语言。如在西裔族人口众多的加州和佛罗里达州，官方文件都有西班牙语的版本，很多街道和商店名都是西班牙语。在有些州，也可以用西班牙语或中文考驾照考试。

61. Which of the following refers to as the U.S. Republican Party?

A. Tea Party

B. GOP

C. DNC

D. Town Hall Meeting

问题：以下哪个是用来称呼美国共和党的？

答案：B. GOP

　　共和党通常被称为GOP（Grand Old Party的缩写）即"老派政党"。另一个是其历史上的对手：民主党（the Democratic Party）。根据CBS（哥伦比亚广播公司）的报道，共和党全国委员会（the Republican National Committee）的缩写首字母可以追溯到1875年，那时候它意味着"老派政党"。它原本是民主党的昵称，但是在1888年，Chicago Tribune《芝加哥论坛报》用GOP来称呼共和党，这下子就改不过来了。而人们也想给民主党来个昵称，可找不到一个合适的，DEMS（来自Democartic）也算个昵称吧。DNC是民主党全国委员会（the Democratic National Committee）的缩写。Tea Party（茶党运动）是共和党内的美国保守派推动的运动。其成员呼吁通过减少政府开支和降低税收来减少美国国债（the U.S. national debt）和联邦预算赤字（Federal budget deficit）。市政厅会议（town hall meeting）是公民和公众人物（public figures）之间的非正式公开会议。地方和国家的政治家们常在竞选活动中或出现重要问题时，与他们的选举区的选民在市政厅会议上见面和发表政见。政府官员也常在市政厅会议上就公众关心的问题（topics of interest）和具体的立法或法规（legislation or regulation），回答公众的问题和听取他们的意见。

62. What are the requirements to be president of the United States?

A. She/He must be 35 years of age.

B. A Natural born US citizen.

C. Lived in the U.S. for at least 14 years.

D. All of the above.

问题：要成为美国的总统，你必须达到哪些要求？

答案：D. 必须达到以上各项要求。

　　根据美国宪法（The U.S. Constitution）第二条第一节（Article II, Section 1）规定，参加总统竞选的人（presidential candidates）有年龄和身份的要求，必须至少满足以下三个条件。第一，竞选的人必须是自然出生的美国公民（a natural born U.S. citizen），而不是归化的移民（a naturalized immigrant）；也就是说，竞选人可以是在国外出生的，但其父母双方都必须是美国公民。第二，竞选的人年纪至少满了 35 岁，至今最年轻的总统候选人是 43 岁。第三，在美国生活了至少 14 年，但不一定是连续的 14。由于前任美国总统巴拉克·奥巴马（Barack Obama）的公民身份和担任总统职务资格的阴谋论（conspiracy theories）引起的争议，促使一些共和党的国家和联邦立法者提出立法，要求将来的总统候选人公布其出生证复印件（birth certificates）。1951 年 2 月 27 日批准的美国宪法第二十二修正案第一节规定，任何人不得当选总统两次以上。在这个修正案之前，美国任期最长的总统是富兰克林·德拉诺·罗斯福（Franklin Delano Roosevelt, January 30, 1882—April 12, 1945）。他在第四任期的三个月后死于脑出血。1932 年，在大萧条时期，纽约州州长罗斯福当选为美国第三十二任总统。他领导美国人民度过了大萧条（the Great Depression）并赢得了第二次世界大战（World War II）的胜利。他经常被学者评为三位最伟大的美国总统之一，其他两位总统是乔治·华盛顿（George Washington）和亚伯拉罕·林肯（Abraham Lincoln）。

63. **What did Martin Luther King, Jr. fight for?**

A. Human rights

B. Women's rights

C. Civil rights

D. LGBT rights

问题：马丁·路德·金是为什么而战？

答案：C. 民权

　　20 世纪 60 年代，Martin Luther King, Jr.（马丁·路德·金）是民权运动（civil right movement）的卓越领袖，他为每个美国人，尤其是为黑人争取平等权利（equality for all Americans，black Americans），反 对 种 族 隔 离（racial segregation）和 歧 视（racial discrimination）作出了不懈的努力。1964 年 10 月 14 日，他因倡导通过非暴力抵抗打击种族不平等而获得诺贝尔和平奖（Nobel Peace Prize）。不幸在 1968 年 4 月 4 日 遭到暗杀（assasinaton）。托马斯·杰斐逊（Thomas Jefferson）在《独立宣言》（*the Declaration of Independence*）中就宣布了"所有的人都是平等的"（all men are created equal）。亚伯拉罕·林肯（Abraham Lincoln）在 1863 年的盖茨堡宣言中也发表了以下有关人权的声明：我们坚持这些真理是不言而喻的，所有的人都是平等的，他们被创造者赋予了一些不可剥夺的权利，其中包括生命、自由和追求幸福。（We hold these truths to be self-evident, that all men are created equal, that they are endowed by their Creator with certain unalienable Rights, that among these are Life, Liberty and the pursuit of Happiness.）然而美国至今不是所有的人都得到了平等的对待，种族歧视依然存在，种族冲突（racial conflicts）时常发生。所谓 Human rights（人权）包括 women's rights（妇女的权利）以及 LGBT rights。LGBT 是 lesbian, gay, bisexual, and transgender peoples（女同性恋、男同性恋、双性恋和变性人）的缩写。美国最高法院（the United States Supreme Court）2015 年 6 月 26 日宣布，在所有的州，除了美属萨摩亚和印第安人的土地以外，同性婚姻（same-sex marriage/gay marriage）是合法的。

64. Which is NOT a U.S.territory?

A. U.S. Virgin Islands

B. Puerto Rico

C. Guam

D. New Mexico

问题：哪个不是美国的领地？

答案：D. 新墨西哥州

　　美国除了 50 个州之外，还有不少领地（territory）。目前美国管辖内的一共有 16 个领地，其中有 5 个大的岛屿：U.S. Virgin Islands（美国维京群岛）、Puerto Rico（波多黎各）、Guam（关岛）、American Samoa（美属萨摩亚）和 Northern Mariana Islands（北马里亚纳群岛）。较小的岛屿有 Bajo Nuevo Bank、Baker Island、Howland Island、Jarvis Island、Johnston Atoll、Kingman Reef、Midway Islands、Navassa Island、Palmyra Atoll、Serranilla Bank、Wake Island。New Mexico（新墨西哥）是美国的一个州，原是美国印第安人居住地，1598 年被西班牙人殖民化，成为西班牙帝国维多利亚皇室的一部分；后来，成为独立墨西哥的一个部分，墨西哥—美国战争（the Mexican–American War）之后，于 1912 年 1 月 6 日成为美国的第 47 个州。美国建国时有 13 个州，后来逐建扩大到目前的 50 个州，美国有两个州不在美国本土大陆，一个是 Alaska（阿拉斯加州），它被加拿大与美国隔开，是美国最大的州，美国在 1867 年 3 月 30 日花了 720 万美元从俄罗斯帝国手中购买过来的，每英亩约 2 美分（4.74 美元/平方公里）。另一个是 Hawaii（夏威夷州），由数百岛屿组成，亚裔人口最多，是最后一个于 1959 年 8 月 21 日才加入美国的州。

65. What is the magic word in daily communication?

A. Thank you.

B. Hi.

C. Bye now.

D. Yea.

问题：哪个词是日常交流中神奇的话语？

答案：A. 谢谢。

在美国的日常沟通（daily communication）中，礼貌（courtesy/politeness）和耐心（patience）将会使你受益匪浅。在小学，有许多被称为神奇的话语（magic words）：please（请）、thank you（谢谢）、excuse me（对不起）、sorry（抱歉）、terribly sorry（非常抱歉）、you are welcome（不用谢/欢迎你）。"不用谢"的通俗表达形式还有：you bet 或 no problem（适合在商店、街上、课堂上或在办公室里使用）。如果你需要帮忙（need a favor）或有一个简单的请求（a simple request），说"请"会更有效。只要你是善意的，与你说话的人很可能会答应你的要求。其他礼貌用语还有：Excuse me, may I borrow your pen?（打扰一下，我可以借用你的钢笔吗？）Yes. Please.（可以的，请用吧。）Excuse me, is the chair（seat）taken（may I sit here）?（对不起，这个座位有人坐吗？）I'm afraid it is taken.（对不起，有人啦。）Hi 是与 Hello 同义的问候语，但 Hello 来得正式一些。同样，Yea 是 Yes 的非正式用词，用得很广泛。Bye now 是再见的意思，与 See you/See you later 和 Good bye 差不多，Good bye 正式一些。

66. Which is the state flag of New York?

A.

B.

C.

D.

问题：哪个是纽约州的州旗？

答案：C

　　纽约州的州旗是C。A是印第安纳州（Indiana）的州旗，B是新泽西州（New Jersey）的州旗，D是德克萨斯州（Texas）的州旗。美国由50个州组成，每个州在加入美国联邦之前都相当于一个独立的小国家，有自己的政府机构、法院、法律、旗帜等。在加入联邦后，都保持了相对的独立性。尤其是在立法方面有很大的区别。每个州的驾照考试要求不一样，购物税也不一样，如有的州有死刑（death penalty），而有的州却没有。对违法行为的判断和量刑有很大差别，如在有些州容许娱乐性吸大麻（entertaining marijuana），而有些州吸大麻是重罪。很多美国人家里都有枪支，但必须有州里颁发的持枪证（a state issued permit）。在有些州，有持枪证的居民可以在公众场合隐蔽携带枪支（a concealed weapon），有的州可以公开携带枪支（open carry）。而在加州、佛罗里达州、纽约州、南卡州、伊利诺伊州是违法的。到美国学习或旅游要特别注意当地的法律，许多社会行为在中国不违法，在美国却是违法的。如将13岁以下小孩单独留在家中，或将婴儿或小孩单独留在汽车中是违法的。任何对儿童或妇女的虐待（child/women abuse）都可能被起诉。刮痧也可能被误认为是虐待造成的。擅自在没有斑马线的地方穿越公路叫作Jaywalk，不但是非常危险的，而且也是违法的。参见美国各州州旗：https://en.wikipedia.org/wiki/U.S._state。

Schools & Studies
学校学习篇

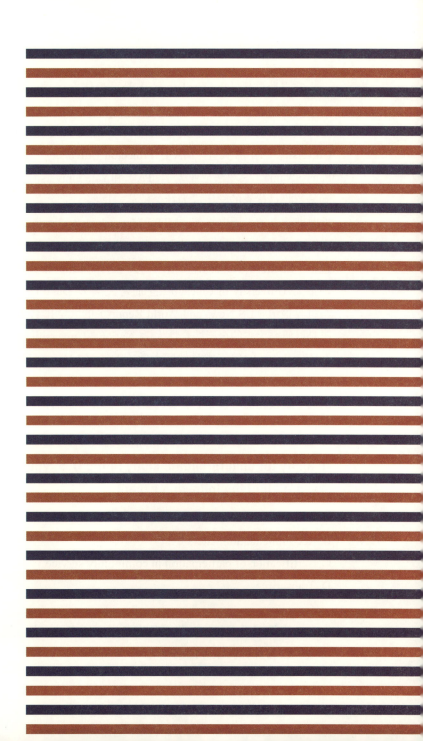

1. Which university does not belong to the Ivy League?

A. Princeton University

B. Harvard University

C. University of Pennsylvania

D. Massachusetts Institute of Technology（MIT）

问题：下列哪个大学不属于常青藤盟校？

答案：D. 麻省理工

　　常青藤联盟（the Ivy League）是一个体育运动的协会，由美国东北部八所著名的私立大学组成：Brown University（布朗大学，RI）、Columbia University（哥伦比亚大学，NYC）、Cornell（康奈尔大学，NY）、Dartmouth College（达特茅斯学院，NH）、Harvard University（哈佛大学，MA）、Princeton University（普林斯顿大学，NJ）、University of Pennsylvania（宾夕法尼亚大学，PA）和Yale University（耶鲁大学，CT）。常春藤盟校的内涵是招收最优秀的学生成为社会精英。这些大学除康奈尔大学（1865）之外，都是在殖民地时期建立的，历史悠久。MIT（Massachusetts Institute of Technology）是最顶尖的工科大学，1861年建于麻省的波士顿，称之为麻省理工。常青藤联盟之外的其他最顶尖的名校还包括：Stanford University（斯坦福大学）、California Institute of Technology-Cal Tech（加州理工）、University of Chicago（芝加哥大学）、Duke University（杜克大学）等。美国新闻与世界报道（US News and World Report）的大学排名（University Rank）为四大类，第一类是以研究为主的全国综合性大学(National Universities)，第二类是文科为主的大学(Liberal Arts Colleges)，第三类是地区大学（Regional Universities），第四类是地区学院（Regional Colleges）。社区大学（community college）没有排名，大多是非本科大学，与中国两年制的大专院校相似。参见下页美国新闻与世界报道的排名介绍。

2. To apply for undergraduate study in the U.S. you must prepare all of the following except:

A. SAT I

B. Recommendation letters

C. Certification of participation in community service

D. Transcripts

问题：申请美国本科生，你必须准备以下所有的文件，除了：

答案：C.参加社区服务证书

美国本科生的入学申请很复杂，要做很多的准备工作。首先是参加SAT考试。SAT原称是Scholastic Aptitude Test（学习能力测验），后改为Scholastic Assessment Test（学习能力评估测试），是由ETS（Educational Testing Service）于1926制定的。近年来ETS对SAT进行了大改革，以前的考试分三个部分：数学、阅读理解和写作。每部分满分800分，共2400分。从2016年开始SAT只有数学（Mathematics）和阅读理解与写作（critical reading and writing）两部分，满分1600分。考试时间是三小时加50分钟的作文。作文部分为选择性的。名校还要求考生考2~3门SAT II 即单科考试，如数学、物理、生物、化学、历史、写作等，每门满分800分。学生可以任意考多少次，以最好的成绩为准。很多美国高中生修许多advanced placement课程，然后参加美国大学理事会（college board）推荐的5分制AP考试。很多大学都接受该成绩，作为入学的参考成绩和大学学分，这样学生在大学里可以少修学分。外籍学生还要考TOFEL，近年来很多美国大学容许用其他英语水平考试如雅思替代TOFEL。参见85页的托福与其他语言考试成绩对照表。申请文件包括2～3封老师的推荐信（recommendation letters）、由学校寄出的成绩单（transcripts）、申请短文（essays）。还有参加各种比赛、活动、义工等获奖或参与证明（certification of participation of community service）。这些证明不是规定的，但对取录很有分量。填写统一的申请表格（common application forms）很花时间，有的学校还要填附加表（supplement），表格都是在网上填写，你可以申请多个学校。不少学校有提前录取申请（early decision），录取率较高，但只能申请一所学校，申请截止日期是11月1号左右。如被录取就一定得去不能改换学校。大部分学校的申请截止日期为12月底。提前录取的通知是在12月中，正常录取通知是在4月1号左右。

美国大学的排名（U.S. University Ranking）

《美国新闻与世界报道》（*US News and World Report*）每年都颁布美国的大学排名，是最具权威的排名。由于每年采用的评分标准有些变化，每年的排名都有所变动。该排名根据大学的类别将美国的大学分为四大类。

第一类是以研究为主的全国综合性大学（National Universities）。其大部分顶尖学校都是私立大学如常青藤联盟，而公立大学都排在20名之后。2018年前20名的大学是：Princeton U、Harvard U、U of Chicago、Yale U、Columbia U、Massachusetts Institute of Technology、Stanford U、U of Pennsylvania、Duke U、California Institute of Technology、Dartmouth College、John Hopkins U、Northwestern U、Brown U、Cornell U、Rice U、Vanderbilt U、U of Notre Dame、Washington U、Georgetown U。最好的公立大学有：UC Berkeley、UCLA、U of Virginia、U of Michigan-An Arbor、U of North Carolina-Chapel Hill 等。该类排名前75位左右的大学都是非常不错的。

第二类是全国文理大学（National Liberal Arts Colleges）。这类大学以本科生教育为主，学校小而精。一般都只有2千学生左右，教学质量一流，丝毫不比第一类学校差。入学的要求有的比常青藤联盟的一些学校还要严。2017 年前 10 名的大学包括 Williams College、Amherst College、Bowdoin College、Swarthmore College、Wellesley College、Middlebury College、Pomona College、Carleton College、Claremont McKenna College、Davison College。这类大学大部分都称为 college。绝对不要误认为 college 比 university 要差，常青藤联盟的达特茅斯学院 Dartmouth College 也是如此。"上大学"的常用英语是 go to college 而不是 go to university! 申请大学不是 university application 而是 college application。美国的大学理事会也叫 College Board 而不是 University Board。

第三类是地区大学（Regional Universities）。主要是以本科生教育为主的综合性大学，有硕士和部分博士学位专业。它以北、西、中西、南四个大区排名。这类大学前十来名的学校都非常好，绝大多数都是私立的。如北区排名中公立大学第一，公私立综合排名第四的新泽西学院（The College of New Jersey）就比该州除普林斯顿大学之外所有第一类排名的大学录取要难。

第四类是地区学院（Regional Colleges）。主要是以本科生教育为主，文科占一半以上，其中有不少很专业化的大学，如美国海岸警卫队学院（United States Coast Guard Academy）和美国商船海洋学院（United States Merchant Marine Academy）。它也是在全美以北、西、中西、南四个大区排名。

社区大学（community college）没有排名，大多是非本科大学，与中国的两年制的大专院校相似，学费非常低。由于近年来美国经济不景气，很多学生就先读两年社区大学，然后转到其他四年制大学，节省很多学费。

对于去美国读硕士或博士学位的学生来说，应该查看《美国新闻与世界报道》的研究生学院（Graduate School）的排名。研究生学院排名的学科有 Business（商务）、Education（教育）、Engineer（工程）、Law（法律）、Medicine（医学）、Nursing（护理学）等。

参见美国新闻与世界报道网页：http://colleges.usnews.rankingsandreviews.com/best-colleges。

3. In American high schools, which of the following events happens more than once a year?

A. Prom

B. Graduation ceremony

C. Homecoming

D. Cheerleading performance

问题：在美国高中的活动中哪个一年举办多次？

答案：D. 拉拉队的表演

在美国的高中，课余时间学生都参加各种学校组织的课外活动（extracurricular activities）和课后项目（after school programs）。与学术有关的有：各学科俱乐部、辩论队（debate team）、剧团等，由学生会主办的活动：fundraising（筹款）、community service（社区服务）等，还有学校的各种体育代表队（Varsity）：football（美式足球）、basketball（篮球）、baseball（棒球）、volleyball（排球）、tennis（网球）、field hockey（曲棍球）、ice hockey（冰球）、golf（高尔夫）、soccer（足球）、swimming（游泳）、track and field（田径）、fencing（击剑）、lacrosse（长曲棍球）、wrestling（摔跤）等。参加这些活动队对今后申请大学很有帮助。如能获得全国或州内大奖，读名校就不成问题了。cheerleading（拉拉队）是学校的热门项目，很多女孩都想参加。她们主要是在足球和篮球比赛期间一展身手。Band（管乐队）也是一样。学校的交响乐队（orchestra）和合唱队（chorus）的规模庞大，几乎每个学生都参加。每个学期都举办表演晚会。美国的初中为三年高中有四年，最后两年分别是junior和senior。这两个年级都会举办舞会，称作prom。prom是promenade的简写，是一个非常正式的舞会。每年一度由senior举办的正式舞会称之为senior prom（毕业舞会）。高中小辈junior参加的舞会称之为junior prom。在舞会上，全校会投票选出一个舞会公主（prom princess）和舞会王子(prom prince)。因此男女学生都事先找好舞伴，身着华丽的礼服,在晚会上竞相比美。homecoming（似水流年）是美国一年一度在高中和大学中举办的传统活动，欢迎校友回母校，通常在9月底或10月初举行。最常见的活动是本校主场的美式足球或者是篮球比赛。活动还包括学校的管乐队和拉拉队的表演、各种游戏以及一个似水流年女王的加冕及舞会等。

4. Which one has nothing to do with college life?

A. March Madness

B. Dead Week

C. Spring Break

D. April Fools' Day

问题：下面哪个答案与大学生活无关？

答案：D. 愚人节

在美国的大学里，通常一个学年和中国一样分为两个学期：秋季（fall semester）和春季（spring semester）。但有些学校是多个学期制称为quarters。暑假（summer vacation）的时间很长，从五月初到八月底为止。夏季很多大学设有夏季课程（summer sessions）供学生修课。在春季，学校都放春假（spring break），时间为一周左右，海滩是很多学生度春假的首选。有的学校还有秋假（fall break）。大部分学校设有国际交流（study abroad）项目，学生可以去国外大学学习半年或一年。通常全日制的本科生（full time students）一学期要修12个学分（四门课），研究生修9个学分（三门课）。在某些学校，本科生12个学分以上的课程免费，所以不少学生每学期都多修几门课来省学费。美国移民局要求外籍学生除了最后一个学期之外，每个学期必须修满全日制学生的学分。另外，要转学的话必须在原录取的学校完成一个学期的学习。大学的考试有quiz、exam、take-home exam（回家做的考试）、finals（期末考试）等。期末考试之前学生突击备考的一周称之为dead week。美国大学强调课堂参与（class participation），课堂发言和讨论是评分的重要依据。美国大学非常重视体育，运动队的比赛是大学生活中一个重要的组成部分，尤其是美国人喜爱的运动项目，如篮球和美式足球，一到赛季，就像过节一般。March Madness（疯狂三月）就是其一，它是美国大学篮球联赛决赛阶段的比赛之象征。可以想象学生球迷那种狂热的程度。April Fool's Day（愚人节）与大学的生活没有直接的联系。在四月一日那天你可以随便开别人的玩笑或搞恶作剧（hoax/make a practical joke）。

5. Which of the following is common on a school supply list?

A. A stapler

B. A desktop computer

C. A file tray

D. A microwave

问题：下列哪一项包括在常见的学习用品清单中？

答案：A.订书机

    在美国，学校开学之前，都给学生发一个要准备的学习用品清单（school supply list）。其中常包括：stapler（订书机）、staples（订书针）、subject-notebooks（分类笔记本）、compositions（作文本）、notepads（记事本）、pens（笔）、pencils（铅笔）、high lighters（荧光笔）、erasers（橡皮）、post-it notes（便笺条）、glue sticks（胶水）、legal pads（长记事本）、folders（文件夹）、binder（活页夹）、index cards（索引卡）、pencil sharpener（卷笔刀）、rulers（尺）、scotch tapes（透明胶带）、hole punchers（打孔器）、calculators（计算器）等。Staplers、Office Depot、Office Max 是提供学习和办公用品（office supplies）的专卖店。每个学期开学前，大量的用品都会打折。常见的学习和办公用品有：desktop computer（桌面电脑）、printer/fax machine（打印机/传真机）、3 in 1 Printer（3 合 1 打印机）、copy machines（复印机）、shredder（碎纸机）、phones（电话）、answer machine（留言机）、typewriter（打字机）。办公家具（Furniture）类：desk（书桌）、bookshelf（书架）、chair（椅子）、bulletin board（公告栏板）、file trays（文件盘）、whiteboard（白板）、file cabinet（文件柜）、desk lamp（台灯）、waster paper basket/bin（废纸篮）。文具类（stationery）：envelope（信封）、manila envelope（牛皮信封）、sticky notes（便签）、message pad（留言簿）、whiteboard marker（白板）笔、paper clips（回形针）、scissors（剪刀）、thumb tacks（大头钉）、pushpin（图钉）、rubber band（橡皮圈）、calendar（日历）等。学校、很多公司和部门都设有休息室或咖啡茶水间、并备有 refrigerator（冰箱）、microwave（微波炉）、coffee pot（咖啡壶）、water dispenser（饮水机）等。

6. Which phrase is not often used in K-3 classroom?

A. Cut and dried

B. Cut and paste

C. Show and tell

D. Turn and talk

问题：在幼儿园至三年级的课堂上，哪个短语不常使用？

答案：A. 拟定好了的

　　美国小学课堂上喜欢做动手型的作业（hands-on activity）。其中之一叫作cut and paste（剪剪贴贴）。另一种常见的活动叫show and tell（展示和讲述），就是教小朋友们带上自己或家庭的照片或实物讲故事。老师让学生们相互交谈时说turn and talk。课堂还常有讲故事时间（story time），小朋友们都围着老师席地而坐，听故事。教室里通常都留有一块空地供讲故事或其他活动使用。任何教室不论是幼儿园还是大学桌椅都不是固定的，可以根据需要临时变动。读书时间可以叫作Dear：drop everything and read。选项cut and dried是个成语，表示常规，拟定好了的。不是课堂中的术语。Although a deal has been agreed, it is not yet cut-and-dried. 虽然交易已经达成协议，但尚未定案。与上课有关的词语有：cut classes（逃课）、play truant（逃学）、tardy（迟到早退）、assignments（作业）、homework（家庭作业）。从中学到大学成绩大都是用A、B、C等来表示，而幼儿园和小学则多用文字表示，如，Exc-Exceeding（超过要求）、Ach-Achieving（达到要求）、Dev–Developing（在发展中）、O/C-Of concern（需注意）和N/A-Not applicable（无关）等。与cut搭配的词语还有：cut（one）loose from somebody/something（解脱）：At last, she cut herself loose from her ex-husband.（她终于从前夫的控制中解脱了。）The exiles had been cutoff from all contact with their hometown.（流亡者被切断了与家乡的所有联系。）cut corners/to take short cuts（抄捷径）：I won't cut corners just to save money.（我不会为了省钱而抄捷径。）Don't cut corners and follow instructions to the letter.（不要图省事，要严格按照说明去做。）cut the crap/Stop the nonsense!（废话少说）：Just cut the crap and tell me what really happened to her recently.（你别废话啦，告诉我近来她到底发生了什么事？）

7. Ashley is very good at reading between the lines. This means she can___.

A. read out loud

B. read for comprehension

C. read extensively

D. read word for word

问题：Ashley非常擅长读懂字里行间的言外之意。
这句话的意思是什么？

答案：B. 她的阅读能力强。

英语阅读（reading）是学习英文的关键之一。但是很多学生和老师对阅读的认识不足，以为阅读就是朗读（read out aloud）；因此上课着重个人朗读和全班朗读。晨读和课堂上常做的读书活动多为朗读或默读（silent reading）。朗读的作用主要是语音的识别（sound decoding/recognition），熟悉词在短语和句子中的发音不是读书的目的，阅读的目的主要是理解（comprehension）而不是语音的识别。在传统教学中，由于只注重在语音即单个词的发音，形成逐个单词的拼读（read word for word），使得语音（phonology）与语义（semantics）的连接脱节，无法提高对短语和句子的理解力。这种阅读的方法应仅在初学时的语音阶段使用。即使在这个阶段也要以理解读的内容，也就是读懂为目的。由于传统教学以一本教科书为主，很少提倡多看书，学习英语变成了所谓的精读（intensive reading）。而真正提高英语能力要大量的阅读即泛读（read extensively）。每个年级都要读至少十几本相同水平的英文原著，从而了解语句、词语的各种用法，这样才有语感，达到理解字里行间的含义（read between the lines）之能力，而靠所谓"精读"是做不到的。在美国，一个学生从幼儿园起，平均每周都看十来本书。一年下来，读的书不是几本而是几十本，甚至几百本，只有这样才能提高阅读水平。中国学生学英语应将"熟读唐诗三百首"的精神转到"读英文书籍三百本"，那效果会让你自己都大吃一惊的。阅读的方法有很多，除了多读之外，另一个问题是如何读。语言和文字都是用来表达思想和传递信息的，所以读书的主要目的就是理解作者的含义，寻找你所需要的信息。简单来说，读书的目的通常是找出诸如以下问题的答案，即找出六个疑问词的答案：who、when、what、where、why、how。朗读或默读都应以理解意义表达方式、词的搭配用法为重点。用自己的话复述（retell）或总结（summarize）看过的内容，对内容提问和讨论都是有效的阅读方法。

8. What school does Psychology belong to?

A. Business School

B. Medical School

C. School of Liberal Arts

D. School of Engineering

问题：心理学属于什么学院？

答案：C. 文理学院

    Psychology（心理学）是美国人爱读的专业之一，属于Liberal Arts（文理学院）。其实，现在心理学应用在很多的领域，包括教育、医学等。Liberal Arts来自拉丁语liberales 是指那些在古代被认为是一个公民必不可少的学科或技能，以履行公民的义务和责任。在古希腊（Ancient Greece），文科的核心包括语法（Grammar）、修辞（rhetoric）和逻辑（logic）三个学科。在中世纪时期又增加了算术（arithmetic）、几何（geometry）、音乐（music）和天文学（astronomy）四个经典的学科（classical subjects），从而构成了中世纪大学课程的七个文理学科。在文艺复兴（renaissance）时期，意大利的人文主义者对文理学科采用了一个更加雄心勃勃的名字：人文主义（humanities）教育。他们排除了逻辑，加入了历史（history）、希腊语（Greek）和道德哲学—伦理学（moral philosophy-ethics）。到了近代，文理教育可以指文学（literature）、语言、哲学、历史、数学、心理学和科学（sciences）等领域，涵盖了生物（biology）和社会科学（social sciences）和人文学科等。通常商科（business）、医学（medicine）、工程（engineering）、法律（law）都是单独的学院。然而，美国大学注重提高所有学生的人文知识，所以大部分学校都要求所有本科生选修一定数量的文理课程（Liberal Arts requirements），如数学、物理、化学、生物、写作、文学、心理、历史、语言等方面的课程，从而提高学生的综合素质。从另一个角度来说，文理课程的学习给学生提供了选择适合自己专业和事业的机会。很多大学生入校之前都没有定专业，在学了一年各种课程后，才决定自己的专业。

9. **A ninth grader is called a____in an American high school.**

    A. freshman

    B. senior

    C. junior

    D. sophomore

问题：在美国的学校里九年级的学生被称作什么？

答案：A. 新生

　　美国的教育体制与中国的大体相同。6 岁开始上小学（Elementary School）。在上小学之前，可以上 preschool（学前班）。学前班又分：为 3~5 岁小孩开的 Pre-kindergarten–Pk（幼儿园学前班）和为 4~6 岁小孩开的 Kindergarten–K（幼儿园）。义务教育（compulsory education）是从幼儿园开始的。小学包括一年的幼儿园和 G（Grade）1~5 年级。有的学区（school districts）分初小（lower elementary school）即 G1~3 和高小（upper elementary school）即 G4~5。中学（middle school）是从 6 年级到 8 年级（G6~8）。高中（high school）有四年，即 9 年级至 12 年级（G9~12）。个别的学校也有把初中和高中合在一起的，称之 Junior High（G6~8）和 Senior High（G9~12）。在四年的高中里，也像大学一样把高一的学生叫做 freshman，高二的学生叫 sophomore，高三的学生叫 junior，高四毕业班叫作 senior。私立学校（private school）的学制也差不多，有不少学校是可以寄宿的，称之为 boarding school。也有以数理化为主的专业高中，如 science/technical academy 等。入读这类高水准的高中，一般都要通过入学考试，对英语的水平要求很高。来美国上私立高中有利有弊，优势在于教学质量高，而且他们与很多名校有关系网，学生较容易被名校录取。但是学费（tuition and fees）昂贵，与读私立大学不相上下，目前大部分好的私立高中一年的费用平均高达 45000 美元。

10. **Which word is different from the other three?**

    A. Calculated

    B. Thought

    C. Measured

    D. Obtained

问题：哪个单词和其他三个不同？

答案：B. 想，思考

在所给答案中，除了 thought，其他的三个单词calculated（计算）、obtained（获取）、measured（测量）都是常用于学术上的动词。学术论文写作常用到的词还有：assumed（假设）、occur（发生）、assign（分配）、emphasize（强调）、execute（执行）、test（测试）、corresponding（相应的）、various（各不相同）、bend（弯曲）、vary（变化）、load（加载）、isolate（隔离）、dissolve（溶解）、refine（精制）、resulting（由此而来）、define（定义）、stress（强调）、illustrates（说明）等。在美国上大学，许多课都需要写很多的文章（essays）或是报告（reports），硕士生要做硕士论文（theses），博士生要写博士论文（dissertations）。一般来说，研究论文都要包括以下几个部分：abstract（摘要）、introduction（引言）、literature review（文献综述）、methods（研究方法）、data collection and analysis（数据收集和分析）、summary/conclusion（总结）、reference/bibliography（参考文献）。而且文章和论文都要按一定的格式来写。最常用的是APA（American Psychology Association）Style（美国心理学协会论文格式）或者是MLA（Modern Language Association）Style（现代语言协会论文格式）（语言类）。APA Style的简介和用法在互联网上很容易找到。如：apastyle.apa.org/www.apastyle.org/learn/tutorials/basics-tutorial.aspx。软件有：Format software：www.styleease.com/www.eazypaper.com/index.cfm/www.refpt.net/。在引用文献Citations方面可参考下面的网站:www.easybib.com/www.liu.edu/cwis/cwp/library/workshop/citapa.htm；www.owl.english.purdue.edu/owl/resource/560/01/www2.lib.unc.edu/instruct/citations/index.html?section=aa&page=1>。

11. "Art washes away from the soul the dust of everyday life." The word "Art"in the sentence means:

A. fine arts.

B. art and science.

C. art gallery, exhibition.

D. works of art.

问题："艺术洗去灵魂中日常生活的尘埃。"这句话中"art"一词的含义为：
答案：A. 艺术，美术。

"Art washes away from the soul the dust of everyday life."（艺术洗去灵魂中日常生活的尘埃。）这句话是西班牙著名画家毕加索（Pablo Picasso）的名言。Art for art's sake.（为艺术而艺术。）古代的艺术主要包括painting（绘画）、sculpture（雕塑）、architecture（建筑）、music（音乐）和poetry（诗歌）五个方面，也包括drama（戏剧）、dance（舞蹈）等。今天的艺术通常还包括如film（电影）、photography（摄影）、conceptual art（观念艺术）和printmaking（版画）。然而，在学院及博物馆里，艺术都只与视觉艺术形式（visual art forms）有关。与艺术有关的用语还有：art auction（艺术品拍卖会）、a piece of art（一件艺术品）、painting（画）、oil painting（油画）、

water and color（水彩画）、ink（墨）、Chinese painting（中国画）、woodcarver（木雕）、paper cut（剪纸）、canvas（帆布画）、Impressionism（印象派）、Abstractionism（抽象派）、art and science（大学里的文理科）、art gallery（艺术画廊）、art exhibition（艺术展览）、works of art（艺术作品）、artist（艺术家）、painter（画家）、calligrapher（书画家）、seal caving artist（篆刻家）、folk art（民间艺术）、decorative art（装饰艺术）。

12. When I see Timothy Kennedy, my instructor, I should greet him with all of the following except:

A. Good morning, teacher Kennedy.

B. Good morning, Professor Kennedy.

C. Good morning, Dr. Kennedy.

D. Good morning, Mr. Kennedy.

问题：当我见到我的导师Timothy Kennedy时，我不应该用下列哪个方式和他打招呼？

答案：A. 肯尼迪老师，早上好。

　　Good morning, teacher. 这完全是中国式的英语（Qing's English 或 Chinglish），即所谓"英语课堂用语"的一种代表性英语用法错误，不是真正英语口语的表达方式。在英语中，teacher（老师）是个职称（position title）而不是称呼（address）或称谓（appellation）。美国称谓的基本礼仪：学校对老师的称呼与在一般公众场合一样，对结婚了的男女称先生 Mr 和太太 Mrs；对没有结婚或是离了婚的女性称小姐 Miss。在书信中，对对方的姓名、性别和婚姻情况不了解时，可用 Ms. 或 Sir and Madam。因此，Good morning, teacher. 应该改为 Good morning, Mr. ×× /Ms. ×× /Mrs. ××. 大学里绝大多数老师具有博士学位，应该称其为某某博士或教授，如，Dr. 或 Professor Kennedy（肯尼迪博士/教授），切记不要用 Mr. Kennedy 或直接用名字 Tim 称呼老师。不然可能会减分。另外，Professor/Prof. 是对所有大学教师的称谓而不是职称。不论是助理教授（asistant prof.）、副教授（associate prof.）还是正教授（full prof.）都一样。其他的领域也是如此，称呼杰克逊工程师，不能说 Engineer Jackson，而应该说 Mr. Jackson, Engineer；介绍王经理或王总工程师，应该说 Mr. Wang, Manager，或 Chief Engineer, Mr. Wang。有些头衔可以直接加在姓之前，如，President Obama（奥巴马总统）、Mayer Blumberg（布隆伯格市长）、Governor Reagan（里根州长）等。除了正式的场合，大多数美国人喜爱亲切自然，结识熟悉之后他们很快就直呼其名字（first name），而不用正式的头衔（formal title）和姓氏（family name）。在极少数正式的场合，开场白用 Ladies and Gentlemen（先生们女士们）。而在许多正式场合，如会议、讲演时都可用如 Good evening, everyone.（大家晚上好。）Good morning. 等问候语开场。男女同学和朋友们之间，常用名字称呼对方，如Jennifer、Timothy、Elizabeth，如果对熟悉的人就常用昵称说：Jen（Jennifer）、Tim（Timothy）、Lisa（Elizabeth）。对很多人可以说，Hi Guys. Hello Guys.

13. Which is prohibited on American college campus?

A. Wearing slippers

B. Being completely nude

C. Riding on scooters

D. Eating in classroom

问题：在美国大学的教室里什么是禁止的？

答案：B. 全裸/一丝不挂

　　美国大学的课堂里，对学生的穿着打扮、发型（hairstyle）等没有要求，可以穿任何式样的服饰，通常穿jeans（牛仔裤）、shorts（短裤）、skirts（裙子）、t-shirts（T恤）、sweatshirts（运动衫）、sweaters（毛衣）等。但是不可以一丝不挂（nude），至少要用遮羞布（loincloth）。夏天穿拖鞋（wearing slippers）和flip flop（人字拖鞋）的学生很多。在作课堂报告、面试等场合，学生可能会被要求穿得较正式些（dressed up）。如你要参加某个特别的活动，最好向主办单位咨询一下什么服装适当（appropriate attire）。在课堂上，可以吃东西和饮料（eating in classroom）。教授们开会时也是如此，上课穿西装的不多。校园里常看到学生蹬着滑板（ride on scooters）去上课。但是教会办的中小学和大学（schools and universities run by Church or religious organization），对男女学生的服饰（dressing codes）、举止、言谈都有严格的制度。美国所有的公立学校（public schools）都没有校服（school uniforms），也没有学生寄宿（boarding），而大多数的私立学校（private schools）都有校服，学生可以寄宿也可以走读。

14. Which of the following is not common in an American elementary school classroom?

A. Posters

B. Pets

C. Computers

D. Smart board

问题：下列哪一项在美国的小学教室里是不常见的？

答案：B. 宠物

在美国，走进小学的教室里就像到了博物馆，什么都有，琳琅满目。大多数的教室备有 smart board（智能板）、chalkboard/whiteboard（黑板：美国的黑板大多是白色或浅绿的）、projector（投影仪）、computers（电脑）、TV（电视）、手动铅笔刀（pencil sharpener）等教学设备。比较富裕的学区，从高小开始就给学生提供苹果平板电脑，中学开始提供手提电脑（lap tops）。教室的墙上常挂满了各种海报（posters）、学习的图片（pictures）、表格（graphics）、学生的作业（assignments）等。有时，空中也挂了不少装饰物。教室里的书架（bookshelves）上有各种读物、字典（dictionaries）、教材（instructional materials）、参考书（reference materials）、学习用的各类纸张、彩笔（color pencils）、记号笔（markers）、蜡笔（crayons）、剪刀（scissors）、胶水（glue）、胶带（tapes）、订书机（staplers）、打孔机（hole punchers）等。教室的角落里还有装学生作业、教具（realia）、资料的文件柜（file cabins）。有的教室还专门设有各种学习园地，如阅读园地（reading center）等。有的老师在地上放一块地毯，让小学生席地而坐，领着读书。美国的教育讲究参与（participation），即学生和老师、学生和学生之间的互动（interaction）。所以教室的桌椅都是可以移动的，分小组而坐便于活动和交流。教室里有宠物（pets）的不多，但有时可以看到金鱼（golden fish）、乌龟（tortoise）、蜥蜴（lizard）等小动物。幼儿园和初小的一些教室还备有自来水的水池（tap and sink）、厕所（toilet）和挂书包和衣物的地方。在教室外的走廊里都是学生的作业和手工栏，各个班级一比高低。

15. Which is not part of the college graduation ceremony in the U.S.?

A. Caps and gowns

B. Diplomas

C. Convocation

D. Commencement

问题：下列哪一项与美国的大学毕业典礼无关？

答案：C. 开学典礼

美国的大学毕业典礼（graduation ceremony）的场面非常壮观，校园里处处张灯结彩，各处都立帐篷提供免费的小吃和饮料，毕业生的亲朋好友都会从各地赶来共贺。毕业生身穿毕业服（caps and gowns），各个大学的毕业服有自己的服饰和颜色。毕业证书（diplomas）一般都是在本专业举行的毕业典礼上颁发，而全校的毕业典礼的学位授予仪式（commencement）最隆重，多数都是在体育馆里举行。入场式犹如奥运会，在传统的进行曲 *The Pompand Circumstance* 的演奏下，由校长、校监和教授领队首先入场，然后是毕业生按院系在家属的欢呼声中入场。*Graduation Walking March*（《威风凛凛进行曲》）是 Sir Edward Elgar 爵士在 1901 年为管乐团创作的，标题取自莎士比亚的名剧《奥赛罗》。（参见 www.youtube.com/watch?v=Kw-_Ew5bVxs。）典礼包括校长讲话、毕业生代表讲话和邀请的名人（Commencement Speaker）讲演。随后是全校毕业生逐个上台领取毕业证书（有的学校）。学校会雇佣专业摄影师（photographer）拍下每个毕业生受校长颁发证书的照片和录像。你可以付费索取。最后由校长确认学位（degree conferring），毕业生届时可以将穗（tassels）从帽子的右侧移至左侧（turns their tassels from right to left），接着把帽子抛向天空表示大功告成，然后是退场仪式。仪式结束后毕业生与亲友、教授、同学们在校园内照相留念。Convocation 通常是开学的典礼集会。

16. Plagiarism does not apply when you___.

A. paraphrase or quote some one's words or ideas
B. copy and paste materials without giving credits to authors
C. use copy right materials without author's consent
D. use other's concepts or ideas without citations

问题：下列哪一项不算抄袭?
答案：A. 复述或引用一些人的话或想法

　　抄袭（plagiarism）在美国是绝对不能容忍的。在大学里如发现学生的作业（assignments）、研究文章（essay/research paper）、论文（thesis）、博士论文（dissertation）等有抄袭的话，学生会受到严厉的处分（punishment），甚至被勒令退学（expelled）。常见的抄袭有 copy and paste materials without giving credits to authors（复制和粘贴材料而没有提到作者），use copy right materials without author's consent（未经作者同意使用了有版权的材料），use any concepts or ideas of others without citations（使用了他人的任何概念或观点而没有表明来源出处）。现在很多美国大学给教授们提供了识别抄袭的软件，很容易就可以知道学生的作业是否有抄袭。如果要引用他人的材料和观点，一是直接引用（quotation），并在文章中表明作者和在参考文献（references）中列出材料的出处。二是用自己的话复述和总结一些人的话或想法（paraphrase or summarize some one's words or ideas），同时表明来源。如何在文章中和文献中标明引用，请参考美国心理学会（American Psychological Association）出版的 *the Publication Manual of the American Psychological Association*（《美国心理学会出版手册》），简称 APA Style。写语言方面的论文，参见现代语言协会（MLA-Modern Language Association）出版的《研究论文作者手册》（*Handbook for Writers of Research Papers*）的文献引用和文献列表的格式要求。

17. What is not the appropriate classroom behavior in the U.S.?

A. Interaction

B. Participation

C. Ask questions

D. Keep silent

问题：在美国的课堂里什么样的行为不适当？

答案：D.沉默不言

这道题与教育的理念有关。不同的教育制度对学生的要求不同。在课堂里，学生的行为和表现受制度的约束。在美国的课堂里，老师特别要求学生积极地参与讨论（discussion participation），促进同学之间和师生之间的互动（interaction），鼓励学生主动提问（ask questions）和发表自己的看法和见解（share their ideas and opinions）。这些都是评分的重要依据，因为美国的教育注重每个人的发展（focus on individual development），尊重个人的见解，培养个性（cultivation of personality）和发挥个人的创造性（creativeness）。在课堂里一言不发保持沉默（keep silent）的表现是消极和不认可的。与老师的眼睛交流（eye contact）也是课堂要求的行为。另外，美国的教育提倡课后多反馈（feedback）与同学之间的交流，参加小组学习（group study/teamwork），多和老师沟通等良好的学习行为。就老师而言，骂学生（abuse students），体罚学生（corporal punishment）是严重的违法行为。老师也不容许触摸学生（touch students）。老师与未成年的学生（minor）发生关系也是违法行为。

18. What health records you must prepare before going to study in the U.S.?

A. CDC

B. Flu shot

C. Vaccination

D. Medical history

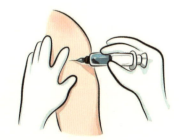

问题：去美国留学，你必须准备哪些健康档案材料？

答案：C. 预防接种

　　进入美国的任何学校，你都必须准备好一份预防接种（Vaccination）证明。幼儿园、中小学要求有出示疫苗的记录。参见下面新泽西州幼儿园至 12 年级学校免疫规定表。美国的幼儿和中小学学生的疫苗都是在自己家庭医生的诊所接种。在幼儿园和中小学里，学校要求发烧或是咳得很厉害的学生不要来校上课，以免传染或影响其他学生。如果学生在校发烧、生病，会马上送到学校护士办公室检查和观察，然后学校会立即通知学生的家长将学生接回家。学校组织校外参观或郊游活动时，学生如需要服药，必须将药连同医生证明交给同行的老师保管，不能自带任何药物。参加任何体育活动都要出示医生签署的健康证（Medical exam）。大学里一般都要递交以下疫苗接种证明才能入学：肺结核TB（tuberculosis）、麻疹（Measles）两剂（doses）、流行性腮腺炎（Mumps）两剂、风疹（Rubella）一剂、B型肝炎（Hepatitis B）三剂。其他答案是：CDC（Centers for Disease Control and Prevention）是美国疾病预防控制中心，学校和社会上出现任何传染病（infectious disease），如肺结核、新型流感（Flu）、脑膜炎（meningitis）、艾滋（AIDS）等都必须立即上报美国疾病预防控制中心。Flu（influenza）shot是流感疫苗，美国大学里每年都提供流感疫苗注射。Medical History是病史。

表2-1　新泽西州幼儿园至 12 年级学生免疫规定（New Jersey K-12 Immunization Requirements）

Minimum Number of Doses for Each Vaccine（每种疫苗的最小剂量）			
Vaccine（疫苗）	幼儿园至 1 年级	2 至 5 年级	6 年级以上
DTaP: Diphtheria（白喉） Tetanus（破伤风） Acellular Pertussis（无细胞百日咳）	4 剂（doses）	3 剂（doses）	3 剂（doses）
Polio（小儿麻痹） Inactivated Polio Vaccine（IPV） （灭活脊髓灰质炎疫苗）	4 剂（doses）	3 剂（doses）	3 剂（doses）
MMR: Measles（麻疹） Mumps（腮腺炎） Rubella（风疹）	2 剂（doses）	2 剂（doses）	2 剂（doses）
Varicella/Chickenpox（水痘）	1 剂（dose）	1 剂（dose）	1 剂（dose）
Hepatitis B（B型肝炎）	3 剂（doses）	3 剂（doses）	3 剂（doses）
Meningococcal（脑膜炎双球菌）			1 剂（dose）

19. "Pros and Cons" stands for all except:

A. In favor and against

B. Advantage and disadvantage

C. Strong point and weakness

D. Problems and concerns

问题："Pros and Cons" 这个短语的意思与下面哪一个不一样？

答案：D. 问题和顾虑

　　pros and cons是拉丁语 pro et contra的缩写，意思是for（in favor of）and against 支持和反对或正反两个方面，常用在对一个事物或事情进行评论时，讲述其优点（advantage/ strong points）或缺点（disadvantage/weakness/shortcomings），即长处或短处。例：He and his classmates debated for hours about the pros and cons of setting up their own firm.（他和他的朋友们就自己创办公司的利弊一起讨论了数小时。）The various arguments in favor of and against a motion.（赞成和反对议案的各种争论。）在会议上做表决时，主持人常会说，Those in favor, raise your hand or say I.（赞同的请举手或说 "我同意"。）The house of representatives are in favor of（in support of）the gun control bill.（众议院赞成的枪支管制法案。）在课堂上或学术讨论时，常常会用到pros and cons这个词语，来阐述一个事物的利弊或得失。例如：Could you do me a favor?（能否请你帮我一个忙？）Favorite是它的形容词，例：Basketball is my favorite sports.（篮球是我最喜欢的运动。）答案D：Problems and concerns 是 "问题和顾虑" 的意思。其他：Alan took advantage of her even after they were divorced.（甚至在他们离婚后，Alan还在占她的便宜。）

20. "I am speechless." means:

A. I am tongue-tied.

B. I am doing tongue twist.

C. I lost my voice.

D. I am so surprised and don't know what to say.

问题："I am speechless." 这句话的意思是什么？

答案：D.我惊讶得不知道该说些什么了。

句子 I am speechless.（我无语。）与 I am so surprised and don't know what to say.（我很惊讶，不知道该说些什么。）的意思相近，也与 I am shocked.（我很震惊。）的意思接近。另外 I am tongue tied.（我的舌头打结了。）可能是因为紧张或其他原因说不出话来了。I feel literally unable to speak（lost my tongue）when I argue with people.（当与人争论时我就成哑巴了。）哑巴（dumb）的英文表达是 a dumb person/man，结巴是 stammer。"哑巴吃黄连，有苦说不出"可以译成 a mute victim 或 A dumb person ate a does of bitter herb, and had to suffer in silence. I am doing tongue twist.（我在说绕口令。）slip of tongue 是滑舌、口误或说漏了嘴的意思。说漏嘴了或泄漏还可以用 give something away 来表示。I lost my voice.（我失声了。）A sarcastic remark was on the tip of his tongue.（挖苦的话到了他嘴边却没说出来。）在美国的中小学都有 speech pathologist/specialist（言语病理学家/言语专家），他们给有语言障碍（speech impediment）的学生提供语言矫正和治疗（speech therapy）。其他相关短语还有：make/give/deliver a（graduation）speech（作讲演）：The specialist gave a speech（talk/workshop）on global warming.（专家作了一场有关全球变暖的演讲。）speech contests（讲演比赛），speaker（讲演者），keynote speaker（主讲人）等。My sister won the first place in the schoolwide English Speech Contests.（我妹妹在全校的英语讲演比赛上获得了第一名。）

21. What is not part of parental involvement?

A. Do homework for your children

B. Participation of teacher/parents conference

C. Participation of classroom activities

D. Read to your children

问题：下面哪一项不是家长参与的一部分？

答案：A. 帮孩子完成家庭作业

在孩子的教育中，家长的作用不能忽视。在美国的学校中，家长和老师及学校的关系不是公司和消费者（company and customers）之间的关系，而是同盟军（allies）。学校十分重视和鼓励家长积极参与自己孩子的教育（participation of their children's education）。在每个学期的开始阶段，学校会在某个晚上举办回校之夜（Back to School Night），让家长与孩子的所有老师见面，了解各门课的内容和要求。每个学期都举行老师与每个家长的会面（teacher/parents conference），交流孩子的学习情况和讨论如何协助孩子提高。学校设有家长教师协会（PTA-Parent-Teacher Association）或家长教师学生协会（PTSA-Parent-Teacher-Student Association）。PTA 旨在促进家长的参与，是由家长、教师和工作人员组成的一个正式组织。老师期待每个家长都能到课堂里参加学生的一些活动（participation of classroom activities），如与学生一起读书（read together）或做游戏（play games）等。老师也期望家长在家里能积极配合老师，协助、检查和监督孩子做家庭作业（homework assignments），但不是帮孩子完成作业（do homework for your children）。孩子的课堂考试卷和作业带回家后都要家长签字后带回学校，这样家长可以了解孩子的学习情况。家长在家里可以做以下事情来帮助孩子的学习，如经常与孩子谈论学校和学习的价值，鼓励孩子以积极的态度上学，尊重教师（respect teachers），给孩子做行为的榜样（model behavior），给孩子读书（read to your children）及听你的孩子朗读（read out），与孩子交谈，询问他们正在学习的东西,问孩子在学校对什么感乐趣、对什么不感乐趣及帮助他们养成良好的学习习惯（strong study habits）等。

22. A School field trip includes the following except:

A. pick up pumpkins on a farm.
B. have activities on a camp.
C. go to Disney World.
D. go to a movie.

问题：学校组织的实地访问活动不包括以下哪个内容：
答案：D. 看电影。

　　美国的中小学常常组织一些实地访问（field trip）的活动，以扩展学生的知识、促进提高学生的社交活动和群体生活的能力。如，在秋季组织小学生去农场摘南瓜（pick up pumpkins on a farm）或者去博物馆（museum）、科技馆（science museum）、海族馆（aquarium）、赫西巧克力工厂（Hersey Factory）参观。有时学校会组织中学生去野外露营地开展各种文体活动（have activities on a camp）。学校要求学生自己准备好行装，如睡袋（sleeping bag）、洗漱用品、换洗衣服等。需要带药品的学生必须要有医生证明而且要将药品交护士保管。通常由学校租长途汽车接送学生，所有的费用由家长负责。也邀请家长自愿参加协助管理和照看学生。不少学校的高中毕业班在毕业前都去迪斯尼乐园（go to Disney World）、六旗公园（Six Flags）、环球影城（Universal Studios）或其他场所游玩。除了实地访问的活动之外，有的学校还组织一些大众体育活动，如去溜冰场（skating rink）溜冰（skating），到纽约的百老汇（Broadway）观看《狮子王》（*Lion King*）或《美女与野兽》（*Beauty and Beast*）等剧目。看电影或球类比赛通常不是学校组织的实地访问活动的内容。但是学校的许多运动队（varsity）和社团（clubs）会募捐（fund-raising）组织参加或观摩比赛。

23. What color is the hood of Medical School gowns in the U.S.?

A. Orange

B. Light Blue

C. Green

D. White

问题：美国医学院毕业礼服的罩袍是什么颜色的？

答案：C. 绿色的

　　美国的校际学位服装局（the Intercollegiate Bureau of Academic Costume）对各个学科领域服饰的颜色进行了规范，并且美国教育理事会（the American Council on Education）在其学位服装码（Academic Costume Code）中予以认可。毕业礼服（gowns/robes）罩袍（hood）的颜色是有规定的。外层（Shell）的颜色与礼服的材料相同，但不论哪个学校都是黑色的。罩袍内衬（Inner lining）的颜色与专业学科所规定的颜色一致。如医学院是绿色（green）、工程学院的是橘色（orange）、文理学院（Humanities）的是白色（white）、教育学院是浅蓝色的（light blue）、商学院是土褐色（drab）、法学院为紫色（purple）、哲学为深蓝（dark blue）、社会科学和自然科学是金黄色（golden yellow）、音乐是桃红（pink）、艺术和建筑是棕色的（brown）。有的毕业生身上带有披肩（stole）来表示学术上的成就或是某个组织的优秀成员，如The Phi Beta Kappa Society（ΦΒΚ）（美国最古老的文科与科学的荣誉协会）。另外优秀的毕业生常配有各种荣誉带（honor cords）。如 summa cum laude（享有最高荣誉），magna cum laude（最优等成绩荣誉），cum laude（优等成绩荣誉）等。请参见各学科的毕业礼服：https://en.wikipedia.org/wiki/Academic_regalia_in_the_United_States。

24. What is the usual number of students in an elementary school class in the states?

A. 15~20

B. 10~14

C. 20~30

A. 30~40

问题：美国的小学里，一个班一般有多少个学生？

答案：A. 15~20 人

在美国，从小学到高中，每班的人数都在 15~20 人左右，极少会超过 25 人，很多的班常常在 15 人左右。幼儿园和学前班的人数更少一些。在许多小学里，老师还配有教师助理（teacher's aid/assistant）。小学里一到五年级，除了 physical education（体育）和 music（音乐）课之外，每个科目即英语、地理、历史、数学等全部课程都是由班主任（homeroom teacher）一人来教。从初中一年级（中国的六年级）开始，老师分科目教 language arts（语文）、mathematics（数学）、social studies（社会学）、science（科学）、world languages（世界语言）、health education（健康卫生教育）、art（艺术）、computer（电脑）、music 音乐。音乐中，老师教乐器（musical instruments）和组织合唱队（chores）、乐团（band）和交响乐队（orchestra），并定期表演（recitals）。从中学开始，由体育老师组织学生参加各种体育活动，并组织运动队，如 cross country（长跑）、boy's soccer（男孩足球）、girl's soccer（女孩足球）、basketball（篮球）、lacrosse（长曲棍球）、field hokey（曲棍球）等。到高中后，各门课都是专业老师上。科目包括：computer graphic design（计算机制图）、English（英语）、social studies（社会学）、physics（物理）、chemistry（化学）、math（数学）、geometry（几何）、biology（生物）、PE（体育）、music（音乐）、world language（世界语）等。体育活动队又增添了 cheerleaders（拉拉队）、football（美式足球）、swimming（游泳）、fencing（击剑）、golf（高尔夫）、volleyball（排球）、ice hokey（冰球）和多个田径项目（track and field events）等。

25. Which is not a financial assistant available for foreign students at American Universities?

A. TA
B. RA
C. Scholarship
D. Federal Financial Aid

问题：在美国大学里哪种经济资助是不提供给外国学生的？
答案：D. 联邦政府的经济资助

在美国读大学，费用是个大问题。近年来，美国大学的学费高涨不停，学生们和家长都怨声载道。通常美国学生都是通过 FIFSA（Free Application for Federal Student Aid）申请 Federal Financial Aid（联邦政府的经济资助），即低息贷款（low interest loan）。而联邦政府的经济支助只提供给美国公民（American citizens）和永久居民（permanent residents），国际学生不能申请。公立大学的学费虽然比私立大学低，但是，国际学生要付外州或高于外州学生的学费（out of state tuition and fees），这样一来与私立学校的费用都差不多了。因此，申请到奖学金（scholarship）来减轻学费负担至关重要。读本科生的外国学生可以申请学校提供的奖学金，读研究生的可以申请TA — Teaching Assistant（助教）或RA-Research Assistant之类的奖学金。通常这些助学金免去学费和学杂费之外还提供全年的生活费用。如申请不到这类的奖学金，到了学校后，仍然有获得资助的一些机会。外国学生允许在校内打工，所以可以申请各类工作，如研究生助理（graduate assistant），做为本专业服务的工作。此外，可以询问有研究项目经费的教授是否需要请一些助手。还可以做学生工（student work），一般是在一些办公室工作，也可以在图书馆工作，以小时计工资。如果是学工科的，还可以在一些实验室、电脑室找到工作。留学一年之后，经济上有困难的国际学生可以申请到校外工作的许可证（working permit）。另外，常青藤联盟和很多私立大学的学费是按学生家庭收入的多少而定的，即need based。以前有位读哈佛大学的中国学生说是拿到了全额奖学金，其实是因为家庭收入低于美国的家庭贫困线（federal poverty line）以下，所以学校免其学费并提供生活费用，并非特别优秀而获得的全额奖学金。2018年家庭年收入的贫困线是：一人家庭为\$12140、两人家庭为\$16460、三个家庭为\$20780，四人家庭为\$25100，五人家庭为\$29420。

26. Which one of the following doctorate degrees does not require a dissertation?

A. Ph.D.

B. M.D.

C. Ed. D.

D. D.B.A.

问题：以下哪个博士学位不需要写博士论文？
答案：B. 医学博士

博士学位有很多种：Ph.D.—Doctor of Philosophy（哲学博士）、M.D.—Medical Doctor（医学博士）、D.M.D.—Doctor f Dental Medicine（牙医博士）、D.Eng.—Doctor of Engineering（工程博士）、Ed.D.—Doctor of Education（教育博士）、D.A.—Doctor of Arts（艺术博士）、D.M.A.—Doctor of Music Arts（音乐艺术博士）、J.D. —Law Doctor/Juries Doctor（法学博士）、Honorary Doctorate（名誉博士）等。不同专业的博士学位课程长短不一，一般为6~8年。博士的课程不多，主要是做研究和写论文。虽然在美国医学博士不用写论文，但是成为医生是一个漫长而艰辛的过程。读医学院（Medical School）首先要完成本科学历，任何学科都可以，但一定要修完医学院入学所规定的必修课，参加MCAT（The Medical College Admission Test，即医学院入学考试）。考试包括生物和生物系统的生物化学基础部分（Biological and Biochemical Foundations of Living Systems），生物系统的化学和物理基础（Chemical and Physical Foundations of Biological Systems）、心理、社会和生物学基础的行为（Psychological, Social, and Biological Foundations of Behavior）及关键分析和推理技能（Critical Analysis and Reasoning Skills）四个部分。很多申请人都已有硕士甚至博士学位，入学率为 3% ~5%，竞争白热化。四年医学院学习期间，还要参加三个步骤的考试，其中包括 8 小时的 USMLE（The Unites States Medical Licensing Examination，即美国医师执照考试），然后申请实习医生（residency programs），这个过程叫 Match。之后至少要在主治医生（attending physicians）的指导之下做 3 年的实习医生，有的专科 specialties 需要 5~7 年的培训（fellowship/specialty training）后才能行医。

27. Which one of the phrases means, "study hard"?

A. Bookworm

B. Book smart

C. Hit the book

D. Bookmark

问题：哪个短语表示努力学习？

答案：C. 刻苦学习

刻苦学习（study hard）的习惯说法是 hit the books 或 pound the books。I gotta go home and hit the books to prepare for the finals.（我得回家温习功课准备期末考试了。）Hit 有不少习惯用法。The missile hit the target.（导弹击中了目标。）Today's biggest hit is Adele's "*Someone Like You*."（当今最热门/流行的歌是阿黛勒的《像你一样的人》。）Let's hit the road.（让我们上路吧。）其他答案：bookworm/bookish 是指书呆子，爱读书的人。book smart 是指很会读书的人。学习不认真的表达有：Nick is very sloppy on his assignments and needs it get on the ball.（Nick 做作业太马虎了，要专心才行。）其他与书有关的词语：bluebook（蓝皮书，指政府官方报告或统计）、bookmark（书签）、textbook（教科书）、book stand/bookends（书挡）、bookshelf/bookcase（书架）、instruction book（说明书）、handbook（手册）、guidebook（指南）、traveler's book（旅行指南）、bookkeeping（记账）、a checkbook（支票本）、a high school yearbook（高中年鉴）、Yellow book（电话簿）、notebook（笔记本）、picture books（图画书）、comic books（漫画书）、composition book（作文本）等。短语用法也有不少，如：We should do it by the book.（我应该按规则办事。）Nicole doesn't look very intelligent, but you can't judge a book by its cover.（Nicole 看上去不是很聪明，但你不能以貌取人。）She has her nose in a book.（她在埋头读书。）She has no secrets, her life is an open book.（她没有

什么秘密，她的生活尽人皆知。）另外 book 可以用作动词，如：book a hotel room（订旅馆）、book airline tickets（订机票），又如 I've booked a table for four tonight.（今晚我预订一张四人的餐桌。）

28. Which of the following is a student's organization usually for men at American Universities?

A. Fraternity

B. Sorority

C. Martial Art club

D. Phi Beta Kappa

问题：在美国大学里以下哪个通常是男学生的组织?
答案：A. 兄弟会

　　在美国的大学里有众多的学生组织（student organizations），如联谊会（fellowship）、会社（societies）和俱乐部（clubs）。他们都是校方认可和支持的。他们给学生提供丰富的机会来提高学生的领导才能、实现自己的目标和价值、自由探索和结社、向他人学习和为他人服务、分享收集个人和共同的价值观和利益，从而促进学生自己全面的发展。最常见的联谊会有兄弟会（Fraternities）和姐妹会（Sorority）。兄弟会顾名思义是男生的组织，而姐妹会是女生的。这些组织颇有历史渊源，他们在 1820 年就从欧洲传到美国。通常都是用由 the International Greek Council（国际希腊理事会）认可，以希腊字母命名组成分会（chapters）。如 Sigma Phi Epsilon,（Σ Φ E）、Alpha Delta Pi（A Δ Π）。各联谊会的章程不同，但基本上都包括以下五个方面（1）保密;（2）单一性别的会员;（3）新成员的选择：审查和试用过程（probationary process）;（4）该联谊会的本科生成员居住和所有权;（5）使用一套复杂的识别符号：包括希腊字母、纹章成就、密码、徽章、鲜花和色彩。在美国，The Phi Beta Kappa Society—Φ B K（优等生协会）被广泛认为是全美最负盛名，历史最悠久的荣誉会社（honor society）。它于 1776 年 12 月 5 日在威廉与玛丽学院（College of William and Mary）成立，现有 284 分会，旨在推动和倡导卓越的文科和理科，吸纳美国大学中最优秀的文理科学生。其希腊字母的意思是"爱学习是生活的指南"（Love of learning is the guide of life.）。要注意的是近年来有些学生组织出现了些违法行为，参加这些组织要审慎行事。

29. Which of the following is different from all other schools?

A. Magnet School

B. Chapter School

C. Public School

D. Private School

问题：哪个学校与其他的学校不一样？

答案：D. 私立学校

　　在美国教育体系中学校分公立（public school）和私立（private school）两种。公立学校的经费主要来源于学校所在社区的地税（property tax）收入。好的区税收多，能雇佣到好的老师，教学设施也齐全，因此教育水平较高。反之，贫困区的教育由于缺乏资金，教育的水平较低。有的学区包括幼儿园（kindergarten）和学前班（preschool）。私立学校的经费主要来源于学生的学费（tuition）和赞助（donation），所以学费昂贵，一般的私立高中年学费高达 4 万~5 万美元，几乎与私立大学的费用相等。大部分私立学校要求学生穿校服（uniform），有的要求住校（boarding school）。较好的私立学校入学要通过考试。大部分私立学校是由教会组织（religious organization）办的，对教会会员优先。特许学校（chapter school）是独立运作的免费公立学校，要求高，课堂内外容许自由创新，注重个性教育，教学质量较高。每个特许学校如正规的公立学校一样由校董事会（school board）管理。董事会由社区、商业和教育的领导组成，制定学校的使命（mission）、合同、课程、学生对象、绩效目标（performance goals）和评估方法（methods of assessment）。尽管有独立性，特许学校及其董事会仍就学生表现和评估对州政府负责（held accountable）。magnet school（磁石学校）是提供特殊或专门课程的公立学校，旨在从整个学区或多个学区吸引学生集中学习某个学科，如 mathematics（数学）、natural sciences（自然科学）、engineering（工程学）、humanities（人文科学）、social sciences（社会科学）、fine or performing arts（美术或表演艺术）以及 technical/vocational/agricultural education 技术/职业/农业教育。入学常需要参加入学考试、面试（interview）、试镜（audition）等。stem schools 指专门提供科学（science）、技术（technology）、工程（engineering）和数学教育（mathematics）的理工科学校，入学需要参加严格的考试。参见美国高中各类学校的排名：http://www.usnews.com/education/best-high-schools/rankings-overview。

30. In the U.S. public schools, special education programs are provided for students with the following except_____.

A. autism

B. dyslexia

C. hearing-impaired

D. vision impaired

问题：在美国公立学校除了_____的学生之外给以下学生提供特殊教育的课程。

答案：B. 有阅读困难

在美国，国家对残疾人（disabilities/handicapped）予以特别的照顾，每年都拨巨款资助他们。大学的特殊教育专业很火热。除了专门的残疾人学校之外，美国的各个学区都给有特殊需求的学生提供特殊教育的课程（special education programs）。国家和州政府都拨专款给特殊教育的课程，除了残疾人之外，有听力障碍（hearing-impaired/hard of hearing）和视力不好（vision impaired）的学生也可以参加特殊教育的课程。通常，学生进入或离开该课程都要通过由老师、辅导员（counselor）、心理专家（psychologist）、特殊教育专业老师（special education teacher）、语言病理学家（speech pathologist）和家长组成的小组鉴定才行。特殊教育的课程是给在身体（physical）、心智（mental）、社会（social）活动十分有限的学生，如给患有自闭症（autism）的儿童提供的。dyslexia是指在阅读或解释文字、字母或其他符号方面有障碍，但智力不受影响的学生之总称。这样的学生不需要上特殊教育的课程，但是应该获得更多的阅读指导。另外，残疾人和需要特殊照顾的学生，参加考试时可以申请给予较长的考试时间。在大学里，国家对患有残疾的学生提供减免学费计划，只要学习认真，还给他们提供免费住房和生活助理生。

31. Which of the following is different from all others?

A. TOFEL

B. IEITS

C. TOEIT

D. ACTFL

问题：以下哪个缩语与其他的不同？

答案：D. ACTFL

ACTFL 是 American Council on the Teaching Foreign Languages（美国外语教学委员会）的简称。该委员会的目标是改善和扩大教学并教授各种语言。会员包括 12500 多名从小学到研究生教育，以及政府和行业的外语教育者和管理者。它设有各种语言的口语 OPI（Oral Proficiency Interview）和写作 WPT（Writing Proficiency Test）的水平等级考试。而题中其他的选项都是英语水平考试（English proficiency tests）。大部分说英语的国家要求留学生申请入学时提供英语考试成绩（English language test score）。目前有很多种英语考试。TOEFL（托福）是美国 ETS-Education Test Service（美国教育考试服务中心）出版的，有笔试 the TOEFL Paper（Paper Based Test）、用电脑考试的 TOEFL CBT（Computer Based Test）和网上考试的 TOEFL IBT（Internet Based Test）三种。ETS 还开发了 TOEIC—The Test of English for International Communication（国际交流英语考试/托业）。该考试是专门设计用来衡量在国际商务环境中（international business environment）工作的人应用英语的能力。所以他们的评分方法都不同。IELTS—International English Language Testing System（雅思——国际英语语言测试系统）是由英国文化协会（the British Council, IDP），澳大利亚雅思（IELTS Australia Pty Ltd）和剑桥英语语言评估（Cambridge English Language Assessment）共同管理。TOEFL, TOEIC, IEITS 的评分标准不一，参见以下由美国教育考试服务中心制作的 TOEFL Equivalency Table（托福与其他语言考试成绩对照表）。

表 2-2　托福与其他语言考试成绩对照表（*TOEFL Equivalency Table by ETS）

TOEIC	TOEFL Paper	TOEFL CBT	TOEFL IBT	IELTS
0~250	0~310	0~30	0~8	0~1.0
	310~343	33~60	9~18	1.0~1.5
255~400	347~393	63~90	19~29	2.0~2.5
	397~433	93~120	30~40	3.0~3.5
405~600	437~473	123~150	41~52	4.0
	477~510	153~180	53~64	4.5~5.0
605~780	513~547	183~210	65~78	5.5~6.0
	550~587	213~240	79~95	6.5~7.0
785~990	590~677	243~300	96~120	7.5~9.0
990	677	300	120	9

* This table is adopted from ETS's Website.

世界上大部分说英语的国家要求英语非母语的留学生在申请大学时，提供英语考试成绩（English language test score）。目前世界上有很多种英语考试。因为他们各有自己的语言测试和计分系统及标准，使用起来很混乱。最常见的语言水平考试有 TOEFL, IELTS 和 TOEIC 三种。ETS 建立了一个成绩对照表供学生参考。

TOEIC—The Test of English for International Communication（托业）

TOEFL—Test of English as a Foreign Language（托福）

TOEFL Paper—Paper Based Test（笔试）

TOEFL CBT—Computer Based Test（电脑考试）

TOEFL IBT—Internet Based Test（网上考试）

IELTS—International English Language Testing System（雅思）

32. Which of the sentences below makes no sense?

A. To be or not to be, that is a question.

B. Colorless green idea sleeps furiously.

C. Read the word, read the world.

D. Language is the tool of tools.

问题：下列哪个句子没有任何含义？

答案：B. Colorless green idea sleeps furiously.

Colorless green idea sleeps furiously.这个句子没有任何含义。其字面直译是"无色的绿理念拼命地睡"。这个句子是世界著名的语言学家Norm Chomsky为证明语义（semantics）与词法（syntax）是可以分离的而造的句子。这个按语法规则造出来的典型例句说明了学习英语光掌握语法是不行的，还必须用词搭配得当，符合英美人的习惯，句子才有可能达意。所以，学英语只背单词毫无作用，记住词与词的搭配和习惯的短语，才能学会地道的英语表达方式。"To be or not to be, that is a question."（生存还是毁灭，这是一个问题。）是大文豪莎士比亚（Shakespeare）的名句。"Read the word, read the world."（认字能了解世界。）是巴西著名的教育家Paula Freire的一句名言。他用来鼓励社会底层的人们提高读写能力（literacy），来认识和解读世界，从而获取力量（empower）。他著有《被压迫者的教育学》（*Pedagogy of the Oppressed*），很有影响力。Lev Vygotsky是当代最有影响力的俄国心理学家（psychologist），他的著作都是在他去世（1934）多年之后，由他人整理出版的。他最有名的著作是*Mind in Society*（1978）和*Thoughts and Language*（1962）。"Language is the tool of tools."（语言是工具之工具）是他的一句名言。他的另一名言也与语言有关：A word devoid of thought is a dead thing, and a thought unembodied in words remains a shadow.（一个字缺乏思想是一个死的东西，而没有体现在文字中的思想只是一个影子。）

33. Which is NOT the responsibility of a school counselor?

A. Helping students in college application.

B. Assisting students who suffer from depression.

C. Giving students advices in selecting courses.

D. Making decisions on what extra-curriculum activities for students.

问题：以下哪个不是学校辅导员的职责？

答案：D.对学生的课外活动做决定。

很多家长和一般公众往往不知道美国学校辅导员（school counselors）是干什么的。在美国的中小学中，学校辅导员扮演很重要的角色。他们必须有学校心理辅导硕士学位（a master's degree in school counseling）并持有州政府颁发的证书（the state certification），秉持着道德和专业标准（the ethical and professional standards）。他们的职责包括帮助所有的学生在学业上获得成功和个人在社会上的发展和职业发展（career development）、指导学生选课（giving students advices in selecting courses）、协助学生申请大学（helping students in college application）、处理换课学生的课程（change courses）或与学生闹事者（trouble makers）谈话、帮助那些患抑郁症的学生（assisting students who suffer from depression）等。但是辅导员不能对学生的课外活动做决定（making decisions on what extra-curriculum activities for students），通常由学生自己选择参加哪种课外活动。

34. To apply for graduate study in the U.S., you usually do the following except:

A. take GRE, or GMAT, or MCAT.

B. contact your potential advisers.

C. have an interview.

D. do school visit.

问题：申请读美国的研究生，你通常要做以下所有事项，除了：

答案：D.参观学校。

报考本科生时，学生和家长都喜欢去理想的学校参观（school visit）。而读美国研究生和申请读本科生的途径很不一样。从入学考试来说，不同的专业有不同的考试。大部分专业要求申请人提供普通的GRE—Graduate Record Examination研究生成绩考试。有的专业要考GRE Subject Test（GRE专科考试）。商科是考GMAT—Graduate Management Admission Test（管理研究生入学考试），少数学校的商学院也接受GRE。读医学院要考MCAT—The Medical College Admissions Test（医学院入学考试）。法学院研究生的入学考试是LSAT—Law School Admission Test。牙医学院入学考试是DAT—Dental School Admissions Test。研究生的专业排名与大学的总排名不完全相对，专业排名前列的不一定都是全美最有名的大学。如德州奥斯丁大学（University of Texas at Austin），总排名是56位，而它的会计专业（accounting）和石油工程专业（petroleum engineering）全美排名都是第一。申请学校时，可以首先从以下研究生学院指南书籍上了解提供自己学科专业的学校的相关信息，如其学科排名、入学要求、学费、生活费用及提供奖学金的情况等。如 *Best Graduate Schools 2018 Guidebook*（《2018年最佳研究生学院指南》），*Barron's Guide to Law Schools*（《拜伦法学院指南》），*Barron's Guide to Medical Schools*（《拜伦医学院指南》）等。然后直接发电子邮件与研究生主任（graduate coordinator）联系，了解是否提供经济资助（assistantship）或奖学金（scholarship），就业等情况。申请博士学位前一定要了解带博士的导师（Doctoral Advisors）、研究项目主管或首席调查员（PI—Principal Investigator），他们的研究方向（research topics）、研究项目（research projects）和经费（budget/grant），然后直接联系导师（contact your potential advisors）。博士的导师基本上能决定是否录取。正式申请后，一般都要面试（have an interview）或网上或电话面试。读大部分理工科的博士学位，如录取都会有奖学金，文科就要因学校而异了。参见美国新闻周刊的研究生专业排名：http://grad-schools.usnews.rankingsandreviews.com/best-graduate-schools。

35. Which of the following is classroom teaching?

A. Teach someone a lesson

B. Teach an old dog new tricks

C. Teach one's grandmother to suck eggs

D. Teach a math class

问题：以下哪个短语是课堂教课？

答案：D.上数学课

　　课堂教学的英语表达有：teach a class或teach a lesson（上课），give a lecture（作报告），give a speech（作讲座），give a presentation（作讲演），give a workshop（教研习班）。Teach（someone）a lesson 是一个成语，意思是教训某人一顿。You can't teach an old dog new tricks. 是个谚语：老狗学不了新把戏（朽木不可雕也）。Teach one's grandmother to suck eggs. 也是个谚语：教奶奶打鸡蛋，意思是班门弄斧。有一个关于如何学习的俗语，对学

习的方法和概念很有解读：Tell me I will forget；teach me I will remember；and involve me I will learn.（告诉我，我会忘记；教我，我会记住；让我参与，我会学会。）learn a lesson（吸取教训/引以为戒）：Yvonne should learn a lesson from her mistakes.（伊婉要从错误中吸取教训。）与 trick 搭配的语句有：It's a tradition in America to play（pull）tricks on people on April Fool's Day（April 1st）.（美国人在愚人节（四月一日）互相开玩笑是个传统习俗。）a bag of tricks（诡计多端/雕虫小技）：Graphic designers have a large bag of tricks！（平面设计师一个个都有很多绝技！）TV program providers are using every trick in the book to stay in the competition.（电视节目提供商想方设法在竞争中生存。）

36. Which of the following is different from all the others?

A. Montessori

B. Phonics

C. Whole Language

D. Child Psychology

问题：哪一选项与其他的不同？

答案：D. 儿童心理学

儿童心理学研究儿童从诞生至青春期间，在生物（biological）、生理（physiological）、心理（psychological）和情绪（emotional）方面发生的变化过程。其他三个答案都是与教育理念或方法有关。phonics（拼音法）是对英语的阅读和写作有帮助的方法之一。拼音的目标是提高读者的语音意识（phonemic awareness），包括：听（listen），识别（identify）和使用音素（phonemes），学会基础语音方面的知识，以便能对新书面文字的解码（decode），掌握拼写（spelling）的模式，对在初级阶段的语音、单词的拼读、拼写方面有一定的帮助。与 phonics 相对的是 whole language（全语言或整体语言）。全语言是一种识字的理念（a literacy philosophy），强调儿童应注重含义和战略指导（focus on meaning and strategy instruction），认为那些在阅读教学和写作中，以拼音为基础，强调解码和拼写的观点是错误的。从整个语言的角度来看，语言是一个决定含义的完整系统（a complete meaning-making system）。整体语言教学工作者倡导开发学生字形和字音（graphophonic）、句法（syntax）、语义（semantics）和语用（pragmatics）等各个方面的语言知识。Montessori（蒙台梭利）教育体系是意大利教育家蒙台梭利博士（Dr. Maria Montessori）在 1870~1952 年开发的教育模式。它强调重点放在培养孩子的独立性（independence），给他们一定范围内的自由（freedom within limits），尊重孩子在心理、身体和社会方面自然的发展（respect for a child's natural psychological, physical, and social development）等方面。教学模式的要点是：1. 强调环境对教育的影响（environment impact），2. 教学以儿童为中心（children centered/ student choice of activity），3. 注重儿童的个性发展（individual development），4. 把握儿童的敏感期（sensitive period），5. 提供丰富的教具（realia），6. 倡导建构和发现（construction and discover），7. 混合年龄教学（mixed age classroom），8. 教室内的行动自由（freedom of movement）。

37. A modern concept of the role of a classroom teacher is all of the following except:

A. a lecturer

B. a learning facilitator

C. a guidance counselor

D. a knowledge dispenser

问题：从现代的概念来看，任课老师的角色，
    除了___之外，应该包括以下各项。

答案：A. 作报告的人

当今在美国，教师的职责随着以学生为中心（student centered）的教育理念的推广而转变。与中国传统式的以老师为中心（teacher centered）、照本宣科（echoes what the book says）、填鸭式（spoon-fed）的教授方式截然不同。美国老师从单一的讲课，重复课本上的字句类似做报告的人，成了多功能的角色。老师是学生成长的指导员（a guidance counselor），了解每个学生的需求（individual's needs），为他们制订个人发展计划（individualized curriculum and plan）。老师是学习诱导员（a learning facilitator），根据教学大纲，拟定好学习的内容，介绍学习的方法和窍门，安排学习步骤和活动，检测学生的学习来促进学习。老师也是一个知识饮水机（a knowledge dispenser），用各种方式展示知识，提供学习的资源。这样的老师在课堂教学，尤其是语言教学中，采用的基本步骤是：1. 展示实际的语言表达方式（give samples of the expressions），强调什么时候用（when do you use it）和在哪儿用（where do you use it）。2. 学生演示（rehearsal）刚学的语言表达方式。3. 布置课后的实战作业（home assignments to use the expressions in real life）。4. 下一次上课时由学生汇报作业完成的结果，老师给予反馈（give feedback）。

38. **Learning activities should be all of the following except:**

A. fun and enjoyable

B. enlightening

C. dull drills or repetition

D. social interaction and hands on

问题：课堂的学习活动除了 ＿＿＿ 之外，应该是以下各项。

答案：C. 单调的操练或重复

　　中国学生到了美国学习后，对课堂教学都会有一种清新的感受。"上课"在中国几乎是"听课"的同义词。学习的要点是听（listen）、记（take notes）、背（memorize），和计算机的记录和储存功能（record it and put it into memory）相似。教师是重复课本上学生上课之前就已经背下的内容，老师和学生之间鲜有交流和沟通，最多就是问些问题，其实就是老师提问学生回答，考学生而已，课堂活动无非是枯燥的练习。在美国的课堂里，是学生提问考老师，向权威和传统观念挑战（challenging authority and convention）。美国的课堂设计更人性化，桌椅可以任意组合。活动活动，动才能活。反之，中国的课堂活动大部分不能"动"，座椅都钉死了，哪能"活"呢？因此，课堂必须有活动的空间。首先活动必须是有意义的（meaningful）而且以引人入胜（fun、enjoyable、enlightening）的方式，展示、讨论新知识的信息处理过程（information processing）。课堂上的互动（interaction）是必不可少的主要活动方式之一，包括学生与老师之间、学生与学生之间、学生与社会之间（social interaction）的互动，而且要有行动、动手做（hands-on）的内容。小组讨论和小组项目（group discussions and projects）、展示（demonstration）、PPT报告（Power Point presentation）、游戏（games）是活动的常态，你想不参与都不可能。活动中还充分利用各种教具（realia），如视频材料（audio-video）、直观教具（visual aid）、图片（pictures）、卡片（fresh cards）等来开展活动，使活动丰富多彩。学习语言应该就是playing the language games（玩语言游戏），学生在游戏和有趣的活动中不知不觉地学到了知识。

39. A textbook is all of the following except___.

A. for intensive reading

B. a curriculum guide

C. a guidance book

D. a resource

问题：教科书不是 ___ 。

答案：A.用来精读的

　　教科书（textbooks）在英国称为教材（course books），是在学习任何一个学科的手册（a manual of instruction）或指南（a guide）。其实就是教育大纲（a curriculum guide）的课堂部分，主要是起指导作用，使教师掌握在该阶段学生应学习的大致内容。教师要根据学生的实际情况作调节，可以作为上课用的材料和学习的资源（resource）之一。不少语言和其他科目的老师常将textbooks作为上课唯一用的材料，翻来覆去地精读（for intensive reading），这是不妥的，尤其是教语言，一本书怎么能展示语言的浩瀚用法呢？就是把教科书一字不漏地背下来，也不可能达到应用该语言的能力。在美国，没有全国统一或统编的教材这种说法。教材都是由许多私营出版公司（private publishing companies）出版。在大学里，教授各自决定用什么书，同专业的同一门课，各个教授用的教材不一样。这就是西方倡导的"学术自由"（academic freedom）的一种体现，是教育成功的关键之一。它鼓励学生和教师在学业、学术上不受拘束（unrestricted），不墨守成规（break etiquette），开拓新思想（fresh thinking），敢于创新（innovation）。美国大多数的K-12（幼儿园至高中教育阶段）公立学校，是由当地学校董事会表决来采用州教育局批准的教科书中的哪一种。教师收到书后发给学生使用，用完后交回老师，给下一年的学生使用。然而，通常学校并不要求教师使用教科书，所以他们喜欢用许多其他的材料代之，而不是就用那本教材。

40. Parents and teachers in the U.S. encourage children to do all of the following except:

A. to be proud of themselves.

B. to have their own identities.

C. to take responsibilities.

D. to compare or compete with their peers.

问题：在美国，家长和老师鼓励孩子们做以下各项，除了：

答案：D.与他们的同龄人相比或竞争。

　　如何教育孩子，东西方的理念有很大的差距。在东方，尤其是在中国，望子成龙（hope one's children will have a bright future）是每个家长的愿望，这无可非议。但是以家长式的（patriarchy）教育方式，按家长的一厢情愿去强加执行家长主导、全盘安排的成功之路，收效不佳，还往往适得其反。反观，美国的家长和老师从小就引导孩子树立个性（to have their own identities），对自己要充满信心和自豪感（to be proud of themselves），所以他们对孩子以鼓励（encouragement）为主，而不是批评（criticism），不是总拿孩子的短处（shortcomings）与邻家孩子的长处（advantages）比或与他们的同龄人相比或竞争（to compare or compete with their peers），不是老盯着孩子学习的分数（scores）或班上的排名（ranking），而是强调参与（participation），注重是否尽了自己的努力，是否在进步之中。至关重要的一点就是他们从小培养孩子要有责任心（take responsibilities），对自己的学习、生活、行为和将来负责（responsible for their own study, life, behavior and future）。这样孩子们就不会有依赖感，具备完全独立生活的能力（independence），并能决定自己的生涯（to choose their own career）。从小家长和老师就容许和鼓励孩子发表自己的意见、见解（to air their own opinions），尊重孩子做出的决定和选择（respect their decisions）。这样孩子才能适应社会变革（social change），并在个性（personality）、情感（emotional）、自我概念（self-concept）、个性的形成（identity formation）等方面得到发展。在美国，报考和上哪所大学都是孩子自己做决定（decision making）。如果孩子整天都在父母、朋友、老师的压力（pressure）之下，他们会成为没有思想、没有主见、没有创造性、不能独立生活的人。

41. Which of the following pairs is different from all the others?

A. Student centered—Students needs

B. Individual battle—Teamwork pride

C. Repeated exercises—Group projects

D. Obey, agree, follow—Challenge, question, lead

问题：下列哪一对与所有其他的不同？

答案：A. 以学生为中心——学生的需求

　　东西方的教育理念不同是众所周知的。最近钱志龙教授（2014）对中国与美国的教育作了精辟的对照分析，令人深思和反省。本题介绍了他提出的几个对照。如，在学习中，中国是强调个人奋斗，而美国是鼓励团队合作精神（Individual battle—Teamwork pride）；中国是死记硬背、拼命做习题，而美国是提倡小组活动相互交流（Repeated exercises—Group projects）；中国的学生要求听从、赞同、遵循老师、家长、权威的意见，而美国培养学生敢于向传统的理念和权威挑战、勇于提出问题、和提高自己的领导才能（Obey，agree，follow—Challenge，question，lead）；中国的教学模式是填鸭式或知识的灌入式，而美国是注重启发式教育（heuristic teaching），点燃学生心灵中的求知欲望（Fill the bucket—Kindle a fire），充分发挥学生的潜力（bring up individual's full potential）等。这些对照对中国改革教育制度、教学理念、教学方法有指导作用。目前中国的教育状况，在很多方面让人担忧，如学校只追求升学率（enrollment rate）和排名（ranking），老师也只能以此为教学目标,结果教学成了以老师为中心(teacher-centered)的局面,把考试作为唯一的检测标准，采用填鸭式、题海战术，补习成风，竞赛成风。从幼儿园起就进入了全面的激烈竞争，其程度都超过古代的秀才备考状元了。儿童的身心健康受到摧残,天真可爱的童年（childhood）生活没有了，应该是享受金色童年的时光，却被繁重的各种功课和自己不愿意做的活动取代了。每天要承受来自老师、同学、家长和社会的巨大压力，现在是该让孩子们回归自然的时候了。

42. After school , the school kids in the U.S. usually do all the following except___.

A. engage in all kids of sports

B. participate volunteer activities

C. do extra schoolwork

D. join community services

问题：放学后，美国的孩子们通常不 ___。

答案：C. 做额外的功课

    在美国，中小学生上课的时间都不一样，高中生最长，早上校车来接的时间最早，上课时间一般从早上 7 点半左右到下午 3 点，初中是 7 点 45 到 3 点，小学是 8 点到 3 点，幼儿园和初小是 9 点到下午 1 点左右。上了一整天的课后，学生需要放松和娱乐，做自己喜爱的活动，而不是做额外的功课（extra schoolwork）。学校布置的家庭作业（homework/assignments）很少。除了少数亚裔之外，很少有学生去像 Kumon（苦闷）之类的连锁补习班学习。很多学校放学后由学校组织课外文体活动（after school programs），从高小开始有乐队（orchestra/band）等，初高中开始，除了参加各个体育队（engage in all kids of sports）的活动之外，很多学生会自己组织开展活动，如学生会（Students' Union）、剧团（theatre troupe）、数学（mathematics）、化学（chemistry）、物理（physics）、生物（biology）、写作（writing）、机器人（robots）、环境保护（environmental）、联合国辩论（United Nations Debate）、录像（video）、校刊（school press）、美食家（gourmet）、尊巴舞（zumba）等学术和文艺俱乐部（clubs）。他们经常参加社区服务（join community services）和志愿者的活动（participate volunteer activities），如教新移民的英语（teach new immigrants English）、为慈善事业筹集资金（raise money for charity）等。放学后，学生通常坐校车回家。学校也提供校车送参加各种课外活动的学生回家，有时需要家长自己接孩子回家（pick up kids）。如需要在上课期间接孩子回家，必须到学校主办公室（main office）签字。学生因生病或其他原因不能去学校上课（absence from school），必须电话或书面通知学校的辅导员（guidance counselor）。

43. The phrase "my two cents" means____.

A. take in

B. my opinion

C. changes

D. valueless

问题：短语"My two cents"的意思是____。

答案：B. 我的见解/看法

　　短语"my two cents"常用在讨论问题时，表示自己的看法（opinion）。而不是我的两分钱，或是找的零钱（change）。put my two cents in...（我的看法是……）That is just my two cents in this issue.（这仅是我对这件事的一孔之见。）表达意见的短语还有：I think...；In my opinion...（我的想法是……）；As far as I'm concerned/know（就我而言/所知……）；In my view...（在我看来……）；I don't think/believe...（我不认为/不相信……）Well, if you ask me...（嗯，如果你问我……）If you want my honest opinion...（如果你想听我的诚实意见……）；According to news report...（据消息报道说……）If you ask me...（如果你问我……）询问别人对某事或问题的表达有：What do you think?（你怎么看？）What's your idea?（你的想法是什么？）How do you feel about that?（你对这件事有什么感想？）Do you have anything to say about this?（你有什么要说的吗？）What are your thoughts on all of this?（你对这一切有什么想法？）I've never come across the idea that...（我从来没有遇到过这样的想法……）。I don't take in the problem.（这个问题我弄不清楚。）On the one hand... on the other hand...（一方面……另一方面……）They claim that...（他们声称……）They also say...（他们还说……）Opinion among teachers is that...（教师的意见是……）That's a matter of opinion.（这是见仁见智的问题。）Ask/seek for a second opinion（征求别人的意见。）I would like a second opinion from a specialist on my illness.（我想找一位专家对我的病进行二次诊断。）

44. When you write an academic paper or essay, you are likely to use the following phrases except_____.

A. support the hypothsis

B. provide a rationale

C. present a finding

D. engage a discussion

问题：在写学术论文和文章时，你常会使用以下除了_____之外的短语。

答案：D. 参加讨论

　　在写学术论文时，有很多常用的术语（terminology），如 support the hypothesis（支持这一假设）：The data in the research report does not support the hypothesis.（研究报告中的数据并不支持这一假设。）provide（give, explain）a rationale（提供理由）：In the introduction, a rationale for the study must be provided.（在导言中，必须提供该项研究的理论基础。）present a finding（陈述一项发现/研究结果），statistically significant（从统计学上看很重要）：The results（research finding）are not statistically significant.（从统计学上看（研究）结果没有什么意义。）学术研究一般分定量研究（quantitative research）和定性研究（qualitative research）两大类方法。Research design in quantitative research is used to control or explain variance while qualitative research focuses on gathering in-depth and detailed data on case studies.（定量研究的研究设计是为了控制或解释差异，而定性研究收集深入和详细的数据进行个案研究。）其他的统计学术语：data analyses（分析数据），standard deviation（标准差），descriptive statistics（描述性统计），percentile（百分比），median（中值），mean（平均值），mode（模式），significance（显著性），P-value（P值：p<0.01 表示研究结果是由于随机机会 random chance 而导致的几率不到 1%），corelation（比对/相关性），correlation coefficient（相关系数），r-value（r值）。engage a discussion（参加讨论）不是写学术论文和文章时用的术语。

45. Which of the following phrases is different from all others?

A. Get knowledge

B. Learn by heart

C. Present a finding

D. Make much progress

问题：下列哪一个短语与其他的不同？

答案：D.取得了很大的进步

所有答案中的短语都与学习有关，但只有make much progress（取得了很大的进步）是老师对学生学习的评估时常用的，与其他短语不同。常用评语还有：show a marked/remarkable/no improvement（显示出明显的/显著的进步或没有进步）；room for improvement（有改进的余地）；a quick/slow learner（接受能力强/弱的学生）；a mental agility（思路敏捷）；a straight A student（全优学生）；a mature student（成熟的学生）；has a natural talent（备具天赋）；demonstrated an ability（表现出一种能力）；a proven ability（确有的才华/能力）；show an initiative in（某个方面表现出主动性）；at the initial, developing, advanced stage/level（处于初级、发展、高级阶段/水平）；need more efforts（需要更努力一些）。学习中，有很多常用的短语搭配，如learn something by heart（记住/牢记），present a finding（展示研究结果），sign up for/enrolled on a number of courses（注册/注册了一些课程）；acquire/obtain knowledge（掌握知识）；thirty for knowledge（渴望知识）。

46. What type of U.S. Visa is for visiting scholars?

A. F-1

B. B-2

C. J-1

D. H-1B

问题：到美国的访问学者是什么类别的签证？

答案：C. J-1 签证

美国的签证基本上分为移民签证（immigrant visa）或非移民签证（non-immigrant visa）两大类。非移民签证包括F-1 Student Visa（F-1 学生签证）：该签证发给读学位的学生或是读学术课程的交换学生，由美国移民局的学生和交换生信息部门（SEVIS-Student Exchange Visitor Information System）签发和负责学生入学后的管理工作。F-1 学生签证在完成学习课程期间都有效。申请表是Form I-20。M-1-Vocational Student Visa（M-1 职业学生签证）：它适用于非学术或"职业课程"的学生，如机械、技术、烹饪课、语言课程、飞行学校或美容课程等。与F-1 签证不同，M-1 签证有效期只有一年，学生可以申请累积延期长达三年。J-1-Exchange Visitor Visa（J-1 交流学者签证）：这类签证适合于来美国进行学术交流和进修或读学位的教授和老师。持J-1 签证的想要在美国移民的话，必须回国服务两年，如想豁免（waiver）的话，必须得到中国驻美使馆出示的证明。B-1 Business Visa（B-1 商务签证）是为了出于商业目的来到美国作临时访问的非移民签证。B-2 Tourist Visa（B-2 旅游签证）：如果你打算去美国度假，看朋友或访问亲戚或进行医疗治病，需要B2 旅游签证。这个旅游签证允许你参加社会、文化和体育活动，但是你不能在你访问过程中工作或上学。打算在美国工作的人员进入美国需要 H-1，H-2，L-1 或其他类的工作签证。H-1B Work Visa（H-1B 非移民工作签证）：它是由雇主给外国专业人士的工作签证，H-1B 签证有效期为三年，可能延长三年。雇主可以协助 H-1B 持有人办理绿卡（Green Card）。持 J-1、B-1、B-2，F-1，M-1 or M-2 签证的，可以使用 Form I-539 申请延长（apply to extend their status）。B-2 旅游签证一般是三个月，可申请延长到半年或一年。持 B-1，B-2，F-1，F-2，J-1，J-2，M-1 or M-2 签证的，可以在美改变身份（Change Visa Status）。但 M-1 的学生不能改成 F-1 学生身份。参见下表的《美国主要非移民签证类别简介》。

表 2-3　美国主要签证类别简介（Types of U.S. Visas）

种类	用途
A	Diplomat or Foreign Government Official Visa（外交签证）
B-1	Business Visa（商务签证）
B-2	Tourist Visa（旅游签证：每次 3~6 个月）
C	Transiting U.S. Visa（过境美国签证）
D-1	Crew Visa（机组人员签证）
DV-1	Visas（the "Green Card Lottery"）（绿卡抽签签证）
E	Commerce/Trade Visa（商业贸易签证）
EB	Employer-Sponsored Immigrant Visa（雇主赞助的移民签证） EB-1：Foreign Nationals of Extraordinary Ability, Outstanding Professors and Researchers and Multinational Executives and Managers（有特殊才能的人，优秀教授和研究人员，跨国高管和管理人员。） EB-2：Workers with Advanced Degrees or Exceptional Ability in the Sciences, Arts or Business（具有高等学历或超凡能力的科学，艺术或商业工作者） EB-3：Skilled Workers and Professionals（熟练工人和专业人员） EB-4：Special Immigrant Visas for Religious Workers（宗教人员的特别移民签证） EB-5：Investor/Employment Creation Visas（投资者/创造就业签证：在新企业中创造 10 个人就业机会的，投资至少 50 万美元的投资者。）
F-1	Student Visa（学生签证：期限按学习计划时间而定，需要填 Form I-20）
H-1B	Temporary Work Visa（临时工作签证：三年，可延长）
H-1C	Nurse Visa（护士签证）
H-2A	Agricultural Workers Visa（农业工人签证）
H-2B	Non-Agricultural Workers Visa（非农业工人签证）
H-3	Special Education Training Visa（特殊教育培训签证）
I	Media, Journalist Visa（媒体/记者签证）
IR	Family-based Immigrant Visa（家庭移民签证）
J-1	Exchange Visitor Visa（交换学者签证：期限一般为半年至 1 年，需要填 Form DS-2019）
K	Fiancées or Spouses of US Citizens Visa（美国公民的未婚夫或配偶签证）
L-1	Intra-company Transferees Visa（管理/公司内部调动签证）
M-1-	Vocational Student Visa（职业学生签证）
O-1	Extraordinary Abilities Visa（特殊才能签证）
P-2	Temporary Entertainer Visa（娱乐人士签证）
Q	International Cultural Exchange Visa（国际文化交流签证）
R-1	Temporary Religious Worker Visa（临时宗教人士签证）

*Adopted from usembassy.gov/visas/visa-directory

47. Which of the following phrases does not mean "agree" with?

A. I wouldn't say that.

B. I'm convinced that...

C. I must admit that...

D. I couldn't agree with you more.

问题：以下短语中哪个表示"不同意"？

答案：A. 我不会那样说的。

      在学习和日常生活中，常要表达自己对事情、事物的看法，是同意（agree）或不同意（disagree）。答案中，只有A选项 I wouldn't say that.（我不会那样说的。）是表示不同意。其他相同的短语还有：It's hard to say.（这不一定。）I don't agree with you at all.（我完全不同意你的意见。）As a matter of fact,...（事实上，……）The way I see it...（我是这样看的……）I don't believe.（我不相信。）I don't think so.（我不相信/不这么认为。）I totally disagree.（我完全不同意。）It seems to me that...（在我看来……）That can't be right.（这是不对的。）It's a fact that...（事实上……）However,...（但是……）Me neither.（我也不同意。）No way.（不可能的。）I beg to differ.（我不敢苟同。）Not necessarily.（不必要。）表示同意的短语和句子有：I'm convinced that...（我相信……）I must admit that...（我必须承认……）I couldn't agree with you more.（我完全同意你的看法。）couldn't...more是习惯用法，是完全肯定的意思。I believe so.（我同意。）I agree with you 100 percent.（我百分之百同意你的意见。）Exactly.（没错。）I totally/partly agree.（我完全/部分同意。）You're right up to a point.（你说的对。）You're absolutely right.（你绝对正确。）That's for sure.（那是肯定的。）No doubt about it.（毫无疑问。）That's exactly how I feel.（这正是我的感受。）I was just going to say that.（我正想这样说的。）I have to side with Mom on this one.（这一点上我必须与母亲一致。）表示有点儿赞同或不赞同，可用以下表达：You could be right/wrong.（你可能是对/错的。）I suppose so.（我想是这样的。）I guess so.（我猜是这样的。）You have（got）a point there.（你说的有些道理。）That's not always the case/true.（这并不总是这样/真的。）I'm not so sure about that.（我不太清楚。）

48. Which tree is your math teacher's favorite?

A. Loblolly Pine

B. Red Maple

C. Flouring Dogwood

D. Geometry

问题：哪种树是你数学老师最喜欢的？

答案：D. 几何

　　这是一个搞笑的题。选择答案中 loblolly pine（萝卜松）、red maple（红枫树）、flouring dogwood（开花的山茱萸）都是美国常见的树，而选项 geometry 是数学老师喜爱的科目：几何。geometry 的英文中最后三个字母——try 的发音跟 tree（树）的发音相近，便成了数学老师喜爱的树了。常用的几何术语有：point（点），line（线），line segment（线段），perpendicular line segment（垂直线），parallel line segments（平行线段），right angle（直角），acute angle（锐角），obtuse angle（钝角），vertex（顶），scalene triangle（不等边三角形），isosceles triangle（等腰三角形），equilateral triangle（等边三角形），radius（半径），diameter（直径），circumference（圆周），chord（弦线），arc（弧）。其他数学常用术语：square（平方/正方形），square feet（平方尺），square foot（平方根），equation（方程式），solve equation（解方程），formula（公式）等。有时与其他词搭配，含义有所不同。fair and square（光明正大），back to square one/start over again（重新开始），out of equation（不可能）。For some reason, Nancy leave her out of the equation.（因为种种原因，南希总是喜欢逃避问题。）美国常见的树还有 aspen tree（阿斯彭树），balsam fir（香脂冷杉），sugar maple（糖枫），white oak（白橡木），douglas fir（道格拉斯冷杉），sweetgum（枫香）等。

49. You should contact_____ if you feel homesick or depressed?

A. Tutoring Center

B. Nurse's Office

C. International Students Office（Services）

D. Counseling Services

问题：当你想家或是郁闷时应该与哪个部门联系？

答案：D. 心理咨询服务中心

在美留学，要做生理和心理方面的调节（physical and psychological adjustment）。由于水土不服（acclimatized），生活习惯不同（different habits and customs），语言障碍（language barriers），学习压力（academic stress）等各种因素，你可能会感到身体不适，想家（homesick），无食欲（lost appetite），出现压抑和郁闷（depressed）等状况，这样会影响你的学习和生活。出现这类情况，你应该打电话或到学校的心理咨询服务中心（Counseling Services）寻求帮助。那儿的咨询师（counselors）会给你提供必要的药物和心理治疗（psychotherapy），来帮你减压和调节生活。如果你在学业上需要帮助，学校的 Tutoring Center 能提供帮助你提高英语或其他的课程的免费辅导。身体不舒服应去学校护士办公室（Nurse's office）去看病，一般的疾病你交的医疗保险都能支付所有的费用，护士办公室每年都提供流感疫苗注射（flu shots）。你如有关于签证（Visa）、住房（housing）、转学（transfer）、在校打短工许可（part time job permission）、申请社会安全卡（Social Security Card）、申请实习（Optional Practical Training-OPT）等事宜，都需要与国际学生办公室（International Students Office/Services）联系办理。

50. In any crises that your life is threatened you should follow the safety tips below except____.

A. call 911

B. fight

C. fleet

D. freeze

问题：在你的人身安全受到威胁时，你不应该遵循以下哪项安全提示？

答案：D. 不动

　　在美国的校园里，如同在任何地方一样，人身安全（personal safety）总是第一位的。每所大学都有校园警察局（campus policy office），警察日夜巡逻来保障全校学生、教职员工的安全；但是随时还是要谨防火灾（fire）、盗窃（theft）、暴力（violence）、校园强奸（campus rape）、醉酒（drunk）等事件的发生。大学校园内各处都设有紧急电话（emergency phones）。学校一般都会举办预防犯罪的讲座（the crime prevention program），介绍保护人身安全的方法和提示（tips），如 fight or flight response（应急反应）。出现恐怖袭击（terrorist attacks）、校园枪击（campus shooting）和其他危害生命安全的危机时（in time of crises），建议除立即打 911 报警电话求助之外，应马上离开现场，或找地方躲避起来（hide）。来不及躲避时，才要 fight，在你死我活的关头，就要为生命而搏斗。使用格斗用具自卫

（self-defense）时，也要了解法律，如了解使用枪支（gun），电击枪（tascr），手电筒（flesh light），辣椒喷雾（pepper spray）的方法和法规等。答案D. Freeze（不动）是下策。夜间上课后，要邀同学一道回宿舍，或事先联系好校警或保安人员来安全护送（safety escort）。安全护送是不需要付费的。大学里有很多学生的学社如兄弟会（Fraternities）和姐妹会（Sorority），参加这类活动对提升社交能力和提高英语水平有益，但也要注意安全。另外，自身保护的另一个方面是穿着，打扮不要过于暴露（exposed）或张扬（show off）。交友更要慎重，不然会引狼入室。

Vocabulary Usages
词汇用法篇

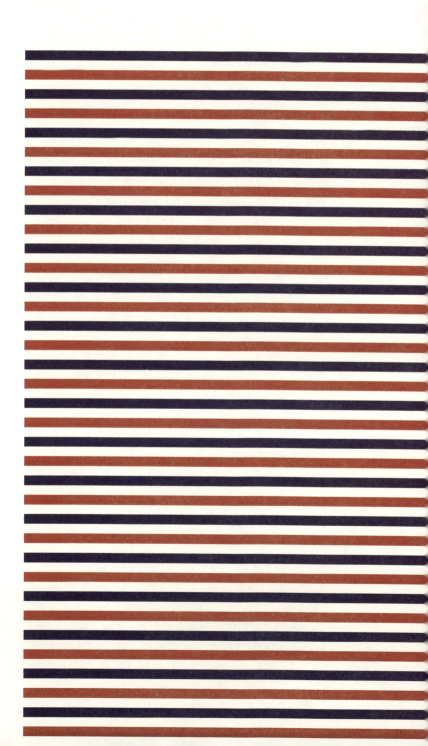

1. What is the longest word in English?

A. Smiles

B. Antidisestablishmentarianism

C. Pneumonoultramicroscopicsilicovolcanoconiosis

D. Gammaracanthuskytodermogammarusloricatobaicalensis

问题：英语中最长的单词是什么？

答案：A. 微笑

　　这是个脑筋急转弯的题，因为smiles这个单词的第一个字母S和最后一个字母S之间有一英里（mile）之遥。真的答案很难确定。通常认为最长的英文字是由凝集方式构成的字，即在词根（root）上加前缀（prefix）和后缀（suffix）而形成的字：如词根establish加上前后缀形成antidisestablishmentarianism（反对教会与国家分开学说）。很多词看来很短，其实他们是很长的短语的缩写（acronym），即词头字转变而来的。如laser（激光）是Light Amplification by Stimulated Emission of Radiation的缩写，有49个字母，比antidisestablishmentarianism还多20个！由于该缩写正巧符合英文的单词拼写规则，就成了一个普通的英语单词。类似的词还不少。如radar（雷达）来自radar detection and ranging。HIV/AIDS（艾滋病）是Human immunodeficiency virus infection/acquired immunodeficiency syndrome的缩写。其实很多科技用语更长。如牛津字典列出的pneumonoultramicroscopicsilicovolcanoconiois（硅酸盐沉着病，硅肺病），还有化学名称如gammaracanthuskytodermogammmarusloricatobaicalensis等。

2. Which of the following phrases means "something easy to do"?

A. A piece of cake

B. A piece of pie

C. A piece of bread

D. A piece of junk

问题：以下短语中哪个表示"很容易的事"？

答案：A. 一块蛋糕

　　英美人遇到很容易做的事，喜欢说a piece of cake，就像吃一块蛋糕一样容易，也常说as easy as a pie（像吃一块饼一样容易）。类似的短语有：a piece of pie（一块饼）、a piece of bread（一块面包）、a piece of shit（一堆屎、没有用的东西或是无用的人—骂人的话）、a piece of junk（一堆垃圾）。junk food是指垃圾食品。英语中的不可数名词（uncountable nouns）常用量词（measure word/numeral classifiers）来表示数量。如：a bag of flour（一袋面粉）、two gallons of milk（二加仑牛奶）、five bars of chocolate（五块巧克力）、a dozen bottles of wine（12瓶酒）、a pile of dirt（一堆土）、a yard of fabric（一匹布）、a bowl of cereal（一碗麦片）、a loaf of bread（一个面包）、a school of fish（一群鱼）、a bit of trouble（有一点麻烦）、a carton of ice-cream（一箱冰淇）、a drop of blood（一滴血）、a glass（cup）of beer/coffee（一杯啤酒/咖啡）、a grain of rice（一粒米）、an item of clothing（一件服装）、a jar of honey/jam/peanut butter（一罐子蜂蜜/果酱/花生酱）、a piece of advice/furniture（一个建议/一件家具）、a roll of toilet paper/Scotch tape（一卷卫生纸/透明胶带）、a slice of cheese/toast（奶酪/烤面包片）、a spoonful of syrup（一勺糖浆）、a tablespoon of butte/ketchup（一大匙黄油/番茄酱）、a teaspoon of cinnamon/medicine（一茶匙肉桂/药）、a tube of lipstick（一支口红）等。可数名词的常用量词有：a sack of books（一麻袋的书）、a group of students（一小组学生）、a crowd of retired workers（一群退休工人）、a pack of mails（一包邮件）、an army of ants（蚂蚁雄兵）、a hive of bees（一窝蜂）、a ring of keys（一串钥匙）、a team of engineers（一个工程师团队）、a deck of cards（一叠字牌）、a herd of cows（牛群）、a flock of swans（一群天鹅）、a swarm of bees（一窝蜂）、a bunch of idiots（一群蠢货）、a cloud of mosquitoes（一群蚊子）、a bouquet of flowers（一束鲜花）、a combination of numbers（数字组合）、three ears of corns（三个玉米棒）等。参见表3-1。

表3-1　常见英语量词一览表（A List of Common English Measure Words）

量词	可搭配词
an ear of	corn（一个玉米）、grain（一穗谷物）、rice（一穗稻谷）
an item of	clothing（一件服装）、expenditure（一项支出）、news（一条新闻）、data（一个数据）
an army of	ants（蚂蚁雄兵）、bees（一大群蜜蜂）、buyers（一大群买主）、refugees（一大队难民）
a bar of	chocolate（一块巧克力）、gold（一块金条）、soap（一块肥皂）、iron（一块铁）
a bag of	gold dust（一袋金粉）、rice（一袋米）、bird feed（一袋鸟食）、bones（骨瘦如柴）
a bit of	trouble（有点麻烦）、cold（有点冷）、luck（有点走运）、a celebrity（小有名气）
a bottle of	milk（一瓶奶）、water（一瓶水）、champagne（一瓶香槟）、ketchup（一瓶番茄酱）
a bowl of	cereal（一碗麦片）、rice（一碗饭）、soup（一碗汤）、beef stew（一碗炖牛肉）
a box of	cereal（一盒麦片）、paper（一盒纸）、candy（一盒糖果）、chocs（一盒巧克力糖）
a can of	meat（一罐肉）、beer（一罐啤酒）、tuna（一盒金枪鱼罐头）、worms（棘手问题）
a carton of	ice-cream（一盒冰淇淋）、orange juice（一盒橙汁）、milk（一盒牛奶）
a couple of	ideas（几个主意）、times（两三次）、weeks（两个礼拜）、hours（两个小时）
a crowd of	retired workers（一群退休工人）、reporters（一群记者）、people（一群人）
a dozen of	eggs（一打（12个）鸡蛋）、chopsticks（十二双筷子）、engineers（十几个工程师）
a drop of	blood（一滴血）、oil（一滴油）、water（一滴水）、perfume（一滴香水）、rain（一滴雨）
a flock of	swans（一群天鹅）、birds（一群鸟）、sea gulls（一群海鸥）、sheep（一群羊）

量词	可搭配词
a gang of	four（四人帮）、youths（一帮小混混）、thugs（一伙歹徒/流氓）
a gallon of	milk（一加仑牛奶）、gas/gasoline（一加仑汽油）、blue paint（一加仑蓝色油漆）
a glass（cup）of	beer（一杯啤酒）、juice（果汁）、wine（酒）、hot chocolate（热巧克力）、coffee（咖啡）
a group of	students（一小组学生）、investers（一批投资商）、protesters（一群抗议人士）
a grain of	rice（一粒米）、sand（一粒沙）、truth（一个真理）、common sense（一点常识）
a herd of	cows/cattle（一群牛）、elephants（一群大象）
a jar of	honey（一罐子蜂蜜）、jam（一罐果酱）、peanut butter（一罐花生酱）、mustard（一罐芥末酱）
a loaf of	bread（一条面包）、sliced bread（一条切片面包）
a piece of	bread（一块面包）、shit（一堆屎）、junk（一堆垃圾）、cake（一块蛋糕）、pie（一块饼）、advice（一个忠告）、furniture（一件家具）、paper（一张纸）
a pack of	mails（一包邮件）、cigarettes（一包香烟）、lies（一派胡言）、wolves（一群狼）
a quarter of	miles（四分之一英里）、population（四分之一的人口）、a year（一个季度）、dollar（25美分）
a roll of	carpet（一卷地毯）、toilet paper（一卷卫生纸）、scotch tape（一卷透明胶带）
a sack of	books（一麻袋的书）、potatoes（一袋土豆）、cement（一袋水泥）
a school of	fish（一群鱼）、dolphins（一群海豚）、philosophy（一个哲学流派）
a scoop of	ice-cream（一勺子冰淇淋）、thin porridge（一瓢稀粥）
a slice of	bread（一块面包）、cheese（一片奶酪）、meat（一块肉）、toast（一片烤面包）、pizza（一块比萨饼）
a swarm of	bees（一窝蜂）、photographers（一群摄影记者）、mosquitoes（成群的蚊子）
a team of	Engineers（一个工程师团队）、experts（一个专家小组）、volunteers（一批志愿者）
a spoonful of	sugar（一勺糖）、syrup（一勺糖浆）、soda（一勺苏打粉）、honey（一勺蜂蜜）
a teaspoon of	cinnamon（一茶匙肉桂）、medicine（一茶匙药）、salt（一匙盐）

3. Which of the following is different from all the other three?

A. Eye to eye.

B. Deed.

C. Madam, I'm Adam.

D. Was it a cat I saw?

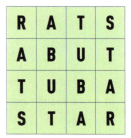

问题：以下答案哪个与众不同？

答案：A. 见解一致。

回文（palindrome）是一种有趣的文字现象，字在词或句子中是左右对称的。如 deed 中的 d 和 e。Was it a cat I saw？（我看到的是只猫吗？）Madam, I am Adam.（女士，我叫雅丹。）选择的答案中只有 A 选项 eye to eye（见解一致）不是回文。最早的回文至少可以追溯到公元 79 年。该回文是用拉丁文写的一个方块句子（word square），参见插图。不论是水平还是垂直读,字和句子完全一样。因此,它们可以被称之为回文阵。英文中的回文字不少,如:dad(父亲)、mom(母亲)、mum(沉默)、nun(尼姑)、level(水平)、pup(小狗)、peep(窥视)等。回文句子还有:Rise to vote, sir.(先生,起来投票。)Do geese see God?(鹅见上帝吗?)Never odd or even.(千万不要奇数或偶数。)Don't nod.(不要点头。)想了解更多的回文阵和回文句请参见 http://www.fun-with-words.com/palin_example.html。其实,中文更好作回文。历代许多诗人都留有美妙的回文诗。如:宋代文学家苏轼有《题织锦图回文》。诗云:春晚落花余碧草,夜凉低月半梧桐。人随雁远边城暮,雨映疏帘绣阁空。倒读则诗曰:空阁绣帘疏映雨,暮城边远雁随人。桐梧半月低凉夜,草碧余花落晚春。

4. **Which of the following is not a homonym?**

A. Seal

B. Bank

C. Fine

D. Pencil

问题:下列哪一个不是同音异义词?

答案:D. 铅笔

英语中有不少字是拼写和发音都一样的同形词(homographs)和同音词(homophones)。这些词叫 homonym。含义往往要根据句子的上下文来判断。如:Seal: Put a seal on the document.(在文件上盖章。)The young seal is very playful.(小海豹很调皮。)LeBron James' three pointer sealed the victory.(勒布朗·詹姆斯的三分球锁定了胜局。)Bank:I have a savings and a checking accounts at the Citizen Bank.(我在公民银行有储蓄和支票账户。)The river bank is in danger of leaking in the hurricane.(河堤在飓风中有泄漏的危险。)Fine:He got a traffic ticket for reckless driving and was fined for $200.(他因鲁莽驾驶而被罚款 200 美元。)Rick is a fine teammate.(Rick 是一个很好的队友。)Pay attention to the fine print in the bottom of the document.(请注意文档底部打印的小字。)They were too close to the door to close it.(他们离门太近了,门关不了。)We must polish the Polish furniture.(我们必须擦亮波兰家具。)常用的同音字还有:left、right、rose 等。

以下是同形同音异义词例句:(摘自 Richard Lederer 的无名诗 *The Anonymous Poem*,"The English Lesson"。参见:https://web.cn.edu/kwheeler/English_hard_2learn.html)

It's time to present the present to the guests.(现在是向客人赠送礼物的时候了。)

The bandage was wound around the wound on his arm.(他手臂的伤口上缠绕着绷带。)

The soldier decided to desert his dessert in the desert.（士兵决定把他的甜点留在沙漠里。）

The wind was too strong to wind the sail.（风太强了摇不动船帆。）

The farm was used to produce produce.（农场是用来产生农产品。）

A bass was painted on the bass drum.（低音鼓上画了条鲈鱼。）

I did not object to the object.（我不反对那个事情。）

A row of oarsmen are ready to row in the race.（一排划桨者准备好划船比赛。）

A sewer fell down into a sewer line.（一个裁缝掉进了下水道。）

5. Which of the following prepositions has the most usages?

A. For

B. Of

C. In

D. At

问题：下面哪个介词用法最多?

答案：B. Of

　　英语介词是最难使用的词之一。它们的用法太多，而且没有多少规律可循。在英国最大的字典 New English Dictionary 中为每个介词列出了其使用的各种含义。介词用法最多的有：1. of 有 63 种，2. in 和 with 有 40 种，3. at 和 by 有 39 种，4. to 有 33 种，5. for 有 31 种，6. on 有 29 种，7. from 有 15 种。虽然介词的用法很多，但是常见的用法不是太多。其实学习介词的最好方法是记住它们与其他词的那些常用搭配，就是说以介词词组来了解含义，记住用法。如就介词 in 而言，与其动词常见的搭配有：give in（放弃）、made in（制造）；与时间词连用：in time（及时）、in the morning（早晨）、in May（在五月）、in 2012（在 2012 年）；与名词搭配：in order（有次序）、in order to（为了……）。又如介词 by：by train（乘火车去）、by the way（顺便问一下）、a book by Shakespeare（莎士比亚写的书）、play by the rule（按规则比赛）、finish it by Friday（星期五完工）、seven multiplied by eight（7 乘 8）。又如介词 at：arrive at（到达）、laugh at（嘲笑）、at night（晚上）、at dawn（清晨）、at first（首先）、at first glance（第一眼）、at large（在逃，逍遥法外）、at any cost（无论什么代价）。介词 of：a cup of tea（一杯茶）、a friend of mine（我的一个朋友）。

6. Which of the following phrases means "be careful"?

A. Look out

B. Go out

C. Get out

D. Speak out

问题：以下哪个短语的含义是"当心"？

答案：A. 当心，留意

短语look out的含义是"当心，留意"与be careful是近义词。careless 是 careful 的反义词。take care（保重）是日常会话中告别时用的短语。out 与很多动词搭配构成新的动词词组，其词义与他搭配的动词的原意不同。go out 的意思是"出去"，如 go out for dinner（到外面去吃饭）、get out of my office（从我的办公室滚蛋）、speak out（说出来）、find out what's wrong with the car（查出汽车出了什么毛病）、act out（表演出来）、sign in and sign out（登录和登出）、figure out the problem（弄清楚问题）。look 与介词和其他词搭配构成的短语动词有：look at（看，检查）：He will look at my engine tomorrow morning.（明天早上他会检查一下我的车引擎。）look after（照料）：She was in charge of looking after his younger brothers.（她负责照顾弟弟们。）look down（upon）（藐视）：Traditionally, strong accents were looked down on（upon）.（通常，口音重的人受到歧视。）look forward to（期待）：The class is looking forward to receiving their individual project grades.（全班都期待拿到他们个人作业的成绩。）look（around）for（寻找）：They are looking for a new home to settle in.（他们在寻找房子定居。）look up（查阅）：I looked the word up in the dictionary.（我在词典中查看这个词。）look into（调查）：They set up a special task force to look into the issue.（他们设立了一个特别工作组来调查这个问题。）look back（回顾）：Many people look back with reminiscence of their days in college.（许多人对大学生时代念念不忘。）

7. "She has her hands full with her three children." This sentence means:

A. She carries too many things.

B. She is quite busy with her children.

C. She has difficulty taking care of her children.

D. She needs helping hands to take care of her children.

问题："She has her hands full with her three children." 这句话的意思是什么？

答案：B. 她忙于照看她的孩子们。

短语Hands full（have hands full）的意思是忙极了。句子She has her hands full with her three children.（她为自己的三个孩子忙得团团转。）与She is quite busy with her children.（她忙于照看她的孩子们）一句的意思相同。The governor has his hands full with the water pollution issues.（州长在水的污染问题上已经忙得不可开交了。）其他选项的意思是：She needs helping hands to take care of her children.（她需要帮手来照料三个孩子。）She carries too many things.（她拿着太多东西。）She has difficulty taking care of her children.（她难以照料三个孩子。）其他有关hand的词语有：hand in（递交）、hand over（上交）、hand to mouth（糊口/生活艰难）：Many African people have a hand-to-mouth existence without medical or other benefits.（许多非洲黑人过着只能勉强糊口的日子，没有医疗补助或其他福利。）hand in hand（手牵手）：He saw the couple making their way, hand in hand, down the path.（他看到他们夫妇手拉手沿着小路往前走去。）The corrupt officials are working hand in glove with the drug traffickers.（贪官与毒品贩子相互勾结，狼狈为奸。）She is the handyman in my family.（她是我家的勤杂工。）其他有关的词语：handle（手柄/把手）、handbag（手提袋）、handbook（手册）、handkerchief（手帕）。现代的美国人很少用手帕，多用tissue（纸巾）或paper towel（厨房纸巾）代替。

8. Which pair is different from all the others?

A. Foot—Feet

B. Goose—Geese

C. Tooth—Teeth

D. Boot—Beet

问题：下列哪一组词与其他组不同？

答案：D. Boot—Beet

英语中许多单词来自拉丁和希腊语，它们的复数（plural）是不规则的，不是在词尾加上 s。答案中 foot—feet（脚/英尺）、goose—geese（鹅）、tooth—teeth（牙齿）都是如此。boot（靴子）的复数不是 beet（甜菜）而是 boots，是规则变化。常见的不规则名词还有：ox—oxen（牛）、child—children（儿童）、man—men（男人）、woman—women（女人）、mouse—mice（鼠）、stimulus—stimuli（刺激）、alumnus—alumni（男校友）、alumna—alumnae（女校友）、syllabus—syllabi（教学大纲）、nucleus—nuclei（核）、focus- foci（焦点）、fungus—fungi（真菌）、thesis—theses（论文）、crisis—crises（危机）、phenomenon—phenomena（现象）、index—indices（指数）、appendix—appendices/appendixes（附录/附件）、criterion—criteria（标准）等。有个别的词单复数一样：deer（鹿）和 sheep（绵羊）。有的名词只有复数形式，但作为单数使用：News（新闻）、linguistics（语言学）、arms（武器）、thanks（感谢）、savings（储蓄）、economics（经济学）、mathematics（数学）。还有的名词没有复数形式却作为复数使用：policy（警察）、cattle（黄牛）。要说一个警察得用另一个词 a policeman。由两部分组成的物品，如 scissors（剪刀）、pants（裤子）、glasses（眼镜）单个时也用复数：Her glasses are broken again.（她的眼镜又弄破了。）请注意，有些名词单数（singular）既可用作单数也可用作复数，要根据上下文而定。如特指每一个成员就用复数否则用单数表示一个整体。如 committee（委员会）、audience（观众）、government（政府）、family（家庭）、class（班级）、crew（船员）、crowd（人群）、jury（陪审团）、parliament（议会）、staff（员工）、faculty（教职员）、the public（公众）。

9. Which of the following expressions shows that someone is all thumbs.

A. Thumbs up

B. Handy

C. Clumsy

D. Thumbs down

问题：下列哪一个词表示某人很笨拙?

答案：C. 笨拙

如果一个人的所有手指都像大拇指一样（all thumbs），可以想象他的手会有多笨。所给的答案中 clumsy 也是指笨拙。其他类似的词还有：awkward（笨拙/尴尬）、slow-witted（反应慢）、stupid（蠢）、silly（傻乎乎）、foolish（愚蠢）。反之，handy 是手巧的意思。如，Her husband is very handy and he can fix his car.（她的丈夫手非常巧，他能修理他的汽车。）come in handy（useful）（迟早有用的）：That key will come in handy if you lock yourself out.

（要是你把自己锁在了屋外，那把钥匙就派上用场了。）表示聪明的词有：clever、smart、bright、intelligent、wise（智慧）、brilliant（卓越）、talented and gifted（有天赋的人）。thumbs up（赞赏）、thumbs down（不好）、green thumb（很会做园艺的人）、a good rule of thumb（好的做法、经验、标准）：A good rule of thumb is to bring two more resumes than you will need for the job fair. （一个好的经验就是去招聘会时，要比你所需要的份数多带两份简历。）

10. "Margaret <u>put on a long face</u> when Jason broke her vase." The underlined part means:

A. make a face

B. have a facelift

C. lose face

D. keep a straight face

问题：“当Jason打破花瓶的时候，Margaret拉长着脸。”这句话中画线部分的意思是什么？
答案：D. 板着脸（生气）

答案中与画线部分 a long face（拉长着脸/生气）最接近的是 a straight face（板着脸，一副严肃的面孔），相当于 make a sad face（一脸愁容）。"Why do you have（pulled/made）such a long face?" "My boyfriend doesn't want to see me any more." （“你为什么愁眉苦脸的？”“我男朋友不想再见我了。”）A poker face（面无表情）：The suspect wore a poker face during police questioning. （在警察侦讯时，嫌疑犯一直面无表情。）lose face（丢面子）、save face（保颜面、爱面子）：He thinks he would lose face if he admitted the mistake. （他觉得如果承认错误，就会很丢脸。）make a face（做鬼面）。facelift（面部整形）。face 一词构成的表达还有很多：face the music（接受责罚）：The boy was caught cheating in an examination and had to face the music. （在一次考试中那孩子作弊被当场抓住，他只能自己承担后果。）face value（面值）：The concert tickets were selling at twice their face value. （这些音乐会的票以其面值两倍的价钱售出。）face to face（面对面）：Parent-teacher conference is a face to face meeting between the parents and teachers. （家长教师会议是家长和老师的面对面交流。）facemask（口罩）：Everyone should wear anti-pollution face masks in such a haze weather. （在这样的雾霾天气里，每个人都应该戴防污染面罩。）Facebook（脸书）：Zuckerberg's Facebook changed the way of human social interaction. （扎克伯格的脸书改变了人类社会互动的方式。）I gave the scoundrel a slap in the face. （我打了那坏蛋一耳光。）

They all had confused expressions on their faces.（他们的脸上表情困惑。）Let's face it, we lost the game.（让我们承认，我们打输了。）Our house is facing the south.（我们的房子是朝南的。）还有一些相关表达，如surface（表面）、face out（面临淘汰）。

11. Which of the following means the right time?

A. In time

B. On time

C. Over time

D. About time

问题：以下哪个短语是表示正是时候?

答案：D. About time

英语多用介词短语表达时间，如在时间（time）一词前加上一个介词，表示不同的时间概念。about time 是正是时候（right time）的意思。He never got to work on time.（他从来没有按时上下班。）The fire fighters arrived at the scene in time and put out the fire.（消防人员及时赶到了现场将火扑灭了。）A nasty incident was prevented by the timely arrival of the police.（警察的及时到来阻止了一次严重事故。）Many workers in the company had to work overtime to complete the project on time.（该公司的许多工人不得不加班来按时完成项目。）time一词还有很多其他的用法：timeout（暂停）、Time flies.（时光荏苒。）、time（岁月）、time bomb（定时炸弹）。Timing is essential.（时机是至关重要的。）Time is money.（时间就是金钱。）It was a race against time（clock）to stop refugees dying from starvation.（为抢救那些即将饿死的难民而分秒必争。）The clock is ticking and time is running out.（钟声滴答时间不多啦。）Is it a good time to talk?（现在好说话吗？）It takes time to adopt her life in a big city.（她需要时间来适应大城市的生活。）Susanne has time off today and wants to kill time by looking around the Mall.（苏珊今天休息想去商场随便看看打发时间。）Time and tied wait for no man.（岁月不饶人。）Time Square（纽约的时代广场）, *New York Times*（《纽约时报》）, *Time Magazine*（《时代周刊》）——美国最具权威的杂志，总部设在纽约市。

12. Which of the sentences is negative in meaning?

A. I can hardly wait for the new school year.

B. You can't pay enough attention to it.

C. Scarcely did he go to Church.

D. His service to the country is valueless.

问题：哪个句子的含义是否定的？

答案：C. Scarcely did he go to Church。

句子"Scarcely did he go to Church."意为他极少去教堂。当带有否定意义的词，如scarcely、hardly、seldom、never出现在句子开头时，句子要倒装，即主谓语要换位。Never is failure quite so frightening as regret.（比失败更令人恐惧的是懊悔。）其他几个选项的意思是：I can't hardly wait for the new school year.（我期盼（等不及）新学年的到来。）这个句子中用了not和hardly两个否定词，双重否定表示肯定，起强调作用。I don't know nothing.（我根本不知道。）You can't pay enough attention to it.（你对此要有足够的重视。）I can't thank you enough.（太感谢啦。）can't help doing something（忍不住做某事）：I can't help feeling sorry for the earthquake victims.（我不禁为这些地震灾民感到难过。）You cannot be too careful while walking in the park after dark.（天黑后在公园散步，你再小心也不为过。）all、every、both、always、quite在否定词no、not和never等后，有部分否定或全部否定的意思。Not all participants enjoyed his speech.（并非所有的参与者都喜欢他的讲话。）His service to the country is priceless.（他对国家的服务是无价之宝。）一般的词加上后缀less后成了反义词。如restless（不安），useless（无用的）。注意美国黑人在口语中，喜欢用双重否定结构表示否定，如，"I didn't do nothing!"（我什么都没做！）

13. Gregg and Jessica are no longer dating, they_____.

A. had a winter break

B. broke up

C. broke a promise

D. broke a leg

问题：Gregg和Jessica不再约会了，他们_____。

答案：B. 分手了

短语no longer dating的意思是不再约会了。break up 是解除约会和分手的意思。如：Jennifer broke up with Frank, her boy friend of eight years.（珍妮弗与她八年的男朋友弗兰克分手了。）所以答案是B。break 是打破东西，如Jim broke an expensive vase by accident.（吉姆不小心打破了一个昂贵的花瓶。）I hope you break a leg（good luck）.（我希望你演出成功。）Having a winter break.（放寒假——圣诞到新年的长假）。spring break是美国的学校在三月中旬为期一周的春假。Nick always breaks his promise.（Nick 总是失信。）The thief broke in and stole his laptop.（小偷闯入盗走了他的手提电脑。）A fire broke out last night and destroyed the factory.（工厂昨天晚上失火被烧毁了。）The struggling restaurant is ready to break the law by tax evasion.（这家挣扎求生的餐厅不惜违法逃税。）"Give me a break." 有两种意思：其一是"别烦我了"，其二是"我才不相信呢"：Jerry won the lottery yesterday. Give me a break!（Jerry 昨天中了彩票。鬼才相信！）No policeman cannot break the law（违法）in order to enforce it.（任何警察都不能为了执法而犯法。）Take a break.（休息一下。）The old lady broke down（失控）and wept when her son died.（老太太的儿子去世时她失声痛哭。）break the ice/the ice break（破冰，打破僵局）、break a record（打破纪录）、break someone's heart/heart break（使人心碎）、a coffee break（休息喝咖啡）、a day break（破晓）、without a commercial break（不插商业广告）、break dancing（霹雳舞）、break out（爆发）。

14. A baby cat is called_____.

A. calf

B. kitten

C. lamb

D. puppy

问题：猫宝宝叫_____。

答案：B. kitten

英语中，许多动物的名称和他们小时候的名称是不一样的。如小猫叫作kitten（cat）、小马是叫colt（horse）、小牛叫calf（cow）、小羊叫lamb（sheep）。其他类似的动物还有：pig—piggy/piglet（小猪）、dog—puppy（小狗）、deer—fawn（小鹿）、goose—gosling（小鹅）、duck—duckling（小鸭）等。其他的动物就可以加上little表示小动物：little tiger（小老虎）、little monkey（小猴子）。注意，如用small的话是通常是形容动物的个头小，而不是年纪小。其他的陆上动物的英文名字是：pandas（熊猫）、lions（狮子）、wolves（狼）、leopards（豹子）、camels（骆驼）、donkeys（驴子）、bears（熊）、giraffes（长颈鹿）、zebra（斑马）、

elephant（大象）、Hippo- hippopotamus（河马）。描绘小东西的词有：tiny（微小）、teeny（绳头）、teeny-tiny（很小很小）、young（年轻）、miniature（微型）等。英语的很多成语中用到动物，如：Lynette was gentle as a lamb when dealing with young children.（Lynette 对待孩子很温顺。）Bob went into the SAT exam room like a lamb to the slaughter.（鲍勃就像上刑场一样进了 SAT 考场。）Dan was a wolf in sheep's clothing, pretending to help but spying for our competitors.（丹是披着羊皮的狼，假装帮助我们实际上在帮竞争对手监视我们。）They are dealing with a wolf in sheep's clothing.（他们是在跟一只披着羊皮的狼打交道。）In market of world smart phones, the Apple has a lion's share.（在世界智能手机市场中，苹果公司占有最大的份额。）When the cat's away, the mice will play.（猫儿不在，老鼠翻天。）

15. Which of the following phrases does not mean a physical space?

A. Make room for me.

B. Make room for the sofa.

C. Have room for improvement.

D. The grand piano takes a lot of room.

问题：下列哪个短语的意思不是指物理空间？

答案：C. 有改进的余地。

答案中唯有 C. Have room for improvement.（有改进的余地）是个抽象的概念。There is no room for error.（不容许有任何差错。）其他三个答案中的 room 都是指具体的物体空间：A. Make room for me.（请让让/借光。）B. Make room for the sofa.（腾个地方摆沙发。）D. The grand piano takes up a lot of room.（三角钢琴很占地方。）其他与 room 有关的词语：classroom（教室）、roommates（室友）、fitting room（试衣间）、roomy（房间宽敞）、locker-room/dressing room（更衣室）。That college charges too much for room and board.（大学的食宿收费太高了。）Can you tell me where is the Ladies'（Men's）room？（你能告诉我女（男）厕所在哪里吗？）I'd like to book a room for two people with a Queen bed next week for three days.（我想下周订一间有大床的房间，住三天。）Get a room.（去开间房。）这是个讽刺而幽默（sarcastic and humorous）的语句，用来告诉一对夫妇或情人停止公开示爱，应该开个房间再继续。

16. Which is NOT the right abbreviation?

A. Oct.

B. Sept.

C. June.

D. Feb.

问题：下列哪个缩写不正确？

答案：C. June.

    很多英语的月份名称很长，使用时人们常用缩写来表示，通常都是取前三个字母作为缩写。唯一例外的是九月，可以用前三个或四个字母：Sep./Sept。月份的缩写：1. January—Jan.；2. February—Feb.；3. March—Mar.；4. April—Apr.；5. May—May；6. June—Jun.；7. July—Jul.；8. August—Aug.；9. September—Sep. or Sept.；10. October—Oct.；11. November—Nov.；12. December—Dec. 英语的月份名称看起来很奇怪没有规律，其实这与他们来自拉丁和希腊语有关。在古罗马时期，月份从March开始，全年分为十个月，共计304天。大约在公元前713年开始,古罗马历法中又在十个月份前加了两个月January（一月）和February（二月）。January（一月）是以罗马神话中门神Janus（雅努斯）命名的，表示一年的开始。February（二月）由拉丁语februarius（februa）演变而成。februa是2月15日罗马人举行的洁净礼日（ritual purification）的名称。March（三月）来自拉丁语Martius，以古罗马的战神Mars（玛尔斯）命名。April（四月）来自拉丁语Aprilli，意为open，是春天花草开放的季节。May（五月）与古希腊神话中生育女神Maia有关，所以五月是个生机勃勃的月份。June（六月）以古罗马女神Juno（朱诺）命名,Juno是掌管婚姻的女神（Goddess of Fertility）。July（七月）是为了纪念出生在七月的恺撒大帝（Julius Caesar）而命名。Julius Caesar逝于公元前44年。在此之前，这个月被称为Quintilis（英语为Quintile），意思是"第五"。在公元前八年，八月份的名称Sextilis（第六）被罗马帝国第一位帝王的名字Augustus（奥古斯都）取代，而成了August（八月）。September（九月）源于拉丁语septem（第七）。October（十月）是古罗马历法中的第八个月,octo在拉丁语中表示"第八"。November(十一月)是古罗马历法中的第九个月,November来自于拉丁语novem,意思是"第九"。December（十二月）来自于拉丁语decem，意思是"第十"。

17. Which English letter is used most frequently?

A. A

B. B

C. S

D. E

问题：哪个英语字母用得最多？

答案：D. E

英语有 26 个字母，简称 ABC 或叫英语字母（English Alphabet），是希腊文中最前面的两个字母 α=Alpha, ß=Beta 合起来读成的 Alphabet（a）。在英语字母中，总体来说 E 字母用得最多，Z 字母用的最少。顺序依次是 e-t-a-i-s-o-n-h-r-d-l-u-c-m-f-w-y-p-g-b-v-k-j-q-x-z。当然这个顺序会因文体不同而有些差异。就字的拼写来说，字首用得最多的字母是 S，也就是说 S 开头的单词最多，最少的是 X。顺序依次是 s-c-p-a-t-d-b-m-f-i-e-h-l-r-w-g-u-o-v-n-j-q-k-y-z-x。字母的形状（shape of letters）从标准印制（printed form）的到手写（handwritten）的有显著的不同，尤其是草书（in cursive style）。根据 wikipedia，英语字母除了 J、V、W 之外，都源于拉丁文，在古英语中开始有 24 个拉丁字母，加上 & 和五个其他的字母：A B C D E F G H I J K L M N O P Q R S T V X Y Z & ⌐ ƿ Þ Ð Æ。到了现代英语阶段，又增加了 U 和从 vv 或 uu 演变而来的 W（double—u），除去了最后的六个共 26 个字母：A B C D E F G H I J K L M N O P Q R S T U V W X Y Z。字母的顺序基本上也是按拉丁文排列的。有人编了个英语字母的笑话（来自互联网）。一个女孩问一个男孩为什么英语是按 ABCDEFG 来排列的。男孩回答说因为：A Boy Can Do Everything For Girls.（男孩能为女孩做任何事。）女孩听了非常感动，非嫁这男孩不可，但是不知道接下来的顺序是 HIJK。He Is Just Kidding.（他只是在开玩笑。）由字母搭配成的词有：ABC（基础），A to Z：An A to Z of Phones（手机指南大全）。I know the event from A to Z.（我对这个事情了解得一清二楚。）

18. What is vowel sound symbol of Schwa?

A. /u/

B. /i/

C. /a/

D. /ə/

问题：中性元音的元音标志是什么？

答案：D. /ə/

美语的元音（vowels）很多，其中有一个元音的用途很广，就是Schwa，即/ə/。许多单元音在非重音的音节中，发弱音/ə/。如：alone/əloun/、above/əbʌv/。或是在词尾：worker、Victor、sir、scholar。中国学生在发一些辅音consonants时，如/t/、/d/、/k/、/g/、/p/、/b/很容易带上元音，尤其是在词尾。如将student/stjudnt/发成/stjudnti/。通常老师会告诉学生，发辅音时声带不震动，其实不然，如果没有一点儿震动，没人能听到清辅音或是浊辅音。所以在辅音后带轻微的元音是正常的，关键是加哪个元音。不是/i/、/a/、/ɔ/、/u/、/o/而是Schwa/ə/。这样student的发音应为/stjudntə/。美国英语有五个双元音（diphthong），除了/ɔi/（单词boy的元音）之外，其他四个和中文的双元音很相似。/ai/就是字母I或中文"哎"字的发音，/ei/就是字母A或是中文"飞/fei/"字的元音发音，/ou/就是字母O或是中文"欧"字的发音，/ao/就是中文"嗷"字的发音。英语的连读（linkage）有一定的规律。两个相连的词，前面的单词如是以元音结尾而后面的词以元音开始时，两词连读：May I、how about、two hours。前面的单词如是以辅音结尾而后面的词以元音开始时，两词也连读：an apple、an example、a lot of、in order to。

19. Which of the following verbs is different from all the others?

A. Do

B. Make

C. Have

D. Study

问题：下列中哪一个动词与其他动词不同？

答案：D. Study

英语的动词有很多种，有一种动词的功能很广。它可以替代很多的动词，也能与其他词构成短语动词（phrasal verb），有万能之功。其中最常见的是do、make、have。如, do homework（做作业）、do me a favor（帮我一个忙）、do laundry—wash clothing（洗衣）、do dishes—wash dishes（洗碗）、do drugs—take drugs（吸毒）、do one's business—defecate（大便）、do（some one's）good（使人受益）、make a breakfast（做早餐）、make up the exam—take the exam again（补考）、make her happy（让她幸福）、make a difference（有所作为）、practice makes perfect（熟能生巧）、have a break—rest（休息一下）、have a meeting（开会）、have a cup of coffee—drink coffee（喝咖啡）等。这三个动词可以接同一个词，在动作的含义上有细微的差别（参见刘迪林博士2008年所著 *Idioms, Description, Comprehension, Acquisition, and Pedagogy*）。如：do a coffee（做咖啡——从咖啡豆开始煮咖啡的整个过程）、

make a coffee（煮咖啡——用咖啡机煮咖啡）、have a coffee（喝咖啡——不需要做什么）。同类的词还有get、take、give等。如, get pregnant（怀孕）、get up（起床）、get caught（被抓住了）、get paid（得到报酬）、get rid of（摆脱）、take care（照顾）、take over（接管）、take a rest（休息一会）、take for granted（觉得理所当然）、take a seat（坐一坐）、take a chance（碰碰运气）、give up（放弃）、give away（抛弃）、give an example（举一个例子）。study（学习）一词的用法就比较有局限。study for the final（准备期末考试）, He studies philosophy.（他主修哲学。）

20. Do you know which word does not have a prefix?

A. Dislike

B. Discipline

C. Dissatisfaction

D. Disbelieve

问题：下列答案中哪一个词没有前缀？

答案：B. Discipline

　　所给的答案中，每个字都是以dis开始，但只有discipline中的dis不是在词根（root）上加的词缀（affix）。英语的构词法中，最基本的方法之一是在词根上加前缀（prefix）或后缀（suffix）。了解和掌握常见的前缀或后缀，可以大大提高词汇量和阅读理解的能力。以dis为例，加上这个前缀词义相反（opposite meaning）：like（喜欢）—dislike（不喜欢/讨厌）、satisfaction（满意）—dissatisfaction（不满意）、believe（相信）—disbelieve（不相信）。表示负面或反义的前缀还有：il-：illegal（非法的）、illogical（不合逻辑的）；in-：incapable（无能的）、invalid（无效的）、inhuman（不人道的）；im-：immature（未成熟的）、impatient（急躁）、impossible（不可能）；ir-：irregular（不规则的）、irresponsible（不负责任的）、irresistible（不可抗拒的）；un-：unhappy（郁郁寡欢）、unemployment（失业）、unusual（不寻常的）、unlucky（不幸的）等。注意, invaluable不是没有价值而是价值无法衡量，说没有价值要用valueless。其他常见前缀还有：re-（again）：reunion（团聚）、review（评论）、recollection（回忆）、reconstruction（重建）、reform（改革）；pre-（before）：preface（前言）、prehistoric（史前）；trans-（across）：transportation（交通）、transform（改造）；inter-（between/among）：Internet（互联网）、interact（互动）、interpreter（翻译）、interview（面试）。最新的前缀有：apple公司的产品：i-Mac（苹果电脑）、i-Phone（苹果手机）、iPad（平板电脑）、iTune（音乐播放器）；e-electronic（电子）：e-mail（电子邮件）、e-business（电子商务）、e-music（电子音乐）、e-book（电子书）。参见下页的常用前缀表。

表 3-2　常用英语前缀（Commonly Used English Prefixes）

前缀 （Prefix）	词意 （Meaning）	词例 （Example）
anti-	against	anti racism（反种族歧视）、antibiotics（抗生素）
auto-	self	automobile（汽车）、autobiography（自传）、autopilot（自动驾驶）
cyber-	Internet	cyberattack（网络攻击）、cyberspace（网络空间）、cybercrime（网络犯罪）
de-	opposite	defrost（去霜）、defence（防卫）、decrease（减少）
dis-	opposite	dissatisfy（不满意）、dislike（不喜欢）、disagree（不同意）
e-	electrolic	email（电邮）、ebusiness（电子商务）、ebook（电子书）
en-,em-	cause to	enhance（加强）、empower（增强）embrace（拥抱）
ex-	out, from	exgirlfriend（前女友）、exwife（前妻）、expresident（前总统）
extra-	beyond	extraordinary（非凡）、extralarge（超大）、extracurriculum（课外活动）
fore-	before	forehead（额头）、forcast（预测）、foretell（预见）
hyper-	extreme	hypertension（高血压）、hyperactive（多动症）、hypersensitive（过敏的）
in-,im-	in	inhouse（内部）、insane（疯了）、immigration（移民）
in-, im-,il-,ir-	not	injustice（不公）、impolite（不礼貌）、illegal（非法）、irresistable（不可抗拒）
inter-	between	interstate（州际公路）、interact（互动）、intervene（介入，干预）
micro-	small	microphone（话筒）、microscope（显微镜）、microprocessor（微处理器）
mid-	middle	midterm（中期）、Mid-autumn Festival（中秋节）、
mis-	wrongly	misunderstand（误解）、misfire（失火）、mislead（误导）
mono-	one,single	monopoly（垄断）、monologue（独白）、monotomous（单调）
multi-	many	multiculure（多文化）、multilingual（多语言）、multimillionaire（千万富翁）
non-	not	nonsense（废话）、nonreturnable/nonrefundable（不能退货）
over-	over	overflow（溢出）、overnight（过夜）、overachiever（成就者）
pre-	before	preface（前言）、preposition（介词）、prehistorical（史前）
post-	after	postwar（战后）、postdoctorate（博士后）、postseason（季后）
re-	again	refund（退款）、reimbursement（报销）、return（返回）
retro-	backwards	retrospective（回顾）、retroactive（追溯）、retros（复古）
semi-	half	semicolonial（半殖民地）、semiconductor（半导体）、semifinal（半决赛）
sub-	under	subway（地铁）、subtitle（副标题）、submarine（潜水艇）
super	above	superman（超人）、superstar（巨星）、superpower（超级大国）
syn-, sym-	together	synchronize（同步）、symphony（交响乐）、synopsis（该要）
tele-	at distance	television（电视）、telephone（电话）、telescope（望远镜）
trans-	across	transplant（移植）、translation（翻译）、transgender（变性）
un-	not	unlikely（不可能的）、unfriendly（不友好的）、unemployed（失业）
under-	under	underwater（水下）、undergraduate（本科生）underclothes（内衣）
up	higher	upstairs（楼上）、upgrade（升级）、uphill（上山）

21. Which of the following pairs is different from all the others?

A. Sea—See

B. Write—Right

C. Night—Knight

D. Bank—Bank

问题：下列中哪一组和其他几组不同？

答案：D. Bank—Bank

答案中的四对词都是同音字（homophones），即每对的两个词的发音完全相同，但三对是词义不同和拼写不同的同音字：sea（大海）—see（看），write（写）—right（对/右），night（晚上）—knigh（骑士）。而只有bank（银行）—bank（河堤）一对不但发音一样而且拼写也一样，与其他几对词不同。其他常见的同音而拼写不同的字还有：to（到）—two（二）—too（也）、carat（克拉）—caret（插入符号）—carrot（胡萝卜）、morning（晨）—mourning（哀悼）、birth（出生）—berth（泊位）、through（通）—threw（扔）、hare（野兔）—hair（毛发）等。有时候一个短语或句子由于音韵的关系，也会有同音而意义不同的现象，叫homophone phrase（同音词语），如ice cream（冰淇淋）与I scream（我尖叫）。有这样的一个流行歌词：I scream. You scream. We all scream for ice cream.（我尖叫，你尖叫，冰淇淋，我们都喊着要。）还有些单词和短语的发音相同，如：urinate（小便）—you are innate（你是天生的）、the sky（天空）—this guy（这家伙）、four candles（四支蜡烛）—fork handles（叉子的手柄）、example（例如）—egg sample（蛋的样品）、some others（其他）—some mothers（有些妇女）—smothers（窒息）、real eyes（真正的眼睛）—realize（实现）—real lies（真的谎言）、a dressed male（身着西服的男人）—addressed mail（有地址的邮件）、them all（他们全部）—the mall（大商场）、whirled（旋转）—world（世界）。

22. Which "it" in the sentences means a real thing?

A. It's hard to tell.

B. It's me.

C. It's cold.

D. It's quite clear that the iPhone changed our way of life.

问题：哪个句子中的"它"指的是真实的东西？

答案：B. 是我。

代词it有许多常见的习惯用法，如表示时间：It's time for dinner.（吃晚饭啦。）It's Sunday.（今天是星期日。）It's six o'clock.（现在六点钟。）有时it不知代表什么，就起一个语法作用。It's cold.（好冷呀。）It's late.（天晚了。）It's over.（结束了。）、it也可以表示一个事物、动作、一件事等。It's a miracle.（真是个奇迹。）It's awesome.（太棒啦！）It's unbelievable.（真是令人难以置信。）It's incredible.（真是令人难以置信的。）It's hilarious.（太好笑啦。）it还可代替一个语法成分，如，It's hard to tell.（这很难说。）it在句子中前置不定式短语to tell，等于to tell is hard。it可以在强调句中代替所强调的词。如，It's the dog that saved the boy's life.（是这条狗救了男孩的生命。）It's at the car exhibition that Frank met his wife.（弗兰克是在车展上认识他妻子的。）当一个句子的主语是个很长的短语或句子时，it还可以代替它们来保持句子的平衡。如，It's quite clear that the iPhone changed our way of life.（很显然，iPhone改变了我们的生活方式。）若该句子不用it引导就会显得头重脚轻：That the iPhone changed our way of life is quite clear. 请注意用it构成的一个不合语法的习惯用法。当你敲门时，房里的人会问你：Who is it at the door?（是谁？）你应回答"It's me."而不是"It's I."

23. Which of the four verbs is a regular verb?

A. Make

B. Put

C. Learn

D. Think

问题：这四个动词中的哪一个是规则的？

答案：C. Learn

很多中国学生对英语的不规则动词（irregular verbs）很是头疼，其实是对不规则动词了解不够。不规则动词的数量并不多，只有200多个，其中有80来个是很少用的。常用的不规则动词使用极广，是日常生活中用得最多的动词。这是因为，这些词来源于拉丁语和希腊语，他们的动词有自己的变化规则。Grabowski & Mindt（1995）的研究表明，160个不规则动词占所有动词使用率的58%；而最常用的20个不规则动词占所有不规则动词使用率的84%；be、have、do三个词的使用率就占这20个不规则动词的84%。20个不规则动词使用率的顺序是be、have、do、say、make、go、take、come、see、know、get、give、find、think、tell、become、show、leave、feel、put。这就完全说明了为什么母语为英语的儿童从小就没有受不规则动词的困扰。中国学生在初学英语时，应该就像英语母语的孩子一样，大量接触和使用并熟练掌握这些动词的用法。天天用这些不规则动词，几年之后，就不会有不规则动词的烦恼了。再加上学会与这些词搭配构成的动词短语（verbal phrases）或短语动词（phrasal verbs），英语的表达能力就能接近母语水平（native proficiency）。

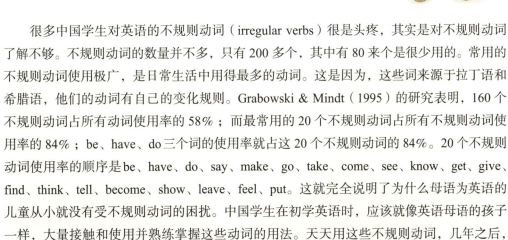

24. When you feel happy, you use the following sentences except:

A. I am like a dog with two tails.

B. I am over the moon.

C. I am as happy as a clam.

D. I am a little down.

问题：你觉得高兴的时候你会说以下句子，除了＿＿＿之外：

答案：D. 我有点失望（不高兴）。

英语中有很多表达高兴的方式。通常说I'm very happy.（我非常高兴。）She is cheerful/joyful.（她性格开朗/快乐。）Emma was overjoyed at her son's return.（爱玛看到儿子回来了欣喜若狂。）I feel good today.（我今天感觉很好。）还有不少习惯的说法：I'm like a dog with two tails.（我就像只两条尾巴的狗。）I am over the moon.（我上月球了。）I am as happy as a clam.（我高兴得像个蛤蜊。）为什么说高兴得像个蛤蜊呢？有人认为是蛤蜊张开时微笑的外观。The little girl is always as happy as a lark.（小女孩总是快乐得像一只云雀。）Nick came back from the birthday party as happy as a pig in shit.（尼克从生日聚会回来快乐得像一头浑身是屎的猪。）还有as happy as a sand boy、as happy as Larry。happy的反义词是unhappy（不高兴）。常用来表示不高兴的同义词和近义词有：She is down.（她不高兴。）Tim put on a long face.（汤姆愁眉苦脸的。）miserable（苦不堪言）：She felt miserable after failing the driving test.（驾驶考试没有过，她觉得很悲伤。）upset（心烦）：I hope she did not say anything to upset you.（但愿她没有说让你不高兴的话。）heart break（心碎）：Michigan State University, the #2 seed had a heart broken lost to #15 seed during the March Madness.（疯狂三月中，2号种子密歇根州州立大学痛心地输给了第15种子。）depressed（心烦意乱）：When depressed, Linda would dramatically eat chocolate and sweets.（情绪低落的时候，琳达就疯狂地吃巧克力和糖果。）troubled（困扰）：The child was troubled/bothered by the noise.（这孩子被噪音所困扰。）其他表示心情的用法有：I am very satisfied with the hotel service.（我很满意酒店的服务。）I feel terrible.（我感觉很糟糕。）He is confident.（他有信心。）She was in a good mood at the party.（派对上她的心情不错。）He is totally occupied with his assignment.（他完全沉浸在他的作业之中。）还有如sad（伤心）、worried（担心）、gloomy（阴沉）等。

25. **What do you see on your right?**

A. A fish

B. Fishes

C. Ghoti

D. Four tails of fish

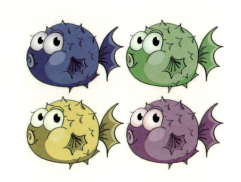

问题：在右边你看到了什么？

答案：D. Four tails of fish

这道题有点难吧？鱼的英文是 fish。fish 是不可数名词。一条鱼不能说 a fish，要用量词 a tail of fish，四条鱼的英文是 four tails of fish。有的时候要表达鱼的种类很多，有人用上复数 fishes，但不常见，最好用 many kinds/variety of fish 来表示。Ghoti 是美国著名心理语言学家 Steven Pinker 在他 Language Instinct（《语言的本能》）一书中创造的一个字，它从语音的角度来描绘英语词的发音和拼写的关系。该书曾被《纽约时代周刊》评为最佳书籍（Best Seller），值得一读。Fish 的发音是 /fiʃ/，而这个音可以拼写成 ghoti。因为根据英语其他单词的发音：gh 在 tough/tʌf/ 中发 /f/；o 在 women/wimin/ 一词发 /i/，ti 在 nation/neiʃən/ 中发 /ʃ/。英文单词的拼写很不规范，其重要的原因是直接应用的外来语太多了，尤其是来自法语的词汇，很多字母都不发音。而且与英语的发音和构词法出入太大。因而英语中单词的发音和拼写不规则的名词和动词数量极大。如 diesel（柴油）来自发明柴油机的法国人 Rudolf Diesel。所以 diesel 一字的发音和拼写不规范。在美国的小学里常举办单词拼写比赛 Spelling Bee 以鼓励儿童熟记不规则单词。参见常拼错的单词：https://coeurdalene-id.aauw.net/files/2012/01/misspelled-words.pdf。

26. **Which one is different from the others?**

A. Novel—new and story

B. Right—wrong and left

C. Fire—shoot and flame

D. Fine—well and penalty

问题：哪一个和其他几个不同？

答案：B. Right—wrong and left

许多英语单词的拼写和发音完全一样，但是有两个或多个不同的含义，也叫同形同音异义词（homonym）。这是因为很多这些词的词源不同而语义相异。如答案 D. Fine:

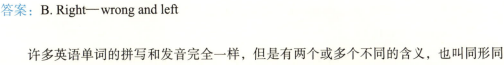

well 好（法语）/penalty 罚款（拉丁语）。又如 box：箱子（拉丁语）/拳打（古英语）。还有 bank：银行（斯堪的那维亚语）—河岸（法语）。有的词源相同而语义相异，如答案 A. Novel：new（新的）和 story（小说），都是来源于拉丁语 novella，词义是新的、新闻、新的短故事。有的很难追溯其来源。fair—light（浅色）/just（正义），fire—shoot（开火）/flame（火焰），story—floor（楼层）/tale（故事），fall—drop（下落）/autumn（秋天），lift—elevator（电梯）/raise（提起）。

英语中常见的同形同音异义词还有：arm（手臂/武器）、ball（球/舞会）、bat（蝙蝠/棒球）、bear（熊/负债）、date（日期/枣）、ear（耳朵/穗）、fan（扇/球迷）、firm（坚硬/公司）、hail（欢呼/冰雹）、last（最后/延续）、lie（谎言/躺）、like（一样/喜欢）、match（比赛/火柴）、miss（小姐/失误）、saw（看到/锯）、seal（密封/章）、sound（声音/健全）、spell（拼写/咒语）、tap（自来水/轻拍）、temple（寺庙/脾气）、well（井/好）、yard（庭院/码）。

英语中有的词有不同的反义词（antonym）。在所给的答案中，B 就是一例。right（对/右）—wrong（错）/left（左）。还有：light（轻的/亮/浅色的）—heavy（重的）dark（黑的/深色的）、hard（硬的/难的）—soft（软的）easy（容易）。参见常用同义反义词分类网站：http://www.smart-words.org/list-of-synonyms/。

27. How many different spellings can /ʃ/ sound represent in English?

A. 3

B. 7

C. 10

D. 20 above

问题：英语中辅音 /ʃ/ 在单词中有多少种拼写法？

答案：D. 20 种以上

英语中辅音 /ʃ/ 在单词中用 20 多种拼写法，可以分为五大类。

1. 词中有 sh：she（她）、shoe（鞋）、Washington（华盛顿）、English（英语）；

2. 词尾有 tion、tial、tient：caution（谨慎）、partial（部分）、potential（潜力）、patient（病人）；

3. 词尾是 cian、cial、cion、cean、cious、ciate、cient：musician（音乐家）、special（特殊的）、official（官方的）、suspicion（猜疑）、ocean（海洋）、delicious（美味）、appreciate（欣赏）、ancient（古代）；

4. 外来词中有 ch、che、chi、sch：Chicago（芝加哥）、mustache（小胡子）、Michelle（米歇尔）、machine（机械）以及 schwa 元音 /ə/；

5. 词中有 sug、sup、sue、sure、scious、sion：sugar（糖）、super（超级的）、suev（控告）、issue（发行）、tissue（组织）、sure（当然）、insurance（保险）、conscious（神志清楚）、mansion（豪宅）。注意，su 后如是 gg 或 pp，则不发 / ʃ/ 音。如 suggestion（建议）、supper（晚餐）等。

28. Which one is different from the others?

A. Color

B. Humor

C. Favor

D. Centre

问题：以下答案中哪个不一样？

答案：D. Centre

美式英语与英式英语在一些字的拼写上有所不同，其原因不明。但根据 D.G. Scragg 2011 撰写的《英语拼写史》（*A History of English Spelling*）一书，在 1828 年之前，许多词语的两种拼写形式，诸如 humor/humour（幽默），defense/defence（防御）和 fiber/fibre（纤维）等，在美国都可接受。1828 年，美国辞典家诺亚韦伯斯特（Noah Webster）在编辑 *Webster's Dictionary* 时，主要负责将美国英语的拼写标准化。他选择了上面每个例子中的前者，并证明他的选择合理，但部分是基于民族主义的理由：他希望美国的拼写与英国拼写不同，并且优于英国的拼写。他去掉了不发音的字母，如 colour — color，把相同的两个辅音字母简化为单辅音，如 program — programme。英美常用的不同拼写有：or — our, er — re, se — ce, m — mme, ize — ise, ll — l。

	美式—英式		美式—英式		美式—英式
幽默	humor — humour	赞成	favor — favour	喜爱	favorite — favourite
颜色	color — colour	罪行	offense — offence	中心	center — centre
汽	vapor — vapour	儿科	pediatrics — paediatrics	分析	analyze — analyse
旅行者	traveler — traveller	平行	program — programme	程序	theater — theatre

参见 http://en.wikipedia.org/wiki/American_and_British_English_spelling_differen-ces。

此外，英美的用词也不尽一样。电梯美语是叫 elevator，而英国称作 lift。汽油：Gas — petrol、行李：baggae — luggage，饼干：cookies — biscuit。美国房子的一楼是 first floor 在英国是 second floor，而一楼是 ground floor。小心！在旅馆里可别走错了房间。以下词的意思完全不一样。

	美式—英式		美式—英式		美式—英式
pants	长裤—内裤	trainer	陪练—跑鞋	restroom	厕所—休息室
football	橄榄球—足球	chips	土豆片—薯条	bird	鸟—女人
braces	牙箍—裤子的吊带	bin	容器—垃圾桶	cider	苹果汁—苹果酒

29. Which of the phrases is correct?

A. A big red real balloon

B. A real red big balloon

C. A real big red balloon

D. A big red real balloon

问题：哪个短语是正确的？

答案：C. A real big red balloon

    当一个英语短语有两个以上的形容词修饰的话，其顺序很难确定。不过美国人不用思考就能随意确定形容词的顺序，通常是靠语感，而说不出个原因。以下是英语形容词顺序的粗略指南（A rough guide for adjective order），供学习者参考。

Size	Shape	Color	Origin	Material	Use	Noun
large	round		home-made			pie
	sleeveless	blue		woolen		coat
small	oval				serving	dishes

美国英语中最常用的 100 形容词

other	national	real	human	free	certain	current	similar	general	religious
new	young	best	local	military	personal	wrong	hot	environmental	cold
good	different	right	late	true	open	private	dead	financial	final
high	black	social	hard	federal	red	past	central	blue	main
old	long	only	major	international	difficult	foreign	happy	democratic	green
great	little	public	better	full	available	fine	serious	dark	nice
big	important	sure	economic	special	likely	common	ready	various	huge
American	political	low	strong	easy	short	poor	simple	entire	popular
small	bad	early	possible	clear	single	natural	left	close	traditional
large	white	able	whole	recent	medical	significant	physical	legal	cultural

参见 http://englishgenie.com/vocabulary/the-top-100-most-common-adjectives/。

30. "His performance is second to none." This sentence means _____.

A. he gave a second rate performance

B. he performed very well

C. he won second place in performance

D. his performance was the best

问题："His performance is second to none." 这句话的意思是_____。

答案：D. 他的表现是最好的。

　　短语 second to none 是第一、最好的意思，等同于 His performance was the best.（他的表现是最好的。）其他选项的含义是：He gave a second rate performance.（他的表演属二流水平。）He performed very well.（他表现得非常出色。）He won the second place in performance.（他获得表演的第二名。）与 second 有关的词语有：second nature（自然，天性）、have second thoughts（改变主意或是开始怀疑），如：Jean seems to be having second thoughts about buying a new iPhone.（Jean 似乎不想买新的 iPhone 了。）Just a second.（稍等一下。）play second fiddle to someone 是成语，含义是做某人的下手。secondary school/education 是中学教育，不是二流教育。在讨论问题或提议作表决时，常说 second 以表示赞同。其他英语序数的用法还有：the third cultural kids（第三种文化的孩子）、first come first serve（先到先得）。

31. Which statement is wrong?

A. Horse is a useful animal.

B. A horse is a useful animal.

C. Horses are useful animals.

D. The horse is a useful animal.

问题：以下哪个陈述是错误的？

答案：A. Horse is a useful animal.

　　"马是一种有用的动物"的英语表达有几种：A horse is a useful animal. Horses are useful animals. The horse is a useful animal 。而 Horse is useful animals. 一句不符合英语的语法法则。英语的可数名词，用单数时，一定得加上冠词。单词的第一个音如果是元音时，即使第一个字母不是元音字母就也要用 an，如：an apple（苹果）、an orange（橘子）、an oven（烤箱）、an icy burger（冰山）、an uncle（叔叔）、an elephant（大象）、an error（错误）、an hour（小

时）、an honor（荣誉）等。有的词第一个字母是元音但不是以元音开始的，不能用an，如：a university（大学）、a union（工会）、a unicorn（独角兽）等。如果这个名词是特指某个物种或物品之一，或是代表一个物种或物品之一时用介词the。要注意，the的发音有变化，一般读/ðə/，但在元音前 读/ðiː/，如：the/ðə/ unit、the/ðə/ book、the/ðiː/ apple、the/ðiː/ orange。名词的单数和复数也能表示一个物种或物品的整体特征。根据统计，冠词the 占冠词使用率的 50%，a 占 20%，使用an 及不用冠词的占 30%。

32. Which sentence has an error?

A. Please pass me a pair of scissors.

B. I'd like to buy pants made of 100% cotton.

C. The burglar surrendered to the police.

D. Jasmine is wearing a pair of sunglass.

问题：下列哪个句子有错误?

答案：D. Jasmine 戴着一副太阳镜。

在答案D中，句子的含义是"Jasmine 戴着一副太阳镜"。"一副太阳镜"的英文应该是a pair of sunglasses，而不是a pair of sunglass。当一件东西是由两个部分组成时，单数也要用复数形式。如scissors（剪刀）、pants（裤子）等。Please pass me a pair of scissors.（请递给我一把剪刀）。I'd like to buy pants made of 100% cotton.（我想买全棉的裤子）。一些单个物品常认为是成双的，要用量词pair of。常见的这种词列表如下供参考。答案C "The burglar surrendered to the police."（盗贼向警察投降。）

a pair of slippers（一双拖鞋）	a pair of cuff links（一对袖扣）	a pair of windshield wipers（一对雨刷）
a pair of shoes（一双鞋）	a pair of swimming trunks（一条泳裤）	a pair of wings（一双翅膀）
a pair of boots（一双靴子）	a pair of earrings（一对耳环）	a pair of dices（一对骰子）
a pair of shoe laces（一双鞋带）	a pair of lungs（一对肺）	a pair of chopsticks（一双筷子）
a pair of skates（一双溜冰鞋）	a pair of kidneys（一对肾脏）	a pair of tweezers（一个镊子）
a pair of socks（一双袜子）	a pair of eyes（一双眼睛）	a pair of headlights（一对大灯）
a pair of trousers（一条裤子）	a pair of glasses（一副眼镜）	a pair of tongs（一把钳子）
a pair of shorts（一条短裤）	a pair of goggles（一副护目镜）	a pair of pliers（一把钳子）
a pair of gloves（一副手套）	a pair of binoculars（一副望远镜）	a pair of skis（一副滑雪板）
a pair of jeans（一条牛仔裤）	a pair of contacts（一对隐形眼镜）	a pair of crutches（一双拐杖）
a pair of pajamas（一套睡衣）	a pair of knitting needles（一对织针）	a pair of speakers（一对音箱）

33. Which of the following means driving a car?

A. She drives me crazy.

B. Don't drive your students up to wall with such a question.

C. We are going to host a blood drive.

D. I drive my children to school everyday.

问题：下面哪个选项的意思是"开车"？

答案：D. 我每天开车送孩子们上学。

      动词 Drive 通常是开车的意思，如选项中只有 D. I drive my children to school everyday. 中的 drive 是指开车。又如, I don't know how to drive a stick shift car. （我不会开手动车。）而在其他的选项中，意思都不是开车。She drives me crazy. （她让我发疯。）与 drive me mad. 同义。Drive someone wild. （使某人极端兴奋。）The trio band drove the crowd wild when they played on campus. （三人乐队在校园的表演让人群疯狂。）Don't drive your students up to wall with such a question. （这是个成语，不是把你的学生开上墙，而是不要用如此难的问题来困扰学生的意思。）We are going to host a blood drive. （我们要举办一个献血活动。）与血有关的词语还有：What is your blood type? （你的血型是什么？）Blood is thicker than water. （血浓于水。) make one's blood boil（愤怒, 热血沸腾）：His blood boiled at the horrified news. （他一听到这噩耗就震怒。）make one's blood run cold/to fill with horror（惊恐，汗毛倒竖）：A terrifying scene in the movie made my blood run cold. （电影中的恐怖情景让我毛骨悚然。）还有一个常用来表示惊恐、害怕的词语叫 freak out：I'm freaking out every time I see a spider. （每次看到蜘蛛我都会吓得要命。）At Rio Olympic Games, the women's volley final between Chinese and Serbia made all audience's emotions ran high and blood boiled, and Chinese team came out on top. （在巴西奥运会上，中国女排和塞尔维亚之间的决赛使所有观众的情绪高涨，热血沸腾，中国队技高一筹取得了胜利。）in one's blood（本性）：Greed for money is in the blood of the corrupt official. （敛钱是此贪官的本性。）The football player's clothes were soaked in blood. （足球队员的衣服被鲜血浸透了。）in cold blood（冷静地，残酷地）：The terrorists killed many innocent people in cold blood. （恐怖分子残忍地杀害许多无辜的人。）Our team needs new blood . （我们团队需要注入新鲜血液。）She suffers from high blood pressure. （她患有高血压。)The visiting team drew first blood.（客队旗开得胜）。blood transmission（输血）、blood bank（血库）。

34. What word do Americans use most frequently when making a pause in a speech?

A. Well

B. And

C. Aha

D. Hum

问题：在美国人讲话时想作短暂停顿时，最常用哪个词？

答案：B. And

　　美国人在讲话中，想作短暂停顿时，常用and，而且字音有时拖得很长，以便思考下面的话题，相当于中国人的"嗯"和"这个""那个"。中国人说英语时要尽可能地去掉它们，而用and。well则是在开始回答问题时，小作思考或是作转折时用。如，Well, so much for today.（那么，今天就到此吧。）Aha是个感叹词，用来表示"弄清啦"。"Aha! So you took the money!"（"啊哈！是你拿走了钱！"）常用的感叹词还有：Hum（哼，嗯），用来表示犹豫（hesitation）、惊喜（surprise）或不悦（displeasure）。oops（哎呀），表示不是有意弄的。Oops! I almost spilled the milk.（哎哟！我差点把牛奶洒了。）Eh（嗯？）表示疑问。Yuck（yech）表示disgusting（厌恶）：Yuck! That's gross.（真恶心！）yeeh! 表示成功时的高兴。uh-oh/oh-oh,（Oh no!）（糟了，糟糕。）Uh-oh, I forgot to bring my lunch today.（糟了，今天我忘记带午餐了。）shh意思是be quiet!（安静。）Wow表示惊讶（amazing!）Wow, it's incredible!（哇，太不可思议了!）man这个词也常用来表示惊讶：Oh, Man! I just missed the school bus!（糟了，我错过乘校车了!）Duh表示犹豫、不快或轻蔑等。

35. When you feel something is funny you would say:

A. It's awesome!

B. It's fantastic!

C. It's hilarious!

D. It's ridiculous!

问题：当你觉得事情很有趣，你会说：

答案：C. 这太搞笑啦！

当美国人觉得一个事情或某人很有趣，很有意思，很好笑，很好玩，他们会发感慨地说：It's hilarious! 如，I like to watch the late night show by Letterman. He's hilarious!（我喜欢看莱特曼的深夜秀。他很搞笑的！）其他类似的有：It's very funny. Eric is such a personality—he is so funny.（Eric 很有个性魅力——非常风趣。）表示惊讶和赞赏的感叹句还有：当看到一个漂亮的篮球进球时，人们会尖叫起来说，It's awesome!（真棒极了！）It's fantastic!（太棒了！）It's unbelievable!（这太令人难以置信了！）It's incredible!（真是难以置信！）Awesome, you got the job!（你得到了这份工作，真棒！）Brilliant, you solved the puzzle!（你解决了这个难题，了不起！）She is still a stunning woman at 55.（她已经 55 岁了，但依然艳丽动人。）You're adorable.（你很迷人。）Hooray!（万岁！）Magnificent!（华丽极了！）表示痛苦或悲哀的有：Ouch, that really hurts!（哎哟，真的好痛！）The media coverage of the current air pollution was shocking.（媒体对目前空气污染的报道令人震惊了。）表示烦躁：I can't figure that out!（我弄不明白这一点！）其他常用的感叹句还有：It's ridiculous!（荒谬至极！）Wow, that was a thrilling（breath taking）ride!（哇，这个过山车太惊险啦！）

36. Do you know which X in the following means extension?

A. X-2345

B. X-ing

C. X-girl friend

D. X-ray

问题：下面哪个 X 是表示电话的分机？

答案：A. X-2345

在美国，电话号码分区域号码（area codes）和地方号码（local numbers）。每个州有一个或多个区域号码。参见全美按州所列的区域号码 http://www.allareacodes.com/area_code_listings_by_state.htm。区域号码之间拨号要加 1. 如从新泽西打纽约的号码 212-888-2828，要拨 1-212-888-2828。号码电话分机 extension 是用 X 加号码表示。如，1-212-888-2828，X-2345。从美国拨打中国的电话顺序是，国际编号（international code），国家编号（country code），省市编号（city code），地方号码（local number）。如打北京要拨 011 — 86 — 10 — 8888 — 8888。X 用在许多常见的表达中。X-ing 是 crossing 的意思，在火车与公路的交叉口，都立有 ▲ 标识，有鹿出入的对段还设有 ▲ deer-crossing 的标识。X-girl friend 中的 X 是 ex-girl friend（以前的女朋友），ex-husband（前夫）。X-ray 中的 X 并不是哪个英文字的缩写。1895 年 11 月 8 日，德国物理学教授威廉·康拉德·伦琴（Wilhelm Conrad Röntgen）发现了一些不常见的光线，它们没有表现出反射或折射特性。因为他不知道它们是什么样的光线，就称他们为X射线，即某种射线。后来这些射线就命名为X射线。X射线是具有高能量和非常短的波长的电磁波，能以不透明的光穿透许多材料。由X射线产生的照相或数字图像（digital image）被广泛用于医疗诊断（medical exam）方面。如X-ray、MIR—magnetic resonance imaging（磁共振成像）等。

37. Which comparison in the phrases given below is not correct?

A. As strong as a cow

B. As clear as crystal

C. As brave as a lion

D. As busy as a bee

问题：下列短语中的比较方式哪个是不正确的？

答案：A. As strong as a cow

　　每种语言都有用明喻（similes）来表示比较的短语。英语和中文有相同比较的用法：如，轻如鸿毛（as light as a feather）、清如水晶（as clear as crystal）、冷如冰（as cold as ice）、像狐狸一样狡猾（as cunning as a fox）、像小鸟一样自由（as free as a bird）、像绵羊一样温驯（as gentle as a lamb）等。但也有很多是不一样的，如中文的"力大如牛"不是答案A. as strong as a cow，而是as strong as a horse（力大如马）。中文用"饿得像狼"，而英文说"饿得像头熊或猎人"（as hungry as a bear/hunter），不是狼（wolf）；中文说"酒醉如泥"，英文是as drunk as a lord（醉如主人）；中文说"甜如蜜"，而英文是as sweet as pie（甜如甜饼）不是蜜糖（honey）。其他一些常见的英文比喻有：as brave as a lion（像狮子一样勇敢）、as easy as pie（容易极了）、as poor as a church mouse（像教堂里的老鼠一样穷 / 一贫如洗）、as quick as a flash（像闪光一样快）。描述高兴的英文是as happy as a pig in shit（快乐得像一头浑身是屎的猪）、as busy as a bee（忙得不可开交）、as white as a ghost/as white as a sheet/as white as snow（像鬼/纸/雪一样白）、as cool as a cucumber（泰然自若/像黄瓜一样凉）、as dark as pitch（黑暗如沥青）。参见：Similes：www.phrases.org.uk/meanings/similes.html。

38. Which of the following expressions is incorrect?

A. In a debt

B. In a hurry

C. Make a fresh start

D. Have a drink

问题：下列表达中哪个是不正确的？

答案：A. In a debt 负债

　　负债正确的表达应该是 in debt。英语中的冠词是最难掌握的，就不定冠词 a 而言，就常常让学生不知所措。通常 a 只有在可数名词单数前使用。可是在由动词或介词接名词的短语中，是否要用冠词 a，似乎无章可循。在题中的短语里，不可数的名词前也加了冠词 a，如：in a hurry（匆忙）。还有：make a start（开始）、in a rage（盛怒）、have a try（试试看）、on a diet（在节食）。而不少短语里的可数名词单数前却又没有加冠词 a，很不可思议。如, make room for me.（借光。）在这种情况下，名词通常是改变了特性成了抽象名词。一般来说，在表明地点、交通方式、就餐的介词短语中不加冠词 a，如：after school（放学后）、at work（在上班）、go to college（上大学）、go to church（上教堂）、go to town（进城）、go to market（上市场）、at home（在家里）、go out for lunch/dinner（出去吃午饭/晚餐）、in town（在城里）、in bed（卧床）、in prison（在监狱里/坐班房）、in market（在市场里）、in hospital（住院）、in person（亲自）、in press（印刷中）、at hand（在眼前）、at table（在吃饭）、on foot（步行）、come to work by bike/bus/taxi/train/boat（骑自行车/公车/出租车/火车/轮船去上班）。有的名词加名词的短语中也不加冠词，如 man and wife（丈夫和妻子）、mother and child（母亲和孩子）、hand in hand（手牵手）、side by side（肩并肩）、arm in arm（手挽手）、day after day（一天又一天）、master and man（主人和仆人）、from door to door（挨家挨户）、sword in hand（剑在手）、cigar in mouth（嘴里叼着雪茄）、from head to toe/foot（从头到脚）、live from hand to mouth（糊口）。美语的习惯用法太多了，记牢词之间的搭配是关键。

39. Which of the following words means eight?

A. Quadrilateral

B. Octagon

C. Pentagon

D. Hexagon

问题：下面哪个字的意思是八？

答案：B. 八角形

如果你知道英语中October是十月，就一般不会想到octagon（八角形）与八字有关。Oct是个表示八的前缀，如八边的（octagonal），章鱼（octopus）等。中国的八仙是The Eight Immortals。英语中，除了用数字表示数量之外，还有些专门表示数量的词。这些词都是来自古拉丁语和希腊语。下面的前缀表会对你了解词义有所帮助。在几何学（geometry）中，涉及物体的图形时，有专门表示角数量的词，如，triangle（三角形）、rectangle（矩形）、square 或 quadrate（方形）、pentagonal（五角形）、hexagonal（六角形）、heptagonal（七角形）、octagonal（八角形）、nine angular（九角形）、decagon（十角形）。美国的国防部常称为五角大楼（Pentagon）。演唱、舞蹈和乐器协奏方面有：quartet（四重奏）、trio（三重奏或三人舞）、duet（二重奏或二重唱或双人舞）。生育方面则有：twin（双胞胎）、identical twin（同卵双胞胎）、twin brothers（双胞兄弟）、triplets（三胞胎）、quadruplets（四胞胎）、quintuplets（五胞胎）等。其他表示数量的前缀见下表：

1	uni-：unify 统一 mono-：monogamy 一夫一妻	2	di-：dilemma，进退两难 bi-：bicycle 自行车	3	tri-：trinity 三合一 triangle 三角形
4	tetra-：tetralogy 四部曲 quandr-：quadrate 方形	5	penta-：pentad 五个一组 quinque-：quinquennial 每五年的	6	hexa-：hexad 六个
7	hepta-：heptahedron 七面体 sept-：septuple 七倍的	8	oct-：octet 八部曲	10	dec-：decade 十年 deci-：decimal 十进制

40. Which of the following acronyms is different from all the others?

A. FAQ

B. DND

C. BTW

D. HTML

问题：下列词中哪个缩写字和其他几个都不同？

答案：D. 超文本标记语言

　　答案 D. HTML（hypertext markup language），意为超文本标记语言，它是一种在网站开发中使用的计算机编程语言（a computer programming language used in development of web sites）。这种语言促进了许多网站的开发，如 Facebook（脸书）、Blog（博客）和 Twitter（推特）等。这些软件的使用正在改变着人类的互动、交流和社交的方式（ways of human interaction, communication and socialization），同时也是对隐私（privacy）和信息安全（information security）的极大挑战（challenge）。另外网络也成了黑客（hacker）犯法的途径。其他选项都与计算机编程语言无关，它们的意思是：FAQ 是常见问题（Frequently asked questions）的缩写，用得很广泛。另一个相似的缩写是 QA—questions and answers（问答）。DND—do not disturb（免打扰，请勿打扰），常挂在办公室和旅馆房门的把手（door knob）上。BTW—by the way（顺便说一句）。

41. Which is not among the top 12 most frequently used lexical verbs?

A. Think

B. Know

C. Say

D. Like

问题：哪一个不是属于最常用的 12 个实义动词之列的？

答案：D. Like

　　答案中除了 like 之外，think（认为，想）、know（知道）、say（说）都是属于最常用的 12 个动词（Ota, 1963）。其他的九个动词是：want、go、get、come、see、make、mean、 fell、take。Bilber 等人在 1999 年所做的研究结果显示，say（说）、get（去/拿）、go（走）、know（知道）、think（想）、see（看）、make（做）、come（来）、take（拿）、want（要）、give（给）、mean（意思）这 12 个动词的使用占会话中动词用量的 45％和学术写作的 11％。这 12 个动词中每个都有几种至几十种用法，以 take 为例，它可以构成众多的动词短语：take train/bus（乘火车/公交车）、take notes（做笔记）、take medicine（吃药）、take a seat（请坐）、take care（照顾）、take a shower/bath（洗澡）、take responsibility（承担责任）、take part in（参与）、take a break（休息一下）、take a look（看一看）、take off（起飞/脱衣服）、take apart（拆散）、take over（接手）、take away from（夺去）等。由此可见，掌握这些常用动词的用法对提高英语听说和写作能力的重要性。like 的用法也不少：Kate likes to read fictions.（凯特喜欢看小说。）He looks just like Harry Potter.（他长的就像哈利·波特。）Like father like son.（有其父必有其子。）How do you like your school?（你觉得学校怎么样？）I'd like to invite you to my son's birthday party.（我想邀请你参加我儿子的生日派对。）Would you like another beer?（您需要再来一杯啤酒吗？）Like it or not, we speak the language where we grow up.（不管我们愿不愿意，我们在哪儿长大就说哪儿的语言。）Something like that.（差不多吧/大概。）You can stay with us tonight if you like.（你愿意的话今晚可以和我们住在一起。）

42. Which one of the sentences is incorrect?

A. Don't raise your voice, please.

B. My boss promised to raise my salary.

C. The prices of consumer goods will rise again.

D. Jeff rose a few questions about the course.

问题：哪一个句子不正确？

答案：D. Jeff rose a few questions about the course.

英语中有很多不规则动词，他们的过去式是不规则变化。raise 一词是规则动词，过去式是 raised，所以答案 D 中 rose 不是 raise 一词的过去式，应该用 raised。Jeff raised a few questions about the course.（杰夫就课程提了几个问题。）其他答案是：Don't raise your voice, please.（请不要提高你的嗓门。）My boss promised to raise my salary.（我的老板答应给我涨工资。）The prices of consumer goods will rise again next week.（下周消费品价格将再次上涨。）raise 还可以表示养育，如，The new development seemed like a good neighborhood to raise my children.（这个新居住区看起来像是一个有利于我的孩子们成长的居住区。）Jessica, a single mother, is struggling to raise three children. (单身母亲杰西卡艰难地抚养着三个孩子。) The church has charity fairs to raise money for people in need. (教会设立慈善日来筹款帮助需要的人群。) raise 的常用搭配有 raise the bar (提高要求/难度): He is surprised that many colleges will raise the bar for their admissions. (他对许多大学提高入学水平感到震惊。) raise a red flag (发出一个潜在的麻烦或危险的信号): Increasing unemployment rate raised a red flag for economic recession. (失业率上升是经济衰退的一个警示。) raise the certain (开始，揭幕)。

43. Which of the following is not formally used to express future?

A. Will, shall, can, might, could, may

B. Simple present

C. Be going to

D. Gonna

问题：下列哪个不是表达将来时间的正式用法？

答案：D. Gonna

　　英文表达时间主要是靠时态 tense 的变化，共有 16 种之多。但是常用的也就 4~5 种。如现在时 (simple present)、进行时 (continues/progressive)、过去时 (past)、将来时 (future) 和完成时 (perfect)。其实还有不少可以表示时间的方式。就将来时而言，除了 will 和 shall (很少用了) 之外，can、might、could、may 也是表示事情发生在将来。不少词的现在时态也能表达将来，如，He is bound to be successful. (他必然会成功。) Jean was about to leave when Tim rang the bell. (Jean 正要离开的时候，Tim 按响了门铃。) Her flight leaves at eight tomorrow morning. (她的航班明早八点起飞。) 一般时态常用来避免在从句中重复使用 will，如，After you finish (wrap up) your homework I will take you to ice-skating. (完成你的功课后，我会带你去溜冰。) be going to 更是用得很广，We are going to see the movie *the Hunger Games* tonight. (我们今晚去看电影《饥饿游戏》。) gonna 是 be going to 的缩写，一种不够正式的用法，但用的人不少。I'm gonna leave now. (我要离开了。) 许多动词都是表示将来：recommend (推荐)、suggest (建议)、advice (忠告) 等。

44. Which of the words below does not have a silent letter?

A. Comb

B. Knee

C. Clutch

D. Think

问题：下面哪个单词没有不发音的字母？

答案：D. Think

　　在英语单词中，有些字母常不发音。有一些规律可以帮助你拼写。字母b在词尾与m相连接时不发音。常见的字有：bomb（炸弹）、climb（攀登）、comb（梳子）、crumb（碎屑）、dumb（哑）、lamb（小羊羔）、limbs（四肢）、plumb（探索）、plumber（管道工）、tomb（坟墓）、thumb（大拇指）等。字母b与t相连接时不发音。如：debt（债务）、debtor（债务人）、doubt（疑问）、doubtful（可疑的）、subtle（微妙的）、subtleness（微妙）等。字母k在词头后接n时不发音。如：knee（膝）、knife（刀）、knight（骑士）、knock（敲）、knot（结）、know（知道）、knowledge（知识）等。字母t后接ch时，不发音。如clutch（离合器）、match（比赛）、stretch（伸展）等。w后接r不发音：wrap（总结）、wreck（沉船）、wrestle（摔跤）、wring（拧）、write（写）、writer（作家）、wrist（手腕）、wrong（错了）等。w不发音的词还有：who（谁）、whose（谁的）、whom（谁）、whole（整个）、whoever（不管是谁）、answer（回答）、sword（剑）、two（二）等。另外在英语的开音节（open vowel syllabus）单词中，词尾的e字母不发音。如：like、make、life、save、pave、space、tube、home等。l不发音的词有：calm（平静）、half（一半）、talk（说话）、walk（走路）、should（应该）、could（可以）、calf（小腿）、salmon（鲑鱼）、egg yolk（蛋黄）、chalk（粉笔）、folk（民俗）、balm（香脂）等。在Psychology（心理学）、pneumonia（肺炎）、psychologist（心理学家）、pseudonym（化名）等单词中的 p 不发音。aisle/ail/（过道）和island（岛）中的 s 不发音。gh是个极难掌握发音的字母组合，在词尾通常发f，如，dough（生面团）、tough（坚韧）、cough（咳嗽）、enough（足够）、laugh（笑）、telephone（电话）、paragraph（段）、alphabet（字母）、phonetics（语音）、sophomore（大二学生），但是在接t后则不发音了：daughter（女儿）、fighter（斗士）、fright（恐怖）、bright（明亮）等。参见下页常见有不发音字母的单词表。

表 3-3　常见有不发音字母的单词表（Common Words with Silent Letters）

B	在词尾与 m 相连接时：bomb（炸弹）、climb（攀登）、comb（梳子）、crumb（碎屑）、dumb（哑）、lamb（小羊羔）、limbs（四肢）、plumb（探索）、plumber（管道工）、tomb（坟墓）、thumb（大拇指）等。与 t 相连接时：debt（债务）、debtor（债务人）、doubt（疑问）、doubtful（可疑的）、subtle（微妙的）、subtleness（微妙）等。
C	ascent（上升）、fascinate（令人着迷）、miscellaneous（杂）、muscle（肌肉）、scenario（场景）、scissors（剪刀）等。
D	handkerchief（手帕）、Wednesday（星期三）、sandwich（三明治）、handsome（英俊）、pledge（誓言）、dodge（逃避）、grudge（怨恨）、hedge（树篱）等。
E	开音节单词词尾的 e 字母不发音：like（喜欢）、make（做）、life（生命）、save（救）、pave（铺）、space（空间）、tube（管子）、home（家）、hope（希望）、drive（开车）、gave（给）、write（写）、site（地点）、grave（坟墓）、bite（咬）、hide（藏）。
G	Champagne（香槟）、foreign（外国的）、sign（标志）、feign（假装）、design（设计）、align（对齐）、cognac（干邑白兰地）等。
Gh	接 t 后：daughter（女儿）、fighter（斗士）、fright（恐怖）、bright（明亮）等。
H	what（什么）、when（什么时候）、where（在哪里）、whether（是否）、why（为什么）、hour（小时）、honest（诚实）、honor（荣誉）、heir（继承人）、choir（唱诗班）、chorus（合唱团）、ghastly（可怕）、ghoul（食尸鬼）、aghast（吓呆了）、echo（回声）、rhythm（节奏）等。
K	在词头接 n 时：knee（膝）、knife（刀）、knight（骑士）、knock（敲）、knot（结）、know（知道）、knowledge（知识）等。
L	calm（平静）、half（一半）、talk（说话）、walk（走路）、should（应该）、could（可以）、calf（小腿）、salmon（鲑鱼）、egg yolk（蛋黄）、chalk（粉笔）、folk（民俗）、balm（香脂）等。
N	在 m 后：autumn（秋天）、solemn（庄严）、column（柱）、hymn（诗等）。
P	psychology（心理学）、pneumonia（肺炎）、psychologist（心理学家）、pseudonym（化名）等。
S	aisle/ail/（过道）、aisle seat（飞机中的过道座位）、island（岛）、isle、islet（小岛屿）等。
T	后接 ch 时：clutch（离合器）、match（比赛）、stretch（伸展）等。在 s 或 f 和 e 之间：fasten（系好）、listen（听着）、hasten（加速）、often（经常）、soften（趋软）。在 s 和 l 或 m 之间：castle（城堡）、whistle（吹口哨）、（thistle 蓟）、bustle（喧嚣）、Christmas（圣诞节）。在法语外来词词尾：rapport（融洽）、gourmet（美食）、ballet（芭蕾）等。
U	在 g 之后：guard（守卫）、guardain（监护人）、guess（猜测）、guidance（指导）、guitar（吉他）、guest（客人）等。
W	后接 r 时：wrap（总结）、wreck（沉船）、wrestle（摔跤）、wring（拧）、write（写）、writer（作家）、wrist（手腕）、wrong（错了）。其他：who（谁）、whose（谁的）、whom（谁）、whole（整个）、whoever（不管是谁）、answer（回答）、sword（剑）、two（二）等。

45. What does "lol" stand for in a text message?

A. Lots of love

B. Lots of luck

C. Laugh out loud

D. Little old lady

问题："lol"在短信中的意思是什么？

答案：C. 笑出声来

　　单词lol是个缩略词（acronym/initialism）：laugh out loud（笑出声来）。第一次用lol这个缩写是在20世纪60年代，当时是Little old lady（小老太太）的缩写。短语lots of luck（总是走运）和lots of love（很多的爱）的缩写也是lol。目前互联网上十个最常用的俚语是：1. SMEXI—smart and sexy（聪明和性感），2. GOMB—Get off my back（饶了我吧），3. CSA—Cheap Shot Artist（偷袭艺术家），4. SIS—slow internet speed（网速很慢），5. UG—Ugly（很丑），6. A1—Top quality（高品质/高质量），7. YT?—You Think?（你觉得呢？你这样认为吗？），8. GIF—Graphics Interchange Format/Picture format（图形交换格式/图片格式），9. TGIF—Thank God is Friday（感谢上帝，是星期五啦），10. SUFI—Super Finger（超级手指）。在网上发短信时，人们用很多简写字，加快信息的传递。如用u代替you、ic代I see，还有如Xmas—Christmas、CU—see you、CYA—see ya、GTG/G2G—got to go、IDK—I don't know—I dunno（我不知道）、JK-just kidding（开玩笑）、THX—thanks、NP—no problem、OMG—oh my God、Sup—What's up、Smiley—☺、TTYL—Talk to you later，还有用数字代词：2—two/to、4—for。

46. Which of the following four verbs is different from all the others?

A. Remember

B. Stop

C. Forget

D. Consider

问题：下列四个动词中哪个和其他几个不同？

答案：D. Consider

　　英语的动词后面常可以接动词不定式to be和现在分词v-ing。有些动词不论接动词不定式或分词其意思基本一样。如begin（开始）：Susan began sharing（to share）her cherries with her friends.（苏珊开始与她的朋友们分享她的樱桃。）其他常见的有：continue（继续）、hate（恨）、like（喜欢）、love（热爱）、prefer（喜欢）、regret（遗憾）、start（启动）、try（尝试）等。有些动词后面却只能接现在分词。如consider（考虑）一词，Hillary Clinton may consider running for next US president in 2020.（希拉里可能会考虑在2020年竞选下届美国总统。）其他例子还有：The boy admitted cheating on the quiz.（男孩承认在测验中作弊。）People nowadays enjoy chatting with friends on wechat.（现在人们喜欢用微信与好友聊天。）其他的动词还有：appreciate（欣赏）、avoid（避免）、defend（捍卫）、deny（拒绝）、enjoy（欣赏）、feel（感受）、finish（完成）、hear（听到）、quit（退出）、recall（回忆）、resume（重新开始）、risk（冒风险）、see（看到）、smell（闻到）等。而有个别的动词则不定式和现在分词都可以接，但是意义完全不同，如remember（记住）、stop（停止）和forget（忘记）。stop to smoke指停下来吸烟，而stop smoking是停止吸烟。remember to bring an umbrella是记得带伞，而remember bringing an umbrella是记得带了伞。forgot to call her指忘了给她打电话，而forgot calling her是忘了已经给她打了电话了。

47. John waited for an answer, but Barbara didn't ___ a word.

A. say

B. tell

C. speak

D. talk

问题：John等着回答，但Barbara一句话也不说。

答案：A. say

　　常用来表示说话的英语动词有say、tell、speak、talk等，但他们的用法及搭配不一样。对某人说话：用say something to somebody，say that...说（接一个句子），say a thing in a language（用某种语言说）。Needless to say, you should spend more time on your assignment.（不用说，你应该在你的作业上花更多的时间。）Say goodbye to something/kiss something goodbye.（与某物告别，不再见到某物。）I can't say for sure.（说不准。）My boss has the final say.（我的老板说了才算。）Let's say...（假定……）Say cheese.（笑一笑——照相时用语）。Never say never.（不一定的！别说绝了。）tell a story/tale（讲故事）、tell the truth（说实话）、tell the difference between（说出……之间的区别）。speak to somebody（与某人说话）、

speak English at a conference（在会议上用英语讲话）。Speak/talk the devil, and in he walks.（说曹操，曹操到。）talk about something（谈论某事）、talk to somebody about something（与某人谈论某事）。Good talking to you.（很高兴和你交谈。）We need to talk.（我们得谈谈。）pillow talk（枕边细语）。表示说话的动词还有shout、yell、scream，意为"大声喊叫"，如yell：Please don't yell at your sister.（不要对你的妹妹大喊大叫。）whisper/murmur（耳语/小声说话）：Keep your voice down, Jack' I whispered.（我轻声说："捷克，小声点儿。"）聊天，闲谈的英语是chat、small talk、casual conversation，比较口语化的词是chit chat。

48. Someone who always tells others to do things＿＿.

A. is friendly

B. is a backseat driver

C. has a big mouth

D. likes gossip

问题：什么人总是教别人怎么做事？

答案：B. 坐在司机后面告诉司机如何开车的人

　　英语中对指手画脚的人称之为a backseat driver，即坐在司机后面告诉司机如何开车的人。Nobody likes a backseat driver!（没人喜欢这种指手画脚的人。）也可以称这样的人bossy、domineering或pushy（跋扈，固执己见。）bossy是指霸道，喜欢指挥别人的人：His old sister is quite bossy and we ran away from her.（他的老姐是相当专横，我们都离她远远的。）对爱说闲话的叫gossip。管不住嘴巴的人是has a big mouth。其他描述人说话的形容词还有talkative（健谈）：He is talkative when he has a few drinks under his belt.（他几杯酒下肚话就多了。）articulate（能言善道）：He is polished, charming, articulate and an excellent negotiator.（他文雅、迷人、能言善辩，是一名优秀的谈判专家。）fluent（流利）：She is a fluent speaker of Hebrew.（她说一口流利的希伯来语。）persuasive（有说服力的）：His arguments in favor of a new swimming pool are very persuasive.（他赞成建一座新游泳池的理由很有说服力。）eloquent（雄辩的）：I heard him make a very eloquent speech at that dinner.（在那次晚宴上，我听到他作了一场非常有说服力的演讲。）其他词语：stutter（结巴，口吃）、non stop talking（说个不停）、talk too much（说话太多）、make a speech（做演讲）、speech competition（演讲比赛）。

49. Okidoki means all the words below except:

A. Okay.

B. All correct.

C. O.K.

D. Not a problem.

问题：Okidoki 的意思包含以下所有选项，除了：

答案：D. 没问题。

英语 okidoki（okidoky, okdokey）一词是从"okey — dokey"派生而来。而且"okay"和"O.K."也都是从 okey — dokey 演变而来的。据说有一位早期的美国总统，他的拼写不太好。当他检查文件时，如果没有发现任何错误，他就在文件上签写 OLL Korrekt（All Correct）。后来他为了方便就缩写成 OK，后人就采用了这个习语。Let's go grab a bite to eat.（让我们去弄点东西吃。）其他相同含义的词还有：sure、alright、sure thing（肯定，好的，当然）Can you get me some ice cream please?（你能不能给我一些冰淇淋？）Sure, what flavor do you want?（当然，你想要什么味道的？）Can I please have a coffee?（我可以来杯咖啡吗？）Sure, would you like regular or decaf?（当然，你愿意一般的或无咖啡因的？）还有 That's fine.（可以/行。）No problem.（没问题。）等。Not a problem.（没问题。）的用法与 OK, okay, all correct 不一样。Don't think that procrastination is not a problem of time management.（不要以为拖拉不是时间管理问题。）

50. Find one sentence below that has an error in using verbs.

A. I would like to make/give some suggestions.

B. Families of the students make/give a contribute to the university.

C. The famous comedian is going to make/give a speech at Oscar next month.

D. Thanks so much for making/giving the arrangement for our visit.

问题：找出下列选项中动词用法不正确的句子。

答案：D. 非常感谢您为我们的访问做的安排。

英语动词 give 和 make 都可以与很多词搭配和互换。如：I would like to give/make some suggestions.（我想提出一些建议。）Families of the students give/make a contribution to the university.（学生的家庭都为大学捐款。）The famous comedian is going to make/give a speech at Oscar next month.（著名笑星将会在下个月的奥斯卡颁奖会上做演讲。）但是，做出安排是 make an arrangement，不是 give an arrangement。Thanks so much for making the arrangement for our visit.（非常感谢您为我们的访问做的安排。）其他不能互换的情况：make an apology（道歉）, make an attempt（进行尝试）, give a try（试试看）。give 的其他常用法有：give away（泄露）：Don't give away your password.（不可泄露你的密码。）not give a damn（毫不在乎）：He does not give a damn about what score on the test.（他根本不在乎考试的成绩。）Don't give up without a fight.（不轻易放弃。）give credit to（给予信任）：No one gave credit to Mary's story.（没有人相信玛丽的话。）give a hard time：The math problems gave the students a hard time.（数学题难倒了学生）。give a heads up（information）（传递消息）：I just want to give you a heads up!（我是来给大家报告最新的信息的/给你提个醒。）give someone a lift/ride（给人搭一程）：Don't you mind to give Shirley a ride to the party?（你不介意搭雪莉去聚会吗？）give a buzz（打电话）：Give me a buzz next time you come to town.（下次来镇上的时候给我来个电话。）give someone a piece of mind（生气）：Jean screwed up everything. His boss gave her a piece of his mind.（汤姆把一切都搞砸了，他的老板很生气。）

51. Which one of the following ligatures is not a word?

A. &

B. æ

C. Œ

D. tʃ

问题：下面哪个连字不是单词？

答案：D. tʃ

在写作和排版（typography）中，将两个或多个字形或字母作为单个字形（a single glyph）来书写和排版的字叫连字（ligature）。如在古英语中使用的连字符 Æ 和其小写 æ，是由字母 a 和 e 接合而成。随着拼写的演变，现代英语的字法中 Æ 不再被视为一个独立的词。例如"百科全书"一字从 encyclopædia 变成 encyclopaedia 或 encyclopedia 了。同样，Œ 和 œ 也是连字，由 o 和 e 连写而成。最常见的连字符号（ampersand）是 &。它是拉丁字 et（其意思是 and）手写将其演变成连字的。这个符号有几种写法，如 etc，&c（and other things（和其他的东西），或 and so forth 等）。由于应用广泛，人们不再将它视为连字，而是 et cetera 的简写（logogram）。答案 D 中的 tʃ 虽也是连字，但只是作为国际音标（International

Phonetic Alphabet）的一个符号。国际音标中大部分使用英语字母标音，而有些音是采用其他符号来表示的。如/ tʃ/、/ dʒ/、/ θ/、/ ð/、/ ʃ/、/ ʒ/、/ ŋ/。中国也有通过合并创造的字符而且历史悠久。然而，这些组合字并不被视为真正的汉字，而是被称为合文或合字。最流行的是用于中国农历新年的装饰品，由"招财进宝"（bring in wealth and fortune）四个字合成的字符，还有"孔孟好学"（to be as studious as Confucius and Mencius）。

52. ____, please welcome our keynote speaker of today's session. What is the missing part in the sentence?

A. That being said

B. Without further ado（adieu）

C. So to speak

D. Well

问题：找出下列选项中哪一项合适：____，请欢迎我们今天会议的主讲人发言。

答案：B. 闲话少说

　　在会议开始前，主持人往往要介绍一下主讲人。然后说，Without further ado（adieu），please welcome our keynote speaker of today's session.（闲话不说啦，请欢迎我们今天会议的主讲人发言。）Without further ceremony, let's get down to business.（不说客套话啦，谈正事吧。）表示要转到正题时，还常用：（The）fun time is over. It's time for home assignment.（玩够啦，该要做功课了。）答案A. That being said（虽然这样说）是个转折语相当于however。相似的短语有having said that/with that said等于连接词nevertheless、though、nonetheless（虽然）的意思。John is not a computer genius. But having said that he is highly skilled in IT and got a well-paid job.（约翰不是电脑天才。但他的IT技术很高明找到了一份好工作。）答案C. So to speak的意思是可以说、可谓。The five students have now all passed, so to speak, their TOFEL test.（可以说，这5个学生现在都已经通过了托福考试。）答案D. Well也是个转折语，但是含义很多，要根据上下文来理解。Well, so much for today.（好吧，今天就讲这么多了。）Well, I'll take your word for it this time.（唔，那我就信你一次吧。）还有一些类似的短语：make a long story short（in short, in a word）（长话短说，简言之）。

53. Which one of the following pairs is different from all the others?

A. Experience—experiment

B. Argument—augment

C. Vacation—vocation

D. Economic—economical

问题：下面哪一对词与其他的不一样？

答案：D. Economic—economical

　　英语的不少单词的拼写很相近，但意思完全不一样，很容易弄错，使用时要格外留意。答案中，experience（经验）—experiment（实验）就是如此。He knew the consequence by experience.（他从经验得知事情的后果。）He obtained the data by experiment.（他是从实验中获取了数据。）argument（争论）—augment（增强）也容易被弄混。Linda works two jobs to augment family income.（琳达打两份工来增加家庭的收入。）vacation（假期）—vocation（职业）。答案D. Economic—economical 这两个词与答案中的其他词不一样，它们是同源词，然而有时词意不一样。economic（经济）：The United States plans to tighten the economic sanctions to North Korea.（美国计划加大对朝鲜的经济制裁的力度。）而economical（节约的，经济的，划算的）：Electric cars are said to be clean, quiet and economical.（电动汽车据说清洁、无噪音而且经济。）

　　常容易弄错的单词还有：adopt（采纳/收养）—adapt（适应）：American families plan to adopt Chinese children.（很多美国家庭打算收养中国儿童。）New immigrants have tried to adapt to local customs.（新移民努力去适应当地的风俗习惯。）effect 和 affect 两词都有影响的含义，但是 effect 是个名词，而 affect 是个动词，用法不同。Oil price change may affect living standard of many people.（油价的波动可能会影响很多人的生活质量。）surly（不友好的）—surely（当然）、contend（争斗）—content（内容）、capital（资本）—capitol（国会大厦）。

54. Which one of the following is different from all the others?

A. Cow

B. Hen

C. Chairman

D. Heroine

问题：下面哪一个词与其他的不一样？

答案：C. 主席

　　英语名词的性（gender）不是很复杂，基本上只有部分人称和一些动物的名称有性的区分。答案中只有chairman（男主席）是阳性的词，其他都是阴性的：hen（母鸡）—cock/rooster（公鸡）、heroine（女主角）—hero（男主角）、cow（母牛）—bull/ox（公牛）。常见的有性别区分的名词有：tiger（老虎）—tigress（母老虎）、nephew（侄儿）—niece（侄女）、Sir（先生）—Madam（女士）、landlord（房东）—landlady（女房东）、god（神）—goddess（女神）、prince（王子）—princess（公主）、lion（狮子）—lioness（母狮子）、emperor（皇帝）—empress（女皇帝）、widow（寡妇）—widower（鳏夫）、host（主人）—hostess（女主人）、lad（少男）—lass（少女）、master（男主人）—mistress（女主人）等。男性/阳性称为masculine，女性/阴性称为feminine。在填写表格时，常要填性别，男性是Male 或以M表示，女性则为Female用F表示。英语里，第三人称单数有she和he的男女之分，但是在泛指时，很不方便，要说 she or he，如，When a new chair is elected, she or he may change the room setting. 现在不少美国人常用s/he来取代she/he。说不准，哪一天s/he真入字典啦。在美国，近年来发动了一场性革命，许多州都通过了同性结婚（gay marriage）法案，2016 年美国最高法院也通过了同性结婚法案。这样一来，性别很难区分了。与性有关的常见词语还有：gay（男同性恋）、lesbian（女同性恋）、homosexual（同性）、homosexuality（同性恋）、safe sex（安全性行为）、condon（安全套）、transgender（变性人）、sexual orientation（性取向）。

55. In which sentence, does the word "good" not mean something "good"?

A. Kobe Bryant left the NBA for good.

B. Good for you.

C. Have a good time.

D. Have a good one.

问题：下面哪个句子中的"good"意思不是"good"？

答案：A. 科比·布莱恩特永远离开了美国职业篮球联盟。

英语单词good好像是初学者都会的字。没学过英语的人也都会随口冒出来个good（好）当头的话：Good bye! Good morning! Good night! 其实good的用法很多，有的根本没有"好"的意思。答案A中的短语for good的含义是永远、永久，没有"好"的意思。下面的两组对话中，"I'm good."的意思完全不一样。Do you want more coffee? I'm good.（您还来点咖啡吗？够了不用了。）How are you? I'm good. Thanks.（你好吗？我很好，谢谢！）带good的常见的短语还有I passed the exam. Good for you.（我通过了考试。做得好！）对某人所做的或得到的东西表示鼓励或赞赏。The Chinese medicine is distasteful but good for you.（中药是良药苦口。）Have a good time.（玩得开心。）Good job.（干得不错！）Have a good（nice）one. 通常用来取代Good morning./Good afternoon./Good night./Good luck.（祝你走运。）Have a good day.（祝你今天愉快。）good at（擅长）：Emily is very good at using her charm to get her way.（艾米丽非常善于利用自己的魅力随心所欲。）good deal（好，行，很划算。）I'll plan on coming around at 3pm. Good deal.（我打算在下午3点来。好。）Good to go/ready to go.（一切就绪，准备好了。）So far so good.（到目前为止，一切顺利。）I need to workout to keep in a good shape.（我需要锻炼身体保持良好的状态。）Don't worry! Your children are in good hands.（别担心，您的孩子们很安全。）

56. What does it mean when you say, "get out of here!" during a conversation?

A. Get out of my room!

B. Unbelievable!

C. You are so bad!

D. You're annoying !

问题：当你在交谈中说"Get out of here!"时，
　　　是什么意思?

答案：B. 难以置信。

　　　在与美国人交谈中，你会听到get out of here! 这个短语，听起来好像是表示"滚出去！"的意思。可别误会，其实是unbelievable（难以置信）的意思，表示对谈到的事情感到特别惊讶和不相信。如果是在房间或办公室里发生争执时说 Get out of here! 或 Get out of the room/my office/my house! 才是表示滚出我的房间/滚出我的办公室/滚出我的家。短语 shut up 也有相同的含义，通常是"住嘴"的意思，有时也表示难以置信。The girl talked too much and I had to shut her up. （这孩子话太多了，我不得不封她的嘴。）Monica: Jessica is crushing on Bob. Jenny: Shut up. Bob is not her type. （莫妮卡：杰西卡迷上了鲍勃。珍妮：不可能，鲍勃不是她喜欢的类型。）其他表示相信不相信的语句有：I don't believe it. （我不相信。）You'd better believe it. （你最好相信它。）用来强调你刚说的。Bill: Man, you're the best player this team has ever had! Tom：You'd better believe it! （比尔：哥们，你是这个团队有史以来最好的球员！汤姆：毫无疑问！）Believe me, I was scared! （这是真的/相信我，我很害怕！）Believe it or not, I finally finished my project. （信不信由你，我终于完成了项目。）Seeing is believing. （眼见为实。）其他的表达：You are so bad! （你坏透了！）You're annoying! （你真烦人！）你还会常听到下面的一些句子：You're kidding me? （你开玩笑吧？）Is that true？（那是真的吗？）I'm serious. （我可没有跟你开玩笑。）

57. "Top notch" means all of the following except:

A. excellent

B. second to none

C. topless

D. first rate

问题："Top notch"这个词的意思除了____之外，
与其他的选项都一样。

答案：C. 袒胸

　　单词topless是袒胸（nude above the waist）的意思。例句：Topless beaches are common in Europe.（赤裸上身的海滩在欧洲很常见。）top notch（顶尖）与其他几个词的意义相同：second to none/No.1/Top One、excellent（优秀）、first rate（第一流）。Li Na plays top notch tennis.（李娜展示顶尖的网球球技。）Tiger Woods is a first rate golfer.（Tiger Woods是一流的高尔夫球手。）His problem solving skill is second to none.（他解决问题的能力是首屈一指的。）Ashley is at the top of her class.（Ashley 在班上排第一名。）最后一名的表达是：at the bottom of（垫底）、the last place。与top搭配的短语很多，如an athlete in top condition（在最佳状态的运动员）。He came to the party dressed top to toe（head to toe）in black.（他来到聚会上，从头到脚都穿着黑色衣服。）Republican Presidential candidate Donald Trump was the top story in this year presidential election.（共和党总统候选人唐纳德·特朗普是今年总统选举中最热门的话题。）Those Nike sports shoes were all top of the line.（这些耐克运动鞋都是顶级的产品。）It was the best solution I could think of off the top of my head.（这是我一时所能想到的最好的解决办法。）topping是指在食品上抹的一层酱油（sauce）、结霜（frosting）、奶油（cream）或其他的装饰物。

58. "He is quite a character." means:

A. He is an actor.

B. He is a character in a Shakespeare's play.

C. He is of distinguishing quality.

D. He is full of humor.

问题："他是个与众不同的人。"这句话的意思是：

答案：C. 他这个人很有特色。

单词character是指人的性格（temperament）、品德（moral）、气质（qualities）等。He is quite a character.（他相当有个性/气质），意思和He is of distinguishing quality. 相同。He is a regular guy（normal, average）.（他是个平庸人。）He is a character in a Shakespeare's play.（他是莎士比亚剧中的一个人物。）He is out of character.（他有些反常。）This guy is quite a smooth character.（这人很世故。）He is full of humor.（他颇具幽默感。）Mozart's music is characterized by its naivety, clarity and cheerfulness.（莫扎特的音乐特色是纯朴、清澈和欢快。）另外character 还有一个词义是书写或印刷的字或符号。中国的汉字叫Chinese characters，简体为simplified Chinese characters，繁体为traditional Chinese characters。其他答案：He is an actor.（他是一个演员。）与演员有关的词语：actress（女演员）、hero（男主角）、heroine（女主角）、director（导演）、crew（剧组）、photographer（摄影师）、makeup artists（化妆师）、fashion designers（服装设计师）、props（道具）、screenwriter（编剧）、audiovisual（音像）、stuntman（替身演员）、special effects/stunt（特技）、producer（制片人）。

59. Which one of the following is different from all the others?

A. Per diem

B. Per annum

C. Per Se

D. Per capita

问题：下面哪一个词与其他的不一样？

答案：C. 本身

　　答案C. Per Se（本身）中的per这个词通常用来表示每一个（every）的意思，如Per Diem——a daily allowance, a daily fee（按日津贴/每日的费用）。He got $36 per diem for meals on his business trip to Europe.（他在欧洲出差时享受了每天36美元的膳食补贴。）Per capita（人均）：The government of Switzerland spends more per capita on healthcare than any other country in the world.（瑞士政府提供的人均医疗卫生费用比世界上任何其他国家的都多。）What country has the highest GDP（gross domestic product）per capita income in all of Europe?（哪个欧洲国家的人均生产总值最高？）Per annum 即annually/per year（每年的）：The golf club membership is $2000 per annum（per year）.（高尔夫俱乐部的会员费是每年2000美元。）The flowers are divided into annual and perennial（per annual）.（花卉分为年生植物和多年生植物。）其他常用的还有：per day（每天）、per month（每月）、per hour（每小时）、per person（每个人）等。Per还可以表示according to/ in accordance with（按照，根据）：Per your request over the conversation, I am sending you his resume for your consideration. (按你来电的要求，我把他的简历寄来供你考虑。) 答案C. Per Se 是一个拉丁语短语，表示"本身""内在"的意思。通常用来表示对之前提到的情况或所使用的术语持负面意见，认为理解不精确，而随后举出解释或理由。例如，Guns are not harmful per se, but they are dangerous to the public when they are in the hands of evils. (枪本身并不是有害的，但是当他们处于邪恶的手中时，对公众的生命安全构成危险。)

60. Which type of storm is caused by weather?

A. Perfect storm

B. Brainstorm

C. Firestorm

D. Thunderstorm

问题：下面哪一个是由天气引起的风暴？

答案：D. 雷雨

　　风暴的英文是storm，它有很多组合词都是与风暴有关。如thunderstorm（雷雨）、snow storm（暴风雪）等。答案A：perfect storm（灾难或严重困难,惊涛骇浪），可以说与天气有关，但不是任何灾难或困境都与天气相关。词中的perfect（完美的）在这里真实表示"严重的/超级"的意思。Now a perfect storm has hit American's manufacturers. (如今一场特大风暴开始影响美国的制造者们。) firestorm是指风暴性的大火，或是争议：The Trump's speech on gun control has resulted in a firestorm of controversy. (特朗普有关枪支控制的讲话已引发了激烈的争议。) brainstorm一词也与天气无关，而是头脑风暴的意思，常用的意思是出谋献策或想办法。The two dropouts meet twice a week to brainstorm and set up their own business. (那两个大学退学生每周聚会两次，在一起出谋献策，来建立自己的公司。) brainstorm 也可以表示头脑发热。Sarah had a brainstorm in the final exam and didn't answer a single question. (Sarah 在期末考试时脑子里突然一片混乱，一个题都没有答上来。) 与storm常用的短语有：take something by storm（使……大为轰动）：The iPhone and iWatch took the world by storm. (苹果手机和手表刮起了席卷全球的风暴。) The performance by Andrea Bocelli, blind Italian tenor took the audience by storm. (意大利盲人男高音歌手Andrea Bocelli的表演使观众为之倾倒。) storm in a teacup（小题大做）：Both patties are trying to present the disagreement on minimum wage as a storm in a teacup. (两党都想拿在最低工资上的小分歧大做文章。)

Entertainment

文艺娱乐篇

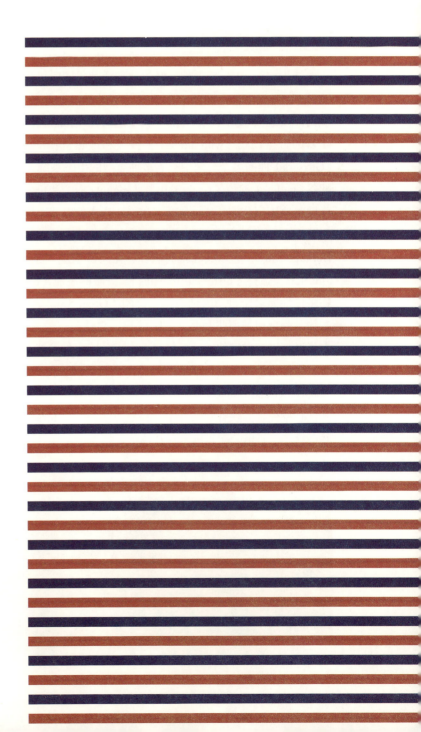

1. Which of the following places is not good for hiking?

A. Yellow Stone National Park

B. Yosemite National Park

C. Grand Canyon

D. Great Smoky Mountains National Park

问题：哪个地方不适合徒步旅行？

答案：C.Grand Canyon

徒步旅行（hiking）是很好的健身活动，同时可以观赏大自然的风光。黄石国家公园（Yellow Stone National Park）是徒步旅行的最好地方之一。它位于美国怀俄明州（Wyoming）境内涉及蒙大拿州（Montana）和爱达荷州（Idaho），是世界上第一个国家公园。公园以丰富的野生动物（wild animals）种类和地热资源（geothermal resources）尤其是间歇泉（Geysers）而闻名。公园中有着多种类型的生态系统（natural ecosystems），其中有黄石湖、峡谷（valley）、河流（rivers）、山脉（mountains）和仍处于活跃状态的黄石火山（volcano）。优胜美地国家公园（Yosemite National Park）以一个印第安部落的名字命名，范围横跨加州（California）中西部，面积为 3080.74 平方公里。1984 年被指定为世界遗产（World Heritage Site），它以其壮观的峡谷、花岗岩悬崖（granite cliffs）、瀑布（waterfall）、冰川（glaciers）遗迹（historical remains）、清澈的溪流（brooks）、巨杉（sequoia）和丰富的生物多样性闻名于世。大烟山国家公园（Great Smoky Mountains National Park），位于美国东部，跨越田纳西州和北卡罗来纳州。它是美东最后一片广大的原始森林，占地 2100 平方公里，以其丰富的物种而闻名。由于公园内的海拔高度变化剧烈，加之降雨量充沛，因而生物极富多样性。由于 441 号公路横贯公园，使得其成为游览人最多的美国国家公园。大峡谷（Grand Canyon）于 1919 年被命名为国家公园。公园坐落在亚利桑那州（Arizona），其核心特征是大峡谷和峡谷中的科罗拉多河（Colorado River），常常被认为是世界七大天然奇景之一，但公园里树木及其他植被稀少、干燥、气温过高，不适合徒步旅行。

2. Which city is the cradle of Rock 'n' Roll in the U.S.?

A. New Orleans, Louisiana

B. Chicago, Illinois

C. Memphis, Tennessee

D. Nashville, Tennessee

问题：美国的哪个城市是摇滚乐的发源地？

答案：C.田纳西州的孟菲斯市

美国是对音乐很狂热的国家，许多城市都以音乐而闻名。路易斯安那州的新奥尔良（New Orleans, Louisiana）可以誉为美国音乐城之首，作为爵士乐的发源地（Birthplace of Jazz），音乐风格至高无上。每年从四月底五月初在那儿举办爵士音乐节（Jazz Fest），是世界最大的爵士音乐节之一，设有各种各样的音乐表演，包括福音（gospel）、蓝调（blues）、摇滚（rock）和路易斯安那州的土著音乐（indigenous music），如Zydeco（柴迪科）。芝加哥市（Chicago）有各种音乐表演的场地，它的特色是蓝调。芝加哥六月的蓝调音乐节（Chicago Blues Festival）值得一去。田纳西州（Tennessee）的孟菲斯市（Memphis）也是以蓝调闻名。比尔大街（Beale Street）是最有名的音乐街道，在那里你会找到最好的现场音乐表演。猫王Elvis Presley于1954年在孟菲斯的Sun Studio录制了他的第一首歌"That's Alright, Mama"，从此孟菲斯成为摇滚乐（Rock 'n' Roll）的发源地。猫王后来成为了世界上第一个真正的摇滚乐明星，他的故居在孟菲斯有9个不同的地址。最有名的是雅园（Graceland），是参观人数最多的景点。田纳西州的纳什维尔市（Nashville）的绰号是"美国音乐之城"，它是美国乡村音乐（country music）和西部音乐（western music）的中心。至今纳什维尔的人们仍然哼唱乡村音乐的乐曲，在其音乐博物馆里游客可以参加现场录音的音乐会、词曲作者的俱乐部和音乐的星光大道，这些都有助于纳什维尔保留它"美国音乐之城"的绰号。

3. Which one of the following is not a TV station in the U.S.?

A. BBC

B. ABC

C. CBS

D. PBS

问题：哪家电视台不是美国的？

答案：A. BBC

　　BBC是British Broadcasting Corporation（英国广播公司）的缩写。BBC的总部设在伦敦（London），是世界上最大的广播公司。ABC — American Broadcasting Company（美国广播公司）是美国三大商业电视网之一，创建于1943年，是世界上收入最多的广播公司，公司总部在纽约市的曼哈顿。NBC — National Broadcasting Company（美国国家广播公司），总部设在纽约市的洛克菲勒中心（Rockefeller Center）的GE大厦，它成立于1926年，是美国历史最悠久的广播网络中心。CBS是哥伦比亚广播系统（Columbia Broadcasting Systems）的英文缩写，它拥有世界上第二大的商业广播电视网络。PBS — The Public Broadcasting Service（公共广播服务）是一个非营利性（non-profit）的公共广播电视网络，它有354个成员电视台，持有集体所有制，其总部设在弗吉尼亚州阿灵顿（Arlington, Virginia）。《芝麻街》（Sesame Street）是PBS最著名的儿童电视节目。现在网络电视（cable TV）与卫星电视（satellite TV）争夺客户日趋白热化。电视节目也越来越数字化（digitalized），费用也年年涨，网络电视的月费加上网费在100美元以上。如不想租网络电视，可以买一个60~100美元左右的室外天线（outdoor antenna）就可以免费收到NBC、PBS和几十个电视台的节目。由于互联网和iPhone及其他智能手机的娱乐功能的进一步扩展，电视网络面临着极大的挑战。

4. Which is a famous sightseeing location in the West Coast of the U.S.?

A. Time Square

B. Golden Gate Bridge

C. Liberty Bell

D. Statue of Liberty

问题：哪一个是在美国西海岸的著名旅游景点？
答案：B. 金门桥

金门桥（Golden Gate Bridge）是加州旧金山（San Francisco）的一个主要旅游景点，在美国的西海岸。旧金山是清末华人到美国淘金（Gold rush）时取的名。旧金山的伦巴底街（Lombard Street）、渔人码头（Fishermen's Wharf）也很有名。在 Pier 39 码头附近，有购物中心、Ghirardelli Square广场、里普利的信不信博物馆（Ripley's Believe It or Not! Museum）、蜡像博物馆（Wax Museum）、海湾水族馆（Aquarium）、旧金山海洋国家历史公园博物馆（San Francisco Maritime National Historical Park）等。渔人码头到处都是活海鲜餐馆，最有名的是珍宝蟹（Dungeness crab）。Times Square（时代广场）是美国的一个重要象征地，位于纽约市曼哈顿中城。时代广场常被誉为世界十字路口（The Crossroads of the World）和宇宙的中心（The Center of the Universe），是世界上最繁忙的行人十字路口之一和全球娱乐产业的主要中心。时代广场原名为朗埃克广场（Longacre Square）。1904 年 4 月《纽约时报》（*New York Times*）将总部迁至新落成的时代大厦时，广场便改名为时代广场。每年元旦前夕（New Year's Eve），成千上万的人聚集在广场，观看一年一度的倒计时（countdown）降球活动（Ball Drop），迎接新年。自由女神（Statue of Liberty）是法国送给美国的，树立在纽约市附近的一个小岛上。自由钟（Liberty Bell）是美国独立的象征，位于宾夕法尼亚州（Pennsylvania）的费城（Philadelphia）市中心。

5. Which of the following famous streets is not in NYC?

A. The Fifth Ave

B. Pennsylvania Ave

C. Wall Street

D. Broadway

问题：下列哪条有名的街道不在纽约市？

答案：B.宾夕法尼亚大道

宾夕法尼亚大道（Pennsylvania Ave）是美国首都华盛顿（Washington D.C.）的一条大道，它从总统府白宫（White House）前穿过，其他三条大街都是在纽约市的曼哈顿岛上。第五大道（The Fifth Ave）是最有名的商业街，Macy 等著名商店都在这条街上。华尔街（Wall Street）是著名的金融街，是纽约证券交易所（New York Stock Exchange）的所在地。原世贸大厦双子楼（World Trade Center）就在金融街的附近，新的世贸大楼（One World Trade Center）已在旧楼的地址上矗立起来，成为纽约及美国最高的建筑物，高达 1776 英尺（541米）与美国的建国之年 1776 相吻合。楼边建有 911 纪念馆（The National September 11 Memorial & Museum）。Broadway St. 以沿着百老汇和林肯中心（Lincoln Center）的百老汇剧院（Broadway Theaters）而出名，拥有 40 个 500 座位以上的专业剧院。百老汇剧院与伦敦西区剧院（West End Theatre）一道被广泛誉为是在讲英语的国家中最高水平的商业剧院。它也是纽约市著名的旅游景点。据报道，2012 年百老汇的门票售出约十亿美元，观看的人数约有 1213 万。

6. "Face the music" means:

A. go to a concert

B. set to music

C. accept the unpleasant results

D. join the musical festival

问题："Face the music" 这个短语的意思是什么？

答案：C. 接受惩罚或自己错误行为所产生的后果

短语 face the music 的意思是接受惩罚或自己错误行为所产生的后果。You've broken the regulation now you must face the music.（现在你已经违反了规定，你必须承担后果。）与音乐有关的词语有：go to a concert（听音乐会）、set to music（谱曲）、join the music festival tour（参加音乐节、巡回演出）、records（唱片）、folk music（民间音乐）、pop music（流行音乐）、country music（乡村音乐）、classic music（古典音乐）、contemporary music（现代音乐）、opera（歌剧）、musical（音乐剧）、solo-concert（独唱演唱会）、composer（作曲家）、music notation（音符）、conductor（指挥）、singer（歌手/歌唱家）、tenor（男高音）、baritone（男中音）、bass（男低音）、soprano（女高音）、mezzo-soprano（女中音）、male and female vocal duet（男女声二重唱）、a cappella（无伴唱/清唱）、chorus/choirs（合唱）。美国最高的音乐奖是Grammy Awards（格莱美奖），最初称为Gramophone Awards（留声机奖），是来表彰美国国家录音艺术与科学学院表彰音乐事业中的杰出成就，第一届在 1959 年举行。美国有不少音乐节目：如，*American Idol*（《美国偶像》）、*The Voice*（《声音》，a vocal talent competition TV show）。美国最好的五所音乐学院是：Indiana University Jacobs School of Music（印第安纳大学雅各布音乐学院），在Bloomington, IN，有 1600 学生；费城的Curtis Institute of Music（柯蒂斯音乐学院），在 Philadelphia, PA，该校免学费（free of charge）；Juilliard School（茱莉亚音乐学院），在 New York, NY；University of Michigan School of Music, Theatre, and Dance（密歇根大学音乐，戏剧和舞蹈学院），在 Ann Arbor, MI；Yale School of Music（耶鲁大学音乐学院），在 New Haven, CT，该校免学费。

7. Which music instrument is different from all the others?

A. Piano

B. Pipa

C. Guitar

D. Flute

问题：哪种乐器和其他几个不同？
答案：B. 琵琶

西方的乐器（music instrument）分弦乐器（string instrument）和管乐器（wind instruments），其中弦乐器有：violin（小提琴）、viola（中提琴）、cello（大提琴）、(double) bass（低音提琴）、harp（竖琴）、guitar（吉他）、banjo（班卓琴）等。管乐有：flute（长笛）、oboe（双簧管）、clarinet（单簧管）、saxophone（萨克斯管）、trumpet（小号）、horn（圆号）、trombone（长号）等。其他的乐器还有：piano（钢琴）、drums（大鼓）、harmonica（口琴）、organ（风琴）、accordion（手风琴）等。与乐团乐队相关的词汇有：orchestra（管弦乐团）、symphony（交响乐团）、band（乐队）、conductor（指挥）、music（乐曲）、movement（乐

章）、notes（乐谱）、music notation（音符）、tuning fork（音叉）、quartet（四重奏）、piano concerto（钢琴协奏曲）、violin solo（小提琴独奏）等。绝大多数的中国的乐器或民族乐器（traditional music instrument）的英文都是音译，如，二胡（erhu）柳琴（liuqin）、芦笙（lusheng）、琵琶（pipa）等。扬琴（yangqin），原名洋琴，来源于Persia，也就是现今的伊朗（Iran）。

8. Which one of the following is not a favorite place for old people to go?

A. Six Flags

B. Disney World

C. Sea World

D. Universal Studio

问题：下列中哪一个地方不是老年人喜爱去的？

答案：A. 六旗游乐园

答案中Six Flags（六旗游乐园）、Disney World（迪斯尼乐园）、Sea World（海洋世界）、Universal Studio（环球影城）都是美国人，尤其是儿童与青少年最喜爱的游乐园（Amusement Park）。但对上了年纪的人来说Six Flags就不是他们想去的地方。因为乐园中主要的游玩项目是各种过山车（roller coasters），还有不少旋转和上下波动的活动车都不适合老人和体弱的人乘坐。在Disney World中，有好几个theme parks（主题公园）：Magic Kingdom（神奇王国）、Epcot（未来世界）、Animal Kingdom（动物王国）等。美国的十大游乐园是俄亥俄州桑达斯基（Sandusky, OH）的Cedar Point（雪松点公园）、宾夕法尼亚州伊利斯堡（Elysburg, PA）的Knoebels公园、佛罗里达州迪斯尼世界中的神奇王国（Walt Disney World's Magic Kingdom）、德克萨斯州（Texas）的Schlitterbahn Water Park（水上公园）、佛罗里达州奥兰多（Orlando, FL）的Universal's Islands of Adventure（环球冒险岛）、加州的Six Flags Magic Mountain（六旗魔术山）、俄亥俄州梅森的Kings Island（国王岛）、威斯康星州（Dells, Wisconsin）的Dells Water Parks（戴尔水上公园）、宾夕法尼亚州的Her shey Park（赫尔希公园）和加州的Knott's Berry Farm（诺氏果园）。

9. You can have the following except _____ when you watch a movie in a movie theater.

A. popcorn

B. soda

C. candies

D. beer

问题：当你在电影院中看电影的时候，除了 _____ 之外，你可以吃以下的食品。
答案：D.啤酒

　　美国是电影（movies，英国用films）的王国。美国大部分的电影院（movie theater）设在大商场内或附近。看电影（go to the movies）往往是儿童青少年聚会的活动之一。影院里出售一些小吃或饮料（beverage），如popcorn（爆米花）、French fries（炸薯条）、pretzels（椒盐脆饼）、candy（糖果）等小吃及soda（苏打）或其他饮料。但是一般不卖hamburgers（汉堡包）等主食，啤酒等酒类是绝对不容许的。观众也不能带任何食品到电影院吃，不然会给赶出剧院的。主要原因是电影院就是靠卖食品赚钱。评价电影的英语表达包括：This movie is so boring, dull and terrible.（这部电影很无聊，差极了。）Titanic's a great movie.（泰坦尼克号是一部非常棒的电影。）The movie is breath taking, very moving.（这部电影惊险，催人泪下，很感人。）I enjoyed it every minute.（我享受了每分钟。/ 太好看了。）I was carried away by the beautiful scenery, by the actor's fantastic performance and acting in the movie.（我被影片中的美丽风光、男主角梦幻般的表现和演技迷住了。）与电影有关的词语如下：director（导演）、producer（制片人）、actors（男演员）、actress（女演员）、feature（故事片）、comedy（喜剧）、tragedy（悲剧）、drama（戏剧）、fantasy（奇幻片）、science fiction（科幻片）、horror（恐怖片）、cartoon（动画片）、documentary（纪录片）、musical（音乐片）、widescreen（宽屏）、tickets（门票）、ticket office（售票处）、make up（化妆）、matinee（日场）、costume（服装）、shoot a movie（拍摄电影）、movie industry（电影业）、Hollywood（好莱坞）、red carpet parade（红地毯游行）、Oscar Award（奥斯卡奖）、Emmy Award（艾美奖）、movie festival（电影节）、movie academy（电影学院）、movie star（影视明星）、popular movie star（当红影星）、movie fans（影迷）等。

10. **Which pair is wrong?**

A. Tennis—U.S. Open

B. American Football—World Cup

C. Golf—Masters

D. Baseball—World Series

问题：哪一组是错的？

答案：B. 美式足球——世界杯

　　在美国，football 是指 American football（美式足球），而中国人常说的足球叫 soccer。美式足球的决赛称作 Super Bowl（超级碗），而世界杯则是 soccer 最重要的比赛。网球的四大赛为 U.S. Open（美国公开赛）、Australian Open（澳洲公开赛）、Wimbledon（温网）、French Open（法国公开赛）。获得四个大赛的冠军叫赢得了 Grand Slum（大满贯）。高尔夫也有四大赛事：The Masters（大师赛）、U.S. Open Championship（美国公开赛）、PGA—Professional Golfers' Association Championship（PGA 锦标赛）、The Open Championship（公开锦标赛），赢得所有这四项大赛也称为大满贯。北美职业棒球大联盟（Major League Baseball—MLB）的决赛叫 World Series（世界大赛），是在美国联盟（American League—AL）和国家联盟（National League—NL）冠军队之间的年度总冠军系列赛。美国全国冰球联盟（National Hockey League—NHL）的决赛叫 the Stanley Cup Finals（斯坦利杯决赛）。每个赛季分为 regular season（常规赛）和 playoffs（季后赛）。NBA—National Basketball Association 的决赛是在东西两个赛区的冠军之间进行，以 7 胜 4 决出总冠军。美国人酷爱打篮球，几乎每家每户的车库边都立有篮球架（basketball stands），孩子们从小就与篮球结缘。适应于各种年龄层次的俱乐部遍及全国。

11. Which fitness exercise is not popular for men in the U.S.?

A. Breakdancing

B. Jogging

C. Sports

D. Yoga

问题：美国的哪一种健身活动男的不常参加？
答案：D. 瑜伽

　　美国人喜爱健身运动（fitness activities）。业余时间都参加各种健身活动，或有氧健身活动（aerobic exercise）来锻炼身体（work out）或减肥（lose weight）。常见的有fitness dance（健身舞蹈）、jogging（慢跑）、ball games（球类）、biking（骑自行车）、swimming（游泳）、yoga（瑜伽）等。瑜伽基本上是女性的活动。由于大多数上班族早上要赶着去上班，许多人都是四点半下班后或晚饭后或周末去活动。人们常在夜晚跑步，几乎没有人在早晨跑步或锻炼。美国的健身房（fitness gym）到处都有，提供各种健身器材：treadmills（走步机）、exercise bike（健身车）、weight bench（举重床）、dumbbells（哑铃）、fitness ball（健身球）等。大众可以付款成为会员（membership），自由前往活动或参加健身房开设的各类课程。除了健身活动之外，现在很流行一种舞叫作breakdancing（地板舞或霹雳舞），也叫B-boying或breaking（街舞），霹雳舞起源于非裔美国人和波多黎各（Puerto Rican）青年街舞（street dance）的风格（style）。舞蹈者称为B男孩（b-boy），B女孩（b-girl）。"霹雳舞"经常用于指流行文化(popular culture)和主流娱乐业(the mainstream entertainment industry)中的舞蹈。还有一种叫Hip Pop（嘻哈）的舞蹈，就是按rap（说唱）的节奏起舞。其他舞蹈有：ballet（芭蕾舞）、tap（踢踏舞）、jazz（爵士舞）、ballroom dance（舞厅舞）、Latin dance（拉丁舞）、modern（现代舞）、flamenco（弗拉门戈舞）等。

12. Which beach is not good for swimming in the U.S.?

A. Myrtle Beach

B. Daytona Beach

C. Half Moon Bay Beach

D. Malibu Beach

问题：美国的哪个沙滩不适合游泳？

答案：C. 半月湾海滩

　　在美国，东、西两个漫长的海岸线上有许多美丽的海滩。美国人喜爱阳光浴，对海滩情有独钟，一有机会就到海滩上沐浴阳光。在大西洋（Atlantic Ocean）海岸有南卡罗来纳州（South Carolina）的 Myrtle Beach（参见 http://www.visitmyrtlebeach.com）和佛罗里达州（Florida）的 Daytona Beach（参见 http://www.daytonabeach.com）。在太平洋（Pacific Ocean）海岸有加州洛杉矶附近的 21 里长的 Malibu Beaches（参见 https://www.malibucity.org/Index.aspx?NID=96）。这些都是很有名的海滩，其沙质优异，海岸线长，适宜各种沙滩活动，而且地处亚热带，夏季温度高，适合游泳等水中活动。这些海滩边都建有度假村（resorts），是学生度春假和暑假的首选之一，也是家庭度假的好去处。而位于南旧金山的半月湾海滩（Half Moon Bay Beach），虽然也很美，但终年水温太低不适合游泳等水中活动。在新泽西和纽约都有很多不错的海滩，但是一年中能游泳和水中活动的日子不多。很多居住在离海边较远的美国人在自家后院建有室内游泳池（indoor swimming pool）和室外游泳池（in ground/on ground swimming pool）。户内外的热水浴缸（hot tub）和按摩浴缸（jacuzzi）也不少。近几十年来，冲浪运动（surfing）愈来愈流行。美国最好的冲浪海滩是位于加州被称为冲浪城（Surf City）的圣克鲁斯（Santa Cruz）。它有适合从初学者（beginner）到职业（professional）各个层次冲浪爱好者的海滩。

13. Which of the following TV programs is not appropriate for children?

A. *Sesame Street*

B. *The Simpsons*

C. *Game of Thrones*

D. *SpongeBob SquarePants*

问题：以下哪一个电视节目不适合儿童观看？

答案：C.《权力的游戏》

美国是电影王国（Kingdom of Movies），每年出版的电影不计其数。2015 年出版的电影就多达 449 部，还不包括文献片（documentary）。（参见 http://www.movieinsider.com/。）据维基百科统计，2015 年美国新上演的电视秀或连续剧有 358 种。*Sesame Street*（《芝麻街》）是儿童们最爱看的 TV 连续剧之一，剧中的角色都是使用木偶（puppets）动物来表演的。从 1969 年 11 月 10 日在 PBS（Public Broadcasting Television Stations）问世以来，至 2016 年已连续了 46 季（seasons）并在 120 多个国家播放。*The Simpsons*（《辛普森一家》）是福克斯广播公司（Fox Broadcasting Company）制作的美国动画情景喜剧（American animated sitcom），很受儿童的欢迎。从 1986 年 10 月 9 日上演以来，至今仍在继续播放。其他受欢迎的还有 *SpongeBob Square Pants*（《海绵宝宝》）、*Disney Little Einstein*（《迪斯尼小爱因斯坦》）、*Power Rangers*（《超级巡警》）、*My Little Pony*（《彩虹小马》）、*Friendship Is Magic*（《友谊是魔术》）等。*Game of Thrones*（《权力的游戏》）是部评价很高的连续剧，但不适合儿童观看。

14. Which of the following is not a Broadway show?

A. *The Lion King*

B. *Les Miserables*

C. *Mamma Mia!*

D. *American Idol*

问题：以下哪一个不是美国百老汇的流行剧目？

答案：D.《美国偶像》

美国纽约曼哈顿（Manhattan）是文体活动的中心地带。每天都有各种 shows（表演）、concerts（音乐会）和 sports games（体育比赛）。42 街周围的百老汇剧院，每天都有成百上千的各类 opera（歌剧）、Musical（音乐剧）、drama（话剧）、comedy（喜剧）等的演出。到了纽约不看一场戏剧会后悔一辈子。剧目前二十位中，有家喻户晓的，孩子们喜爱的 *The Lion King*（《狮子王》）、*Aladdin*（《阿拉丁》）、*Les Miserables*（《悲惨世界》）、大人爱看的 *Mamma Mia!*（《妈妈咪呀！》）、*The Phantom of the Opera*（《歌剧魅影》）。还有 *The Book of Mormon*（《摩门之书》）、*Wicked*（《妖兽》）、*Chicago*（《芝加哥》）、*Jersey Boys*（《泽西男孩》）等。*Matilda*（《明德》），*Kinky Boots*（《淫靴》）、*If/Then*（《如果/然后》）、*Beautiful*（《美丽》）、*The Carol King Musical*（《卡罗尔国王的音乐》）、*An American in Paris*（《一个美国人在巴黎》）、*Finding Neverland*（《寻找梦幻岛》）、*Doctor Zhivago*（《日瓦戈医生》）、*On the Town*（《在镇里》）、*Honeymoon in Vegas*（《拉斯维加斯蜜月》）等。票价根据

时间、座位而定,在 30 美元到 200 美元之间。周末,即星期五到星期天的票价比平日高很多。所以最好是在平日去看。有的剧目有日场,另外有减价(discount)的团体票。(参见 http://www.broadway.com/。) *American Idol*(《美国偶像》)不是百老汇剧院的剧目而是电视系列(series)节目。这个电视系列展示了想当歌星的人为唱片交易而竞争。评判小组中包括最妙趣横生而又以毒舌著称的西蒙·考威尔(Simon Cowell),由他们审查表演者是否有天赋,然后由在家的观众为自己喜爱的潜力新星(favorite potential stars)投票。该节目对艺术家(artists)凯莉·克拉克森(Kelly Clarkson)、凯莉·安德伍德(Carrie Underwood)、詹妮弗·哈德森(Jennifer Hudson)和亚当·兰伯特(Adam Lambert)的职业生涯帮助很大。

15. Who is not a host of a famous TV Night show?

A. David Letterman

B. Jimmy Fallon

C. Larry King

D. Jay Leno

问题:以下哪一个不是美国晚间电视脱口秀的主持人?

答案:C. Larry King

　　美国的电视脱口秀(TV Talk Show)多达 383 个。其中全国几家最大的电视公司播出的喜剧类(comedy)包括近年来 NBC 在洛杉矶播出,由 Jay Leno 主持的 *The Tonight Show*(*The Tonight Show with Jay Leno*),该节目始于 1954。Jimmy Fallon 从 2014 年 9 月开始在纽约市洛克菲勒中心(Rockefeller Center)6B 演播室(Studio),取代 Jay Leno 主持 *The Tonight Show with Jay Leno*。Jimmy Fallon 之前主持了另一个 NBC 脱口秀,叫 *Late-Night Talk Show*,现在的主持人是 Seth Meyers。NBC 还设有 *Saturday Night Live*(*SNL*)的节目,它从 1975 年就开始在洛克菲勒中心播出,是一种综合性的表演。主持人经常变换,很多名人都担任过主持,在美国是播出时间最长的网络电视节目之一。David Letterman 是 CBS 的主持人,从 1993 年 8 月 31 日开始主持,是电视脱口秀主持年限最长的,他主持的 *The Late Show with David Letterman* 在 2002 年电视指南(TV Guide)评出的历来 50 个最佳电视节目中排第 7 位。节目在下午录制,晚上 11：35 播放。地址是纽约百老汇 1697 号。*Larry King Live* 是 Larry King 主持的直播节目,从 1985 年至 2010 年播放,是 CNN 收视率最高(most watched)、播出时间最长的节目,每晚拥有超过百万的观众。Larry King 在 CNN 的洛杉矶工作室以电台采访(radio interview)的方式,每个晚上采访一个或多个名人,包括政客或商人。并通过全国的网络播出,有超强的影响力。

16. Which is not a popular TV game show in the U.S.?

A. *Jeopardy*
B. *Wheel of Fortune*
C. *Family Dues*
D. *Modern Family*

问题：以下哪一个不是美国电视游戏节目？
答案：D.《摩登家庭》

　　答案A. *Jeopardy*（《危险边缘》）是电视主持人、演员、歌手梅尔夫·格里芬（Merv Griffin）创造的美国电视游戏节目。每次都有三个参赛者，以抢答方式回答包罗万象的知识问题。主持人判定答案正确与否，给答题人加分或减分。NBC在1964年3月30日第一次播出，1984年9月10日开始播全新版本的 *Jeopardy*。可以说它是目前所有节目中最成功的。它播出超过6000集，赢得了创纪录的31次艾美奖，并且是唯一获得皮博迪奖的游戏节目。它现在的主持人是亚历克斯（Alex Trebek）。*Wheel of Fortune*（《命运之轮》）也是梅尔夫·格里芬创办的，1975年1月6日在NBC首播，播出了34季，超过6000集。电视指南（TV Guide）称之为收视率最高（top rated）的游戏节目。它每次有三个参赛者，他们轮流旋转一个巨大的嘉年华轮，然后猜出字母解开填字游戏谜。根据嘉年华轮上的标记赢取现金和奖品（cash and prizes）。游戏结束时，获得最多金额的参赛者还有机会猜词语获得大奖。现在的主持人是Pat Sajak和Vanna White。*Family Feud*（《家族问答》）是Mark Goodson创造的电视游戏节目，由ABC于1985年6月14日开始播出。节目由两个家庭各派五名成员参加，就民意调查（survey questions）的问题，说出最流行的答案（popular answers）来赢取现金和奖品。Rubin Ervin是现在的主持人。*Modern Family*（《摩登家庭》）是ABC从2009年9月开始播出的美国电视系列，不是电视游戏节目。它是一种仿纪录片（mockumentary）的电视剧，以戏剧或喜剧的纪实形式来打造虚构的事件。

17. Which is the Academy Award?

A. Emmy Awards

B. The Oscars

C. Grammy Awards

D. Tony Awards

问题：以下哪一个是美国的学院奖?

答案：B. 奥斯卡奖

　　答案都是美国最著名的文艺奖项。美国这个电影王国，每年都对电影（cinema）的成就颁布各种奖项（awards）。奖项被分为三大类：批评家的奖（critics' awards）由一群批评家来投票；电影节（festival awards），奖项颁发给在一个特定的电影节所示的最佳影片；行业奖项（industry awards），由电影业的一些分支机构工作的专业人士评选，在全国的网络播出，有深远的影响力。从 1929 年开始，好莱坞的学院奖（Hollywood's the Academy Awards）即 The Oscars（奥斯卡奖）每年举行颁奖典礼，表彰电影界的成就。颁奖典礼（award ceremony）之前的红地毯（red carpet）活动是最受人关注的。被提名的获奖人都接受采访，演员们也身着艳丽的服装争妍。Tony Award（托尼奖）正式的名称是 The Antoinette Perry Award，表彰百老汇剧院（Broadway theatre）的现场舞台表演成果。该奖项由美国剧院翼（the American Theatre Wing）和百老汇联盟从 1947 起每年在纽约市举行颁奖仪式。Grammy Awards（格莱美奖）是奖励音乐表演成就。第一届格莱美奖颁奖典礼在 1959 年 5 月 4 日举行，由美国国家录音艺术与科学学院（the National Academy of Recording Arts and Sciences（NARAS）of the United States）颁奖。Emmy Awards（艾美奖）表彰在电视行业中的卓越成就，美国电视艺术与科学学院（the Academy of Television Arts & Sciences，ATAS）从 1950 年开始颁发此奖项。

18. Which activity is illegal in the United States?

A. Gambling

B. Hunting

C. Horse racing

D. Recreational drugs

问题：以下哪一种活动在美国是非法的?

答案：D. 软性毒品

　　美国是个自由的国家，很多活动都是容许的，如赌博（gambling），但不是每个州都容许的。私设赌场是违法的（illegal）。内华达州（Nevada）很贫瘠，所以设有著名的拉斯维加斯（Las Vegas）和里诺（Reno）赌场，赌场的收入是该州主要的经济来源。在不少美国印第安人的保留地（Indian Reservations）也容许设立赌场。新泽西州（New Jersey）的大西洋城（Atlantic City）也是有名的赌城。赛马（Horse racing）也是一种赌博。在美国，最有名的赛马比赛是肯塔基德比（Kentucky Derby），每年 5 月的第一个周六在肯塔基州路易斯维尔（Louisville）的丘吉尔·唐斯（Churchill Downs）举行。普里克内斯锦标赛（the Preakness Stakes）两周后在马里兰州巴尔的摩（Baltimore, Maryland）的皮姆利科马场（Pimlico Race Course）举行。三个星期后，普里克内斯（the Preakness）比赛在纽约长岛（Long Island）的贝尔蒙特公园（Belmont Park）举行。这三个马赛形成三年纯种赛马的三冠王赛（the Triple Crown）。Hunting（狩猎）是美国人传统的娱乐文化。从牛仔文化（cowboy culture）开始至今，枪是不可缺的。大多数家庭都有枪，爱狩猎的人众多，持枪和狩猎都必须要有执照，否则是犯法的。近年来，新泽西州鹿（deer）和黑熊（bears）的数量剧增，影响居民行车和住家的安全，州政府发令让狩猎人在规定的时间和范围内捕杀一部分鹿和黑熊。在美国贩卖和使用软性毒品（recreational drugs）是违法的。但是近年来有些州通过法律容许居民买卖和使用某些软性毒品，如华盛顿州和科罗拉多州等十个州就容许为治病或娱乐性地使用大麻（marijuana）。

19. Which is the least favorite sport in the U.S.?

A. Basketball

B. Football

C. Baseball

D. Volleyball

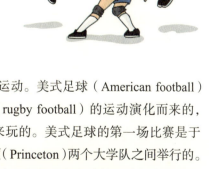

问题：以下哪一个不是美国人最喜爱的球类运动？

答案：D. 排球

　　答案中除排球之外都是美国人最疯狂的三大球类运动。美式足球（American football）是从美式足球联赛（Association Football）和橄榄球（rugby football）的运动演化而来的，与足球（soccer）完全不同，美式足球基本上是用手来玩的。美式足球的第一场比赛是于 1869 年 11 月 6 日，在罗格斯大学（Rutgers）和普林斯顿（Princeton）两个大学队之间举行的。美式足球是一个椭圆形的球（an oval ball），类似橄榄球。职业比赛中球的尺寸与大学和高中的稍有不同。职业的和大学的足球比赛共 60 分钟，分为 4 节（four quarters），每节 15 分钟，半场 30 分钟。而高中比赛的时间共 48 分钟，分 4 节，每节 12 分钟，半场共 24 分钟。得分是将球带入对方端线内，叫touchdown（达阵），得6分，加踢1球（pat）得1分，field goal（任意射门）得3分。篮球（basketball）起源于美国，相当是国球。美国在奥林匹克等国际篮球比赛中常胜无敌手。NBA职业篮球更是云集了几乎世界上所有的高手。每年NBA的Slam Dunk Contest（扣篮比赛），Three-Point Contest（三分球大赛）和All Star Game（全明星比赛）更是受世人关注。棒球（baseball）也是美国人喜爱的球类活动，棒球场各个社区都有，孩子们从小都爱打棒球。女子打的叫垒球，打法和规则与棒球很相似，只是场地较小，球大一些，比赛只有七局而非九局，使用腋下投球（underarm pitching）。排球不是很流行，但是近年来沙滩排球（beach volleyball）在美国发展很快。

20. What is an official called in a baseball game in the U.S.?

A. A judge

B. A referee

C. An umpire

D. An arbitrator

问题：在美国，棒球裁判的名称是什么？

答案：C. An umpire

　　裁判是执行游戏和比赛规则，维护游戏和比赛秩序的官员（an official）。也包括计分员（scorers）和计时员（timekeepers）。各类比赛裁判的称呼不同。在棒球比赛中裁判称为umpires，常简称为UMP，负责主持比赛，是做出判断（make judgment calls）、处理和处分的人（handle the disciplinary actions）。裁判都有特定的服装（uniform）。篮球比赛的裁判叫referees，通常有1个主裁判，1至2个副裁判（umpires）组成裁判组（the umpiring crew）。很多比赛项目的裁判都称为referees，如游泳，但是位于泳池的两侧观察游泳指定样式规则，匝数和回转的督察称为行程裁判（judges of stroke）。确定到达终点的顺序（order of finish），确保游泳者按照规则完成终点触壁的裁判称为（finish judges）终点裁判。美式足球（American football）的主裁判叫referee，定位在防守方的裁判叫umpire，他观察确定场上不超过11个进攻球员，监视进攻和防守线球员之间的接触等。背面裁判定位在防守队后，裁判(umpire)的后面。确保球队的防守一方不超过11名球员，并确定踢的三分球是否有效。还有边线裁判（the line judge）等。裁判为referee的体育项目还有田径（track and field）等。在网球（tennis）比赛中坐在高椅上的主裁判叫（head judge or chair umpire）。还常设有line judges和a net judge。花样滑冰（figure skating）、击剑（fencing）、体操（gymnastics）等的裁判叫judges。仲裁员（arbitrator/arbiter）是在比赛出现争端时，由比赛组织机构正式任命以解决争端（to settle a dispute）的人。

21. Which is not an extreme sport in the U.S.?

A. Cliff diving

B. Mountain climbing

C. Base jumping

D. Sky diving

问题：哪个项目不是美国的极限运动？

答案：B. 登山

　　美国人喜欢冒险（adventure），参加各种充满危险的极限运动（extreme sports）。在水上进行的极限运动有：drifting（漂流）、scuba diving（水肺潜水）、surfing（冲浪）、windsurfing（帆板）、white water rafting（激浪漂流）、standup paddleboarding（立桨冲浪）、cliff diving（悬崖跳水）、kayaking（皮划艇）、water skiing（滑水）等。从高空跳跃的极限运动包括：Base jumping（定点跳伞）、Bungee jumping（蹦极）、sky diving（跳伞）、cliff jumping（跳悬崖）、paragliding（滑翔伞）、parascending（滑伞）、kite surfing（风筝冲浪）等。在山地和平地进行的极限运动有：skateboarding（滑板运动）、rock climbing（攀岩）、bouldering（抱石）、backpacking（背包旅行）、mountain biking（山地自行车）、ski board（滑雪板）、snow boarding（单板滑雪）等。（参见http://www.buzzfeed.com/alejandroalba/extreme-outdoor-activities-to-try-before-you-die#.uk6Jab9z9。）

22. Which sport is of American origin?

A. Car racing

B. Baseball

C. Rodeo

D. Basketball

问题：哪个项目起源于美国？

答案：D. 篮球

　　答案C. rodeo是一种牛仔竞技表演，产生于西班牙（Spain）和墨西哥（Mexico）放牛（cattle herding）的工作实践中。随后传到美国、加拿大（Canada）、南美（South America）、澳大利亚（Australia）和新西兰（New Zealand）。rodeo当今在整个美国西部盛行。在怀俄明州（Wyoming）、南达科他州（South Dakota）和德克萨斯州（Texas）为官方体育项目。auto racing（赛车），也被称为car racing/automobile racing。世界上第一次赛车比赛是由两个自供电的道路车辆于 1867 年 8 月 30 日凌晨 4：30 在规定的路线上进行的，比赛路段从英国德阿什顿安德莱恩（Ashton-under-Lyne）到老特拉福德（Old Trafford），全长 8 英里，由艾萨克·瓦特博尔顿的车辆赢得比赛。美国的第一次赛车比赛（the first U.S. motor race）于 1878 年 7 月 16 日在威斯康星州举行，赛程为 200 英里。棒球（baseball）是美国人最喜爱的球类运动之一。棒球是用棒子打球的比赛（bat-and-ball games），各方有九名队员，两队轮流击球和防守。棒球的来源和演变难以精确跟踪，一般认为今天的棒球是从盛行于英国（Great Britain）和爱尔兰（Ireland）的圆场旧游戏在北美发展起来的。篮球是美国的国球。詹姆斯·奈史密斯博士（Dr. James Naismith）是一名加拿大的体育教授，为了让他的学生在雨天和漫长的新英格兰冬季保持健身的正常水平，詹姆斯·奈史密斯于 1891 年 12 月初在美国马萨诸塞州（Massachusetts）的斯普林菲尔德学院（Christian Association Training School）制定了篮球基本规则，将篮筐（hoop）定为直径 18 英寸（46 厘米），离地 10 英尺（3.048 米），装在场地两端的篮板上。

23. **Which is not part of a man's life?**

A. Beauty Pageant

B. Bachelor party

C. Baby shower

D. Wedding Ceremony

问题：哪个不是男人生活中的一个部分？

答案：A. 选美

　　在男人的一生中，会经历很多活动，尤其是在婚礼（wedding ceremony）前后。首先就是单身派对（bachelor party）。单身派对是在订婚后，举行的一次庆祝他的"最后一个自由的晚上"（last night of freedom）的聚会，未婚妻不会参加，他们在聚会上是尽情喝酒或雇用脱衣舞表演（hiring a stripper）。拉斯维加斯是单身派对和婚礼的热门地方。结婚后，在妻子怀孕后或婴儿出生前要举行迎婴聚会（baby shower）。迎婴聚会是为了庆祝孩子的出生（birth of a child）或近期分娩，也是为了庆祝一个女人转变为母亲的聚会。有些婴儿淋浴是为未来的父亲（the future father）而举办的。聚会上常是喝啤酒、观看体育比赛、钓鱼、或玩视频游戏。准爸爸的朋友们会送来尿布等婴儿用品作为礼物，为孩子的出生做好准备。选美（beauty pageant）不是男人生活的一个部分。世界上四大选美是英国的 Miss World

Pageant，美国的 Miss Universe，位于菲律宾的 Miss Earth 及位于日本的 Miss International。选美获胜者称为 A Beauty Queen（绝代佳人）。美国小姐选美（Miss America Pageant）是今天最古老而且仍然在运作的选美比赛。1921 年新泽西州当地的商人为吸引游客前往大西洋赌城而开始举办选美比赛。选美的竞争标准历来侧重于选手（contestants）的体形相貌（physical attributes）、泳装（bikini swimsuit）、化妆（make up）、发型（hair）、个性（personality）、仪态（deportment）、礼服（gowns）、智力（intelligence）、才能（talent）：唱歌（singing）、舞蹈（dance）、乐器演奏（music instrument）等和回答法官（judges）的提问和个人访谈（interview）。与此相对的男人比赛是健美比赛（bodybuilding contest）。

24. When your book is ranked first it is called: ____

A. MVP

B. Best seller

C. Best album

D. MIP

问题：书排名第一时称为：____

答案：B. 最畅销书

《纽约时代周刊》（*The New York Times*）每周都发布各种书籍的排名，称为 best seller。其中分 e-books（电子书）、paperback（简装）、hardcover（精装）、graphic Books（图书）、children's books（儿童书籍），又分有 fiction（小说）和 non-fiction（非小说）。（参见 http://www.nytimes.com/best-sellers-books/。）best album（最佳录音专辑奖）是格莱美奖的项目之一，是美国国家录音艺术与科学学院（NARAS）表彰以英语语言为主的音乐产业的杰出成就。MVP 是 most valuable player（最具价值选手）的缩写，相当于 best player，通常是体育集体项目中表现最佳的运动员。champion（冠军）可以是体育比赛或任何比赛的第一名。大部分的体育比赛都颁奖给前三名的运动员，分别是金牌（gold medal）、银牌（silver medal）和铜牌（bronze medal）。MIP 是 most improved player（进步最快球员）的缩写。Hall of Fame（名人堂），是为表彰对于一项体育运动有杰出贡献的球员或教练而设立的。Lifetime Achievement Award 为终生成就奖。

25. What is the net on the right for?

A. Keep birds

B. Keep pets

C. Catch crabs

D. Catch mice

问题：右边的网状笼子是做什么用的？

答案：C. 钓螃蟹

美国人喜爱户外活动，如钓鱼（fishing）、打猎（hunting）、钓螃蟹（crabbing）等。右边的网状笼子就是专门用来钓螃蟹的，不是用来养宠物（keep pets）、逮老鼠（catch mice）或养鸟（keep birds）的。美国的海岸线很长，在沿海的海湾和河沟螃蟹（crab）遍地都是，每年的 4~10 月都可以钓螃蟹。当然 7~9 月是钓螃蟹的最佳时间，先在网上查找好钓螃蟹的地点，通常都是在近海的小桥上和河道边。笼子在沿海的百货商店可以买到，再买几磅鸡腿（chicken drums or quarters）或 2~7 寸的鱼。将他们逐个绑紧在笼子里，笼子用结实的长绳子链接，然后将笼子从桥上或河道边抛入，笼子的四周到水底时会展开，让螃蟹进入吃诱饵（bait），过 10~20 分钟就可以收了，收时动作要快，准备好夹钳（tongs）和桶子捉蟹入桶。在美国钓螃蟹不需要执照（license），但是要注意，政府规定 4.5 寸以下的螃蟹和待产籽的母螃蟹要放回大海。钓到的螃蟹洗净后，蒸好，配上姜、酱油、醋、辣椒等调料，就是美味佳肴了。在美国钓鱼通常需要执照，钓鱼时不用蚯蚓或其他活的诱饵，而是人造的假小鱼、虾（shrimp）、昆虫（insect）等。美国的鱼似乎很蠢，分不清真假食物，很容易上钩。

26. Which of the following is not a rating for movies in the U.S.?

A. R

B. PG-13

C. PG

D. P

问题：以下哪一个不属美国的电影分级制度？

答案：D. P

美国电影协会（The Motion Picture Association of America, MPAA）制定了电影的分级制度（film-rating system），分为 G、PG、PG13、R 和 NC-17 五个级别。

•G 级适宜于普通观众（General Audiences）。票房会注明：任何年龄都可以观看（All ages admitted）。G 级电影中没有家长担心不适合儿童观看的内容（Nothing that would offend parents for viewing by children.）。

•PG 级是建议在家长指导下观看的电影（Parental Guidance Suggested）。票房会注明：电影中有一些内容可能不适合儿童观看（Some material may not be suitable for children.）。

•PG-13 级是家长需特别注意的电影（Parents Strongly Cautioned）。票房会注明：电影中的一些内容可能不适合 13 岁以下的青少年（pre-teenagers）观看（Some material may be inappropriate for children under 13.）。

•R 级是受限观看的电影（Restricted）。票房会注明：17 岁以下儿童要求随家长或监护人一同观看（Under 17 requires accompanying parent or adult guardian.）。这类电影包含一些成人内容（Contains some adult material.）。呼吁家长们在带他们年幼的孩子去观看以前更多地了解这部电影（Parents are urged to learn more about the film before taking their young children with them.）。

•NC-17（Adults Only）是仅限成人观看的电影。票房会注明：17 周岁或以下的禁止观看（No One 17 and Under Admitted.）。儿童不得入场（Children are not admitted.）。除了级别之外，电影和电视还要注明所含有的不良内容，如裸露（nudity）、暴力（violence）、成人的场景（adult scene）、肮脏的语言（dirty language）等。

27. Which one is not a popular pet in the U.S.?

A. Pigs

B. Lizards

C. Spiders

D. Snakes

问题：在美国哪个不是流行的宠物？

答案：C. 蜘蛛

美国人爱养宠物（pets），到处都有宠物店，如 PetSmart、Petland 等。店中出售各种宠物食品、用具、玩具甚至衣服。过万圣节时，有的主人还给宠物打扮一番。有的宠物店提供给狗、猫等动物的剪毛（shearing）、训练（training）、看病（medical care）、清洁（cleaning）等服务。据 2007~2008 年 Pet Owners Survey 的数据统计，美国人最爱养的宠物是 dogs（狗）、cats（猫）、fresh water fish（淡水鱼）、birds（鸟）、rabbits（兔子）、mice（老鼠）、hamster（仓鼠）、guinea pigs（豚鼠）、reptile（爬虫）、equine（马）和 saltwater fish（海鱼）。reptile（爬虫）包括 snakes（蛇）、lizards（蜥蜴）、crocodiles（鳄鱼）、turtles（乌龟）以及 tortoises（陆龟类）等冷血脊椎动物（cold-blooded vertebrate）。它们具有干燥鳞状皮肤（dry scaly skin），并且通常在陆地上产软壳蛋（soft-shelled eggs）。美国人还喜欢把猪（pigs）作宠物养，也有人养蜘蛛（spiders），但不普遍。很多宠物如狗和猫都要接种狂犬病疫苗（rabies vaccine）。如被动物咬伤、抓伤要立即去医院和诊所注射狂犬病疫苗。兽医（veterinarian）的收入不凡。

28. In the States, it is illegal to do the following, except:

A. Catch birds
B. Grow vegetables
C. Kill cats
D. Cut trees excessively

问题：在美国，除了____之外，以下的各项都是违法的。
答案：B. 种菜

　　美国对动物（animals）、植物（plants）和环境的保护（environment protection）做得很好。除了对濒临灭种（on the verge of extinction）的动植物严加保护外，对大部分动植物都是一样，不容许随意破毁和捕杀。所以 catch birds（捉鸟）、abuse pets（虐待宠物）、kill animals（杀害动物）、cut trees excessively（乱伐树木）都是不容许的。违法会被罚款和监禁。在美国不论是在平原还是山区，树木和植被（vegetation）都受到很好的保护，上百年的参天大树到处可见。除了大城市老建筑群的地域之外，很少见到没有树木草地覆盖的空地。加上对工厂污水和废气的严格管理和控制，水和空气的质量优良。几乎全美的自来水都可以直接饮用。公共场所到处都设有自来水的饮水器（water fountain/water dispenser）。在自己的后院种菜（grow vegetables）是容许的。很多美籍华人都开菜园子（vegetable garden），种植美国没有或稀有的中国蔬菜，如空心菜（water spinach）、苋菜（amaranth）、长豆（long beans）、扁豆（hyacinth bean）、丝瓜（luffa/sponge gourd）、冬瓜（wax gourd/winter Melon/white Gourd）、苦瓜（bitter melon）、韭菜（leek）、中国芹菜（Chinese celery）等。从中国带种子来美是违法的，菜种可以在中国商场买到或在网上邮购。美国人喜欢种花草，大部分住宅都用花草树木将前后院美化（landscape）成小花园（flower garden）。园丁所用的各种工具（garden tools）、花卉（flowers）和肥料（fertilizer/manure）等都可以在 Home Deport（家得宝）和 Lowe's Home Improvement 等商场买到。常用工具有：耙（rakes）、手推车（wheelbarrow）、锄头（hoes）、手铲（hand trowel）、铁锹（spade）、4齿耙（tine forged cultivator）等。

29. Which of the following museums is in New York City?

A. Metropolitan Museum of Art
B. National Gallery of Art
C. National Museum of Natural History
D. Museum of American History

问题：哪个博物馆在纽约市？
答案：A. 大都会博物馆

    Metropolitan Museum of Art（大都会艺术博物馆），俗称"the Met"，位于纽约市，是美国最大的艺术博物馆，也是世界上参观人数最多的艺术博物馆之一。一年有 500 万左右的人次参观。它的永久收藏品（permanent collection）超过 200 万件，分布在古埃及、珍宝、名画、亚洲、动物、雕塑等十七个展览区。它位于曼哈顿中央公园（Central Park）的东部边缘，是世界上面积最大的美术馆之一。在曼哈顿上城（Upper Manhattan）的堡特赖恩公园（Fort Tryon Park）的修道院博物馆（The Cloisters），还有一个展示中世纪艺术（Medieval Art）的小展览馆。参观是免费的，但是售票处人员希望你购票捐钱，你可以给一两美元，不给也可以。National Gallery of Art（国家艺术画廊）及其连接的雕塑花园（Sculpture Garden）是位于华盛顿特区国家广场（the National Mall）的国家艺术博物馆，免费向公众开放（open to the public and free of charge）。博物馆收藏了大量艺术珍品，包括从中世纪到现在的油画（paintings）、素描（drawings）、版画（prints）、照片（photographs）、雕塑（sculpture）、奖牌（medals）和装饰艺术（decorative arts），包括达·芬奇（Leonardo da Vinci）在美洲的唯一绘画，每年有 420 万人次参观。National Museum of Natural History（美国自然历史博物馆）和 Museum of American History（美国历史博物馆）也都在华盛顿特区国家广场，而且也都是免费的。美国自然历史博物馆，尤其是动物部分是儿童了解大自然的最佳去处。还有儿童喜爱的美国国家航空航天博物馆（National Air and Space Museum）。美国的很多城市都有很不错的各类博物馆。（参见 http://www.ranker.com/list/the-best-museums-in-the-united-states/nychick。）

30. Which of the following is different from all other media carriers?

A. Comcast

B. Verizon

C. Sprint

D. Dish Network

问题：下面哪个电视公司与其他的不同？

答案：D. 卫星电视公司

美国的有线电视公司（Cable TV Company）很多，最大而最有名是Comcast、Verizon、Sprint三家。目前这三家公司竞争激烈。而Dish Network则是一家提供卫星电视节目（Satellite TV Programs）的公司。Dish在这里是指圆盘式卫星电视天线（Satellite Dish）。现在这些公司都提供多方位的服务：电视节目（TV programs）、电话（telephone）和互联网（Internet）。你可以购置其中之一或全部服务项目。但通常是互联网加上一些电视节目比较合算。因为手机的功能越来越多，很多家庭都不再使用电话座机（home phone）了。另外，你也可以购买一个好的天线（antenna），一百多美元的就可以了，架设在自家的阁楼上就可以免费收到几十个本地电视台的节目。在美国看中文电视节目不是很方便。在大城市，如纽约、旧金山、洛杉矶、波士顿等的本地电视网上都有中文电视台；但是中小城市里，就收不到中文电视节目。现在有一些有线中文电视公司，如I talk BB公司，还有小米盒子等能通过互联网观看中文电视，它提供包括中国中央和地方电视台的电影、电视剧、文艺节目等。

31. Which of the following is not equivalent to Hall of Fame?

A. World Championship

B. Hollywood Walk of Fame

C. Lifetime Achievement Award

D. Wall of Fame

问题：哪个答案与Hall of Fame不相等？

答案：A. 世界冠军

Hall of Fame（名人堂）和Wall of Fame（名人墙）是为了表彰在体育、科技、电影、音乐、艺术等领域做出杰出贡献的人士，通常是在该人士退休或职业生涯的尾年颁发的终生成就奖（Lifetime Achievement Award），如 Basketball Hall of Fame（篮球名人堂）、United States Astronaut Hall of Fame（美国宇航员名人馆）、Grammy Hall of Fame — for recordings（格莱美名人堂——唱片）、College Football Hall of Fame（大学足球名人堂）、National Baseball Hall of Fame and Museum（美国国家棒球名人堂暨博物馆）。在美国的电影娱乐界（entertainment industry），名人堂的表达方式是将杰出的演员、音乐家、导演、制片、音乐和戏剧团体和其他人的名字印在洛杉矶的好莱坞大道（Hollywood Boulevard），即星光大道上，称为 the Hollywood Walk of Fame。名人的名字是嵌在水磨石和黄铜铸成的五角星上。星上有五种分类的徽记代表不同的奖项：古典摄影机代表电影（Classic film camera—motion pictures）、电视接收器表示广播电视（Television receiver —broadcast television）、唱片表示录音或音乐（Phonograph record —audio recording or music）、无线话筒代表无线电广播（Radio microphone —broadcast radio）、喜剧/悲剧面罩代表戏剧/现场演出（Comedy/tragedy masks—theatre/live performance）。星光大道与落日大道（Sunset Boulevard）相邻，长 2.1 公里，目前共有 2500 多颗星，每年有上千万的人去参观。World Championship（世界冠军）与名人堂不相等。

32. "Skate on thin ice" means:

A. Figure skating

B. Skate on a frozen lake

C. In a dangerous situation

D. Run high risk

问题："在薄冰上溜冰"是什么意思？
答案：D. 冒高风险

　　短语 skate on thin ice 指如履薄冰，与 run high risk（冒高风险）含义相近，如 It warns that parents run a high risk of losing their investment.（告诫说，家长有很大的风险失去自己的投资。）其他选项：in a dangerous situation（处境危险）、Skate on a frozen lake（在冰冻的湖面滑冰。）figure skating（花样滑冰）是一项冬季体育活动，但是在美国，各处都有室内溜冰场（indoor ice rink），所以全年都可以进行冰上活动，如溜冰、花样滑冰、冰上舞蹈（ice dance）、冰球（ice hockey）比赛等。冰上的体育活动还有：speed skating（速滑）、curling（冰壶）比赛。很多冬季室外的活动都与雪有关，美国人也很喜爱滑雪（ski）。在美国有很多天然的滑雪避暑胜地（ski summer resorts），最有名的是：怀俄明州（Wyoming）的 Jackson Hole Resort，该处的滑雪索道不到 10 分钟就能将 100 名乘客运载达 4000 英尺高处，从杰克逊机场仅 35 分钟即可赶到滑雪场。位于犹他州（Utah）的雪鸟滑雪和避暑山庄（Snowbird

Ski and Summer Resort）的雪粉充足得难以置信，是全国最大的滑雪地点之一。而同在犹他州的 Alta（阿尔塔）滑雪度假村，具备了度假村滑雪场所需要的一切，被誉为美国最佳滑雪圣地，滑雪者的天堂。犹他州的优越滑雪场所曾为之赢得了 2002 冬季奥运会（Winter Olympic Games）的举办权。冬季奥运的项目有：ski jumping（跳台滑雪）、speed skating（速滑）、luge（雪橇）、snow boarding（雪地滑板）、freestyle skiing（自由式滑雪）、bobsleigh（有舵雪橇）、cross country skiing（越野滑雪）、alpine skiing（高山滑雪）、nordic combined（北欧两项）、figure skating（花样滑冰）、short track speed skating（短道速滑）、skeleton（骨架）、ice hockey（冰球）、biathlon（冬季两项）、curling（冰壶）等。

33. Which of the following is an event of the Summer Olympic Games?

A. Frisbee

B. Lacrosse

C. Golf

D. Cricket

问题：下面哪项体育活动是夏季奥运会的项目？
答案：C. 高尔夫球

在美国，不少人们喜爱的体育活动不是奥运会的比赛项目。如中学生和大学生常在室外进行的 frisbee—flying disc（飞盘）比赛。比赛各队出七人，传递飞盘，在对方端线接到飞盘就得分。这项活动是弗雷德•莫里森（Fred Morrison）于 1938 年第一次推出的，他在康州纽黑文出售 25 美分的蛋糕盘子，供人们在海滩上玩。现在有很多的飞盘俱乐部，说不定哪一年会成为夏季奥运会（the Summer Olympic Games）的项目。lacrosse（长曲棍球）也是一项美国的中学生和大学生的团队体育活动，与曲棍球很相像，长曲棍球使用小橡皮球和长柄棒，曲棍球棍的头部有一个网兜，用来接球和传球，球员需要佩戴头盔和护肩，比赛的目标是通过射门，把球打入对手的球门。cricket（板球）是一种类似棒球的体育比赛，只在英联邦国家之间举行，美国没有这项体育活动。夏季奥运会有 41 个正式项目：archery（射箭）、athletics（竞技）、badminton（羽毛球）、basketball（篮球）、boxing（拳击）、canoe slalom（皮划艇激流回旋）、canoe sprint（独木舟冲刺）、BMX（小轮车）、beach volleyball（沙滩排球）、cycling mountain bike（山地自行车赛）、cycling road（车道自行车）、cycling track（场地自行车）、diving（跳水）、equestrian dressage（马术盛装舞步）、equestrian three（马术三项）、equestrian jumping（马术场地障碍）、fencing（击剑）、

football（足球）、golf（高尔夫球）、gymnastics artistic（竞技体操）、gymnastics rhythmic（艺术体操）、handball（手球）、hockey（曲棍球）、judo（柔道）、modern pentathlon（现代五项）、rowing（划船）、rugby（橄榄球）、sailing（帆船）、shooting（射击）、swimming（游泳）、synchronized swimming（花样游泳）、table tennis（乒乓球）、taekwondo（跆拳道）、tennis（网球）、trampoline（蹦床）、triathlon（铁人三项）、volleyball（排球）、water polo（水球）、weightlifting（举重）、wrestling freestyle（自由式摔跤）、wrestling Greco-Roman（古典式摔跤）。

34. Which of the following is a popular video game for children in the U.S.?

A. Assassin's Creed

B. Minecraft

C. Battlefield

D. Game of Thrones

问题：下面哪项视频游戏是美国儿童喜爱的?

答案：B. Minecraft

　　现在是电脑游戏的时代，高科技的发展使视频游戏（videogames）变得更逼真（real life like），更有互动性（interactive）和挑战性（challenging）。使用的平台（platforms）有：PC、Mac、PS4、Xbox、Nintendo Wii 等。儿童（children）、青年人（teenagers）甚至很多成人（adults）都成了痴迷视频游戏的奴隶。当下青年人和成人喜爱的有Assassin's Creed、Battlefield、Hardline、Batman、Arkham Knight、Game of Thrones等。目前儿童爱玩的视频游前九名（2015）是：1. Disney Fantasia：Music Evolved，2. Minecraft，3. Zoo Tycoon，4. Just Dance 2015，5. Angry Birds：Star Wars，6. Farming Simulator 15，7. LEGO Marvel Super Heroes，8. Child of Light，9. Portal 2。网上的游戏有：www.nick.com/games/，www.nickjr.com/games/。适合幼儿的有www.sproutonline.com/games等。有的网站上提供各个年级学生学习用的游戏（参见https://www.turtlediary.com/）。就英语教育而言，视频和网络游戏也在不断增加，包括英语发音、拼写和阅读，如starfall.com。

35. Which of the following is a most popular leisure activity in the U.S.?

A. Watching TV

B. Engaging sports or exercises

C. Reading

D. Socializing and communicating

问题：下面哪项是美国人最普遍的休闲活动？

答案：A. 看电视

　　根据美国劳工部（U.S. Department of Labor）统计局（Bureau of Labor Statistics）2010年的数据，几乎每个 15 岁以上的人每天都在进行某些休闲活动（leisure time/pastime）如看电视（watching TV）、社交活动（socializing）或锻炼（exercising）。在休闲活动中，男性平均每天花 5.8 小时而女性花费 5.1 小时。最普遍的休闲活动是看电视，占所有休闲时间的一半以上，每天约 2.7 小时。其次社交活动：访友（visiting with friends）、参加或主办社交活动（attending or hosting social events）、与朋友一起吃饭（eating and drinking with friends）、玩棋盘游戏（playing board games）、去餐馆或酒吧（going out to restaurants or bars）等。每天平均花费 3/4 小时。其他娱乐休闲包括去电影院看电影（movies）、看脱口秀（watching talk show）或看戏剧表演（theaters）、参加音乐会（concerts）、使用因特网（using the internet）、听音乐（listening to the music）、听收音机节目（listening to to radio talk shows）、玩视频游戏。从事体育和锻炼（engaging sports or exercises）也是很普遍的休闲活动。其他的户外（outdoor activities）休闲活动还包括钓鱼（fishing）、划船（boating）、徒步旅行（hiking）、野营（camping）、跑步（running）、骑自行车（cycling）、攀岩（rock climbing）、游泳（swimming）等活动。阅读书籍和杂志（reading books and magazine）也是一部分人的休闲活动。

36. Which of the following is the biggest Aquarium in the U.S.?

A. Monterey Bay Aquarium

B. Georgia Aquarium

C. National Aquarium

D. Shedd Aquarium

问题：下面哪个是美国最大的水族馆？

答案：B. 佐治亚水族馆

　　水族馆（Aquarium）是成人和儿童都喜爱参观又能增长知识的地方。美国的五大水族馆中，位于亚特兰大（Atlanta）的 Georgia Aquarium（佐治亚水族馆）是美国也是世界上最大的水族馆，占地 550000 平方英尺，有 800 万加仑水，展出 60000 动物，并设有一个屡获殊荣的海豚水下观景窗，还有动物表演。水族馆的展览部分 25% 是专门为教育服务的，采用 4D 数字投影，特技和 3D 电影技术让参观者感觉是在水下与动物接触。水族馆一年 365 天开门，成人票价大约是 40 美元，儿童 30 美元。其他的水族馆还有北加州蒙特利湾水族馆（Monterey Bay Aquarium），有 550 个不同的物种和超过 100 个水箱。父母和孩子都喜欢蒙特里湾水族馆的水溅区戏耍，那儿装有 45 个互动展览，对九岁以下儿童是最完美的选择。成人票价大约是 40 美元，儿童 25 美元。National Aquarium（国家水族馆）在首都华盛顿，水族馆除了海洋生物之外，还在屋顶设有热带雨林，游客可以在那里搜索异国情调的鸟类和其他树木生物。票价在 25~40 美元之间。Shedd Aquarium（谢德水族馆）在芝加哥市（Chicago），建于 1930 年。Audubon Aquarium of the Americas（美洲奥杜邦水族馆）在路易斯安那州的新奥尔良市（New Orleans, Louisiana）。世界最大的水族馆的排名是：1. Georgia Aquarium（6.3 million gallons）；2. Dubai Mall Aquarium（2.64 million gallons）；3. Okinawa Churaumi Aquarium（1.98 million gallons）；4. L'Oceanografic（1.85 million gallons）；5. Turkuazoo（1.32 million gallons）；6. Monterey Bay Aquarium（1.2 million gallons）；7. uShaka Marine World（about 1 million gallons）；8. Shanghai Ocean Aquarium（about 1 million gallons）。

37. In which sports the lowest score wins?

A. Soccer

B. Tennis

C. Golf

D. Baseball

问题：哪种体育比赛分数最低的获胜？
答案：C. 高尔夫球

　　高尔夫（golf）是所列体育项目中唯一的以得分最低（lowest score）获胜的球类运动。正规的球场（golf court）设有 72 个洞，有 4 轮，每轮 18 个洞的比赛中，使用的杆数最少的高尔夫球员获胜。与其他球类运动相反，球员和教练都在一直想方设法帮助他们获得较低的成绩。golf 运动的术语不少，如 hole/cup（洞）、birdie（比设定少一杆进洞）、caddie（球童）、eagle（比设定少两杆进洞）、bogey（比设定多一杆进洞）、ace（一杆打进三杆的洞）、bunker（沙坑）、par（平杆）、flagstick（旗杆）、green/putting area（推杆区）、iron（高尔夫球杆）、match play-playoff（决胜/加赛）、tee（每个洞开球时将球提高的小装置）。有些休育项目的比赛也是以最低的成绩为胜者，尤其是竞赛项目，如各个短跑（dash）、长跑（long distant running）项目、马拉松（marathon）、游泳（swimming）、ice-skating（溜冰）、cycling（自行车）、racing（赛车）等，时间用得最少的获胜。也有的比赛既要分数高又要发的时间少，如 diving（潜水）、rope jump（跳绳）等，而举重（weight lifting）项目，胜者则是举的重量最大而且体重最轻的。

38. Which of the biggest zoo in the U.S.?

A. San Diego Zoo

B. Bronx Zoo

C. Columbus Zoo & Aquarium

D. Henry Doorly Zoo & Aquarium

问题：下面哪个是美国最大的动物园？

答案：A. 圣地亚哥动物园

　　动物园在美国已经有近 150 年的历史，它吸引着每一个家庭。当今全球有超过一千家的动物园而在美国就有 2400 多家。根据总面积、动物数量和参观人数，美国最大的动物园在哪里？位于纽约的布朗克斯动物园（Bronx Zoo）在 1899 年首次开放时，是全美最大的城市动物园，占地 265 英亩，拥有 650 多种类的 4000 多只动物，每年吸引超过 200 万游客。哥伦布动物园和水族馆（The Columbus Zoo and Aquarium）是一个巨大的综合体，包括一个水上公园和一个以美国最著名的动物园管理员命名的游乐园。哥伦布动物园和水族馆位于俄亥俄州（Ohio）北部州府，总面积达 582 英亩，拥有超过 575 类 10000 多只动物，通常被认为是世界上最好的动物园之一。亨利门动物园和水族馆（Henry Doorly Zoo & Aquarium）位于内布拉斯加州（Nebraska），成立于 1894 年，占地 130 英亩，拥有来自 962 个种类的 17,000 只动物，以及世界一流的展览，游乐设施和其他景点。曾经被誉为世界上最好的动物园，包括世界上最大的室内沙漠以及世界上最大的室内沼泽园。San Diego Zoo（圣地亚哥动物园）由《旅行顾问》命名为世界上最好的动物园，拥有世界上最多的珍稀濒危动物（rare and endangered animals）。它位于圣地亚哥有名的巴尔博亚公园（Balboa Park）内，占地 100 英亩，共有超过 650 个种类的 3500 多只动物，包括迷人的大熊猫（giant panda）和澳大利亚以外的最多的考拉（koalas）。动物园的其他亮点是极地熊（polar bear）、猎豹、大象奥德赛的现场表演和两个 4D 剧院。该动物园于 1915 年开业，还负责监管著名的圣地亚哥野生动植物保护区（wildlife sanctuary），占地近 1800 英亩，拥有超过 300 种类的 3000 多只动物。

39. When an athlete is doping it means she/he is taking_____.

A. Steroids

B. Stimulants

C. Cannabis

D. Any of the above

问题：运动员吸毒是指他在服用____。

答案：D. 以上任意一种

当今的体育比赛越来越商业化（commercialized），为了提高成绩（enhancing performance）来赢得奖金，运动员服用兴奋剂的丑闻（drugs scandal）不断。服用禁药（prohibited drugs）严重地危害了体育运动的健康发展。由于科技的发展，禁药的种类繁多，反兴奋剂的检测（anti-doping testing）措施也在加强。常见的非法药物/禁药（illegal drugs）有 steroid（类固醇）即 sex hormone（性激素）、stimulants/uppers（兴奋剂）、agonists（激动剂）、gene doping（基因药物）、cannabis（大麻）、cocaine（可卡因）等。另外，控制血液和血液组合（manipulation of blood and blood components）的方式也是禁止使用的。

以下是一些与禁药有关的常用句子：

Some athletes from Canada, the United States and the Czech Republic also were either disqualified or banned for drug use.

（加拿大、美国和捷克共和国的一些运动员也因使用禁药而被取消比赛资格或禁赛。）

The most important reason for using prohibited drugs is the winning bonus, however, there will be negative effects physiologically and mentally.

（使用禁药的最主要理由是为了奖金，但使用禁药会对身心产生负面影响。）

She was stripped of her Olympic Hundred Meters gold medal after testing positive for steroids.

（类固醇检测呈阳性后，她的奥运百米金牌被收回。）

40. Which of the following phrases is different from all the others?

A. Keep the ball rolling

B. Hit a buzzer beater

C. Suffer a concussion

D. Join a fencing club

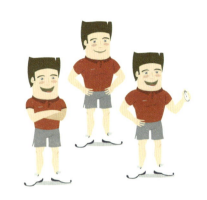

问题：以下哪个短语与其他的不同？

答案：A. Keep the ball rolling

  答案选项中，只有Keep the ball rolling与体育活动没有直接的联系。它的意思是保持项目的活动水平和热情（maintain a level of activity in and enthusiasm for a project）。Hit a buzzer beater是进了个压哨球。如Curry of Golden State Warriors hit a game winning three pointer buzzer beater（金州勇士队的Curry投了一个制胜的压哨三分球）。美国人不论男女老少都酷爱体育运动。家长从小就极力鼓励孩子参加各种体育活动和俱乐部（sports clubs），时间和钱的投入堪比中国的数理化奥赛（Academic Olympics）。其中一个因素是体育方面的表现是大学入学和获得奖学金（scholarship）的一个重要的因素。体育活动对身体有益，但是不少运动容易受伤（injuries）。如美式足球（American football）的肢体冲突大，虽有头盔（Football helmet）和身体保护服（body protection）等，运动员还是常出现脑震荡（suffer a concussion），肌肉拉伤（muscle strain），骨折（fracture），踝关节扭伤（ankle sprain）等伤情。近年来，美式足球运动员脑震荡的人数大增，引起了广泛的关注。脑震荡的症状有Headache（头痛）、Dizziness（头晕）、Nausea and/or vomiting（恶心和/或呕吐）、Slurred speech（言语不清）、Sensitivity to light（对光敏感）、Delayed response to questions（对问题的反应迟缓）等。出现以上症状要及时就医。常见的运动损伤有：Hip Flexor Strain（髋屈肌拉伤）、ACL（anterior cruciate ligaments）Tear or Strain（前交叉韧带撕裂或拉伤）、Groin Pull（腹股沟拉伤）、Hamstring Strain（跟腱拉伤）、Tennis or Golf Elbow（网球或高尔夫球手肘）、Shoulder Injury（肩关节损伤）等。由于大多数东方人个头较小，因此多数选择身高体重要求不高，身体碰撞（body collision）不大的体育项目，如参加击剑俱乐部（Join a fencing club）和体操（Gymnastics）、花样溜冰（Figure skating）、跳水（Diving）、飞盘（Frisbee）、武术（Martial arts）、跆拳道（Taekwondo）、长跑(Distance running)、足球(Soccer)等体育活动。不过参加任何一项体育活动都要小心，充分做好准备活动（warm up），循序渐进。

Idioms & Proverbs
习惯用语篇

1. "She woke up on the wrong side of the bed this morning."This sentence means:

A. She fell off the bed.

B. Her bed has many sides.

C. She jumped out of her bed.

D. She is not feeling well.

问题：句子"她早上醒来发现床掉了个头"的意思是：

答案：D. 她感觉不舒服。

　　句子"She woke up on the wrong side of the bed this morning."的意思是表示身体感到不舒服，与句子"She is not feeling well."相同。其他类似的表达方式还有："She is under the weather.","She is not herself today.","She is sick/ill."。表达身体具体某个部位不适的方式有：got a cold（感冒了）、flu（患了流感）、sore throat（喉咙疼）、cough（咳嗽）、a diarrhea（拉肚子）、headache（头痛）、running nose（流鼻涕）、stomachache（胃痛）、chest pains（胸口疼）、a fever（发烧）或是I am running a fever.（我在发烧。）I vomited（threw out）.（我呕吐了。）I feel dizzy.（我头昏。）等。身体好的表达有：She feels well. She is in good health. She is in good shape.在西方和美国看病很少去医院（go to hospital），而是到自己的家庭医生（family doctor）的诊所（doctor's office）看病，而且要事先预约（make an appointment）。医生也称为Physician。只有在需要看急诊（emergency）时或需要住院动手术（surgery或operation）时，才去医院或急诊中心（emergency room）。现在有一种新设立的小型急症诊所叫Urgent Care Center，突发疾病时，可先上这种急症诊所看病，很便捷。另外家庭医生的诊所里是没有药（medicine）的。病人看病后，要带着医生开的处方（prescription）到药店（drug store）去买药。医用表达：take your temperature(量体温）、take your blood pressure(量血压）、listen to your lung（听听你的肺部）、take a deep breath（做深呼吸）、hold your breath（屏住呼吸）、air out（呼气）、open your mouth（张开嘴巴）、check your nose and ears（检查你的鼻子和耳朵）、measure your height and weight（测量你的身高和体重）、lie down（躺下）。

2. "It's raining cats and dogs." means:

A. rain checks.

B. a heavy rain.

C. prepare for a rainy day.

D. a rainy season.

问题：句子"天上下猫下狗"的意思是?

答案：B. 下大雨。

天上下狗下猫是不可能的，除非是遇到龙卷风了。"It rains dogs and cats"是个成语，描绘雨下得铺天盖地。通常说下大雨是"It's raining hard.","There is a heavy rain/downpour/torrential rain."。与雨相关的词语有: drizzle（毛毛雨）、shower（阵雨）、thunderstorm（雷雨）、storm（风暴）。在美国中南部常常有龙卷风（tornado/cyclone）。在佛罗里达州和墨西哥湾附近的州，夏天常遭受hurricane（飓风）和typhon（台风）的袭击。其他与雨雪天气有关的词语有：heavy fog（大雾）、foggy（雾天）、lightening（闪电）、thunder（雷鸣）、strong wind（大风）、gusty wind（阵风）、hail（冰雹）、frost（霜）、snow（雪）、flora/snowflakes（雪花）、ice（冰）、black ice（一层薄冰）、freeze rain（冰雨）、rain coat（雨衣）、umbrella（伞）、rainy season（雨季）。另外美国的 Weather channel 及网页www.weather.com不仅提供世界各地的天气预报（weather forecast），还提供交通信息，及各地的风土人情和奇景，值得一览。其他常用表达：Prepare for a rainy day.（未雨绸缪，以备不时之需。）rain checks 是在美国许多大商店里可延期，留作下次继续用的票据。当某件降价物品卖完了，顾客还想买的话，商店可以给你开出一个 rain check。新货到了，你可用它按当时降价的价格买到该物品。这是美国商店讲究信用的一种体现。

3. "She had butterflies in her stomach." means:

A. She got a stomachache.

B. She ate some butterflies.

C. She loved butterflies.

D. She liked to play with butterflies.

问题："她的胃里有蝴蝶"的意思是什么?

答案：A. 她胃疼。

句子 She had butterflies in her stomach. 这一个成语，表示胃痛。sick to stomach 是想吐，throw up/vomit 为呕吐。其他的句子表示的意思为：She ate some butterflies.（她吃了一些蝴蝶。）She loved butterflies.（她喜欢蝴蝶。）She liked to play with butterflies.（她喜欢玩蝴蝶。）与疾病和身体有关的习语还有：An apple a day keeps doctors away.（一天吃一个苹果，不用看医生。）My mom is finally back on her feet after being sick for months.（我妈妈病了好几个月后终于恢复了她的健康。）Get well.（早日恢复健康。）The football player blacked out after being hit by other player.（这位足球运动员被其他球员撞了之后昏了过去。）My brother came down with a flu.（我的哥哥感冒了。）The lady went to the drug store to fill a prescription/get medicine.（这位女士拿处方到药店去取药/拿药。）I had my annual（medical）check-up（a physical examination）last week.（上周我做了年度体检。）The old lady has one foot in the grave（at death's door）.（那位老人已是风烛残年。）die a natural death（自然死亡）、pass out/faint（昏倒）、take a sick leave（请病假）。

4. "Kill two birds with one stone." means:

A. a stone's throw.

B. the Stone Age.

C. a heart of stone.

D. solve two problems at one time with a single action.

问题："用一块石头打死两只鸟"的意思是什么？
答案：D.一箭双雕。

短语 kill two birds with one stone 是个成语，与中国的成语"一箭双雕"异曲同工，意为 solve two problems at one time with a single action（用一个方法同时解决两个问题）。其他的答案是：a stone's throw（一石之遥/短距离）。The beach is only a stone's throw away from my house.（海滩离我家很近。）The Stone Age 意为石器时代。a heart of stone 指一颗石头的心，铁石心肠：Her love is enough to melt a heart of stone.（她的爱足以软化铁石心肠。）与鸟有关的用语还有：birds of a feather（一丘之貉）、flock together（物以类聚）。The early bird catches the worm.（早起的鸟儿有虫吃/一分耕耘，一分收获）。A bird in hand is worth two in the bush.（一只鸟在手胜过在丛林中的两只：到手的东西更有价值/天上仙鹤不如手中麻雀）。A little bird told me.（一只小鸟告诉我——这个句子意味着说话人不想让你知道是谁告诉他的。）a bird's eye-view of the city（全城的鸟瞰/全景图）。常见的鸟类有：swallow（燕子）、sparrow（麻雀）、magpie（喜鹊）、thrush（画眉）、robin（知更鸟）、peacock（孔雀）、

parrot（鹦鹉）、pigeon/dove（鸽子）、owl（猫头鹰）、woodpecker（啄木鸟）、eagle/hawk（老鹰/鹰）、crow（乌鸦）、pheasant（野鸡）、wild duck（野鸭）、crane（鹤）、egrets（鹭鸶）、swan（天鹅）。其他：feather（羽毛）、claw（爪）、wing（翅膀）、birdcage（鸟笼）。

5. "The kid seems like a puppy with two tails." It indicates that the kid ____.

A. is very happy.

B. likes dogs.

C. is a lucky dog.

D. likes to play with puppies.

问题："这个孩子像个有两条尾巴的小狗。"
这句话的意思是这个孩子____。

答案：A. 非常高兴。

短语a puppy with two tails（两条尾巴的小狗）是个俚语，表示高兴极了。表示玩得高兴的词语有：have a good time（玩得很痛快）、enjoy every minute of it（享受了每一刻）、joyful（快乐）、entertaining（有趣）。其他答案：lucky dog（幸运儿）、likes to play with puppies（喜欢和小狗玩）、likes dogs（喜欢狗）。与tails有关的词句有：I can't tell heads or tails of her.（我看不懂她。）tuck your tail between your legs（夹紧尾巴做人）：Behave yourself and tuck your tail between your legs.（检点一些，要夹紧尾巴做人。）Frank came back with his tail between his legs.（Frank垂头丧气地回来了。）heads or tails（头或尾巴/正面或反面）。通常是在两者之间做出选择的时候，掷硬币（toss a coin/flip a coin）来决定。比赛时裁判会说，Let's just flip a coin to decide who plays first. Do you want heads or tails?（我们来掷硬币决定谁开球。你要正面还是反面？）每个参与的人选择硬币的一面，即"头"和"尾"，朝上那一方被认为是获胜者。

6. The meaning of "pulling someone's leg" is___.

A. teasing somebody.

B. get in a fight.

C. stretch the legs.

D. bullying someone.

问题：英语中，"拉某人的腿"的意思是什么？

答案：A. 开个玩笑。

　　短语pulling someone's leg不是中文中"拖后腿（hold back/hinder）"的意思，也不是打架（get in the fight）中拖对方的腿的意思，而是说开个玩笑（teasing/joking/fooling）。其他表示开玩笑、取笑等的表达有kidding：I'm not kidding, Eric. Ashley got 2400 in SAT（Eric、我是说真的，阿什利的SAT得了满分。）crack（tell）a joke（说笑话）：Frank cracked a joke to lighten a tense conversation.（弗兰克讲了个笑话来缓解谈话的紧张气氛。）play a trick（捉弄）：The boys hid Jone's iPhone to play a trick on him.（孩子们把乔恩的苹果手机藏起来捉弄他。）make fun of someone 是取笑某人：It was miserable of you to make fun of the disabled.（你取笑残疾人，这是可耻的。）tease 也有取笑捉弄的意思：Jack is a tease, ignore him.（对杰克爱捉弄人别搭理他。）leg 还用在一些习惯语中：stretch legs（放松）：We stopped at the next station and got out the bus to stretch our legs.（我们在下一站停下来，下车活动活动腿脚。）on one's last legs—extremely tied, close to collapsing（累极了）：After moving furniture all day they are on their last legs.（搬了一天家具他们都累瘫了。）Fresh legs, I know it's not the job for you, but at least you can use it to get your foot in the door.（新来的，我知道这对你来说不是一份理想的工作，但至少你入门了。）It's difficult to get a foot in the door of mobile business.（加入移动电话行业是很难的。）其他与脚有关的词语有：She would clean the kitchen from top to toe（bottom）.（她会把厨房彻底打扫一下。）The X-ray results show that Jim's only a minor ankle sprain without friction.（X—光照片结果表明，吉姆的脚踝只是轻微的扭伤没有骨折。）常用词还有：instep（脚背）、thigh（大腿）、foot cramps（脚抽筋）、foot print（脚印）、athlete's foot（脚气）。bullying someone意为欺辱某人。

7. "He opened a can of worms." means:

A. He is in hot water.

B. He did something to cause a future trouble.

C. He likes animals.

D. He is very naughty.

问题："他开了一罐蠕虫"的意思是：

答案：B. 他造成了很多的麻烦。

短语opened a can of worm是个成语，意思就是如果你打开一罐蠕虫/蚯蚓，这将导致很多问题，即可能会造成更多的麻烦（cause a future trouble），所以答案是B。麻烦（trouble）一词有不少用法。These guys have the freedom to make trouble all over the place without fear of punishment.（这伙人可以肆意到处惹是生非，而不用担心受到惩罚。）He is a trouble maker.（他是个捣蛋鬼。）Never trouble trouble till trouble troubles you.（不要自找麻烦。）其他的答案中，He is in hot water.是个暗喻，意思是他有麻烦了（in trouble），而不是说他在泡热水澡。泡热水澡的英语是take a hot tub/buddle bath。He screwed up.（他搞砸了。）He likes animals.（他喜欢动物。）He is very naughty.（他很调皮。）常见的昆虫（insects）有：bees（蜜蜂）—as busy as a bee（忙如蜜蜂）、wasps（黄蜂）、bugs（臭虫）、lady bugs（瓢虫）、computer bugs（计算机错误）、firefly（萤火虫）、mosquitoes（蚊子）、flies（苍蝇）、beetle（甲虫）、cockroach（蟑螂）、spider（蜘蛛）、butterfly（蝴蝶）、snail（蜗牛）、locust（蝗虫）、grasshopper（蚱蜢）。Japanese beetles（日本甲虫）在美国很疯狂，像蝗虫一样，有时几天时间可以将住宅周围的花草树叶一扫而光，很有破坏性。

8. "Once in a blue moon" means:

A. a full moon.

B. a half moon.

C. moon eclipse.

D. a rare chance.

问题："Once in a blue moon"是什么意思？

答案：D. 千载难逢的好机会。

短语 once in a blue moon 是稀有、稀少（very rare）的意思。I saw him drinking once in a blue moon.（我几乎没见到他喝过酒。）Here comes a rare chance to appreciate the trio Tenors!（千载难逢的好机会！快来欣赏三大男高音。）There's still a（little）slim chance that he may become a mayor.（他仍然有一丝希望当上市长。）LA Lakers would have a fat chance（no chance）beating the stronger Golden State Warriors.（洛杉矶湖人队不太可能击败实力更强的金州勇士队。）by chance（碰运气）：Life gets better not by chance, but by hard work.（生活变得美好，不是偶然，而是我们努力奋斗的结果。）The reporter of *New York Times* seized the chance to interview President Obama about this issue.（《纽约时代周刊》的记者抓住机会就这一问题采访了奥巴马总统。）The golfer blew the chance to win the PGA championship at the last hole.（那位高尔夫球员在最后一洞失去了赢得PGA锦标赛的机会。）

与月亮有关的词语有：moonlight（月光）、crescent moon（新月）、full moon（满月）、Middle Autumn Festival（中秋节）、moon cake（月饼）等。

李白的名诗：《静夜思》A Quiet Night Thought（Wikipedia）

床前明月光（Moonlight before my bed），

疑是地上霜（Perhaps frost on the ground）。

举头望明月（Lift my head and see the moon），

低头思故乡（Lower my head and pine for home）。

9. "Katherine is a pain in the neck." This sentence means:

A. She has a neck pain.

B. She causes a lot of inconvenience to others.

C. She suffers from a neck injury.

D. She has a neck problem.

问题："凯瑟琳的脖子不舒服"的意思是：

答案：B. 她给别人造成了诸多不便。

短语 a pain in the neck 是指像脖子疼那样令人讨厌的意思，与真正的脖子疼无关。与答案B的意思相同：She causes a lot of inconvenience to others.（她给别人造成了诸多不便）。She always stirs up/make trouble.（她总是惹事。）表示厌恶的同义词还有：unpleasant（令人不快）The newly painted room has an unpleasant smell.（那个新油漆的房间有股很难闻的气味。）offensive（反感）：His words were horribly offensive to the audience.（他的话语让听众非常反感。）disagreeable（讨厌）：Don't listen to him. He is a shallow, disagreeable man.（别听他的。他是个肤浅、难相处的人。）sick to one's stomach（恶心）：I felt sick to my stomach after heard the dirty language in the movie. （听到电影中这些污言秽语，我感到恶心。）distasteful（讨厌）：She found his manner distasteful. （她觉得他的举止不雅）。还有displeasing（不快）、off-putting（倒胃口）、undesirable（不可取）等。其他选项都与脖子有关：She has a neck pain. （她颈部疼痛。）She suffers from a neck injury in a car accident. （她在一次车祸中颈部受了伤。）She has a neck problem. （她脖子出了问题。）necktie/tie（领带）、necklace（项链）、bottleneck（瓶颈/受限制），也指很难解决的问题。

10. "The detective had a nice lead but ended up with a wild goose chase."This sentence means:

A. The detective did not lose the trace.

B. The detective looked after a group of geese.

C. The detective had a hopeless pursuit.

D. The detective was successful in chasing the wild geese.

问题："这位侦探有了好线索，但结果成了漫无边际地追逐大雁。"这句话的意思是：

答案：C. 侦探跟踪无望。

　　答案是The detective had a hopeless pursuit. （侦探失去了跟踪的目标。）a wild goose chase的意思是无望的追求、高不可攀的东西。其他选项的含义是：The detective did not lose the trace. （侦探没有失去跟踪目标。）The detective looked after a group of geese. （侦探在照顾一群大雁。）The detective was successful in chasing the wild geese. （侦探追逐大雁成功。）He hired a private detective in an attempt to find his losing daughter. （他雇了一名私人侦探，试图找到自己失散的女儿。）在美国有两大国家的情报机构：FBI和CIA。FBI—Federal Bureau of Investigation（联邦调查局）是美国的一个政府调查机构,专门负责调查破坏国家法律（a national law）或让国家的安全（the country's security）受到威胁的事件。FBI在美国司法部的部门管辖下运行，现兼管美国情报界、两个总检察长和国家情报部门。CIA—Central Intelligence Agency（中央情报局）是美国政府的一个平民对外情报局（foreign intelligence service），主要职责是通过人的智力（human intelligence：人际网）在世界各地收集、处理和分析国家安全的信息（gathering, processing and analyzing national security information）。与联邦调查局（FBI）相对，CIA是国内安全服务（domestic security service）机构，没有执法职能，只给国家情报总监、总统和他的内阁提供情报。9•11袭击事件（September 11 attacks）之后，美国的反恐、反间谍和刑事调查机构的力度越来越大，成立了美国国土安全部（The United States Department of Homeland Security, DHS）。其主要职责是保护美国的领土（protecting the American territory），应对恐怖分子（responding to terrorist attacks）的攻击、人为事故（man-made accidents）和自然灾害（natural disasters）等。

11. "She <u>made a detailed arrangement</u> for the visiting delegation." The underline part means_____.

A. screw up something

B. set things up

C. mess up something

D. shake things up

问题："她为来访的代表团<u>作了周密的安排</u>。"

句子中的画线部分的含义是_____。

答案：B. 把事情准备好

　　短语 set things up 的含义是将事情安排好、准备好，意思与 make an arrangement 意义相同。相似的表达有 keep things in order（井井有条）、keep things tidy（保持整洁）。而 screw up 和 mess up 的意思恰好相反，是弄糟、搞乱或打扰某人。例如：I hope Mary won't mess up this time.（但愿玛丽这次不会把事情弄砸了。）The UPS crewed up and delivered the package to a wrong address.（快递公司搞错了，把包裹送错了地址。）The boy messed up his room and his mom asked him to clean it up.（男孩把房间弄得一塌糊涂，母亲叫他将房间整理干净。）选项 D. shake things up，shake up 意为动摇，是打乱原有秩序，作出重大调整的意思。如 The slow downs in the national economy shake thing up in the heavy industry.（国民经济的放缓使重工业动荡不定。）许多动词都可以与 up 搭配构成短语动词。如 keep your chin up/to keep one's spirits high/to act brave and confident（鼓起勇气，不灰心）Keep you chin up, Helen, things will be improving.（海伦，不要气馁，情况会改善的。）The terrorists blew up the subways and causes severe casualty.（恐怖分子炸毁了地铁，造成严重的伤亡。）wrap up（圆满完成，总结，包裹）：We will wrap up this project in a week.（我们会在一个星期后完成这项计划。）To wrap up, the presenter high-lighted the three major issues she discussed in the session.（总结时，主讲人重申了她在会议中讨论的三个主要问题。）其他常见用法有：It's（The decision）up to you.（你来决定/随你的便。）相当于 ball is in your court.

12. "The Mayer of Houston is in hot water." This sentence means the Mayer is____.

A. in trouble

B. in a heated pool

C. in a hot tub

D. in a hot shower

问题："休斯敦市长在热水中"的意思是市长____。

答案：A. 有麻烦了

短语 in hot water 的意思是有麻烦了（in trouble），处于困境之中。其他答案的含义是 in a headed pool（在加热的游泳池游泳），in a hot tub（在一个热浴盆中/在洗澡），in a hot shower（在冲热水澡），take a shower/take a bath（洗淋浴）。其他与水有关的词语：waters（水域）、ice water（冰水——美国的餐厅中常喝的饮料）、water bottle/bottle water（瓶装水）、to water flowers（浇花）、fountain water（喷泉饮用水）、spring water（矿泉水）、Tap water（自来水）。She is hot. 的意思是 She is very attractive（迷人）。baby shower（迎婴派对——在孩子出生前举办的特殊派对）、take a cold shower（洗个冷水澡）、a surprisingly chilly reception（出奇冷清的招待会）。If you tell someone to take a cold shower, you mean they should do something to stop themselves thinking about sex.（如果你告诉别人洗个冷水澡，你的意思是他们应该做一些事情来阻止自己想到性。）She's clearly not interested, so why don't you just take a cold shower?（她显然不感兴趣，那么你为什么不去洗个冷水澡呢/降温？）April showers bring May flowers.（四月的雨带来五月的花。）

13. Which of the following phrases means "No matter what happened."?

A. Come up short.

B. Come what may.

C. Come away empty handed.

D. Come through.

问题："No matter what happened." 这句话的意思是什么？

答案：B. 无论发生什么事。

句子 "No matter what happened." 的意思是 "无论发生什么事"，和 come what may，no matter what/whatever 的意义相同。come up short 是没能实现自己的目标或功亏一篑。The students tried to raise $1,000 for a field trip, but they came up short.（学生计划募捐 $ 1,000，但他们没达到目标。）come away empty handed（无功而返）：Both sides held a new round of talks but went away empty-handed.（双方的代表进行了新一轮的谈判，但是毫无成果。）The robbers fled empty-handed.（抢劫犯一无所获地逃走了。）come through（度过）：The country had come through the worst of the recession.（该国已经度过了经济衰退最糟糕的时期。）与 no matter 搭配使用的例句诸如：No matter when（whenever）you come you are welcome.（随时欢迎你来访。）No matter who（whoever）did it, he is responsible for the consequence.（不管是谁干的，他都要对此负责。）No matter how the invaders come, they will be wiped out clean.（无论侵略者怎样入侵，他们必将被消灭得一干二净。）No matter where（wherever）you travel in the States, you can easily find a Starbucks.（无论你在美国何处旅行，都很容易地找到星巴克。）Taking drugs is bad for your health, no matter why people do it.（无论是为了什么，吸毒对身体都是不好的。）

14. "We are in the same boat." This sentence means:

A. on board the same ship.

B. it's time for boarding.

C. have the same boarding pass.

D. in the same situation.

问题："我们在同一条船上" 这句话的意思是：

答案：D. 处境相同。

短语 in the same boat 是处境相同或面临同样的问题（having the same problem）的意思，与中文中 "上了同一条船" 的暗喻相似。乘坐同一条船上的英语是 on board the same ship。其他的交通工具也可以用 on board，如 on board a plane（上飞机）、ship（轮船）、bus（公共汽车）、shuttle bus（往返客车）等。The speed train pulled out of the station after all passengers were on board.（所有乘客都上了车后，高速火车开出了车站。）It's time for boarding.（现在开始登机/登船）。Have your boarding pass and passport ready.（请把你的登机票和护照准备好。）Have the same boarding pass.（持有相同的登机牌。）The four astronauts on board will spend three months in space.（飞船上的 4 名宇航员将在太空中度过 3 个月。）Welcome on board Air China flight 88 to New York.（欢迎乘坐中国民航飞往纽约

的 88 号航班。）On board 也表示在或加入一个组织：Ms. Smith, welcome on board our team.（斯密斯女士，欢迎加入我们的团队。）He is serving his third term on the school board.（他第三次担任学校董事会会员。）表示船只的英语有：boat（小船）、raft（竹筏）、cruise ship（游轮）、spaceship（太空船）、warship（军舰）、submarine（潜水艇）、aircraft carrier（航母）、helicopter carrier（直升机航母）等。board 的常用法还有：room and board（吃和住）、boarding school（寄宿学校）、board of directors（董事会）、chairman of the board（董事长）、chalkboard/green board（黑板）、smart board（智能黑板）。

15. He is very easy to <u>lose his temper</u>. The underlined phrase means ___.

A. lose his cool

B. get mad

C. lose control of himself

D. lose his mind

问题：他很容易发脾气。画线的短语是什么意思？
答案：A. 失去了冷静

短语 lose one's temper 是发脾气 to become angry at someone or something 的意思，与 lose one's cool/nerve 失去了冷静意思相同。其他选项是：get mad（发疯，疯狂）。She wept with rage (strong anger).（她气哭了。）lose confidence（失去信心）、lose control of oneself（失去控制）、cool down and get a grip（冷静下来并控制住情绪）。lose his mind 是 become crazy（发疯了）的意思。例句：Taking a child on a motorbike without a helmet! Have you completely lost your mind?（骑摩托车带孩子不戴头盔，你真疯了！）其他与 lost 有关的词语还有：After graduation from high school, she lost touch with her classmates.（中学毕业后她与中学同学失去了联系。）Suffering from a stroke, the artist lost his touch.（由于中风，艺术家失去了他的创作能力。）We always lose in Los Angeles.（我在洛杉矶老是迷路。）Lost and Found（失物招领）、lose face（丢面子）、lose appetite（没有食欲）、Lost Generation（迷惘的一代——通常指在第一次世界大战期间成年的一代人）。I'm sick of having you in my face so get yourself lost!（我讨厌你在我面前晃来晃去，离我远点/别烦我）！

16. **What is the picture on the right?**

A. An apple

B. The Big Apple

C. An apple of one's eye

D. An apple a day keeps the doctor away

问题：右边的图片是什么?

答案：B. 大苹果

The Big Apple（大苹果）是纽约市的一个绰号，1920 年由约翰•J.菲茨杰拉德（一个体育作家）在纽约晨报上第一次使用。由于纽约会议及旅游局在促销活动中使用了该绰号，因而在 20 世纪 70 年代广泛流行。许多英文用语都与苹果有关，如：Her daughter is the apple of his eye.（他的女儿是他的掌上明珠。）An apple a day keeps the doctor away.（一天吃一个苹果不用看医生。）美国人在谈到两个东西截然不同（two entities that are not similar），不能相提并论时，喜欢说他们是apples and oranges（苹果和橘子）。Fred and Ted are not in the same breath! They're like apples and oranges.（Fred 和 Ted 不能同日而语! 他们就像苹果和橘子一样，完全不同。）美国人喜欢吃苹果汁（apple juice）和苹果派（apple pie）。Jack is as American as an apple pie.（杰克是个地道的美国人。）常见的水果：pear（梨）、banana（香蕉）、grape（葡萄）、cherry（樱桃）、mango（芒果）、orange（橘子）、carambola（杨桃）、pomegranate（石榴）、persimmon（柿子）、plum（李子）、apricot（杏子）、litchi（荔枝）、watermelon（西瓜）。另外，an apple of love 是西红柿（tomato）而不是爱情的果实。a bad（rotten）apple是指坏蛋。谚语：a bad apple spoils the bunch.（一个坏苹果糟蹋了一堆。）

17. **"The search for the missing girl left no stone unturned."**
   The underlined part means all except:

A. Search high and low.

B. Looked every where/every corners.

C. Tried every ways and measure.

D. Turned over all the stones.

问题：他们<u>不遗余力</u>地寻找失踪的女孩。

　　　　哪个选项与画线部分的含义不同?

答案：D. 把所有的石头都翻了过来。

短语 left no stone unturned 是个成语，表示千方百计、尽了一切努力。除了答案 D 之外，其他几个选项的含义都是全力寻找的意思。search high and low（所有的地方都找遍了）、looked everywhere/every corner（每个角落都找遍了）、tried every way and measure（用尽了所有的方法和渠道）。all out/an all-out effort 也是表示全力以赴，相当于 with all one's strength/ability/resources, not holding back（使用自己所有的力量，能力或资源，没有留一点余地）。如 They are going all out fund-raiser a success.（他们正在全力以赴使筹款获得成功。）答案中只有 turned over all the stones（把所有的石头都反过来了）的意思与画线的短语不同。与石头有关的词语有：Stone Age（石器时代）、stone cold（冰凉）。My apartment is a stone's throw from the campus.（我住的公寓离校园不远。）A rolling stone gathers no moss.（一个滚动的石头不会长出苔藓。）a rolling stone（永远停不下来的人）：Kate's lived in ten cities and she's a real rolling stone.（凯特住过十个城市，她是一个真正的滚石。）*Rolling Stone Magazine*（《滚石》），其内容包括：music reviews（音乐评论）、movie reviews（电影评论）、musical artists（音乐艺术家）、免费 MP3 音乐和流行文化（pop culture entertainers）的艺人照片。

18. "Wake up and smell the coffee."
This sentence means:

A. Stay focused and listening.

B. Pay attention to what's going on.

C. Take coffee after waking up

D. The coffee smells good.

问题："醒来后闻闻咖啡"的意思是什么？
答案：B. 要注意在发生的事情。

短语 wake up and smell the coffee 的意思是 pay attention to what's going on（认清事实，要注意在发生的事情），而不是字面的意思。与 smell 有关的短语或句子有：The coffee smells good.（咖啡的味道不错。）Everyone else in the firm lost money in the real estate deal, but Bob came out smelling like a rose.（公司里的其他人都在房地产交易赔了钱，唯有鲍勃赚了钱。）The politician survived the sex scandal smelling like a rose（to seem innocent）.（遭遇性丑闻的政治家显得很无辜。）The detective did not think it is an accident and he smelled a rat soup tonight/had a fishy smell.（今晚的汤有种鱼腥气。）smell bad/stinky（臭气熏天）：Where is the stinky smell coming from？（那股臭味是从哪里传来的？）smell blood（闻到血

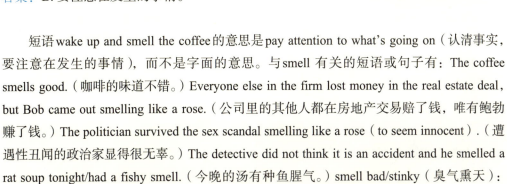

腥味）. Sharks can smell blood over a long distance.（鲨鱼隔着很远的距离仍能嗅到血腥味。）My parents warned us to stay away from drugs.（我父母告诫我们要远离毒品。）This is my business（name）card. Let's keep stay in touch.（这是我的名片，让我们保持联络。）Take coffee after waking up.（醒来后喝咖啡。）

19. **"The mayor is a very honorable man who always keeps his word." The under-lined part means all except:**

A. keeps his promise.

B. lives up to his words.

C. true to his word.

D. always forgets his word.

问题："市长是位值得尊敬的人，他总是信守诺言。"
　　与画线部分意思不同的是：
答案：D. 总是忘记他说的话。

　　短语 keep his word（信守诺言/不食言）与 keep his promises 意思相同。live up to 是不辜负的意思，如 live up to his reputation/expectation（不辜负他的名声/期待）。true to one's word（说真实的话），always forget his word（总是忘记他说的话）。与 keep 搭配的短语很多，如 keep track of something（跟踪）：As an engineer, Brooks has to keep track of the latest developments in technology.（作为一名工程师，布鲁克斯必须了解技术的最新发展动态。）keep in touch with（保持联系）：She's still keeping in touch with her ex-boy friend.（她仍旧与前男友保持着联系。）keep in mind（记住）：Keep in mind you're going to be fighting lots of terrorists.（记住你要和许多恐怖分子交手。）keep a low profile（保持低调）：Before appointed as the committee chair, Bob kept a low profile.（鲍勃在获委任为委员会主席前一直保持低调。）keep fit（保持健康）：We should work out regularly to keep fit.（我们应该经常锻炼身体以保持健康。）Congress complains about being kept in the dark about the Middle East peace talks.（国会抱怨中东和谈之事被蒙在鼓里了。）Smith managed to keep my parents in the dark about this.（史密斯设法对我的父母瞒下了此事。）Do you know how to keep a secret?（你知道如何保守秘密吗？）keep up the good work（再接再厉）、keep one cool（保持冷静）、keep an eye on（密切注视）、keep someone posted（有消息随时通报）。

20. "We should save some money for a rainy day." This sentence means:

A. Save the day.

B. Put something aside for a time of need or adversity.

C. Money talks.

D. Good save！

问题：我们应该为下雨天存点钱。这句话的意思是：

答案：B. 节省一些钱以备不时之需。

选项的意思是"我们应节省一些钱以备不时之需"，有点接近"有备无患"的意思。save 的常用短语有：save the day（解围），如 They had forgotten the knife to cut the wedding cake, but Elizabeth arrived with one and saved the day.（他们忘了带刀切结婚蛋糕，幸好伊丽莎白带了一把刀来，真是有惊无险。）谚语：A stitch in time saves nine.（小洞不补，十洞吃苦/一针不补十针难缝。）A timely effort will prevent more work later.（及时努力将减少更多的工作。）A penny saved is a penny earned（省一分钱就是赚一分钱。）save 的其他用法：save time（省时间）、save a lot of trouble（减少麻烦）、save life（救命）、Good save！（这球救得好！）、save face（保全面子）、savings account（储蓄账号）、save money（省钱）、lose money（赔钱）、Time is money.（时间就是金钱。）money talks（有钱能使鬼推磨）：The formula in entertaining business is simple—money talks.（娱乐产业的生存规则很简单，就是金钱万能。）pocket money/spending money（零钱）：Many kids spends most of their pocket money on PlayStation games.（许多孩子将大部分零花钱都用来买 PS 游戏了。）not for love or money = never/under no circumstances（无论如何）：He would not take the job, for love or money.（不管怎样他也不做这工作。）

21. "Meet someone halfway" implies:

A. make concession.

B. meet someone on the way home.

C. meet someone unexpectedly.

D. run into someone.

问题："Meet someone halfway" 的意思是什么？

答案：A. 妥协。

　　短语meet someone halfway 是妥协、让步的意思，如If you can meet us halfway, we could sign the contract.（如果你们能让一步，我们便可签协议。）make concessions也是妥协的意思。The territorial dispute was finally settled by concessions on both sides.（领土争端终于由于双方的让步而解决了。）另一个同义词是 compromise：Don't compromise your principles.（不要在原则上妥协。）其他答案：meet someone on the way home（在回家的路上遇到了某人）、meet someone unexpectedly（意外遇到某人）、run into someone（碰到某人）。meet一词的用法很多，常见的有：Nice（Glad）to meet you.（很高兴见到你。）I'd like you to meet my coach, Mr. Ma.（我想给你介绍/让你认识 我的教练，马先生。）make ends meet（维持开支）：She has three kids and barely earns enough money to make ends meet.（她有三个孩子，几乎挣不到足够的钱以维持开支。）meet one's expectation（满足自己的期望）：The best way to meet the customers' expectation is to improve the quality of our products.（为满足客户的期望，最好的办法就是提高我们产品的质量。）meet the requirements（符合要求）：Most high school seniors in the district met the college requirements.（大部分高中毕业班的学生达到了读大学的要求。）Highway 95 and Highway 295 meet in the city outskirts.（95 号公路和 295 号公路在城市郊外相交。）

22. "Told you so!" means:

A. You forgot what I told you!

B. Did you hear what I said?

C. I already warned you that it would happen!

D. I don't tell you again!

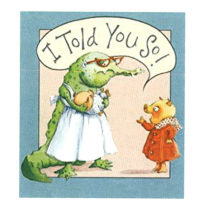

问题："Told you so! "这句话的意思是什么？

答案：C. 已经警告你那个事件会发生的。

　　句子"Told you so!"是"I hate to say I told you so."的原句，意思是说"You were already warned that a certain event would happen."（已经警告你那个事件会发生的。），与"See, I was right!"（瞧，我说对了吧！）的含义相近。在美国报道天气时，常发出大风警报（typhoon warning）、龙卷风警报（hurricane warning）、海啸警报（tsunami warning）、大雾警报（fog warning）、山火警报（wild fire warning）、洪水警报（flood warning）等。Emergency alert, flash flood warning this area till 3pm EST this afternoon. Avoid flood areas.（紧急警报，山洪警报在这个区域将持续到美国东部今天下午 3 点为止，避免去洪灾地区。）Amber Alert（安珀警报）是美国和加拿大在发生绑架小孩（abduction of a child）事件时，通过商业电台（commercial radio）、手机通知公众，希望协助的紧急通知。其他答案的选择是：Did you hear what I said?（你没有听我说的吗？）You forgot what I told you!（你忘记我告诉你的事了。）I don't tell you again!（我不会再说一遍！）"Don't ask, don't tell（DADT）!"（不问，不说）是美国官方对同性恋者（homosexual）在军中服役的政策，政策禁止军事人员歧视（discriminating）或骚扰（harassing）未公开的同性或双性（bisexual）服务人员或申请人，同时禁止公开的男同性恋（gay）、女同性恋（lesbian）或双性恋（bisexual）服兵役（military service）。

23. The phrase "leave him alone!" means:

A. Stop bothering him.

B. Let him stay at home by himself.

C. Let him do it by himself.

D. Let's get out of here.

问题："让他一个人待着！"这个短语的意思是：

答案：A. 不要烦他。

句子"Leave him alone."是"不要烦他，别缠着他"，即 stop bothering him 的意思。同样的说法有：Don't bother me!（别吵我！）Leave me alone!（别烦我！）其他选项：Let him stay at home by himself.（让他一人留在家里。）Let him to do it by himself.（让他自己做好了。）Let's get out of here. Don't leave a child alone near an open fire, a pool or pond.（不要让小孩单独靠近明火、泳池或池塘。）在美国，父母让 13 岁以下的孩子独自待在家中（home alone）是违法的（illegal），一定要有成人照看。同样，出门在外时，让 13 岁以下的小孩子独自待在汽车中也是违法的。因为由于酷热和严寒的（extreme hot and cold）天气可能会对在车中小孩的身体和生命造成威胁。也有可能被坏人拐骗走（kidnap）。在家中父母也不能体罚（corporal punishment）或动手打孩子（beat child），也不能让孩子挨饿（go hungry）。一旦被发现，就要上法庭，还可能失去对孩子的监护权（lose custody of the child）或判刑（sentence）或罚款（fine）。小孩不舒服，不要给他们刮痧（scrapping），因为老师和其他美国人会把刮痧留下的痕迹误认为是受到家庭暴力和虐待（domestic violence and abuse）所造成的，很有可能因为这个把你告上法庭（file a law suit against you）。

24. "What goes around comes around" means all of the following except:

A. You will get back what you give out.

B. You get what you sow.

C. Coming and going.

D. Kindness will be rewarded.

问题：下面哪个短语与"善有善报恶有恶报"的意思不同？

答案：C. 来来往往。

句子"What goes around comes around."是个谚语，意思是"善有善报恶有恶报"或是"种善因得善果"（Kindness will be rewarded.），一报还一报（you get what you sow/you will get back what you give out）等含义。There is an old saying, what goes around comes around.（有这样一句古老的谚语，所付出的终将会回归。）

与come搭配的词语很多，How come?（怎么会呢？）I came across an old classmate in high school at a conference.（我在会议上偶然遇到了一位中学同学。）How is your paper coming along?（你的文章写得怎么样啦？）My son came down with flu.（我儿子患了流感。）Come over to join us for a BBQ party this Sunday!（这个星期天来我家参加我们的烧烤派对！）come up with（想出、提出）：Several of the board members have come up with suggestions of their own for the new school budget.（有几位董事会成员就学校新的财政计划提出了自己的建议。）

与动词go搭配的常用短语有很多。go mad/crazy（发狂）：Fortunately, I'm interested in geometry, otherwise I'd go mad.（我很庆幸自己对几何有兴趣，不然我会疯掉的。）The new student goes by Bill.（新来的学生叫比尔。）The story goes back to his childhood.（这个故事可以追溯到他的童年。）How things going?（事情进展如何？）How about go shopping this weekend?（周末去逛街怎么样？）as time goes by（时光流逝）：As time goes by my vision seems to get worse.（随着时间的流逝，我的视力似乎越来越差了。）all set to go（准备就绪）：All my bags are checked in. I believe I'm all set to go.（我的行李托运了，看来我一切都办好啦。）

25. "You can't teach an old dog new tricks."
This sentence means:

A. Old people cannot learn new things.

B. The dog is not clever enough to learn anything.

C. You are not a good teacher.

D. You are not able to train dogs.

问题："你不能教一只老狗新把戏"的意思是什么?

答案：A. 上年纪的人学不了新玩意。

句子 You can't teach an old dog new tricks 的意思是上年纪的人学不了新东西（Old people can not learn new things.），不能直译为：你无法教老狗新把戏。The dog is not clever enough to learn anything.（狗是不够聪明，学不到什么东西。）You are not a good teacher.（你不是个好老师。）You are not able to train dogs.（你不会训狗。）与狗有关的词句或短语有：lucky dog（幸运儿）、clever dog（聪明人）、live a dog's life（过着贫困的生活）、walk a dog（遛狗）、Every dog has its day.（凡人自有出头日。）与 tricks 有关的词语有：play tricks（hoax）on somebody（作弄某人）。dirty trick（使坏）。I'm in a rather tricky position.（我的处境很尴尬。）Use every trick in the book, all possible means.（使用了书中每一个技巧，用尽伎俩）。

26. Which of the following phrases means stopping a phone conversation?

A. Hang in there.

B. Hang on.

C. Hang out.

D. Hang up.

问题：下列哪个短语的意思是结束电话谈话?

答案：D. 挂断电话。

动词 hang 可与许多介词搭配，挂断电话是用 hang up，如 It's not clear. Hang up and I will call you back again.（声音不清楚。挂掉电话我再打过来。）打电话的常用语有：Hello, May I speak/talk to Professor Smith? This is he（she）speaking.（你好，我可以和史密斯教授谈谈吗? 我就是。）Sorry, Rick is not here right now. Do you want to leave a message?（对不

起，瑞克现在不在。你想留个口信吗？）Sorry, Michelle stepped out of the office, please call back in half an hour.（对不起，米歇尔刚走出办公室，请在半小时后再打回来。）Hello, this is Admission office. What can I help you?（这是招生办。我能帮你什么吗？）Hold on, John is on another line and will talk to you shortly.（请不要挂线，约翰在另一条线上，很快就会和你说话了。）美国人爱用留言电话，你会常听到这样的留言：This is Dr. Smith's office. I am sorry. I am not able to pick up the phone. Please leave me a message. I will get back to you as soon as possible.（这是史密斯博士的办公室。对不起。我现在无法接电话。请给我留言，我会尽快回复你。）Sorry, Dr. Smith is not available please leave a message after the tone.（对不起，史密斯博士不在，请听到铃响后留言。）在听到以上电话录音的时候，一定要留言。在很多情况下，你要找的人在家，只是不想接不熟悉的电话号码。你留言通报姓名后，他很可能就会接你的电话。留言时可以这样说：This is Jennifer Wong. I'd like to talk to Dr. Smith about my project. Please call me at 609-777-1234 at your convenience. Thanks. Have a nice day.（我是Jennifer Wong。我想和史密斯博士谈谈我的项目。请在您方便的时候给我打电话。我的号码是609-777-1234。谢谢。祝你今天愉快。）其他的常用搭配有：hang in there（挺下去，坚持下去）hang on（紧紧抓出/坚持）。Jimmy always hangs out with Amy.（Jimmy总是和Amy出去玩。）Some jobless youth hang around the street corner all day long.（一些没有工作的年轻人整天在街头闲荡。）hang by a threat（千钧一发）。hang本身也有很多含义，如hangers（衣架），hang certain（挂窗帘），The murderer was hanged.（杀人犯被处绞刑。）。

27. "Don't count your chickens before they hatch." means:

A. Don't rely on something before you are positive and sure that it will happen.
B. Not all chicken eggs hatch.
C. Be patient when hatch your chickens.
D. It is difficult to count chickens.

问题："不要在鸡还没有孵出来之前就去数。"这句话的意思是什么？
答案：A. 事情没有完全确定之前不要急着做决定。

Don't count your chickens before they hatch. 的意思是 Don't rely on something before you are positive and sure that it will happen.（事情没有完全确定之前不要急着做决定。）其他答案的意思是：Not all chicken eggs will hatch.（不是所有的鸡蛋都会被孵化出来。）Be patient when you hatch your chickens.（当你孵小鸡时要有耐心。）It is hard to count chickens.（鸡很难计数。）下结论的其他表达还有：find a quick conclusion（找到一个快速的结论）、draw/come a conclusion（得出结论）、in conclusion（结论是）。hatch（孵化）：A huge number of sea turtles have hatched (out) on Jersey shore.（大批的小海龟在新泽西海滩上破壳而出。）急躁的表达有：inpatient（急躁）、shot tempered（心急）、impetuous（毛躁、浮躁、急躁）、rash（草率、鲁莽）。耐心的表达有：patient（耐心）、calm down（别急躁）、cool down（冷静）、chill out（冷静下来）、sit tight（耐心）：Just sit tight and everything will turn out well.（耐心等着，一切都会好转的。）More haste less speed./Haste makes waster.（欲速而不达。）

28. "Her father had to work three jobs to <u>make ends meet</u>." The underlined phrase means:

A. make something from scratch.

B. buy a house.

C. make a good life.

D. live from hand to mouth.

问题："她的父亲不得不打三份工来达到<u>收支平衡</u>。"
　　　画线的短语是什么意思？
答案：D. 收支平衡。

　　　短语make（both）ends meet是个成语，表示收支平衡，即to earn and spend equal amounts of money的意思，也就是说挣的钱仅够你必须支付的。所以答案是D. Live from hand to mouth（生活只能糊口）。其他选项的意思是：make something（start）from scratch（从头开始）、buy a house（购房）、make a good life（生活富足）。人身体的部分常用来丰富语言的表达，如keep your mouth shut / keep silent（保持沉默）。Don't tell Nancy any secret —she's got a big mouth.（别告诉南希任何秘密，她是个大嘴巴。）Watch your mouth/tongue/language. Do you know who you're talking to?（说话客气一点。你知道你在跟谁说话吗？）hand这个字的用法尤其多：caught red handed（当场抓获/人赃俱获）：The armed robber were caught red-handed.（抢劫犯在一家商场被当场逮到了。）get out of hand（control）（一发不可收）：The air pollution got out of hand in many major cities in China and their vicinities.（空气污染在许多中国的大城市及其附近地区到了无法控制的地步。）hand in（上交）、hand out（发给）、handout（讲义）、hand over（拱手）、an old hand（老手）、a green hand（新手）、have a big hand（鼓掌）、made by hand（手工制作）、hand in hand（携手并进）、hand off（别碰）、in good hand（受到照顾）、hand stand（倒立）、on the other hand（其他方面）、a handful of（几个）、raise your hand（请举手）、hand-up（举手）、left handed（左撇手）、hand-on activity（动手的活动）等。

29. Which of the following means <u>have a day off</u> ?

A. Off the air

B. Off duty

C. Off the hook

D. Off the top of one's head

问题：下列哪个短语的意思是有一天休息？

答案：B. 休班

　　短语off duty的意思是下班/休班，off the air（电台、电视台的停播）：Many radio station go off the air after midnight.（很多广播电台后半夜停止广播。）off the hook（解脱，逃脱）：Richard counted on his friends to get him off the hook.（理查德指望朋友们帮他摆脱困境。）off the hook（是电话没有挂好的意思）：Jack left the phone off the hook so that he wouldn't be disturbed.（杰克不把电话挂上，以免受到干扰。）off the top of one's head（不假思索）：Off the top of my head., I can only name about three female plliticians.（要我马上说的话，我大概只能说出三个左右的女政治家的名字。）a head start（先拔头筹/良好开端）：A good early childhood education gives your child a head start in life.（良好的幼儿教育会让你的孩子在人生中比别人领先一步。）from head to toe（从头到脚）：She coated herself from head to toe with sun lotion.（她给自己从头到脚都抹上了强效防紫外线晒露。）Stop daydreaming! Get your head out of the clouds and watch while you are driving!（别做白日梦了！当你在开车的时候，别想胡思乱想，好好看路。）Put heads together.（一起想办法。）He laughed his head off when he read the letter.（当他看那封信的时候，他狂笑不止。）

30. "The corrupt officer was put in jail for 10 years. <u>Serves him right!</u>" The underlined sentence means:

A. He did it right.

B. He deserves it.

C. He received a good service.

D. He did not do his service.

问题："那个腐败官员被判10年监禁。<u>活该！</u>"画线部分的意思是什么？

答案：B. 他罪有应得。

句子 Serves him right!（罪有应得，活该！），与 "He deserves it." 的意思相同。其他选项 He did it right.（他做得对。）He received a good service.（他得到了很好的服务。）He did not do his service.（他没有尽他的职责。）First come first served.（先到先得）这个说法是很古老了，第一次使用是在 1545 年。另一个相似的谚语是 "早起的鸟儿有虫吃"（Early bird gets the worm）。in jail/prison/jailhouse（监禁/在狱中），相关表述还有 put behind the bar（判监禁）、sentence to jail time、lock up（关起来）、serve jail time/term（坐牢/服狱）、get out of jail（出狱）、bail someone out of jail（给人保释出狱）：My friend, John was in jail. I had to go down to the police station with some cash to bail him out.（我的朋友约翰在监狱里。我只好带了一些现金去警察局将他保释出来。）serve the purposes of（为宗旨）：Well, it isn't a very pretty car, but it should serve the purposes of our mission.（嗯，这不是一个很漂亮的车，但它应该能帮我们达到目的。）But mom, I want a smartphone!（妈妈，我要一个智能手机！）Nonsense, the cell phone you have serves the purpose just fine.（胡说，你的手机就够用啦。）

31. "<u>Take it easy</u>! Everything will be fine."
Which is the opposite of the underlined part?

A. Calm down!

B. Got on your nerves!

C. Chill out!

D. Relax!

问题："<u>放松些</u>！一切都会好的。"

哪个选项和画线部分的意思相反？

答案：B. 使你心烦意乱！

句子 Take it easy!（慢慢来）和 Relax!（放松些！）的意思相似。calm down 和 chill out/cool off 同义，都是 "冷静下来" 的意思。keep cool/calm（保持冷静）。唯有 get on your nerves（使你心烦意乱/神经紧张）的意思与 take it easy 相反。例句：She got (took) a lot of nerve to speak at the graduation.（她够胆大，敢在毕业典礼上作演讲。）He is always nervous before an exam or interview.（在考试或面试时他总是很紧张。）与 easy 搭配的短语有 as easy as pie: My brother is very handy. He won't have any problems assembling your new bike—it's as easy as pie.（我哥哥手很巧。他给你组装的新自行车不会有任何问题——对他来说太容易了。）easy money（快钱，赚钱容易）。Winning the lottery, that's easy money!（买彩票中大奖，那是轻松赚钱！）easy come, easy go（来得容易去得快，来也匆匆，去也匆匆）：Readily won and readily lost. Easy come, easy go, that's how it works in the stock market. (股市上就是这样来得容易去得快。) I'm easy (to please). (我很随和/很容易满足。) I am not particular. (我不挑剔。) Tom, do you care if we get a sausage pizza rather than mushroom? (汤姆，我们点一个腊肠比萨而不是蘑菇比萨，你说好吗？) Fine with me (That's okay with me.). I'm easy. (我不在乎，随便。)

32. "Put up a good fight." means:

A. fight for a good cause.

B. try hard against a stronger opponent.

C. fight a losing battle.

D. a dogfight.

问题：" Put up a good fight." 这句话的意思是什么?

答案：B. 努力对抗更强的对手。

短语 put up a good fight 意为 try hard against a stronger opponent (努力对抗更强的对手)。其他选项的意思是：fight for a good cause/justice (为正义而战), fight a losing battle/tried but failed (打一场必败/毫无希望之仗/尝试但失败了)。For years it seems many countries in Africa have been fighting a losing battle against poverty and hunger. (多年来，非洲很多国家似乎一直在打一场抗贫困和饥饿败仗。) The two gangs got into a street fight. (两大帮派在街头斗殴。) an uphill battle/fight/struggle (一场艰苦的战斗)：Environmentalists face an uphill battle/fight convincing people to use their cars less to reduce air pollution. (环保人士面临一场苦斗来说服人们少使用汽车以减少空气污染。) be fighting for your life (求生存)：One of the passengers was fighting for her life last night after a car collision. (一乘客在昨晚的车碰撞后多处受伤，她与死神作战求生存。) You can't fight City Hall. (你打不赢市政府/你无法抗拒市政府), 这个句子的意思是 There is no way to win in a battle against a bureaucracy. (没有办法在反对官僚主义的战斗中取胜。) I won't give up without a fight. (我不会轻易放弃/束手就擒。) Don't give up easily. (不要轻易放弃。) 其他有关的词语：fighting spirit (斗志)、cockfighting (斗鸡)、bullfight (斗牛)、battlefield (战场)、fighter (战斗机，斗士)、dogfight (空战/搏斗)。

33. "In the long run" it is good for your health.
The quoted phrase means:

A. in the end.

B. a long distance.

C. run for a long time.

D. run a Marathon.

问题："从长远看"，这有利于你的健康。引用部分短语的意思是什么？

答案：A. 最后，最终。

短语in the long run（长远来说）与in the end（最后）同义。其他选项的意思是：a long distance（很长的距离）、run for a long time（跑了很长一段时间）、run a Marathon（跑马拉松）。与run 有关的词句还有：The runner-up of the US beauty pageant is Miss Florida.（美国选美比赛的第二名是佛罗里达小姐。）Hillary is running for president.（希拉里在竞选总统。）The bullet train runs between Beijing and Shanghai.（高速列车运行于北京和上海之间。）We ran out of gas.（我们的车没有油了。）We are running a bit late.（我们迟了一点。）Still waters run deep.（宁静的人往往思维缜密。）ran short of manpower（人手不够）：The insurance company ran short of manpower.（保险公司人手短缺。）run into a stone/brick wall（碰上了（砖）墙/遇到难以逾越的屏障）：Allan ran into a brick wall in learnning a foreign language.（艾伦在学习外语中遇到大难题了。）run into someone（巧遇某人）：I ran into Mike, my high school classmate, on seventh avenue.（我在第七大道上碰到了我的高中同学迈克。）其他词：running water（自来水）、running mate（竞选伙伴）、run away（逃跑）、runner（跑步的人）、a boy with running nose（流鼻涕的男孩）。

34. "That's my final offer. Take it or leave it."
The underlined part means:

A. take something or someone for granted.

B. take its toll.

C. take this one or none.

D. take chances.

问题："这是我的最终报价。要么接受，要么拉倒。"画线部分的意思是什么？

答案：C. 没有选择。

短语take it or leave it是没有选择，即take this one or none / have no choice的意思，有选择是have chances / choices。take chances（冒险）：Never take chances.（不应冒险。）take something for granted（认为某事是理所当然的），比如说有人帮助了你而你没有表示感激，往往是因为他们经常帮助你。Don't take for granted the love that she has for you.（她对你的爱视为理所当然）。take one's toll to sb意思是对某人造成伤害，例句：Their separation takes its/a toll to their children.（他们的离异对他们的子女造成了伤害和痛苦。）take一词的用法实在太多，不可能逐个列举，常用的有：take turns（轮流）：Sue and her brother take turns（at）doing the dishes and laundry.（苏珊和她的兄弟轮流洗盘子和洗衣。）take place（发生）：Presidential Elections will now take place on November the forth.（总统选举现定于11月4号举行。）take advantage of（充分利用）：Take advantage of of low-season airfares to Hawaii.（利用淡季廉价飞机票去夏威夷。）take off（起飞，腾飞）：The decades of 1980-2010 witnessed China's economy taking-off.（1980至2010年是中国工业快速发展的30年。）never take no for an answer（不轻言放弃）：Hillary is iron lady forceful, aggressive, unwilling to take no for an answer.（希拉里是个女强人，强硬决断，咄咄逼人，不达目的誓不罢休。）take a big/deep breath（做一个深呼吸）、take a bath / shower / break（洗澡/淋浴/休息）、take charge（负责）、take notes（做笔记）、take care of（照顾）、take one's life（自尽）、take back（收回）、take a sick leave（请病假）。

35. There's no such thing as _____.

A. a free press

B. a free lunch

C. a free college education

D. free of charge

问题：句子"There is no such thing as"后接什么？
答案：B. 免费的午餐

　　答案B.There is no such thing as a free lunch.（天下没有免费的午餐。）是一句流行的格言（adage/saying/proverb），表示任何获得都是有代价的。It is impossible to get something for nothing.（不可能不劳而获。）当然，美国中小学给家庭生活困难的儿童发放免费的午餐（free lunch）是个例外。美国实行幼儿园至高中的免费教育（free education）其实也不是真正的免费，学校的大部分费用都是来自每个家庭交的地税（property tax）。business lunch（商务午餐），指一边吃一边谈工作的午餐。lunch hour是美国的午间就餐和休息时间，一般为 12 点至 13 点。free of charge（免费）：All the immigration forms are available online free of charge for downloading.（所有移民表格可在网上免费下载。）Holiday Inn offers free WIFI，free parking and complimentary continental breakfast.（假日酒店提供免费WIFI上网，免费停车场和免费的简便早餐。）I got two concert tickets for free.（我有两张免费的音乐会门票。）Please feel free to contact me.（请随时与我联系。）free press/no government censorship（新闻自由/无政府的审查）。People should enjoy freedom of speech，press，religion.（人们应该享有言论自由、新闻自由和宗教自由。）freedom的同义词是liberty，在纽约的自由女神像叫Statue of Liberty。I took the liberty of writing this letter to you.（我冒昧地给您写了这封信。）

36. Which of the following idioms means you use all your strength in doing something?

A. All over.

B. All out.

C. All right.

D. All of a sudden.

问题：下列哪个俗语的意思是你竭尽全力做某件事？

答案：B. 全力以赴。

短语All out、use、all strength and efforts意为全力以赴、竭尽全力。例句：They went all out to complete the project by next Friday.（他们全力以赴，赶在下周五之前完成这个项目。）all over（遍地、到处）：I looked all over but could not find it. 意思相同的短语还有：everywhere、everyplace、far and wide、high and low、throughout。all of a sudden/all in once（突然）、all right（好吧）。与all 搭配的短语还有：all time（所有的时间）、not all there（不是所有的在那里）、all around（全面、全能）：Michael won all around（AA）State champion in Gymnastics.（迈克尔赢得了州体操全能冠军。）all the same（即便如此）：Thank you all the same.（同样感谢！）All night long/throughout the whole night：I couldn't sleep all night long.（我昼夜不眠。）by all means（当然、务必、绝对）：Emergency room doctors are tying by all means to save the dying.（急诊室的医生采用一切手段试图抢救那个垂危的病人。）all year round（全年）：The public in-door swimming pool can be used all year round.（公共室内游泳池可全年使用。）

37. "She was fed up with her sister."
The sentence means the following except:

A. She was bothered by her sister.

B. She was annoyed by her sister.

C. She was tired of her sister.

D. She fed her sister.

问题："她厌烦她的妹妹。"下列哪句话不是这个意思？

答案：D. 她喂她的妹妹。

　　句子 She was fed up by her sister.（她厌烦她的妹妹。）与其意思相近的选项有：选项 A. She was bothered by her sister.（她被她的妹妹困扰着。）选项 B. She was annoyed by her sister.（她让妹妹给惹恼了。）选项 C. She was tired of her sister.（她厌倦了她的妹妹。）其他打交道方面的用语有：She had a hard time to deal with（cope with）her sister.（她很难与她的妹妹打交道。）He is annoying/irritating.（他烦死人了。）I am busy with my assignment, don't bother me.（我在忙着赶作业，别吵我。）用 "Sorry to bother you." 比用 "Excuse me." 更客气一些。Sorry for the trouble.（打扰/麻烦了。）It's no bother（trouble）at all.（一点不麻烦。）与人交谈中，没有听清对方的话时，也可以用 "Pardon me." 或 "Pardon?" 或 "Excuse me." 相当于 "I did not hear you clearly, please repeat." 或 "Say it again, please."（我没有听清，请重复。）在就餐和开会之中要离开一会，如上卫生间时，应该说 "Excuse me."。请别人原谅时，"Forgive me." 比 "Excuse me." "Pardon me." 更显诚意。There is no excuse for his absence.（他的缺席没有任何借口。）

38. "She is in love with an actor."Which of the
following does not match to the underlined?

A. She fell in love with an actor.

B. She developed a romantic relationship with the actor.

C. She lost her heart to the actor.

D. She is married to the actor.

问题："她和那个演员相爱了。"下列哪个选项和画线部分意思不同？

答案：D. 她嫁给了这位演员。

选项 A、B、C 都是说她在热恋一位演员。She fell in love with an actor.（她爱上了一名演员。）Mary says she'll never have a crush on anyone again.（玛丽说她再也不会迷恋任何人了。）She developed a romantic relationship with the actor.（她与男演员发展了浪漫的关系。）She lost her heart to the actor.（她的心给了这位演员。）与爱情和婚姻（marriage）有关的用语：girl friend/boy friend（女友/男友）、lover（情人）、bride/bridegroom（新娘/新郎）、husband and wife（夫妻）、your better half（尊夫人/先生）、ex-husband/ex-wife（前夫/前妻）、cohabit/live together（同居）、have a（love）relation/a relationship with（与某人有恋情）、have a fair with（婚外情）、propose a marriage（求婚）、engaged（订婚）、get married（结婚）、walk down the aisle（结婚、步入婚姻的殿堂）、divorce（离婚）、Their wedding took place in church.（他们的婚礼在教堂举行。）attend wedding（banquet）（参加婚宴/喝喜酒）、wedding anniversary（结婚周年纪念日）、marriage certificate（结婚证书）。婚誓：

I,（Bride/Groom）, take you（Groom/Bride）, to be my（wife/husband）, to have and to hold from this day forward, for better or for worse, for richer, for poorer, in sickness and in health, to love and to cherish; from this day forward until death do us part. Do you take＿＿ as your wife/husband?（bride/bridegroom）I do. I now pronounce you Husband and Wife! You may now kiss the bride!

我（新娘/新郎）嫁/娶你（新郎/新娘）为我的（妻子/丈夫），从今日开始，无论是好还是坏，家境贫富，生病和健康，从今天直到死亡我们恩爱和珍惜永不分开。你愿意取/嫁给＿＿为你的妻子/丈夫吗？（新娘/新郎）我愿意。我现在宣布你们成为夫妻！现在你可以亲吻新娘了！

39. Which of the following is not a curse word?

A. You son of a bitch.

B. Fuck you.

C. Thank goodness.

D. An asshole.

问题：下列哪句不是骂人的话？
答案：C. 谢天谢地。

答案 C.Thank goodness. 这句话比用 Thank God. 要委婉些，来得没那么冲动，不是骂人的话。Thank goodness, it is Friday.（谢天谢地，终于到礼拜五了。）英语中有不少骂人的粗痞话，不应该学，但应该知道他们的含义。You son of a bitch.（狗娘养的东西/王八蛋。）Fuck you（去你妈的）。做爱（make love/sexual intercourse）也常被称作 F word. Holy

Fuck 与 Holy shit（狗屎）的意思相同，都是来表达愤怒、轻蔑、厌恶或惊异"礼仪亵渎"。Bull shit（狗屁），即 nonsense（胡说八道）。He is a piece of shit.（他是一块狗屎。）Her boy friend is an asshole.（她的男朋友是个大混蛋。）Kick your ass（butt）.（打败你，揍你/踢你的屁股。）Go to hell!（见鬼去吧！）Damn it!（真该死！糟糕！）I'm pissed off！（我气死了！）Shame on you!（你真丢脸！）What a shame.（多可惜，多可耻。）常用来表达惊讶的口头语有：Holy crap!（哇！）Wow!（噢！）Oh, my gosh!（我的天！）

40. The lady was <u>under house arrest</u>. The underlined phrase means:

A. lost freedom.

B. have a vacation.

C. not allowed to leave her home.

D. placed under arrest.

问题：这位女士"under house arrest"。画线部分短语的意思是什么？

答案：C. 不准离开她的家（软禁）。

  答案 C.not allowed to leave her home（不准离开她的家）是 under house arrest（软禁）的意思。under arrest/placed under arrest/take into custody（逮捕）：The main opposition leaders were either arrested or placed under house arrest.（反对派的主要领导人都遭到了逮捕或软禁。）The authorities will arrest any suspects.（当局将逮捕所有的疑犯。）put the criminal in jail/behind bars（把罪犯关入监牢）：He was sentenced（判刑）to twenty years behind bars after being convicted for armed robbery.（他被认定犯武装抢劫罪，判二十年监禁。）与法律有关的词语还有：bail（保释金）、subpoena（传票）、search warrant（搜查证）、appeals（上诉）、court（法庭）、judge（法官）、prosecutor（检察官）、case（案件）、lawyer（律师）、private detective（私人侦探）、jury（陪审团）、witness（证人）、the suspect（嫌疑犯/犯罪嫌疑人）、evidence（罪证）、booty（赃物）、lethal（致命）、weapon（凶器）、guilt/guilty（有罪）、innocent（无罪的）、compensation（索赔/赔偿金）。例句：The jury determined that the murder suspect convicted of three counts.（陪审团判定谋杀嫌疑犯三项罪名成立。）He is guilty of child abuse.（他犯虐待儿童罪）。打官司的英语：file a lawsuit against（对某某提起诉讼）、go to court/appear in court（出庭）、litigate/litigation（诉讼）、handcuffs（手铐）。选项 B.having a vacation 意为在度假。

41. "Do you want to go see the new movie?" "I guess so."
Which is not the meaning of the underlined part?

A. I think so.

B. I believe so.

C. I suppose.

D. I hope so.

问题：“你想去看那部新电影吗？”“我想是的。”哪个选项和画线部分的意思不同？

答案：D. 我希望如此。

句子 I guess so. 是回答 Yes（是）的一个模糊的方式（a vague way），表示有可能性（probably or possibly）但不想用 Yes 时，用 I guess so / I think so / I believe so.（我相信是这样。）如，Bob：I guess it's going to rain. Bill：Oh, I don't know. Maybe so, maybe not.（鲍勃：我想这是要下雨了。比尔：哦，我不知道。也许是这样，也许不是。）表示一种假设的短语还有：I suppose（我想）、I suspect（我怀疑）。通常在讲话时，suppose 说成 spose，suspect 说成 spect。John：You want some more coffee? Jane：I spose. Alice：Ready to go? John：I spect. I hope so。（约翰：你想要一些咖啡吗？简：可以。爱丽丝：准备好了吗？约翰：我希望如此/但愿如此。）与搭配相关的词组还有：in the hope of（希望，为了）：Emily returned to the college in the hope of finishing her degree.（艾米丽为完成学业回到了学校）。give up（all）hope（绝望）：The climbers had given up all hope when a miracle happened.（攀登者们放弃所有的希望时，奇迹发生了。）Never give up hope. There's always a chance.（绝不要放弃希望。总是有机会的。）Hope for the best and prepare for（expect）the worst.（抱最好的希望，做最坏的准备。）

42. Which of the phrases means
"a long evening of fun"?

A. Paint the town red.

B. Burn the house down.

C. An overnight party.

D. Had too much to drink.

问题：下列哪个短语的意思是“a long evening of fun”？

答案：A. 痛快地玩了一个晚上。

短语paint the town red是个成语，意思是to go out and enjoy yourself in the evening（晚上出去，享受自己），经常是喝大量的酒和跳舞（often drinking a lot of alcohol and dancing）。它与短语a long evening of fun（痛快地玩了一个晚上）意思一样。Jack finished his exams today so he's gone out to paint the town red.（今天杰克考完了试，所以他出去痛快了一番。）"玩个痛快"的英语表达还有：have fun、have a good time、enjoy yourself。*Hunger Game* is my favorite movie and I enjoyed every minute of it.（《饥饿游戏》是我最喜欢的电影，我非常喜欢它。）bring the house down通常这个短语是把房子弄倒了，如The hurricane brought town many houses near the shore.（飓风吹倒了靠近岸边的许多房屋。）如果是在看表演或戏剧时，意思就截然不同了。The first episode of the new TV show *Games of Thrones* brought the house down.（新的电视节目《权力的游戏》的第一集赢得满堂喝彩。）had too much to drink（酒喝得太多），overnight party（昼夜聚会）。"玩得不愉快"的英语表达有：The game was so boring.（比赛很无聊。）His speech is deadly dull.（他的讲话死气沉沉。）It was very unpleasant experience.（这是非常不愉快的经历。）It is totally a waste of time.（这完全是在浪费时间。）The last night talk show was tedious and not funny at all.（昨晚的脱口秀很乏味，一点也不好笑。）It's wrong to make fun of the disabled/cripple.（嘲笑残疾人是错误的。）

43. "Jump to conclusions" is to _____.

A. give a quick assumption

B. find a quick conclusion

C. draw a conclusion

D. come to a conclusion

问题："jump to conclusion" 的意思是什么？

答案：A. 妄下结论

短语jump to conclusion是指妄下结论，即在没有足够的信息之下作出判断（judge a situation without enough information about it）。它和give quick assumption（很快做出假设）的意思接近。find a quick conclusion（找到一个快速的结论）。短语draw a conclusion（得出如下结论）和come to a conclusion（得出结论/作出决定）的意思相同。The policy find it difficult to draw a conclusion on this accident.（警方觉得此事故难下结论。）The Rio Olympic Games has formally come to a conclusion.（巴西奥运会的比赛正式结束。）in conclusion（总之，综上所述）：In conclusion, jogging is a cost free, safe, enjoyable and readily available form of exercise.（总而言之，慢跑是一种不花钱、安全、愉快的锻炼方式，而且随时随地都可以

进行。) in summary（总的来说）：In summary, it is my opinion that this complete treatment process was very successful.（总的来说，我认为整个治疗过程非常成功。）与jump搭配的词语有：long jump（跳远）、high jump（跳高）、trip jump（三级跳远）、jump rope（跳绳）等。

44. "Michael Jackson, the greatest singer of our time passed away last night."The following are equivalent to the underlined phrase except:

A. kicked the bucket.

B. died.

C. committed suicide.

D. has gone forever.

问题："我们这个时代最伟大的歌手迈克尔·杰克逊昨晚去世了。"下面哪个选项的意思和画线部分不同？

答案：C. 自杀。

　　答案C是自杀（committed suicide/kill oneself）的意思，其他的词语都是问句中passed away（去世）的同义词。passed away是正式用语，kicked the bucket是俚语。其他的表达方式有died（归天）：Countless soldiers died for freedom.（无数的士兵为自由而献身。）He is dead.（他死了。）He ended his life.（他结束了他的生命。）"He has gone forever." 是指一去不复返，也有去世的含义。homicide（杀人）：Eric is a missing person's case, not a homicide case.（埃里克是失踪案，不是谋杀案。）To this day, it's unclear whether he shot himself or if he was murdered.（至今尚不清楚他究竟是饮弹自杀还是被谋杀的。）assassinate（政治谋杀、暗杀）：Would Martin Luther King be the first black president of USA if he had not been assassinated?（如果马丁·路德·金没有被暗杀，他可能成为美国的第一位黑人总统吗？）slaughter（残忍地杀害）：The barbaric slaughter of whales is inhuman.（对鲸的野蛮屠杀不人道。）butcher（残杀）、massacre（大肆掠杀无辜）：Japanese killed thousands of innocent people at Nanjing Massacre during the World War II.（日本在二战期间杀害了数万名无辜的南京人）。murder（谋杀/谋杀犯）、killer（杀人犯）、kill（杀害）。有时kill的含义不一定是杀。如：My back is killing me.（我的背痛得要命。）Old women like to do crossword puzzles to kill time.（老年妇女喜欢玩填字游戏来消磨时间。）闲聊也是消磨时间：They spent the whole evening to breeze/kill time with idle chit-chat.（他们整个晚上都在闲聊。）

45. "The kids <u>kept in contact</u> with their teachers in the fourth grade." The underlined phrase means:

A. keep in touch.

B. keep in mind.

C. keep fit.

D. keep calm.

问题："孩子们与他们四年级的老师保持着联系。"
　　画线短语的意思是什么?

答案：A. 保持联系。

　　短语 keep in contact 和 keep in touch 都是保持联系的意思。keep 的常用短语还有：keep in mind（请记住）、keep fit（保持健康）、keep（stay）calm/cool（保持冷静）、keep calm and carry on（保持冷静继续进行）。人们常用 keep calm 加上一词来制成海报，鼓励人们做某事，如 Keep calm and play music（保持冷静和播放音乐）、Keep calm and stay strong（保持冷静和坚强）、Keep calm and follow your dream（保持冷静去追逐你的梦想）、Keep calm and be cool（保持冷静并保持酷）、Keep calm and stop dreaming（保持冷静并停止梦想）、Keep calm and enjoy life（保持冷静和享受生活）等。其他的用法还有：keep someone in the loop（让某人知情或参与），相当于 keep someone informed or involved、keep track of somebody/something（对某人/某事跟踪）、keep someone posted（不断给某人提供消息）、keep an eye on（注意）、keep a low profile（保持低调）、keep hands off（别碰）、keep a diary（写日记）、keep a secret（保密）。Here is $10, keep the change.（这里是十块钱，不用找啦。）Keep off the grass!（请勿踩草地!）He kept his promise/word.（他履行了他的诺言。）It won't keep you long.（不会耽误你很多时间/一会儿就好啦。）

46. The meaning of "That's out of the question." is___.

A. no question

B. no problem

C. not possible

D. no brainer

问题："That's out of the question." 的意思是什么?

答案：C. 不可能。

短语Not possible. 与That's out of the question.（不可能/不容许）的意义相近，就是说没有必要讨论了，都已经决定啦。If something is out of the question, it is not possible or not allowed. 例句：A trip to Disney World is out of the question this summer.（今年夏天不可能去迪斯尼世界。）No problem指没有问题。与question有关的短语很多：no question（毫无疑问）、beyond question（这是毫无疑问的）。His royalty to the company is beyond question.（他对公司的忠心是无可怀疑的。）burning questions（焦点）。open to question（有疑点/问题）：The decision on this case is open to question.（本案的判决仍有待进一步讨论。）no questions asked（不问任何问题）：The police will pay $100 for every gun turned in, no questions asked.（每上缴一支枪，警方将支付100美元，不会问任何问题。）You can return the shoes as long as you keep the receipt, no questions asked.（只要你保留收据，你就可以把鞋子退回，不用说明原因。）Q&A = Questions and Answers（问题解答专栏）。FAQ = frequently asked questions（常见问题的解答）。question mark（问号）。no brainer（太简单的问题）：His proposal of marriage was a no-brainer. She turned him down flat on the spot.（他的求婚是没有头脑的。他被她当场拒绝了。）brain twister（脑筋急转弯）：The girl is very good at the brain twister game.（这个女孩很擅长猜脑筋急转弯的题。）brain teaser（动脑筋）：I would like to leave you with a brain teaser.（最后，大家来动动脑筋。）blow one's brains out—kill someone with a gun（用枪杀死某人）。brain dead/stupid（脑死亡/愚蠢的）。

47. "I will have to <u>start</u> the experiment <u>again from scratch</u>."
The underlined part means all of the following except:

A. start at the very beginning.

B. start all over again.

C. start a different experiment.

D. do it again from the beginning.

问题："我将不得不<u>从头开始</u>做这个实验。"
以下哪个答案与画线部分的意思不同？

答案：C. 开始一个不同的试验。

短语start...from scratch与以下词组的含义相近：start all over again（从头再来）、start at the very beginning（从头开始）、do it again from the beginning（从头再做一次）。start a different experiment（开始一个不同的试验）。scratch的用法还有：Your research paper only scratched the surface of the problem.（你的研究论文只触及问题的表面。）常用搭配有：

scratch paper（草稿纸）。start的搭配用法有：They are thinking of starting a family.（他们在考虑生孩子——不是成家的意思）。from start to finish = from beginning to end（自始至终）：It was a fantastic performance from start to finish.（这真是一次从头到尾梦幻般的演出。）start 和begin 常可以互换，但指发动汽车时，只用start the car/engine。in the beginning of 和at the start of 都是表示"开始时"，但用的介词不一样。Her team got off to a good/bad start.（她的小组旗开得胜/出师不利。）kick off 也是开始的意思：They kicked off the celebration of their wedding anniversary with a bottle of champagne.（他们打开一瓶香槟酒，拉开了他们的结婚周年庆祝活动的序幕。）jump-start（启动车——用电线将两辆车的电瓶连接后充电帮助没电的车启动）：My（car's）battery is dead. Could you give me a jump-start?（我的车电池没电了，请帮我启动一下。）Don't get me started on your dating, okay?（别逼我说你的约会故事好不好？）There are five starters on each team for a basketball game.（篮球比赛中每个队有先发五虎。）

48. "I am off today." This sentence means:

A. I am on an errant.

B. I am on duty.

C. I am on vacation.

D. I am off duty.

问题："I am off today." 这个句子的意思是什么？
答案：B. 今天我休假。

句子I am on vacation.（我休假）与I am off today.（我今天不上班/休班）意思一样。take a day off也是休息一天。on an errant（出差）：I asked her to run an errand for me.（我要她为我办了件事。）take a vacation（休假），on vacation（在休假）：Dick and his family are on vacation in Hawaii.（迪克和他全家去夏威夷度假了。）summer/winter vacation（暑假/寒假）。on duty（值班）：There were hundreds of policemen on duty in and around the Time Square.（在纽约时代广场内及周边有好几百名警察在值勤。）I am at work.（我在上班。）与work 搭配的常用词语有：work out = find a solution for（行得通，找到一个解决方案）：I hope the new schedule works out for you.（我希望新的工作时间表对你合适。）Bill: I'm so miserable! Cheer up! Mary said to a gloomy Bill: Things will work out all right（for the best）.（比尔：我可惨啦！玛丽对悲观的比尔说：振作起来，事情会很顺利的。）workout（锻炼）：Victor goes to the gym to workout every other day.（维克多每隔一天去健身房锻炼一次。）In the current economic crisis, many people in Western Europe are out of work—unemployed.（在当前的经济危机中，西欧很多人失业了。）work around the clock（全天候工作）。work full time/part time（全职/半工）。work against the clock（分秒必争地工作）。

49. "Let's <u>keep our fingers crossed</u>." This sentence means:

A. good luck.

B. bad luck.

C. point the finger.

D. finger food.

问题："让我们把手指交叉。"这句话的意思是什么？

答案：A. 好运。

　　短语keep one's fingers crossed/cross one's fingers 做指头交叉的动作，即将中指与食指（index finger）交叉，中指在上。其含义是希望某人好运或某事成功（to wish for luck for someone or something）。这个短语用得很广泛，如 I hope you win the race Saturday. I'm keeping my fingers crossed for you.（我希望你赢得星期六的比赛。祝你好运。）good luck是祝你好运，与keep hope的意思一样。bad luck（霉运、倒霉）：The home team lost the game was purely by bad luck.（主队输了比赛纯粹是运气不好。）point the finger/index finger（指责）：Don't point the finger at me!（不要把矛头指向我！）Past elections involved clashes of ideas and angry finger—pointing between the two parties.（刚刚过去的选举中包含了两党派之间的想法冲突和相互指责。）其他有关finger的常用短语有fingerprint（指纹）：At the immigration office, all visitors will have their pictures and fingerprints taken before entering the United States.（在入境处，所有访客在进入美国之前他们会被拍照和提取指纹。）lay a finger on somebody—to touch someone as a threat of hurting them（碰，冒犯）：If you lay a finger on my sister, I'll break your arm!（如果你碰/欺负我姐姐的话，我会打断你的胳膊！）fingernails（指甲）、finger food（小吃）。五个指头的英语名称：the thumb（拇指）、index finger（中指）、middle finger（无名指）、ring finger（食指）、little finger（小指）。

50. The sentence, "Are you kidding me?" means:

A. Are you joking?

B. Are you lying to me?

C. Do you trust me?

D. Are you making believe?

问题："Are you kidding me？"这句话的意思是什么？

答案：A. 你在开玩笑吧？

句子 Are you joking?/You must be joking.（你在开玩笑吧？）和 Are you kidding me? You have got to be kidding me.的意思相同。play a joke on somebody（开某人的玩笑）、play a practical joke/hoax（搞恶作剧）：On April the first, many people play hoax/mischief.（很多人在四月一日愚人节时玩恶作剧。）There is no joke, it is a serious matter.（没有开玩笑，这是个严重的问题。）Are you lying to me?（你是在骗我吗？）Are you trusting me?（你信任我吗？）Are you making believe?（你在骗人吧？——一个无辜的、俏皮的假装）。laugh at somebody（笑话/嘲笑某人）。mock on somebody（取笑某人）。tease somebody（捉弄人）：She likes to tease the boys to death.（她喜欢狠狠地捉弄男孩们。）play a trick on somebody（取笑/作弄/逗某人）：Richard hid Eric's skating board to play a trick on him.（理查德把埃里克的滑板藏起来捉弄他。）You'd better not tease George. He can't take a joke.（你最好不要去逗George，他可开不起玩笑。）笑的表达有：smile（微笑）、laugh（笑）、giggle（傻笑）。He who laughs last, laughs longest./He, who laughs last, laughs best.（谁笑到最后，笑得最好。）The comedian made the audience laugh their heads off.（喜剧演员让观众笑得前仰后合。）

51. "My nose is running." The sentence means:

A. I just follow my nose.

B. Keep your nose out of other people's business.

C. I caught a cold.

D. I have to pay though the nose.

问题："我在流清鼻涕"这句话的意思是：

答案：C. 我感冒了。

"I caught a cold." 意思是我感冒了。 其他句子的意思是: I just follow my nose/instinct. (我只是跟着直觉走。) Keep your nose out of other people's business. (别管闲事。) Keep yourself out of trouble. (别惹麻烦。) 和 nose 相关的短语和句型有: It's not polite to pick your nose in public places. (在公众场合抠鼻子不礼貌。) running nose (流鼻涕)、blow nose (擤鼻涕)、nasal mucus (鼻涕)、nasal sound (鼻音)、snuff bottle (鼻烟壶)。My nose is bleeding. (我在流鼻血。) My nose is buried in a book. (我在读书。) I have to pay though the nose. (我不得不多付钱)。See no further than the end of nose. (目光短浅。) Look, there it is, your iPhone is right under your nose! (瞧, 那不是, 你的手机就在你面前!) 欧美人的鼻子很高又大, 注意: 高鼻子的英文不是 high nose 而是 big (huge) nose。当女人说 I am going to power my nose. 时, 她是要上洗手间去, 而不是给鼻子打粉。除了鼻子之外, 人的五官之一耳朵的英文 (ears) 也有很多常用的搭配用法。如, turn a deaf ear to (充耳不闻/不理): It is not wise to turn a deaf ear to other's criticism. (对别人的批评充耳不闻是不明智的。) I am all ears. (仔细倾听。) Walls have ears. (隔墙有耳。) hearing aid (助听器)、earrings (耳环)、earwax (耳垢, 耳屎)、deaf (耳聋)。

52. The sentence, "You have nothing to lose." means:

A. You lost everything.

B. You are a loser.

C. You can take any risk and won't suffer losses.

D. You are not afraid to lose anything.

问题: "你不会失去任何东西" 的意思是什么?
答案: C. 你可以冒任何风险而不会遭受损失。

句子 "You have nothing to lose." 表示你不会有任何损失, 即 You can take any risk and won't suffer loses. (你可以采取任何风险而不会遭受损失/不会吃亏)。其他句子: You are not afraid to lose anything. (你不怕失去任何东西。) You lost everything. (你失去了一切。) You are a loser. (你是一个失败者。) 和 nothing 搭配的常用词语有: nothing to prove (没有什么需要证明的): We've got nothing to prove and we know what we did is legal. (我们不需要证明什么, 我们所做的一切都是合法的。) come to nothing (落空): Her years' efforts came to nothing. (她多年的努力成了泡影。) good for nothing (一无是处): Dick is a good for nothing guy and he could not even take care of such an easy job. (迪克就是个废物, 这点小事都做不来。) lose 一词可以与许多词构成短语, 如 lose temper (发脾气): It is easy for her to lose temper after a long day's hard work.（在一天的艰苦工作后她很容易就会发脾气。）lose one's cool（失去冷静）、lose heart to someone（爱上／倾心于某人）、lose one's mind（失魂落魄）、lose confidence（失去信心）、lose face（丢面子）、lose money（赔钱）、lose trace of（失去踪迹）、lose contact with（失去了联系）、lose appetite（没有食欲）、lose patient（失去了耐心）、lose time（浪费时间）等。

53. "There is <u>a short cut</u> to the castle." The underlined part means:

A. There is a cut on her arm.

B. Cut corners.

C. Turn the corner.

D. He is cornered.

问题："到城堡去有一条<u>近路</u>。"画线部分是什么意思？

答案：B. 走捷径，抄近路。

短语 cut corners 和 short cut 一样，都是走捷径、抄近路的意思，即 to do something in the easiest, quickest, or cheapest way（以最简单、最快捷和最便宜的方法做事）。与 cut 相关的短语还有 cut short（中断）：The career of a figure skater was cut short by accident.（花样滑冰运动员的运动生涯被意外断送了。）The company needs to cut down expenses.（公司需要削减开支。）You had your hair cut. It looks great.（你理了发后，看起来很棒。）The power line was cut off by a falling tree.（电线被一棵倒下的树给切断了。）There is a cut on her arm.（她的胳膊上破了一个口子）。to cut（make）a long story short（简言之）：To cut（make）a long story short, I decided to stay for another day.（简而言之，我决定再住一天。）take turns（轮流）：Let's take turns to clean the bathroom.（让我们轮流打扫浴室。）turn the corner（境况好转）：I wonder if the situation in Syria has turned the corner.（我不知道叙利亚局势是否已走出谷底。）Drive carefully and slow down before you turn the corner.（在拐弯前要小心，把速度降低。）He is cornered.（他走投无路。）Christmas is around the corner.（圣诞节就要来临了／指日可待。）Athletes came from all corners of the world to attend the Winter Olympic Games in Sochi.（运动员从世界各地来到索契参加冬季奥运会。）

54. "She kept changing her mind on what cloth to wear for the birthday party." It means she_____.

A. kept an open mind

B. had a hard time to make a decision

C. had a master mind

D. was absent minded

问题："对于生日晚会上穿什么衣服，她拿不定主意。"

这句话的意思是她____。

答案：B. 很难做决定。

短语has a hard time to make a decision意为很难做决定，它与题目中的短语keep changing her mind（拿不定主意）同义。make up your mind.（拿定主意）是其反义词。mind一词有许多的用法：keep an open mind（保持开放的心态）：It's a good idea for you to keep an open mind on the problem.（对这个问题你最好是不要抱偏见。）master mind（智囊团）：President sent his top aide to mastermind peace negotiations between the opposing parties.（总统派出他的高级助手去组织安排对立派别之间的和平谈判。）absent minded（恍惚、心不在焉）：She was absent minded and a little slow on reaction.（她心不在焉，反应有点迟钝。）I often do absent minded things, particularly when I'm worried.（我常做些心不在焉的事，尤其是在我焦虑不安时。）Mind you own business.（少管闲事）。Don't you mind if I use your iPhone to make a call?（你不介意我用你的苹果手机打个电话吧？）Never mind.（没有关系。）You are out of your mind.（你疯了！）bear/keep in mind that（记住）：You have to keep in mind that we are on your side.（你要记住我们支持你。）mind goes blank（头脑一边空白）：I stood beside her bed numbly while mind went blank.（我那样呆呆地立在她床前,脑子里一片空白。）Her boss was criticized for being boring and narrow minded.（她的老板被指无趣乏味和心胸狭窄。）

55. "To make thing worse" is equivalent to all except:

A. Add fuel to the fire.

B. Add ice to the snow.

C. Pour salt on the wound.

D. Pour salt on the road.

问题："使事情变得更糟"与以下哪个短语的意义不相同？

答案：D. 往道路上撒盐。

　　问题中的短语to make thing worse是"使事情变得更糟"的意思。类似的短语还有pour salt in the wound（往伤口上抹盐）、add fuel to the fire/pour oil over the flames（火上浇油）、add ice to the snow（雪上加霜）、one disaster after another（灾难不断/雪上加霜）。Tom added fuel to the fire by bringing up old grudges while they were arguing.（在争吵中，汤姆火上浇油，翻出了旧账。）在美国的北部和东北部，冬季常常是漫天的大雪，冰冻的天气持续很久。市政和地方政府都及时出动大量的铲雪车（snowplow）清理公路的积雪，然后往道路上撒盐（pour salt on the road）防止道路结冰，保障道路畅通。大部分主要道路在下大雪后几个小时就可以重新开通。每家每户门前的道路也是由市/镇政府负责清扫，但自己要扫门前雪，包括自己的车道（driveway）和人行道（sidewalk）上的雪，不清扫会罚款的。worse的用法还有：for better or worse（不管是好还是坏）、if worst comes worst（如果出现最坏的情况的话）、go from bad to worse（每况愈下），转好的英文是turn for the better。Tony：What happening, Fred? Fred：Things could be worse not as bad as it might be.（托尼：弗雷德，你怎么回事？弗雷德：事情还不是太糟。）

56. The sentence , "I put my foot in my mouth." means:

A. I started off on the wrong foot.

B. I made my hair stand on end.

C. It made my skin crawl.

D. I regret what I said.

问题："我把一只脚放在嘴里"的意思是___.

答案：D. 我后悔不该说那些话。

短语 "put one's foot in one's mouth" or "put one's foot in it" or "stick one's foot in one's mouth"（把一只脚在一个人的嘴里面）是个成语，表示你后悔（regret）说了一些愚蠢（stupid）、侮辱（insulting）或伤害（harmful）的话。如，When I told Anna that her hair was more beautiful than I had ever seen it, I really put my foot in my mouth. It was a wig.（我告诉安娜，她的头发是我见过的最漂亮的。我真愚蠢，她那是假发。）I started/stepped off on the wrong foot.（我一开始就错了脚/出师不利。）It made my hair stand on end.（这让我毛骨悚然。）It made my skin crawl.（这让我害怕/恶心。）与foot搭配的词语或句式有：You're one's foot in the door.（你完成了第一步。）have a foot in the grave（快死了）。shoot yourself in the foot（搬起石头砸自己的脚），意思是to do or say something stupid which causes problems for you（做了蠢事或说了蠢话招来麻烦）。He shot himself in the foot by suggesting that women politicians were incompetent.（他暗示女政治家们无能，砸了自己的脚啦。）My car broke down and I had to get back home on foot.（我的车抛锚了，只好步行回家。）The NCAA football championship game had the crowd on its feet all the time.（全国大学体育协会橄榄球冠军赛让全场观众群情激昂。）

57. "That kid has ants in his pants." means_____.

A. some ants got into his pants

B. the kid plays with ants

C. ants are dangerous

D. the kid is not able to keep still

问题："有些蚂蚁钻进了那个孩子的裤子"

这句话的意思是 ___。

答案：D. 这孩子坐不住

问题 "That kid has ants in his pants." 这个句子字面的意思是有些蚂蚁钻进了他的裤子，即 "Some ants got into his pants."。实际上，这个成语表示由于激动（agitated）或兴奋的（excited）事情而静不下来、坐立不安或焦躁不安。它与The kid is not able to keep still.（这孩子坐不住）的意思相近。表示焦躁不安的方式还有：The patient exhibited symptoms of anxiety.（病人表现出焦躁不安的症状。）The panda presented hyperactivity and restlessness.（熊猫呈现出多动和焦躁不安的情绪。）The suspect shifted uneasily on his chair.（犯罪嫌疑人坐在椅子上焦躁不安地动来动去。）其他答案是：The kid plays with ants.（小孩玩蚂蚁。）Ants are dangerous.（蚂蚁是危险的。）

58. "Pay your dues" means ＿＿＿.

A. you get what you pay for

B. pay for membership，club or organization fees

C. pay your outstanding bill

D. your payment is due

问题："Pay your dues" 这句话的意思是＿＿＿。

答案：B. 支付会员、俱乐部或组织费

短语 "pay your dues" 的意思是缴纳会员、俱乐部或某个组织的会费。支付账单是 pay bill：Pay your outstanding bill.（支付你的未付账单。）due 这个词有很多常见的用法。Your payment is due next Monday.（你的付款期限是下周一。）I have two assignments due tomorrow.（明天我要交两个作业。）Megan's due date is next Wednesday.（Megan 的预产期是下个礼拜三。）Due to inclement weather schools are either closed or delayed opening.（由于天气恶劣，学校或者停课或者推迟上课。）Jack finally got his long due promotion.（杰克终于获得了盼望已久的提升。）与 pay 有关的用法：payroll（工资单）、pay back（还款）、pay a lum sum（支付一次性付款）。pay back（归还）：My father worked his fingers to the bone till he paid back all the debts.（我的父亲拼命地工作直到把借款还清为止。）Please write a check of $ 50 payable to Starbucks.（请写一张支付给星巴克的 50 美元支票。）pay off（付清/偿还）：Many American college graduates took more than ten years to pay off college loan.（很多美国大学毕业生要花十多年的时间来偿还大学贷款。）You get what you pay for.（一分钱一分货。）也就是说你要买廉价的东西，其品质就不会高（cheap and low quality）。

Daily Life
日常生活篇

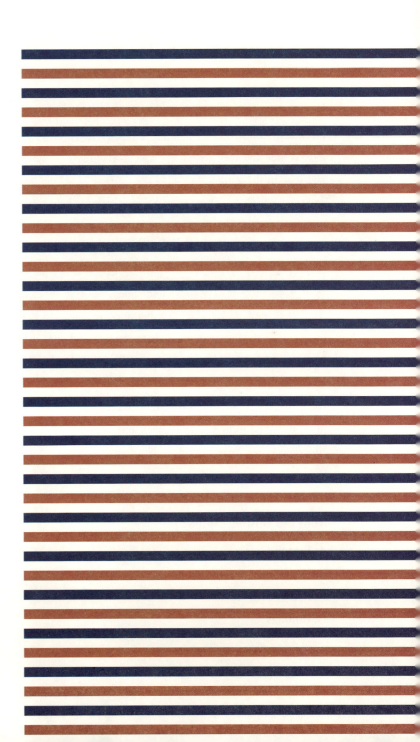

1. Which pair of words below is different from all the others?

A. Shoes and socks

B. Rich and poor

C. Black and white

D. Butter and bread

问题：下列词组中哪一对不一样？

答案：A. 鞋袜

英语中有些习惯用法是没有道理可讲的。词的一些搭配和顺序不能调换。如答案中 black and white（黑白）的顺序与中文的相同，不能改成 white and black。顺序和中文一样的还有 hide and seek（捉迷藏/先藏起来再找）：When we were children, we used to play hide-and-seek in the garden.（小时候我们常在花园里玩捉迷藏。）up and down（上上下下）、east and west（东西）：There is an obvious contrast between the cultures of East and West.（东西方文化之间存在着明显的差异。）cups and sources（茶杯和茶碟）、deaf and mute（聋哑）、law and order（法纪）、eat and drink（吃喝）、here and there（这儿那儿）、old and young（老少）。有的顺序与中文不一样，中国人说穿鞋袜，而英美人刚好相反，他们认为是应先穿袜子再穿鞋子，所以说 socks and shoes，而不是 shoes and socks。题中的其他词的顺序都与中文的不一样，如，只能说 butter and bread（面包和黄油）、rich and poor（贫富）：With urbanization the disparity widen between rich and poor.（伴随着城市化的推进，贫富差距日益扩大。）类似的还有如 rain or shine（无论晴天还是下雨）：Frances walks her dog every day, rain or shine.（弗朗西斯无论晴天还是下雨，每天都出去遛狗。）stop and go（走走停停）、spoon and fork（叉子和调羹）、right and left（左右）、north and south（南北）、land and water（水陆）、back and forth（前后）、back and belly（腹背）、sooner or later（迟早）。表示方位的词也是如此：Southeast（东南）、Northwest（西北）、Northeast（东北）。

2. Which of the following is not originally from the United States?

A. French Fries

B. Hamburger

C. Barbecue Wing

D. Hotdogs

问题：下列哪种食物不是起源于美国的？

答案：A. 炸土豆条

热狗（hot dog）、炸土豆条（French fries）、汉堡包（hamburger）、烧烤鸡翅膀（barbecue wing）都是美国人百吃不厌的食品。烧烤鸡翅膀是美国人的发明。很多家庭在后院里都有烧烤灶（barbecue grill/stoves），在搞聚会时给客人做烧烤食品。不要以为炸土豆条（French fries）有 French（法国）一词就误认为是法国的食品。据说炸土豆条起源于比利时（Belgian），后来美国士兵在第一次世界大战时到比利时吃到它，因为比利时人说法语，而误称之为法国土豆条。汉堡包不是来自德国的汉堡市（Hamburg），而是由路易斯·拉森于 1900 年在美国康涅狄格州（Connecticut）纽黑文的午餐店首创的。hot dog 是美国的德国移民在 19 世纪创造的。它通常是指夹有熟香肠（sausage）的三明治面包（sandwich），一般会配上芥末（mustard）、番茄酱（ketchup/tomato juice）、洋葱（onion）、蛋黄酱（mayonnaise）、奶酪（cheese）、辣椒（hot peppers）、酸黄瓜（pickled cucumber）等，风味各异，能满足不同人群的需求，备受青睐。美国人其他爱吃的食品（popular foods）都是来源于其他国家：苹果饼（apple pie）源于英国，冰淇淋（ice-cream）可能是源于古希腊，巧克力（chocolate）来源于墨西哥的玛雅人，但是巧克力曲奇冰淇淋（Chocolate Chip Cookie Dough Ice Cream）是美国麻州的 Ruth Graves Wakefield 在 1937 年发明的，塔科（taco）来自墨西哥，牛排（steak）来源不明，比萨（pizza）和意面（pasta）是意大利面食。

3. Which of the following measurement units is not used in the US?

A. Pounds

B. Inches

C. Fahrenheit

D. Meters

问题：在美国，不用以下的哪个度量衡单位？

答案：D. 米

美国人使用的度量衡单位（the units of measurement）与世界上大多数国家不一样，不是十进制（decimal）而是英制的。长度单位有 mile（英里）、foot（英尺）、inch（英寸）。1ft. = 12in; 1yd = 3ft = 36in; 1mi = 5280ft.。重量单位有 pound（磅）、ounce（盎司）。1 1b（磅）= 16 oz.（盎司）。体积（液体）单位有 gallon（加仑）、fluid ounce（液盎司）、cup（杯）。1 gal（加仑）= 128 fl oz.（液盎司）。

美国使用的是英制的长度、重量、体积单位，与中国的不同。参见下列对照表。

	英制	公制	中国
长度单位	1 mile, mi（英里）	1.6093 kilometer, km（千米）	3.2186（里）
	1 foot, ft.（英尺）	0.3048 meter, m（米）	0.9144（尺）
	1 inch, in（英寸）	2.54 centimeter, cm（厘米）	0.726（寸）
重量单位	1 pound, 1b（磅）	0.4536 kilogram, kg（千克）	0.90718474（斤）
	1 ounce, oz.（盎司）	28.35 gram, g（克）	
体积（液体）单位	1 gallon, gal（加仑）	3.785 liter, L（升）	
	1 fluid ounce, fl oz.（液盎司）	29.57 milliliter, ml（毫升）	
	1 cup, c（杯）	236.6 milliliter, ml（毫升）	

4. What is 24 Centigrade in Fahrenheit?

A. 80 ℉

B. 93 ℉

C. 75 ℉

D. 55 ℉

问题：摄氏 24 度是华氏多少度？

答案：C. 75 ℉

世界上多数国家是采用摄氏（Centigrade）来测量温度（temperature），而美国例外，是用华氏（Fahrenheit）。摄氏与华氏的换算方式如下。

华氏换成摄氏：℃＝（℉－32）×5÷9。

例如华氏 85 度：℃＝（85－32）×5÷9＝29.4℃。

摄氏换成华氏：℉＝9×℃÷5＋32。

例如摄氏 40 度等于华氏：℉＝9×40÷5＋32＝104 ℉。

类别	华氏（Fahrenheit）	摄氏（Centigrade）
冰点	32 ℉	0℃
人体常温	98.6 ℉	37℃
沸点	212 ℉	100℃

人体常温是 37℃左右＝98.6 ℉左右。发烧时体温在常温以上，40℃的高烧是 104 ℉。

与温度有关的词语有：He is running a fever/having a（high）temperature. 他在发（高）烧。use ice or take a shower to bring down the temperature 用冰或洗个澡来降温。其他短语：take temperature（量体温）、change in temperature（温度变化）、drop or fall/rise in temperature（温度下降/上升）。

5. You can take money any time from all of the following accounts except:

A. Checking account

B. Savings account

C. Joint account

D. IRA account

问题：以下的哪个账号不能随时取钱?

答案：D. 个人退休账户

     在美国，你存在IRA account（individual retirement account）个人退休账户里的钱，只能在退休后才能取钱，提前取钱会受罚税款。这是为了保障你在退休之后有足够的钱生活。支票账户（checking account）主要是用来进行现金存取、转账结算等活期存款账户，通常没有或利息很少。开户时银行提供支票本和ATM，即Automatic Teller Machine（自动提款机）卡。用ATM卡时需要输入4位数的密码（PIN，Personal Identification Number）。借记卡（debit card）也是一种银行提供的可以自动存取款的卡。除了在提款机上使用外，在很多商店可以像信用卡（credit card）一样使用，不同的是借记卡不能帮你建立信用。储蓄账户（Savings account）主要也是用于存钱和取钱，但一般都有利息，没有结算功能。储蓄账户分普通储蓄（regular saving）和货币市场储蓄（money market savings）两种。后者开户要求高，利息也高。联名账户（joint account）可以是夫妇也可以是生意合伙人。还有一种账户叫定期账户（certificate of deposit）或CDs。有长期（long term）和短期（short term）的，利息较高，但是如果在到期前取出会收罚金。银行开户时的惯用语有：I'd like to open an account.（我想开一个支票账户。）What is the minimum deposit for opening a checking account?（开支票账户的最低储蓄限额是多少？）Is there any monthly fee for the savings account?（储蓄账户有月费吗？）What documents are required to open an account?（开户需要哪些文件？）

6. Which one of the following fruits is different from all the others?

A. Strawberry

B. Blackberry

C. Blueberry

D. Raspberry

问题：以下哪种水果与其他的不同?

答案：A. 草莓

strawberry（草莓）、blackberry（黑莓）、blueberry（蓝莓）、raspberry（山莓/覆盆子），还有cranberry（蔓越莓）都是berry（浆果）类水果，营养丰富，味道可口，是居家喜爱种植的水果。除了草莓之外，其他的都是bush（灌木）。草莓很像蔬菜，长得很矮，没有枝干，靠藤蔓式根系向四周延伸扎根。果实个大是其他浆果的好几倍甚至十来倍。黑莓和山莓很相像，就是颜色不同而已，果实很软，不易采摘和保存。蓝莓的果实圆而光滑，与黑莓和山莓的形状完全不同。草莓、黑莓、蓝莓和山莓等常用来做milkshake（奶昔）或smoothie（冰沙）。人们将这些浆果制成strawberry jam（草莓果酱）、raspberry jam（山莓果酱）、blackberry jam（黑莓果酱）、blueberry jam（蓝莓果酱）。草莓果酱、山莓果酱、苹果酱（apple jam）和葡萄果酱（grape jam）是美国人吃面包时都爱抹上的果酱。这些果酱做成各种各样的浆果派（berry pie），也很受欢迎。holly tree（冬青树）在冬季结果，树叶深绿色，果实小圆红艳，是圣诞节时常用的装饰品。但是要特别小心，holly berry（冬青浆果）是有毒的（poisonous），不要让小孩接近它们，吃一两颗没有什么问题，如果吃上20颗会有生命危险。

7. Brian brought a second hand car. His car is＿＿＿.

A. brand new one

B. a lemon

C. stick shift

D. a used car

问题：布莱恩买了辆二手车。他的车是个＿＿＿.

答案：D. 二手车

使用过的汽车英语叫作a second hand car（二手车），也就是a used car。有严重问题的新车叫a lemon指有缺陷的（defective）. Tom's new car turned out to be a lemon.（汤姆的新车原来是个柠檬车/有缺陷的车）。车的类型包括：truck（卡车）、pickup truck（小型卡车）、jeep（吉普）、mini-van（微型面包车/商务车）、convertible（敞篷车）、sports car（跑车）、taxi（出租车）、limousine（limo）或a luxury sedan（豪华轿车）、shuttle bus（摆渡车）、school bus（校车）、hybrid（电动车）、ambulance（救护车）、fire engine（消防车）、garbage truck（垃圾车）等。车的类型主要有：stick/hand shift（手动车）、automatic（自动车）、four way drive（四轮驱动）、hybrid vehicle/cars（混合动力汽车）等。与车有关的词语有：windshield wiper（雨刷）、head lights（前大灯）、power window（电动车窗）、steering wheel（方向盘）、power steering（动力转向）、GPS—The Global Positioning System（导航系统）、parallel parking（平行停车）、break（刹车）、accelerate（油门）、hand break（手刹）、trunk（后舱）、mileage gauge（里程计）、fog lights（雾灯）、beam（聚光灯）、sun/moon roof（阳光

顶窗）。美国的加油站（gas station）提供全方位（full service）的服务，你也可以自己加油（self service）。有几个州是不能自己加油的，如新泽西州就只有 full service。一般的加油站都设有汽车保养如 oil change（更换机油）、air filter change（换空气过滤器）、tire change（更换轮胎）和其他修理业务。如你自己会修车，可以到废车场（junk yard）去买汽车配件，很便宜，但你自己得在旧车上把需要的部件取下来。

8. Which one of the following pairs is different from all the others?

A. Buffalo/bull/cow—Beef

B. Hen/cock—Chicken

C. Sheep/goat—Mutton

D. Horse/colt—Horse meat

问题：以下哪个选项和其他的不同？

答案：D. Horse/colt—Horse meat 马/小马——马肉

在学习英语时，也许你会感到有些困惑，为什么 buffalo（水牛）、ox/bull（公牛）、cow（母牛）和牛肉（beef）的英语不是同一个单词。另外小牛叫 calf，小牛肉却不叫 calf 或 beef，而是叫 veil。这种差异的来源要追溯到法国诺曼人（French Normans）11 世纪对英国的入侵和占领（occupation）。当时动物的名称都是来自盎格鲁-撒克逊（Anglo-Saxon）族群，而动物肉类的名字，则来自诺曼法语，源于拉丁语。常见的解释是，被征服后，盎格鲁-撒克逊人经常被限制在卑微的角色，如牛郎（cowboys）、织女（weavers）、猪倌（swineherds）等。他们在牧场上用原有的动物名称，而他们的诺曼主人在餐桌上，用的是法文的动物名称，沿袭下来，活的动物是英文名而餐桌上的肉却是法文。如：母鸡（hen）/公鸡（cock）—鸡肉（chicken）；绵羊（sheep）/山羊（goat）—羊肉（mutton）；猪（pig/swine）—猪肉（pork）。西方人不常吃的家禽家畜就没有这种问题。如鸭和鸭肉（ducks）、鹅（goose/geese）、兔（rabbits）、hares（野兔）也一样。另外，马（horse），小马（colt），而马肉是（horse meat），只是因为马通常是骑士的战骑或牧人的工具，不是法国人或英国人的食肉。狗和猫都是西方人最爱的宠物（pets），当然绝不会出现在餐桌上。另外野生动物也没有这种现象。与肉类有关的词语还有：tripe（牛肚）、brisket（牛腩）、steak（牛排）、ribs（肋骨）、pork chops（猪排）、trotters/pig feet（猪蹄）、chicken feet（鸡爪）、chicken breast（鸡胸肉）、chicken wing（鸡翅）等。常见的美国肉类食品有：ham（火腿）、smoked ham（熏火腿）、sausage（香肠）、smoked turkey（熏火鸡）、salami（意大利腊肠）、bacon（培根）等。

9. DIY means you do the following at home except:

A. decorating your house

B. fixing your car

C. painting your room

D. repairing household items

问题：DIY 的意思是你可以在家做以下所有的事情，除了____之外。

答案：B. 修理你的汽车

　　DIY 是 Do-it-yourself（自己动手做）的缩语，主要是指在家中自己动手进行家居的装饰和改造，而不是请专业人士来做。如 decorating your house（装饰你的房子）、painting your rooms（油漆你的房间）、repairing household items（修理家用物品）等。在美国这是一种时尚（fashion），对许多家庭的主人们来说，还是一种很好的业余爱好（good hobby）。美国有专门提供房屋建造（building）、维修（home maintenance）、装修（renovation）、装饰（decoration）材料的大型商场，如 Home Depot（家得宝）和 Lowe's 等连锁店。也卖家用电器（appliance），如空调（air conditioning）、冰箱（refrigerator）、炉灶（stove）、微波炉（microwave oven）、饮水器（water dispenser）等。商店还提供 DIY 指南，以及一些项目的免费课程。美国人花很多的钱购置各种工具（tools），在很多家庭的车库（garage）里，都摆满了常用的工具，如起子（screwdriver）、电锯（saw）、电钻（drill）、榔头（hammer）、钳子（pliers）、管钳（wrenches）、扳手（spanner）、楼梯（ladder）等。常见的 DIY 有设置窗帘（set up window curtains）、装饰墙壁（decorate walls）、灯光（lighting）、给房间粉刷不同的颜色（repaint rooms with different colors）。有些手巧的主人（handy man）还能装修瓷砖地板（install ceramic floor）、装修阁楼（attic）、把地下室（renovate the basement）建成家庭电影院（family theater）和健身房（fitness room）等。修理汽车是需要专业人士来做的。一般不是 DIY 的内容，当然，不少人能够给汽车换机油和空气滤清器（change oil and air filter）、给轮胎打气（inflate tires）和加冷却剂（coolant）等日常维修项目。

10. Which one of the following food is not a common breakfast for American kids?

A. Milk

B. Pancakes

C. Cheerios

D. Cookies

问题：下列中哪一种食品不是美国孩子常吃的早餐？

答案：D.曲奇饼

美国的孩子早餐爱吃的食品之一是牛奶（milk）冲脆谷乐（cheerios）——用麦片做成各种形状和颜色的脆片。有的脆片中还加了草莓（strawberry）、葡萄干（raisins）等，既营养又方便。pancakes是用鸡蛋与面粉煎成的小饼，淋上蜂蜜吃，味道不错。曲奇饼（cookies）是美国人爱吃的一种饼，形状和味道有点像中国的桃酥饼，由面粉、鸡蛋和糖做成。在英国和其他地方cookies称为biscuits。cookies的种类很多，如chocolate chip cookies（有巧克力片的曲奇饼）尤其受欢迎，是公司、学校开会时提供的点心、小吃和饮料中最常见的。但不是天天早餐吃的食品。很多美国的家庭主妇都会做cookies。有聚会时，很多人都会带上自己做的曲奇饼供大家享用。其他常见的家庭制作的点心有：brownies（布朗尼，一种用巧克力粉做的糕点）、cupcake（杯形饼）、cheesecake（奶酪蛋糕）、apple pie（苹果饼）、waffles（华夫饼）、muffin（松饼，类似cupcake但大一些），常加有strawberry（草莓）、blueberry（蓝莓）、raspberry（山梅）等。美国人的早餐大多是吃面包和喝牛奶，把面包在烤面包机上烤好之后，抹上butter（黄油）和jam（果酱），或者是peanut butter加jelly做成PB&J（花生酱和果冻三明治）。当然对成人而言，早上一杯咖啡是必不可少的。另外酸奶（yogurt）是营养价值高的健康食品，愈来愈多的人都喜爱将其作为早餐和中餐。橙汁也是家庭早餐上的常见饮料。

11. Which one of the following is not a real dog in the US?

A. Boxer

B. Greyhound

C. Spot

D. Hot dog

问题：下列中哪一种不是真正的美国狗？

答案：D. 热狗

热狗（hot dog）是美国人爱吃的一种食品，不是真的狗。狗的种类繁多，如greyhound（灰狗）、spot（斑点狗）、boxer（巴儿狗）。在美国，Greyhound（灰狗）还是一家最著名的长途汽车公司的名称，其业务遍及全美。美国的公共交通系统（public transportation system）不是很发达，基本上只有从城郊和乡村至城市的公交车线路（suburban lines），而小镇至小镇之间鲜有公车。因此没有私车很不方便。铁路虽然四通八达，但是非常陈旧，速度很慢。目前还没有高速铁路（high-speed railways）。全国性的铁路（national railway）有Amtrak（参见 http://www.amtrak.com/home）。很多州都有自己的铁路系统（railway system），如费城（Philadelphia）是 SEPTA，新泽西是 NJ Transit，旧金山（San Francisco）的叫 Bart。很多铁路系统进出站都不检票，上了车后，乘务员（conductors）挨个检票。检票时票会被收走，如需要报销，一定要在购票时要求开收据。如果乘车前来不及买票的话，可以在车上补票。城市的铁路公交车线路都有对老人（senior citizen）（一般为 62 岁以上）、儿童和残疾人的票价优惠。如新泽西的火车，周末和假日儿童是免费乘坐的。很多大城市都有地铁（subway），但大部分都是有历史的了。如，纽约地铁称为 subway，华盛顿、洛杉矶和芝加哥的都叫 metro（metropolitan subway），出入口附近都有 M 标识。很多城市的地铁不一定全在地下运行，常有一段是在地面运行。

12. Which of the following is different from all the others?

A. Subway

B. Fridays

C. MacDonald's

D. Wendy's

问题：下列中哪一个答案与其他的不同？

答案：B. Fridays

供选择的答案中，除了 Fridays 是一家普通餐馆连锁店（restaurant chain），其他的都是美国人喜爱的快餐店（fast food restaurant）。其中 Wendy's 2011 年超过麦当劳（McDonald's）成为美国最受欢迎的快餐店。其有名的食品叫作 frosties，还包括传统的汉堡包、薯条和厚厚的奶昔（milkshakes）。Cheese Factory（奶酪餐馆）以其奶酪糕点的特色在 2010 被评为美国中等餐馆第一位，Red Robin（红罗宾餐馆）则以其 20 种以上的汉堡包及热三明治而夺得第二名。Subway（赛百味）提供的是各种现做现卖的面包。其他有名的快餐店还有 Burger King（汉堡王）、KFC—Kentucky Fried Chicken（肯德基）、White Castle（白色城堡）。美国第一家快餐店可以追溯到 1912 年在纽约开张的 Automat，一家用五分硬币自动购买简单食品和饮料的餐厅。美国最大的四家比萨饼连锁店是 Pizza Hut（必胜客），第二是 Domino's Pizza（达美乐比萨饼），第三是 Papa John's Pizza（约翰爸爸比萨饼）和第四的 Little Caesars（小凯撒比萨饼）。他们都提供外卖（take out/deliver）服务。比萨饼上配料（topping）的种类有：cheese（奶酪）、meatball（肉丸）、pepperoni（意大利辣味香肠）、mushroom（食用菌）、bell pepper（柿子椒）、Sausage（香肠）等，带多种配料的叫作 combo。美国十大著名的快餐店食品如下：French fries（炸薯条）、burger（汉堡包）、pizza（比萨饼）、fried chicken（炸鸡）、grilled chicken（烤鸡）、taco（塔科，玉米饼快餐店，是墨西哥食品，提供由软玉米饼包上各种肉类和蔬菜组合的玉米卷饼）、burrito（卷饼）、hot dog（热狗）、tuna sandwich（鲔鱼三明治）及 Ice-Cream and Sundae（雪糕和圣代）。其他还有 fish（鱼）、sandwiches（三明治）、pitas（皮塔饼）、chicken nuggets（炸鸡块）、ice cream（冰淇淋）、chili（辣椒）、mashed potatoes（土豆泥）、salads（沙拉）等。在美国餐厅就餐，餐巾（napkin）是不用收费的，随便用。不少快餐店的饮料是按杯子大小交费，可以免费添加（free refill）。

13. **"What do you want for your coffee?"**
   "Half and half, please."
   Answered Tom. Tom wanted_____.

A. a half cup of coffee

B. decaffeinated coffee

C. sugar for his coffee

D. milk and cream for his coffee

问题："您想在 coffee 中放点什么？"汤姆回答说"请放一半一半"。汤姆想要_____。
答案：D. 在咖啡里放一点牛奶和一些奶油

　　本题是问 Tom 想在他的 coffee 中放什么？ Tom 的回答是"half and half"，全意是 half milk and half cream，即在咖啡里放一点牛奶和一些奶油。现在很多人都喜欢喝不含咖啡因（decaffeinated）的咖啡。因为咖啡较苦，大部分人都在咖啡中放些糖。英美人早餐吃得很少，上班族端上一杯咖啡就上班去了。在中餐之前都想再喝杯咖啡提神。美国人喝咖啡就如中国人喝茶一样是每天必不可少的。最有名的咖啡店叫 Starbucks（星巴克）。通常咖啡店都备有糖、牛奶、奶油，随便顾客自己加的。常用语：Coffee（with milk），please.（请来杯（加牛奶的）咖啡）。Is there an internet café（coffee shop）near here?（这附近有咖啡网吧吗？）美国的家庭中都有 coffee pot 和 coffee maker（咖啡壶）。常用词有 coffee beans（咖啡豆）、caffeine（咖啡因）、instant coffee（速溶咖啡）、coffee break（茶歇）、make coffee（煮咖啡）、cafeteria（自助餐馆）。茶的作用与咖啡差不多，都有很多的功能。一部分美国人也爱喝茶，但不会泡茶，所以较喜欢袋装的茶（tea bags）。如送茶给美国人，最好指点一下泡茶的方法。在美国带点甜味的冰茶（ice tea）很受欢迎。美国人爱喝冷饮，他们不习惯喝开水。在家庭、办公室、旅店、医院等地方都没有暖水瓶（thermos bottle），但常备有电热壶，可用它来冲茶。

14. "Getting the sack." It means all the following except:

A. Your contract is not renewed.

B. Get the sack of books.

C. You are fired.

D. Here is your last pay stub.

问题："背上你的包"，这个短语除了____之外与其他三个的答案的意思一样。

答案：B. Get the sack of books

Getting the sack. 是英语的一个俚语，意思是背上你的包走路吧，即被炒鱿鱼（fired）。被开除的说法还有：AT&T has laid off 2000 workers because of the drop in sales.（AT&T 由于销量下降而解雇了 2000 名员工。）You are fired.（你被解雇了。）Your contract is not renewed.（你的合同不再续签。）Because of the current economic crises, many workers lost their jobs.（由于当前的经济危机，许多工人失去了工作。）Here is your last pay stub/pay check.（这时你最后的一张工资单。）自动辞职是 resign：The Mayor was under pressure to resign.（市长承受着被迫辞职的压力。）Mr. Morgan has offered his resignation and it has been accepted.（摩根先生已经递交了辞呈，并已获准。）在美国，通常工资是每两个星期发一次，失业的人在找到另一份工作之前，可以到失业局（unemployment service）领取失业救济金（unemployment benefits）来维持基本的生活。那儿协助失业者介绍工作，提供职业培训，国家还给失业的人重新就业提供免学费读大学课程的计划（tuition waiver program）。对经济困难的新移民，所在社区提供免费的英语课和就业课程。与工作有关的词语：失业（be unemployed）、找工作（look for job/job hunting）、申请工作（apply for jobs）、雇用（hire）、工作面试（job interview）。很多商店或工厂招人，都在互联网上、报刊上登招聘广告，或挂招牌上面写着：Help wanted（雇人）、Now Hiring（现正招募）。

15. The sports car cost him an arm and a leg. This sentence means:

A. He spent a huge sum of money on the car.

B. He injured his arm and leg in a car accident.

C. Buying the car is really beyond his budget.

D. He lost an arm and a leg in a car accident.

问题：这辆跑车使他失去了一只手和一条腿。这个句子的意思是：

答案：A. 他花了大价钱买车。

俚语 cost him an arm and a leg 与 spent a huge sum of money 一样，是花了大价钱的意思。cost a fortune（价值连城）：A bottle of Lancôme French perfume must have cost a fortune.（一瓶法国兰蔻香水一定很昂贵。）其他几个句子不是这个含义。He injured his arm and leg in a car accident.（在一次车祸中他的手臂和腿部受了伤。）Buying the car is really beyond his budget.（买车远超出了他的预算。）美元（dollar）的符号是 $，现金（cash）分硬币（coins）和纸币（bill）两种。其中硬币有一元（one dollar）、25 分（a quarter）、10 分（a dime）和 5 分（a nickel）。纸币有 $100、$50、$20、$10、$5、$2 and $1。与钱有关的俚语有：two bucks（二美元）、3K（3000 美元）、make money（赚钱）、have money to burn（有花不完的钱）、short of money（缺钱）、money talks（有钱能使鬼推磨）。与钱有关的词语：money order（汇票）、change（零钱/找的钱）、traveler's check（旅行支票）、foreign currency（外汇）、currency exchange（外币兑换）、exchange rate（外币兑换率）。一些国家的货币：pounds（英国）、Euro（欧元）、yen（日本）、won（韩国）、dollar（加拿大）、ruble（俄罗斯）。

16. Which one of the following do you need to bring when you see a doctor?

A. Health Insurance card

B. Prescription

C. Blood test results

D. Doctor's note

问题：看医生时你必须携带哪样文件？

答案：A. 医疗保险卡

在美国，每人都有自己的医生。看病要先与医生的诊所预约（make an appointment），然后按时去诊所（Doctor's office）看病。去时一定要带上你的医疗保险卡（health insurance card），如是第一次看病，还要带上你的驾照或其他身份证，填写本人资料和病史的表。看病前，先要登记，秘书要核对你的医疗保险卡，然后坐下休息等候。排到时护士会叫你，带你到诊室，通常一个医生有 3~5 个诊室。护士会给你量血压（take blood pressure）、体温（check temperature）、脉搏（heart beat）、体重（weight）、身高（height）等。通常还会问你来看病的原因、病史、服药情况和对哪些药物有过敏（allergic to medicine）反应等。医生看完病之后，会给你开药方（prescription）、验血单（blood test）、验尿单（urine sample）、心电图 ECG（electrocardiogram）、X 射线（X-ray）、CT 扫描（CT scan）、磁共振成像 MRI 或其他试验单，必要时开医生（休假）证明（doctor's note）。药要到药店（pharmacy）去买。做试验或化验（lab work）都要去专门的化验中心（lab/medical center）。美国的药店有 CVS、Walgreens、Rite Aid、Kaiser 等连锁店。大型的超市里，如 Wal-Mart、Costco、Kmart、Shoprite、Safeway、Kroger、Target 都有药房。如要住院的话，医院里提供药和化验。如没有医疗保险，看病和治疗的费用十分昂贵。如流感之类的预防针（vaccination）可以在诊所注射。如果你的病需要看某个专科（specialist），你的医生就会推荐专家给你，然后你再去与该专家预约看病。常见的专科有：medicine（内科）、surgical（外科）、cardiovascular（心血管）、gynecology（妇科）、pediatrics（儿科）、dermatology（皮肤科）等。常见疾病的表达有：diabetes（糖尿病）、pulmonary/lung disease（肺病）、stomach disease（胃病）、hypertension（高血压）、heart disease（心脏病）、cancer（癌症）等。如发急病时，应马上打"911"急救电话，附近的医院会立即派救护车（ambulance）送病人去医院的急诊室（emergency room）救治，同时会与你的家庭医生取得联系。

17. "He is armed to teeth." means:

A. He brushes his teeth.

B. He has a toothache.

C. He is fully armed.

D. He wears a brace.

问题："He is armed to teeth." 这句话是什么意思？

答案：C. 他全副武装。

短语 armed with teeth 是全副武装的意思与 fully armed 相同。牙齿是人体中非常重要的一个部分。保持牙齿的完好和清洁对身体健康大有好处。每天都应该刷两次牙（brush teeth twice）。吃完饭后绝对不要用牙签（tooth pick）清理牙缝中残留的食物，这样会破坏牙龈（gum），引发牙周炎（Periodontitis/gum dieses），并导致掉牙，应改用牙线（floss）清理。Brush your teeth after each meal and floss daily.（餐后要刷牙，而且每天要使用牙线清洁牙缝。）每天还应该用防腐剂李施德林（antiseptic Listerine）之类的漱口水（mouthwash）漱口，来除去口臭（bad breath）、牙菌斑（plaque）和牙龈炎的细菌（gingivitis germs）。12 岁以下的儿童不宜使用这种漱口水。儿童的牙齿更需要保养，牙齿长得不齐的，要及时地矫正（teeth correction），配上牙套（braces），一年内至少上牙医（dentist）那洗牙（scaling/cleaning）一两次。与牙有关的词语有：tooth brush（牙刷）、toothpaste（牙膏）、tooth powder（牙粉）、wisdom tooth（智齿）、front teeth/incisor（门牙）、canine tooth（犬齿）、molar teeth（磨牙）、cavities（虫牙）、permanent teeth（换牙）、extractions/take out teeth（拔牙）、fillings/fill cavities（补牙）、denture（镶假牙）、toothache（牙痛）。She has a sweet tooth.（她爱吃甜食。）

18. Last night Kobe Bryan was on fire. He got 80 points! This means he was___.

A. caught on fire

B. burned himself

C. was unstoppable

D. playing with fire

问题：昨天晚上Kobe Bryan的状态极佳。他投进了80分！这句话的意思是____。

答案：C. 势不可挡

通常on fire意指起火了。房子着火了（The house is on fire. / The house was caught on fire.），在句子Last night Kobe Bryan was on fire. He got 80 points! 中on fire是一种俚语表示"很火/状态极佳"。意思是Kobe在昨晚的篮球比赛中神了，狂得了80分，不可抵挡（unstoppable）。burning himself是指烧伤了自己。Their house was burned down by arson.（他们的房子被纵火烧毁。）play with fire（玩火）。在美国，住宅的每个房间都必须装有火灾报警器（fire alarm），每层都要装灭火器（Fire Extinguisher）。家庭住宅的每层楼还必须装二氧化碳报警器（Carbon dioxide alarm）以防中毒。学校每年都进行消防演习（fire drills）。其他与火有关的用语有wild fire（野火）：Fire fighters are trying to bring the wild fire in South California under control.（消防人员正在试图控制南加州的野火。）forest fire（森林火灾）、make fire（生火）、set something on fire（点上火）、fire department/brigade（消防队）、fire engine（消防车）、fire fighter（消防员）、fire hydrant（消防龙头）、put out the fire（灭火）、fireplace（壁炉）、bonfire（篝火）、fireworks（烟火）、be fired（被解雇了）、add fuel to the fire（火上加油）。其他用法：The police opened fire on the protesters.（警方对示威者开枪。）The Governor's new budget is under fire from the opposition.（州长的新预算受到反对派的猛烈攻击。）No smoke without fire.（无风不起浪。）

19. Which one is not a favorite name brand clothing store for teens in the U.S.?

A. American Eagle

B. Aeropostale

C. Forever 21

D. Calvin Klein

问题：下列哪个服装品牌不是美国青少年所喜爱的?

答案：D. Calvin Klein

在美国不同年龄和层次的人对服饰有一定的讲究，尤其是青少年更是如此。teens 即 teenager，是指 a person aged from puberty to maturity 从青春期（puberty/adolescence）到成熟之间的人，即年龄为 13 到 19 岁（thirteen，fourteen，fifteen，sixteen，seventeen，eighteen and nineteen）。teenagers 和年轻人（youth）喜欢的名牌商店有：Aeropostale、Forever 21、Hollister、Abercrombie and Fitch、Ed Hardy（T shirt 衬衣）、Levi's、Lee、American Eagle、Pac Sun、Juicy Couture、Tilly's. H&M、True Religion、Tommy、Lacoste 等。Calvin Klein 是成年人喜欢的服装品牌，白领特别爱穿 Ralph Lauren Polo 的服装。女性爱逛的商店有 Victoria's Secret、Burberry、Juicy Couture 等品牌店。儿童的有 Polo、Old Navy、Oshkosh。对体育爱好者来说，当今最时髦名牌有 Under Armour、Nike、Adidas、Puma、Reebok、Sketcher、New Balance 等。目前 The North Face 的秋季便装和冬装如大衣（overcoat）和夹克（jacket）最受欢迎，男女老少人人都爱穿。

20. "Amy got terrible jet lag after flying across the Pacific Ocean." means:

A. She lags behind.
B. She suffered from her long flight.
C. She is car sick/has motion sickness.
D. She is sea sick/airsick.

问题："在飞过太平洋之后，Amy 的飞行时差反应很大。"这句话的意思是什么？
答案：B. 长途的飞行使她很疲劳。

短语 jet lag 是指经过长途的飞行之后的时差反应、时差感和疲劳的感受。jet lag occurs when the body clock does not readjust immediately to the time change.（由于人体生物钟不能迅速对时差作出调整，因而产生了飞机时差反应。）长途乘坐交通工具旅行很多人都会感到 motion sickness，如晕机（airsick）、晕船（seasick）、晕车（carsick）等。长期出远门，你还会想家（homesick）。lag 的另一个常用用法：She lags behind.（她落后了。）从北京飞到纽约需 13~14 小时，到旧金山或洛杉矶也需 12 小时左右。冬季北京比纽约早 13 小时，比洛杉矶早 16 小时，夏季则分别早 12 和 15 小时。通常要 4~5 天才能将时差倒过来。上飞机后你可以试着吃一片安眠药（sleeping pill）来减少时差反应。美国的夏令时从 3 月的第二个星期日开始，到 11 月的第一个星期日结束。美国夏时制起止时间是统一的，没有东西部之分。美国有 6 个时区（time zones）。洛杉矶与纽约有 3 个小时的时差（time difference）。乘飞机，尤其是需要转机（make connections）时，要特别小心留意时区的变化，以免误机。参见以下美国时区与北京的时差表。

时区 Time Zones	包括的区域 Included Places	与北京的时差	
		其他时间	夏天
Eastern Time	Washington, New York, Boston, Atlanta, Philadelphia, Miami	— 13	— 12
Central Time	Chicago, St.louis, New Orleans, Houston, etc.	— 14	— 13
Mountain Time	Phoenix, Denver, etc.	— 15	— 14
Pacific Time	Los Angeles, San Francisco, San Diego, Las Vegas, Seattle	— 16	— 15
Alaskan Time	Alaska	— 17	— 16
Hawaii Time	Hawaii	— 18	— 17

21. How do you want your beef done?
Your answer could be all except:

A. Half-done.

B. Spicy.

C. Medium-done.

D. Tender.

问题：你要的牛肉要几成熟？你的回答除了____之外都可以。

答案：B. 辣一点。

在美国的餐厅（restaurant）就餐点菜（order）时，服务员（waiter/waitress）会问你，你要的牛肉要几成熟 How do you want your beef done? 你可以回答：medium-done/half-done（中等熟）、tender（嫩一点）、half-baked（烤个五成）。英美人通常就点一个主食（main dish），如 roast beef（烧牛肉）、pork ribs（猪排）、stewed fish（煎鱼）、roast chicken（烤鸡）等。主食上可以选 1~2 种配菜，如 mashed potatoes（土豆泥）、French fries（薯条）、beans（豆类）等。面包（bread）先上，有时面包是不包括在主食中的，要另外点。然后加上一盘色拉（salad）、一杯酒或一瓶酒。主食最后上。餐后，通常来一杯咖啡（coffee）或再吃点甜点（dessert），如蛋糕（cake）、冰淇淋（ice cream）等。餐厅中常用的句子有：Here is the menu.（请看菜单。）What would you like to drink?（您要点什么饮料吗？）I'd like to have a couple of French red/white wine/soda/beer/ice water/champion/cocktail/Vodka/Sake.（我想来两杯法国红葡萄酒/白葡萄酒/苏打/啤酒/冰水/香槟/鸡尾酒/伏特加/日本米酒）。Are you ready to order?（您可以点菜了吗？）Care for any dessert?（您需要甜点吗？）Anything else（do you like）?（您还要点什么吗？）Is everything okay?（满意吗？）Very delicious！（很好吃！）Taste good.（味道不错。）salty（咸）、sour（酸）、sweet（甜）、bitter（苦）、spicy（辣）、hard（硬）。Please pass me the salt/sugar.（请把盐/糖递过来。）Bill, please.（请拿账单/付账。）通常小费为 10%～15%。有时小费是包括在账单内（included in the bill），有时可直接交给男女服务生（waiter/waitress）或留在账单夹内。

22. When you drive in the U.S. you must have all of the following except:

A. valid driver's license

B. valid insurance card

C. personal ID

D. valid car registration

问题：当你在美国开车时，你必须带上以下所有的证件，除了____之外。

答案：C. 身份证

    在美国开车你一定要随身携带驾照（driver's license），不用带身份证（personal ID）。车上要有有效注册卡（valid registration card）和汽车的保险证明（car insurance），还必须有汽车年检标志（car inspection sticker）。驾照在美国是最重要的身份证，考驾照要在DMV（Department of Motor Vehicles）通过笔试和路考（road test）及视力检查，佩戴正确的眼镜。路考通常有K-turn（掉头）、U-turn（倒车）和平行停车（parallel parking）等。每州的笔试和路考及驾照都不一样。现在大部分的笔试都是在电脑上做。华人多的城市可以用中文考。路考与中国的相比是太容易了。16岁考过笔试就可以学开车，17岁可以拿到临时驾照，18岁就可以换成正式驾照。高中大都专门为学生开设交通知识课，考试过关就等于过了驾照的笔试，可以学开车了。美国的交通制度很严，任何时候你都一定要系安全带（fasten your seatbelt）。现在很多州都不容许开车打电话和发短信（text message）。汽车要年检（Car Inspection），一般新车两年后才要年检。汽车每年都要缴纳州政府的注册费。中国公民持有中英文对照的驾照，可以在美国短期开车或租车自驾游。每个城市的机场或其他地方都可以租到车，用完之后可以将车还到租车处，也可以还到该公司在任何地点的分公司，十分便利。美国公民租车时不用买保险，因为他们自己购车时买的保险可以用于租车，中国公民租车时要买保险。租车公司有：Enterprise、Hertz、Alamo、Dollar、Budget、National、Thrift等，直接上这些公司网站查询和租车就可以了。

23. When kids say "Yummy" while eating something, it seems:

A. The food is delicious.

B. The food is oily.

C. The food is tasteless.

D. The food is juicy.

问题：当孩子们吃东西的时候说"Yummy"是什么意思？
答案：A. 很好吃。

单词Yummy 是东西好吃（delicious/tasty）的意思。其他常用的评价食品的用语有：crunchy（香脆）、bitter（苦）、sour（酸）、salty（咸）、sweet（甜）、soft（软）、hot（热）、spicy（辣）、crispy（脆）、hard（硬）、tender（嫩）、juicy（多汁）、oily/greasy（油腻）、creamy（滑腻）。常用的 dressing（调料品）有 oil（油）、soy sauce（酱油）、vinegar（醋）、brown sugar（红糖）、rock sugar（冰糖）、sesame oil（麻油）、oyster sauce（蚝油）、chili oil（辣椒油）、wie（料酒）等。美国人常用来做菜的油是 vegetable oil（菜油）、canola oil（菜籽油）、olive oil（橄榄油）。中国人爱用的配料有：ginger（姜）、garlic（大蒜/蒜头）、preserved bean/salt black bean（豆豉）、onions（葱）等。其他的调料品有 catchup（番茄酱）、cinnamon（肉桂）、mint（薄荷）、rosemary（迷迭香）、purple perilla（紫苏）、mustard（芥末）。美国人喜欢在色拉中加不同的色拉调料（salad dressing）。根据 The Apple Food Channel，2010 年前十名的色拉调料是：1. Ranch Dressing，2. Vinaigrette，3. Caesar Dressing，4. Italian Dressing，5. Bleu Cheese Dressing，6. Thousand Island Dressing，7. Balsamic Vinaigrette，8. Honey Mustard Dressing，9. French Dressing，10. Greek Dressing。

24. Which sentence has nothing to do with a traffic jam?

A. To avoid getting stuck in traffic you should not drive during rush hour.

B. There is heavy traffic on Route 1 south, pump and pump.

C. Many people drive convertibles in the summer.

D. The traffic is building up at interstate highway 95 and is expected to ease off in two hours.

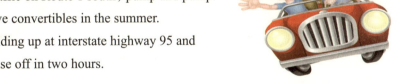

问题：哪个句子和堵车没有关系？
答案：C. 许多人喜爱在夏季开敞篷汽车。

堵车（traffic jam）是现代城市的交通问题。熟悉交通术语能帮你在电台的广播中了解交通状态，避开堵车路段。To avoid getting stuck in traffic you should not drive during rush hour.（为了避免遇上交通堵塞，你不应该在交通高峰的时段开车。）There is a heavy traffic on Route 1 south, pump and pump.（目前 1 号公路往南交通流量很大，走走停停。）The traffic is building up at interstate highway 95 and is expected to ease off in two hours.（95 号州际高速公路上车流量增大，预计畅通需两小时。）美国的公路分为州级高速公路（interstate highway）、州内高速（state highway）、本地公路（local route）等。美国收费的高速公路叫 tollway/toll road，有的 turn-pike 也收费。进时取卡，出时缴费。你可以买 E-ZPass 从快速通道进出高速公路，免去排队之烦恼。保障长途开车安全的方式之一是每开两小时停车休息一下。美国高速公路每隔几十英里就有一个休息处（rest area），供路人休息和吃便餐，很方便。较大的休息处设有餐厅、小商店、加油站等。公路沿线都设有加油站、餐厅和旅店。公路上有限速标志（speed limit），超过了会被开罚单（traffic ticket）。罚单注有交罚单的期限、数额或上法庭（appear in court）申述的方式。注意美国每个州都有自己的交通规则和驾照，一般来说在其他州逗留时间在三月之内，你不用换驾照。开车要注意交通灯（traffic lights）、交通指示牌（traffic signs）、交通管制（traffic control），避免 traffic accident（交通事故）。特别要留意的交通标识有：One Way（单向行使——许多城市中的街道都是单行的）、Detour（绕道行使）、No double parking（不能双停车）、Tow away zone（拖吊区）、No stopping any time（任何时间不能停车）、Four Way（四向停车——先来后到）、Wrong Way（错道/反向）等。通常在安全的情况下，你在十字路口是可以随时右转的。但在美国繁忙的十字路口常立有 No Turn On Red（红灯不能右转）的交通牌，你只能等到绿灯才能右转。同样有左转信号灯（left turn signal）时，即使直行是绿灯还是不能左传。闪黄灯，看道路安全时再行走。闪红灯，先停，路道安全时再行走。

25. Which of the following is different from all the others?

A. Federal Express

B. UPS

C. USPS

D. First class mail

问题：下列哪一个与其他的不同？
答案：D. 第一类邮件

　　美国主营快递业务的公司有 Federal Express（联邦快递）、UPS—United Parcel Services（美国联合包裹服务）、USPS—United States Postal Services（美国邮政局）。目前的网上邮购大部分商品都是由这三间公司提供上门递送（door to door）服务。美国的邮局（Post Office）每周一至周五全天营业，周六半天营业。信件和包裹都分 First Class、Express Mail（快件）、Priority Mail（优先邮件）及 Overnight（第二天送到）邮件等。你可以在邮局租用邮箱（mailbox）。其他与邮局有关的词语：What's the postage for registered mail to China?（寄到中国的挂号邮件的邮资是多少？）How long does it take to send a parcel to California?（寄

一个包裹到加州要多长时间？）其他和邮政有关的词汇还有：postcard（明信片）、stamps（邮票）、postage（邮资）、postman/postwoman（邮差）、parcel（包裹）、package（盒装邮件）、bulk mail（群发/大批邮件）、snail mail（平信）。美国郊外每个家庭的邮箱（mailbox）都是树立在住家车道边。邮差开邮车（post car）挨家挨户将邮件放到邮箱里。大部分邮箱上有一个红色可移动的箭头。你如有要寄出的邮件，就把邮件放入邮箱，竖起箭头。邮差下次来送信时，会将你的邮件带走。其他有关的词语：junk mail（广告邮件）、e-mail（电子邮件）、spam mail（网络上的垃圾邮件）。blackmail（勒索）：The letter she received was a blackmail.（她收到一封勒索钱财的信。）The check is in the mail.（支票已经寄出。）

26. Who cut the cheese? This question means:

A. Someone bought the cheese.

B. Someone cut the cheese into pieces.

C. Someone has farted.

D. Someone is a big cheese.

问题：谁切了奶酪？这个问题的意思是什么？

答案：C. 有人放了屁。

Who cut the cheese?是个俚语，不是问"是谁切的奶酪"，而是说"谁放了屁"（Who farted？），另一种说法是break wind。The politician is talking the greatest nonsense.（这位政客完全是在放屁。）a big cheese（大奶酪）也是俚语，指重要或有影响的人，相当于a big fish或是a big shot。cheese是美国人和西方人最爱吃的食物之一。奶酪是乳蛋白质的酪蛋白凝固后衍生的食物。它包括牛奶中的蛋白质和脂肪（protein and fat）。在生产过程中，牛奶通常酸化，并加入酶凝乳凝成固体后压制成最终的形式。美国的奶酪是一种加工奶酪（processed cheese），有橙色、黄色或白色的，味道略甜，具有非常低的熔点。cheese是美国人不可缺少的食品，在蔬菜、沙拉等很多的食品中都放奶酪。cheese burger（奶酪汉堡包）、cheese pizza（奶酪比萨饼）、cheese cake（乳酪蛋糕）等就自然成了美国人所喜爱的食品。macaroni and cheese（通心粉加奶酪）也是美国人最爱吃的食品之一。就是在照相时，美国人也忘不了奶酪。Is everybody ready? Say cheese!（大家准备好了吗？笑一笑！）中国人一般都不喜欢吃奶酪，更不愿意在照相时说"气死（cheese）"。那还能笑得出来吗？后来人们发现说"茄子（eggplant）"的口型与cheese很像，所以在照相时就用茄子取代了奶酪。成语：You can't have your cake and have it.（两者不可兼得——不能既要吃饼，又要把饼保存。）

27. An American standard kitchen has all of the following except:

A. oven

B. gas/electric burner（stove）

C. toaster

D. heater

问题：在美国标准的厨房里以下哪一个没有？

答案：D. 暖气设备

　　暖气设备不是厨房的一部分。美国家庭中的厨房都备有各种用具（appliance）：烧煤气或电的炉灶（cooking range / gas / electric stove）、微波炉（microwave）、烤箱（oven）、冰箱（refrigerator）、洗碗机（dishwasher）、带热水龙头的水槽（sink）、抽油烟机（hood）、橱柜（cabinet）及储藏室（pantry）。有的厨房还设有冷冻箱（freezer）和中心岛（a center island）。中心岛上可以设有水槽、炉灶、烤面包机（toast）和咖啡壶（coffee maker），搅拌机（blenders/mixers）也很普遍。大部分家庭都有餐厅（dining room），不过早上一般是在厨房里的早餐桌或中心岛上用餐。美国人不怎么炒菜做饭（cooking），家用抽油烟机大部分效果都很差，有很多只是抽风机（ventilator），不能将油烟抽到房子外面去。常用的炊具（cookware/cooking utensil）有：frying pan（炒菜锅）、lid/cover（锅盖）、spatula/turner（锅铲）、tongs（钳夹）、balloon whisk（打蛋器）、peeler（削皮器）、spoon（调羹）、fork（叉子）、non-stick pot（不粘锅）、boiler（蒸锅）、cutting board（砧板）、knife（菜刀）、bowls（碗）、dishes（碟子）、cups（杯子）等。东方人爱用rice cooker（电饭煲）、slow cooker（慢炖锅）、wok（炒锅）、chopsticks（筷子）等。She packed everything but the kitchen sink for a field trip tomorrow.（她把明天郊游需要的东西全都准备好了。）

28. The thunderstorm finally passed and the rain <u>eased off</u>. The underlined part in the sentence means:

A. tapped off

B. stopped

C. scattered

D. lift up

问题：雷雨终于过去，雨势<u>减弱</u>。句子中画线部分的意思是什么？

答案：C. 雨散了

答案中tape off、lift up、stop都是雨停了的意思。只有scatter（雨势减弱，雨散了）和 ease off意思最相近。常用谈天气的语句有：What's the weather today?（今天的天气如何？） It's nice and warm.（天气很温和。）sunny、cloudy、hazy、smoggy、foggy、sultry、hot、cold（晴天、阴天、阴霾、雾霾、闷热、热、冷）It's very changeable in the spring.（春天的天气变化无常。） Quite before the storm.（暴风雨前的宁静）与天气有关的词语有：weather station forecasting （气象站预测）、weather channel（气象频道）、climate change（气候变化）、global warming （全球气候变暖）、rain（雨）、torrential rain（暴雨）、drizzle（毛毛雨）、heavy rain（大雨）、 light rain（小雨）、scattered shower（阵雨）、freezing rain（冻雨）、wind（风）、mild wind （和风）、gust wind（阵风）、breeze（微风）、tornado（龙卷风）、thunder storm（雷雨风 暴）、dust storm（沙尘暴）、lightening（闪电）、thunder（雷鸣）、snow（雪）、heavy snow （大雪）、light snow（小雪）、freeze（冰冻）、icy（冰）、hail（冰雹）、frost（霜）、dew（露 水）、cloudy（多云）、dense of cloud（密集的云）、muggy（闷热）、sultry（闷热）、high temperature（高温）、heat wave（热浪）、flood warning/watch（洪水警告）、umbrella（雨伞）、 raincoat（雨衣）、poncho（雨披）。

29. Rebecca has relations with Kevin. This sentence means:

A. Rebecca has an affair with Kevin.

B. Rebecca is dating with Kevin.

C. Rebecca is a remote relative to Kevin.

D. Rebecca wants to rupture a relation with Kevin.

问题：Rebecca has relations with Kevin. 这句话是什么意思？

答案：A. 瑞贝卡与凯文有男女之间的关系。

短语has relations with someone 与has an affair with都是有男女关系的意思，所以答案 是A选项。相同的表达还有：has an intimate relation with（有亲密关系）、sexual relations occurred outside of marriage（婚外情）。其他选项：Rebecca is a remote relative to Kevin.（瑞 贝卡和凯文是远亲。）Rebecca wants to rupture a relation with Kevin.（瑞贝卡要和凯文断绝 关系。）Rebecca is dating with Kevin.（瑞贝卡在与凯文约会。）My wife and I first met on a blind date arranged by a friend, both were a little nervous.（我和妻子的初次会面是朋友安排的， 双方都有点紧张。）date的一些用法：We need an up to date schedule of the final project.（我 们需要一份最新的项目日程表。）We'll keep you up to date（posted on）with any development of this grant.（我们有该基金的新进展就会告诉你。）Your passport is out of date therefore invalid.（你的护照过期了。）CNN will update you on today's top news stories.（CNN将为您 提供今天的重要新闻的更新消息。）

30. Which color of traffic signs is NOT for warning in the U.S.?

A. Red

B. Blue

C. Yellow

D. Brown

问题：在美国，哪个颜色的交通标志不是警告标志？

答案：B. 蓝色

在美国开车必须熟知交通规则（traffic regulations）和交通标志（traffic signs）。交通标志以颜色和形状分类。各州的交通标志都有些不同。大部分警告标志的颜色为黄色（yellow）或红色（red）或棕色（brown），多为圆形、菱形和三角形。最重要的警告标志有：Stop sign 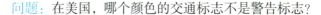（交叉口停车）、Do not enter sign （不可进入）、Yield sign （让先）、Pedestrian （行人过道）、One way street （单行道）、Detour （改道）、School zone （校区）、Speed limit sign （限速等）。在住宅和学校附近的限速多为15~25英里每小时。开车时，遇到停在路边的校车（school bus），绝对不能超越。如有救护车（ambulance）和消防车（fire engine）经过，一定要马上在路边停下让他们先通过。如果车道前面有警车闪亮，必须转到其他车道（move over），保障执行公务的警员的安全。不然会吃大罚单。公路的信息标志牌是深蓝色的，提供停车休息、加油、就餐、住宿等信息。高速公路上悬挂的大型路牌多是绿色的。 是州际高速公路的标志（interstate highway sign）， 是州内高速公路的标志（state highway sign）。很多高速公路是要收费（toll）的，在进出口设有Easy pass/E-Zpass （快速通道），购买了快速通道卡就可以不用排队交费。一般的收费道路是在收费站按键拿卡在出口处缴费。注意，有的道路，如新泽西的Garden State Parkway在一些收费点是无人收钱，需要在收费网中投放正确金额的硬币（exact change）。所以要先准备好硬币。在美国，人们非常遵守交通规则，交通法也十分严厉，抢道的情况很少见，道路上很少听到汽车鸣笛。在美国大部分的州际公路，东西走向的为双数，如40、70、80、90号，西南和东南走向的为单数，如5、75、85、95号等。

31. Which U.S. size for women's shoes is equivalent to size 37 in China?

A. 7-1/2

B. 10

C. 8

D. 6

问题：哪一个美国鞋子的尺码相当于中国的 37 码？

答案：D.6

美国人使用的衣服、裤子、鞋帽等的尺码与中国的都不一样。成人男女鞋子的尺码对照表如下：

中国女人	35.5	36	37	37.5	38	39	39.5	40	41	41.5	42	43
美国女人	5	5.5	6	6.5	7	7.5	8	8.5	9	9.5	10	10.5
中国男人	35	36	37	38	39	40	41	42	43	44	45	46
美国男人	5	5.5	6	6.5	7	7.5	8	8.5	9	9.5	10	10.5

衣服的尺码一般分儿童和成人两种。儿童的衣服裤子一般都是按年龄算：婴儿的按月份、重量和高度：NB（new born）、5~8lb、less than 21-1/2 inch（新生儿、5~8 磅、身高少于 21.5 英寸）。男女儿童的尺寸有点不同，如 10 号的衣服适合身高 57 英寸的女孩（1.45 米左右）和 54 英寸的男孩（1.37 米左右）。成人男式和女式衣裤的尺码标法不同。衣服一般分小号 S（small）、中号 M（media）、大号 L（large）、特大号 XL（extra large）、超大号 XXL（extra/ extra large）等，衬衣则是根据衣领大小而定的，如 38、40、42、44 英寸等。男式裤子则按腰围和长度而定，如 30×32 是腰围 30 英寸（78 公分）裤长 32 英寸（81 公分）。但女式的尺码有的分得很细，比较复杂（可参见 http://en.wikipedia.org/wiki/US_standard_clothing_size）。

	XXS	XS	S	M	L	XL	2XL	3XL
Chest胸	29-31	30-32	34-36	38-40	42-44	46-48	48-50	50-52
Waist腰	27-29	28-30	30-32	32-33	33-34	36-38	40-42	44-48

32. What do you want for your cash? This question is likely heard in___.

A. a bank

B. a grocery store

C. a post office

D. a drug store

问题：你是要大的还是小的钞票？这个问题很有可能在哪里听到？

答案：A. 在银行

　　你在银行（bank）取现金（cash）的时候，银行职员会常问：What do you want for your cash?（你是要大的还是小的钞票？）你可以回答：Three 100 dollar bills and five 20s, please.（三张 100 块的，五张 20 块的。）其他与银行有关的用语有：open/close an account（开/撤销账户）、savings account（储蓄账户）、checking account（支票存款账户）、loan（贷款）、interest（利息）、withdraw（取款）、deposit（存款）、transfer money（转账）、bank transfer（银行汇款）、IRA account（个人退休账户）、retirement account（退休账户）、education account（教育账户）、joint account（联名账户）、money order（汇票）、traveller's check（旅行支票）、bank check（银行支票）。在杂货店（grocery store）里，收银员（cashier）会问你"交现金还是信用卡"（"cash or credit?"）。信用卡组织有Master、VISA、American Express等。常见的用语还有：Swipe your card, please.（请刷卡。）Sign your name here（在这里签名）。Enter your PIN number（输入密码）。顾客也可以用debit card（银行支付卡）或是food stamp（粮食券）付钱。food stamp 是一种国家发给贫困家庭的救济金，只能用来买食品。付钱时收银员可能会说Do you want cash back? 是问你是不是需要取些现金，而不是退钱给你。在药店（drug store）买药通常都要出示医疗保险卡。你把药方交给药剂师（pharmacist），病人只付很少的钱，即按保险条例共同支付的部分。如果没有医疗保险，药费很贵的。

33. A typical single American house has the following except:

A. family room

B. living room

C. kitchen

D. sunroom

问题：典型的美国独栋房不包括下列哪种房间：

答案：D. 日光浴室

在美国，独栋的住房一般有两层，包括以下的房间：living room（起居室/客厅）、family room（家庭房间）、kitchen（厨房）、master bedroom（主卧室）、1~4 bedrooms（卧室 1~4 间）、powder room（化妆间，通常也叫 half bath）、utility room（意为杂物间，放有烧水的锅炉（boiler）、暖气设备（heater）、冷气机（air conditioner）、洗衣机和烘干机（wash room）洗衣间等。主卧室通常都带有淋浴（shower）和澡盆（bathtub）的卫生间（bathroom）及衣帽柜（closet）或步行衣帽间（walking closet）。较大的卧室如公主房间（princess'suit）也常带有卫生间。大部分居家都有 2~4 个卫生间。有的房子还配了其他的房间：attic（阁楼）、conservatory（音乐厅）、study/library（学习室/书房）、playroom（游戏室）、sunroom（日光浴室）、bay window（窗台）、foyer（门厅）、garage（车库）、deck/porch（阳台）、basement（地下室）、walkout basement（带出口的地下室）等。车库前的路叫 drive way，房子前后院（front yard and back yard）有草地（lawn）。常见的房屋类型有殖民式（colonial）、双层式（bi-level），牧场式（range），现代式（contemporary）等。townhouse 是指联排别墅，室内结构与单独的别墅差不多但小些，也带车库。condominium 是较豪华的公寓，一般不带车库，apartments 即公寓。在美国，所有的新建房屋，不论是单独别墅或公寓都是装修好了的，不容许卖毛坯房。对自己的房屋改造也要提交方案交当地政府审批。

34. Which of the words is not frequently used in daily shopping?

A. Loan

B. Discount

C. Coupon

D. Rain check

问题：下列哪个单词不是日常购物中常用的？
答案：A. 贷款

一般来说，美国的商品是物美价廉，遇上节假日或促销，常有减价（on sale）。减价的折扣（discount）表示方法与中国的正好相反。5% discount，意思是中国的 95 折，25% discount 则是中国的 75 折。很多公司发放折扣券（coupons），可以在减价折扣的基础上再减价。大部分折扣券都是以广告方式由邮局送到各家各户，许多家庭主妇都带着很多收集起来的折扣券上街购物。许多仓库型超市如 Costco、Sam's Club、BJ's 等每月都发放折扣券本（Coupon books）。在很多大型商场里，如果减价的商品在减价期内售完（sold out）的话，你可以要商店开出（rain check）专用减价单，你可以凭此单在新的货品到了之后，按减价时的价格购买该商品。另外，如你对所购的商品不满意或发现有瑕疵（defect），尤其是在大商店购买的，你可以在规定时间内随时调换（exchange goods）或退货（return the goods），非常讲信用。如果你的发票不见了，有的商店也让你退货，但是只能将退款放在该店的消费卡上，供你今后在店内使用。loan（贷款）一词在一般的购物时不常用。但是，如你要购买大的商品，如家具、大型电器、汽车等，商店可以让顾客以分期付款（installment）的方式付费。购房屋的费用巨大，大多数人都是选择贷款方式付费。值得注意的是，用贷款方式购物，你要付很高的利息（interests），你最终支付的费用往往是全款的两倍以上。

35. What is "十万" in English?

A. A hundred thousand

B. Ten thousand

C. A million

D. A thousand

问题：汉语中数字"十万"的英语是什么？

答案：A. A hundred thousand

中文的数字分个、十、百、千、万、十万、百万、千万、亿等位数，而英文的数字表示法有所不同。one（个）、ten（十）、hundred（百）、thousand（千）没有区别，但英文中没有"万"这个数位，而是用"千位"来代替，所以一万的英文是ten thousand（十个千），十万是a hundred thousand。英文一百万叫a million，一千万是ten million，一亿是a hundred million，十亿是a billion。英文基数和序数的发音、拼写和缩写：one—first/1st、two—second/2nd、three—third/3rd、four—fourth/4th（从四之后都是在数字后加上th）、five—fifth/5th、six—sixth/6th、seven—seventh/7th、eight—eighth/8th、nine-ninth/9th、ten—tenth/10th、eleven—eleventh/11th、twelve—twelfth/12th、thirteen—thirteenth/13th、fourteen—fourteenth/14th、fifteen—fifteenth/15th、sixteen—sixteenth/16th、seventeen—seventeenth/17th、eighteen-eighteenth/18th、nineteen—nineteenth/19th、twenty—twentieth/20th、thirty—thirtieth/30th、forty—fortieth/40th、fifty—fiftieth/50th、sixty—sixtieth/60th、seventy—seventieth/70th、eighty-eightieth/80th、ninety-ninetieth/90th。一般数字的读法是：街道号码和房间号码通常都按两位数来读，如房号218,读two, eighteen，而不是two hundred and eighteen，街牌1365读成thirteen, sixty-five。2018年读成two thousand and eighteen 或twenty eighteen。

36. A vegetarian is a person who___ .

A. does not eat meat

B. likes vegetables

C. grows vegetables

D. eat both meat and vegetables

问题：素食主义者是指什么人？

答案：A. 不吃肉的

　　素食主义者（vegetarians）是不吃肉的（does not eat meat）的人。一般来说，他们吃鸡蛋和奶制品，如牛奶和奶酪。一般的人都吃肉类和蔬菜（eat both meat and vegetables）。现代人重视食物对身体健康的影响，都减少肉类而多吃蔬菜。美国人爱吃的蔬菜有：lettuce（生菜）、spinach（菠菜）、broccoli（西兰花）、cauliflower（花菜）、carrot（胡萝卜）、bell pepper（柿子椒）、cucumber（黄瓜）、celery（西芹菜）、radish（萝卜）、onion（洋葱）、bean（豆类）、hot pepper（辣椒）、potato（土豆）、tomato（西红柿）等。但他们是不大会做菜的，常把蔬菜煮得烂烂的很难吃。他们大部分的时候都是将蔬菜洗净后，切小混合成沙拉（salad）放入酱（sauce）或沙拉酱（dressing）后生吃。也可以加上鸡块（chicken）、虾（shrimp）、奶酪（cheese）、水果（fruit）等做成各类的沙拉。中国的很多蔬菜美国没有，就是翻成英文美国人也听不懂，需要再解释。如，豆角译成（long bean）、中国芹菜（Chinese celery）、苦瓜（bitter gourd）、丝瓜（loofah/sponge gourd）、冬瓜（wax gourd）、空心菜（water spinach）、豆芽（bean sprouts）、包菜（white cabbage）、油菜（rape）、上海青（Shanghai green）、韭菜（leek）等。一般的美国人就知道白菜（Chinese cabbage），称之为bok choy（粤语）。所以碰到蔬菜翻译时，就说是一种青菜（green vegetable）就好了。种菜（grows vegetables）、菜园子（vegetable garden）。

37. Which of the sentences below is not involved in renting an apartment?

A. How much is the monthly charge?

B. Does it include utilities?

C. I am looking for two bedrooms with a basement.

D. Show me your insurance card.

问题：以下哪个句子和租房无关？

答案：D. 让我看看你的保险卡。

How much is the monthly charge?（月租是多少？）Does it include utilities?（是否包括水电费？）I am looking for two bedrooms with a basement.（我想找有两间卧室带地下室的住房。）以上句子都与租房有关。唯有Show me your insurance card.（让我看看你的保险卡。）这句话与租房无关。租公寓时，要签合同（sign a contract），大部分要求租半年以上，先要交两个月的租金（rent），其中一个月是押金（deposit），最后一个月就不用交了。租前一定要了解清楚，租金是否包括utilities fees（水电费：electricity and water）、air-conditioner（空调）、heater（暖气）、the Internet（互联网）、cable（有线电视）、recycle（回收）和gabbage fee（垃圾）等的费用，还要了解厨房是否有 range hood（抽油烟机），灶是 electric stove（电炉）还是 gas stove（煤气炉），是否配有 furniture（家具），如：bed（床）、mattress（床垫）、chest/cabinet（衣柜）、table（桌子）、chair（椅子）、sofa（沙发）、washing machine（洗衣机）、dryer（烘干机）、lamp（灯）等。可以这样问：Do you have furnished apartments?（有带家具的公寓吗？）因为许多公寓的房间是没有任何家具的，除了厨房、浴室、厕所、车库、地下室之外，其他房间的灯也要自己备。还有就是看公寓有没有停车位（parking lot）。在看房的时候要仔细检查，看是否有被损坏的地方。也可以用手机把各个房间拍个照。离开时，要把房间，尤其是厨房打扫清理好，以免扣押金或罚款（fine）。租金要按时交，不然就会罚滞纳金（late fee），还可能会被赶出去。房子租好后，往往需要打电话给电话、有线电视、水电或煤气等公司接通电话、电视、水电、煤气等。

38. "Do you want to eat here or to go?" "To go" in this sentence means:

A. take the meal with you.

B. have a box lunch.

C. deliver the food.

D. have a potluck party.

问题："Do you want to eat here or to go?"

"to go" 在这个句中的意思是什么？

答案：A. 带走食品

在美国的快餐店，常听到店员问订餐的顾客说 "To go?"，意思是 "你打算在这里吃还是带走？"（Do you want to eat here or to go?）如是带走（take the meal with you），店员会将食品用纸袋装好给你。在店里吃的话，吃后要将餐盘（food plate）放到指定处，把垃圾丢到垃圾桶（garbage can）里。有些餐厅有外卖服务，你可以打电话订好餐，他们会将饭菜送上门（deliver）。potluck party（便饭聚会）是很多企业、公司、学校、社区、街坊等举办的一种常见的聚会形式。

每个参加聚会的人都准备一种食品（多数是自己做的homemade），或带饮料（drinks）、糕点水果（cake and deserts）、餐具（utensils）等和大家一块分享。这种聚会温馨随意，很受欢迎。box lunch是盒饭的意思。美国的午餐时间（lunch break/hours）一般是12点到下午1点或2点。大公司有自己的餐厅（cafeteria），但大部分人会到外面餐厅就餐，也有些自己备好午餐盒（lunch box/box lunch），有三明治（sandwich）、热狗（hot dog）、酸奶（yogurt）、香蕉（banana）、苹果（apple）之类的水果等。中午是没有午休的，美国人也没有睡午觉（take a nap）的习惯。所以到4点或4点半，大多数的公司和企业都下班了。另外，一般的商店，除餐厅之外晚上7点就关门，个别的到9点左右也都打烊了。夏季开门的时间相对长一些。周日上午许多商店不开门，都上教堂做礼拜去了，开门的商店大都在下午4点左右关门。

39. Kent's family is <u>going abroad</u> next semester. The underlined phrase means:

A. go on board an airplane.

B. go overseas.

C. go on board a bus.

D. go to a boarding school.

问题： 肯特一家打算下学期<u>出国</u>。
　　　 画线部分短语的意思是什么？

答案： B. 去海外。

短语go overseas（去海外）与go abroad/go to a foreign country的意思一样。go on board an airplane（登机），如CA 981 to New York now is boarding.（前往纽约的中国民航981号航班现在开始登机。）go on board a bus（上公车），go on board a ship（上船）。与乘飞机旅行相关的用语有：Passport and ticket, please.（请出示机票和护照。）Would you like an aisle seat or window seat?（你想要靠过道的座位还是靠窗的座位？）Attention, please. UA 830 to Los Angeles is delayed.（请注意。联合航空公司前往洛杉矶的UA1493航班因故延迟起飞。）check in counter（检票柜台）、boarding pass/gate（登机牌/登机口）、book e-ticket online（网上订电子客票）、departure/arriving gate（离境/到达口）、check-in baggage（托运行李）、carry-on baggage（随身携带行李）。飞机上用语：What would you like, noodle/pasta or chicken or beef?（您要面条/意大利面，或鸡肉/牛肉？）Anything to drink?（想喝点什么饮料？）Orange juice with ice and a bottle of red wine, please.（请来一杯加冰橙汁和一瓶红酒。）其他饮料有：Canada Dry、Pepsi、Sprite、cola、diet coke、apple juice、tomato juice、water、tea。keep your seatbelt fastened（保持你的安全带/系紧的状态）、fasten your seatbelt（系好安全带）、

lavatory occupied/empty（厕所占用/无人）。Please turn off all electronic equipment.（请关闭所有的电子设备。）Serve beverage and dinner/lunch.（供应饮料和晚餐/午餐。）Please keep your seatbelt fasten while the plane is still taxing.（飞机仍在滑行，请系好你的安全带。）

40. "Where is the restroom?" "Around the corner." The person who asked the question wanted to_____.

A. take a bath

B. take a rest

C. take a shower

D. use the toilet

问题：“厕所在哪里？”“在那个角上。”

问话人想要_____。

答案：D. 用卫生间

答案是D.use the toilet（上卫生间）。go to John's（use Johnny on the spot, a portable toilet）。上卫生间（使用便携式厕所）。use the restroom也是指上卫生间，不是想休息一会（take a rest）。take a rest in a rest room.（在休息室小歇一下。）飞机上卫生间标识的英文是lavatory。找卫生间时，通常女士们问Where is the Lady's room? 男士则说Where is the Man's room。WC 也是厕所的标志，是water closet的缩写，通常是指带抽水马桶（flush toilet）的卫生间，是英国用语。bathroom 也可以指卫生间，但是指带有洗澡盆（tub）或淋浴（shower）的。其他有关的用语有：take a bath（洗澡）、take a shower（洗淋浴）、go for a pee.（去撒尿/小便，urinate/piss）。拉大便的表达是：I want to poop/move bowels/empty bowels. He is pooping.（他在大便——俚语）。拉肚子的表达是：I had diarrhea four time today.（我今天拉了四次。）I am having the runs.（我拉肚子。）相关词汇还有：hand soap/sanitizer（洗手液）、paper towels（纸巾）、tissue（手纸）、hand dryer（干手器）、wastebasket（纸篓）、flush the toilet（冲马桶）、dog shit（狗屎）、bull shit（牛粪/胡说八道——骂人的话）。I am fed up with your bull shit, cut the crap.（真是受够了，废话少说。）

41. "I'm in the shower, please answer the door!"
The speaker means all except:

A. someone rang the doorbell.

B. someone knocked at the door.

C. someone is at the door.

D. the telephone rang.

问题："我在洗澡，有人来了请去开门。"

说话人的意思不是说：

答案：D. 来电话了。

　　说话人是听到了门铃响（bell ringing）或敲门声（knocks at the door），知道有人来访了（someone is at the door/you have a visitor），叫人到门口看看谁来了（answer the door/bell）。相关短语有：ring the door bell（按门铃）、door keeper（看门人）、door stopper（门吸/门碰——挡住不让门自动关的东西）、security door（安全门）、door to door（挨门挨户）。在美国不能随意到别人家拜访，一定要事先当面或电话约好，不然不单是不礼貌，有时还会引起麻烦或危险。打电话用语：answer（pick up）the phone/call（接电话）、hang up the phone（挂电话）。Hold on, I will get him for you.（别挂电话，我去叫他接电话。）I will call you back later.（我待会儿给你打过来。）在美国接电话时，应先报自己姓名或是工作单位。如，Hello, this is Mr. Carter.（我是卡特先生。）Hello, this is Mr. Smith's residence.（这是史密斯先生家。）Good morning,（this is）Dr. Murphy's office.（早上好，这里是 Murphy 医生的诊所。）询问对方是谁时说：May I ask who is calling?（请问你是谁？）对方问你 May I speak to Mr. Li?（我找李先生）或 Is Mr. Li available/at home?（李先生在家吗？）如你就是李先生，你就回答：This is he/Speaking.（我就是。）美国的电话绝大多数都是留言电话，如没有接，就可以留言。May I leave a message?（我可以留言吗？）另外，很多美国人就是在家也不一定接你的电话，一是商业电话太多，再就是有选择的接，所以你一定要留言。说不定你要找的人在家里呢！常用词还有：phone bill（电话账单）、yellow book/phone book（电话簿）。

42. Which is a typical food for an American family?

A. Salad

B. Pizza

C. Barbecue ribs

D. Buffalo wings

问题：下列哪种是美国家庭的典型食品？

答案：A. 沙拉

　　美国是个移民国家，每个民族都带来了有自己特色的食品和烹饪方法（recipe），很难说哪个食品是最典型的美国家庭食品。人们说美国是"melting pot（熔炉）"，即美国化（americanization）或同化（acculturation），其实是不正确的。用"salad bowl（沙拉碗）"来描述会更贴切，因为各个种族保留了自己的特点。salad platter（沙拉拼盘），是美国喜爱的食品，几乎餐餐都有。最常见的是蔬菜沙拉（vegetable salad），沙拉中有新鲜的蔬菜（fresh/raw）：lettuce（生菜）、spinach（菠菜）、kale（羽衣甘蓝）、radish（小红萝卜）、celery（西芹）、cherry tomato（樱桃番茄）、bell pepper（柿子椒）等，还常加有 olive（橄榄）、cheese（奶酪）、croutons（油炸面包块）等。fruit salad（水果沙拉）and coleslaw（卷心菜沙拉）也很流行。答案中的食品美国都爱吃。其他爱吃的食品有：macaroni and cheese（通心粉和奶酪）、fried chicken with mashed potatoes（带土豆泥的炸鸡）、pizza（比萨）、barbecue ribs（烧烤排骨）、buffalo wings（布法罗鸡翅）、pasta（面食）等。参见美国最爱吃的 50 种食品（American food：The 50 greatest dishes）：http://travel.cnn.com/explorations/eat/best-usa-travel/top-50-american-foods-513946。参见 15 种美国传统食谱（15 traditional American recipes）：http://www.realsimple.com/food-recipes/recipe-collections-favorites/american-recipes-00000000061159/。

43. Which is not a common activity for all members of an American family to do on the weekend?

A. Mow the lawn.

B. Have a BBQ party.

C. Go to a park.

D. Go to a movie.

问题：哪个不是美国家庭所有成员在周末的活动？

答案：A. 剪草坪。

　　在美国，除了城市之外，几乎每个家庭都有带草坪（lawn）的独立住房。到了周末，常常要推着割草机（lawnmower）剪草（mow grass）。一般每两到三周割一次。基本上都是男主人来干，有时女主人也帮着做。天气热时，还要天天用水管或安装的自动浇水系统（sprinkler）浇水，每年还得施肥（fertilizer）和杀虫（pesticide）。家庭条件好的就请保养草地（lawn care）的公司来做。在前院，大部分都种了观赏的树木和花草（landscape），如雪松/柏（cedar/cypress）、日本红枫（Japanese maple）、樱花（cherry）、梨花（flowering pear）、山茱萸（dogwood）及每年生（annual）和多年生（perennial）的花草、黄杨木（boxwood）、玫瑰（rose）等。美国的华人大都在自己的后院有菜园子（vegetable gardens），种上美国市场上没有或少见的中国蔬菜，如空心菜、长豆角、丝瓜、扁豆（hyacinth bean）等。美国人对工作和休息是分得很清楚的。一到周末，就是家庭的生活，如邀请亲朋好友来家聚会吃烧烤（have a BBQ party）。带孩子们到公园（take kids to a park）或主题公园（theme park）去玩，如迪斯尼乐园（Disney）、六旗游乐园（Six Flags）、环球影城（Universal Studio）等，或去看电影或球赛（go to a movie/game），完了之后便上馆子（go out to eat），也有的家庭驱车到外地旅游和访友。

44. The sign on the right means all of the following except:

A. parking for handicapped.

B. automatic door for handicapped.

C. wheelchair.

D. reserved for disabled persons.

问题：右边的标志与哪个答案不相符合？

答案：C. 轮椅

　　在美国，残疾人（the handicapped or persons with disabilities）受到广泛的尊重和帮助，无论在何处人们都为他们提供方便。右边的那个画有轮椅的标志是专为所有的残疾人设计的，而不光是为坐轮椅（wheel chair）的人。每个地方都有这个标志。在停车场，它表明是提供残疾人专有的停车位（parking for handicapped 或 reserved for disabled persons）。残疾人的车都带轮椅标志的残疾人车牌（license plate）和挂在后镜上的残疾人卡。占用残疾人专有的停车位的罚款比任何交通违章都重。在大楼门口，它是残疾人用自动门（automatic door for handicapped）的标志。所有大楼、机场、车站、运动比赛场地都有方便轮椅的通道（wheelchair path）。残疾人在美国享有最好的福利，他们读书是全免费的。学习成绩达到要求的还享有免费的起居生活方面的护理（living assistance）。毕业之后，找工作不成问题。在学区和学校里，都设有特殊教育班（special education classes）。国家还拨款帮助在某些方面有小缺陷的儿童，如患自闭症的（autism）、眼盲（blind）、耳聋（deaf）、哑（dumb）、阅读上有困难的（reading disability）、听力弱的（listening deficits）、说话有困难的（speech difficulties）等。学校对残疾学生的鉴定十分严谨，要由教师、心理专家（psychologist）、语言病理学家（speech pathologist）、特殊教育教师（special education teacher）、辅导员（counselor）、家长或监护人（parents or guardian）组成的小组进行鉴定。对于英语不是母语的学生ELL（English Language Learners）也要进行笔试和面试来确定上哪种班级，通常有ESL、Bilingual和Mainstream Pull out ESL等选择。

45. In the U.S., you must wear a helmet in all the following situations except:

A. riding a bike.

B. riding a scooter.

C. doing ice skating.

D. working on a construction site.

问题：在什么情况下你不必戴头盔?

答案：C. 溜冰。

　　美国的法律要求每个人，不管是大人或小孩，在街上骑自行车（riding a bike）、骑摩托车（riding a motorcycle）、玩滑板车（riding a scooter）、滚轮溜冰（roller skating）时都必须戴头盔（helmet）以保证安全。除此之外，最好也穿上显眼的服装，引起路上车辆驾驶人的注意。很多的街道都设有自行车车道（bike lane）方便骑自行车的人。夜间骑车一定要配有手电筒，不然会被处以罚款。许多自行车上都带有荧光反射标识（fluorescent reflective logo），骑自行车的人也往往穿上有荧光反射的衣服。美国的上班族常常喜欢在傍晚跑步（jogging）和散步，为了安全，很多人都穿浅色或有荧光反射的衣服。在溜冰场溜冰（ice skating）不一定要戴头盔，但打冰球（ice hockey）是一定要戴的。在美国很多项体育运动也都必须戴上头盔或面具（mask），如美式足球（American football）、长曲棍球（lacrosse）、冰球（ice hockey）、棒球（baseball）、击剑（fencing）等。而且有的还要穿防护服（protesting cloth）来保护肩膀（shoulder）、手肘（elbows）、膝盖（knees）等部位。消防员（firefighters）和在建筑或其他工地上工作（working on a construction site）的人，也必须戴上安全帽（head protection must be worn.）或（all personnel must wear a hard hat.）。

46. In the U.S., what must you NOT do when involved in a traffic accident?

A. Call 911 and wait for policemen and/or ambulance.

B. Argue with the other driver or policemen.

C. Write down the plate number of the other vehicle and the driver's license.

D. Find a safe place and wait for help.

问题：在美国遇到交通事故时，你不应该做什么？

答案：B. 和另一个司机或警察争论。

在美国遇到交通事故，首先要自救或可能的话救助他人。但一定要在第一时间拨打 "911" 报警电话。等待警察和救护车（call "911" and wait for policemen and ambulance）。同时离开公路，找一个安全的地方，等待救援（find a safe place and wait for help）。不要与对方争论（argue with the other driver）谁的过错，交警来后自有公断。如果警察一时来不了，可以记下或用手机拍下对方车辆的牌照和驾驶证号码，以及汽车损坏的情况（write down the plate number of the other vehicle and the driver's license），并记下目击者（witness）的姓名电话等为今后打官司用。同时马上与你的保险公司联系（contact your insurance company），告知事故情况和警察提供的事故报告（police report）。如果在开车时被警车叫停，要立刻在路边停下来，绝对不要与警察争执（argue with policeman）。当然最重要的是如何预防事故的发生。首先应严格遵守交通规则（follow traffic laws and regulations）。绝对不要酒后开车（never drink and drive）、超速行驶（drive over the speed limit）、累了也不要开车（don't drive if you are fatigued）、开车时不能用手机，绝对不要发短信（don't use cell phone or text messaging）。开长途时，每两个小时停车休息（stop and take a break every couple of hours），司机和所有的乘客全程都要系安全带（The driver and passengers should have their seatbelts fasten at all times.）。其他用语：rare-end（追尾）、reckless driving（鲁莽开车）、crash/collision（撞车）、head on collision（对头撞车）、run a red light（闯红灯）、hit and run（交通肇事后逃逸）、defensive drive（防御性驾驶）。He was arrested for drunk driving/driving recklessly.（他因酒后开车/鲁莽开车被捕。）

47. Which of the words is different from all the others?

A. U-Haul

B. Ryder

C. Penske

D. Alamo

问题：哪个词与其他的词不同？

答案：D. Alamo

　　题中所有的选择都是美国的汽车出租公司（car rental company），不同的是U-Haul、Ryder、Penske出租的是专门用来搬家（moving）和货运用的货车（trucks）。租金一般从一天20美元起，根据车型大小而异，通常不以里程计费（free mileage），用完之后，可以还回到新驻地附近的同一公司，这些公司还提供付费的包装纸盒（packing boxes）。Alamo是轿车、面包车/商务车（van）、小型卡车（small trcuk）等日用车的出租公司。其他类似的出租公司有：Hertz、Enterprise Rent a Car、Thrifty、Dollar、Hotwire。用有英文的中国驾照就可以租车，与搬家车出租一样，用完后可以将车还到同一公司的任何出租店，十分便利，保险（insurance）费用也不高。开走之前要仔细检查一下车的状况，还车之前加满油（fill up the tank）。现在很多在网上订飞机票的公司都把飞机订票、旅馆订房及租车合为一体。有这类公司中较好的有：hotwire.com、Kayak.com、Vayama.com、BookingBuddy.com。较有名的网上旅馆订房公司有airbnb.com和hotel.com。hotel.com也提供打包服务（packages），如订飞机票、租车、订房间的度假套餐（vacation Packages）。如果你订满十间房还可以免费住一间房。有不少旅行社提供廉价机票，如Student universe，Scott's cheep flights等。另外，很多公司时不时有促销活动（promotion），所以在不同的时间查看不同的公司网站，说不准能幸运地找到廉价机票或最划算的租车或旅店的价格。

48. Which of the following beverages usually does not contain alcohol?

A. Soda

B. Beer

C. Champion

D. Red wine

问题：哪种饮料通常不含酒精？

答案：A. 苏打水

单词beverage（饮料）指 any drink, usually other than water or any drinkable liquid, 即指任何饮料液体，通常不包括饮用水。alcohol（酒类）：white wine（白酒）、red wine（红葡萄酒）、champion（香槟）、bear（啤酒）、fizz（发泡性饮料，特指香槟酒）等。soft drinks（软饮料）与酒类饮料（hard drink）相对，一般没有酒精含量：如压榨水果/果汁（fruit crush/juice）：orange juice（橙汁）、apple juice/cider/cyder（苹果汁）、tomato juice（番茄汁）、fruit punch（果汁饮料）、smoothie：a thick smooth drink consisting of fresh fruit pureed with ice cream or yoghurt or milk（用新鲜水果加冰淇淋或酸奶或牛奶打碎搅拌做成的冰沙饮料）。其他的软饮料有：Coca-Cola（可口可乐）、Sprite（雪碧）、Diet coke（健怡可口可乐）、Pepsi（百事可乐）、Dr Pepper（胡椒博士）、ginger ale（姜汁汽水）、tea（茶）、coffee（咖啡）、fizzy drink（碳酸饮料）、lolly water（冰棍水）、soda/soda pop（苏打水）、tonic（奎宁水、滋补饮料）和mineral（矿泉水）。美国人喝饮料往往加冰块（with ice cubs）。近年来，由于对身体健康的关注，越来越多的人选择矿泉水和果汁而取代人为加工而且多糖的饮料，如可乐、雪碧等。与drink有关的语句有：Could I buy you a drink?（请你喝一杯?）I'll drink to that.（我同意你的意见。）Let us drink to Becky's new job.（让我们为贝基的新工作干一杯。）

49. Which of the following is not normally related to "a physical"?

A. Take CAT scan/MRI.

B. Measure blood pressure.

C. Do blood work.

D. Take X-ray.

问题：以下哪一项通常与"体检"无关?

答案：A. 做CAT扫描/MRI磁共振成像

在美国，每年一度的身体检查（take physical exam）都是在自己的私人医生诊所做的。一般都包括量体重（measure weight）、量血压（take/measure blood pressure）、常规验血（do blood work）、尿检（take urine sample）、听听心肺（listen to heart and lungs）、做心电图（electrocardiogram-ECG）等。照X光（X-ray）虽不是一般年检的项目，但是学校的新生体检一定要做X光检查，看是否有肺结核病（tuberculosis -TB）。而CAT Scan（CT扫描）和MRI-magnetic resonance imaging（磁共振成像）只是在某些疾病诊断时做的检查，不在体检项目之内。定期的乳腺癌检查（breast cancer screening）也要到医院和专门的诊所去做。大部分的私人诊所不能做常规验血和尿检，所以都得去验血中心（Lab Center）做。一般的验血都在早上和上午，要求不吃早餐。中心的医务人员都会问你，早上没有吃东西吧？（Are you fasting?）去的时候要带上医生开的处方、医疗保险卡（medical insurance card）、驾照（drive license）或其他身份证（ID）及信用卡（credit card）。首先到窗口签到，如是第一次去，要填好几页的注册表。上面要填上你的医生姓名、医疗保险卡的信息、自己的病史、身体状况、用药情况等。医务人员在你注册时会反复核对你的身份。抽血之前还会核对你的姓名和出生日期。检查结果会直接送到你的医生诊所。

50. Which is not a cooking utensil for preparing Chinese food?

A. Cutting board

B. Turner

C. Can opener

D. Salad bowls

问题：以下用具中哪个不是做中国餐用的炊具？
答案：D. 沙拉碗

在选择的答案中，D. 沙拉碗（salad bowls）不是烹饪（culinary）中国饭菜用的炊具（cooking utensil）。西餐中，沙拉是不可少的一道菜。它是由不同种类的蔬菜洗净混合而成，吃的时候再按各自的喜爱淋上配汁沙拉酱（dressing）。在开招待会（reception）或聚会时，也常配有很多的（salad bowls）。西方人做饭基本上不会炒菜（fry），蔬菜就会生吃或水煮（cook），肉食就靠烘（bake）和烧烤（grill）等。而中国的烹饪花样繁多，有：煮（boiled）、蒸（steamed）、炖（braised）、溜（leavened）、焖（stew）、红烧（fried）、清炖（stewed）、烧（roast）、烤（baking）等。通常东西方烹饪都用的炊具有：菜刀（kitchen knife）、菜板（cutting board）、锅铲（turner）、开罐器（can opener）、高压锅（pressure cooker）、开瓶器（bottle opener）等。西方人做饭用平底锅（pans）而中国人用炒菜锅（Chinese Wok）。现在多用电饭煲（rice cooker）煮饭，用慢炖锅（slow cooker）煮粥炖肉。用于烹饪菜肴的厨具（cookware）还有：肉叉（meat fork）、量杯（measuring cups）、量匙（measuring spoons）、食品加工器（food processor）、钳（tongs）、开槽锅铲（slotted turner）、壶（pots）、刨皮器（peeler）、打蛋器（whisk）、瓢（ladle）、切碎机（copper）等。常用的佐料有：盐（salt）、糖（sugar）、冰糖（sugar）、黄糖（brown sugar）、酱油（soy sauce）、醋（vinegar）、料酒（cooking wine）、豆豉（fermented soybeans）、姜（ginger）、蒜（garlic）、蒜头（garlic）、八角（star anise）、茴香（fennel）、紫苑（asters）、香菜（parsley）、辣椒（hot pepper）、花椒（Sichuan pepper）等。

References
参考文献

1. Broukal, M. (1994). *Idioms for Everyday Use.* National Textbook Company.

2. Celce-Murcia, M. , Brinton, D. & Goodwin, J. M. (2010). *Teaching Pronunciation Paperback with Audio CDs (2): A Course Book and Reference Guide 2nd Edition*. Cambridge UP.

3. Celce-Murcia, M. & Diane Larsen-Freeman, D. (1999, 2nd Ed.) *The Grammar Book: An ESL/ EFL Teacher's Course*. Heinle and Neinle.

4. Cowan, R. (2008). *The Teacher's Grammar of English: A Course Book and Reference Guide*. Cambridge UP.

5. Craig, R. P. & Hooper, V. F (1986). *1001 Pitfalls in English Grammar. Barraon's Educational Serious*. Longman.

6. *English-Chinese Dictionary*. (2002). 2nd edition, Longman.

7. Freeman, D.E. & Freeman, Y. S. (2004). *Essential Linguistics: What You Need to Know to Teach Reading, ESL, Spelling, Phonics, and Grammar*. Heinemann.

8. Liu, D. (2008). *Idioms: Description, Comprehension, Acquisition, and Pedagogy/Edition 1*. Taylor & Francis.

9. Liu, D. (2013). *Describing and Explaining Grammar and Vocabulary in ELT: Key Theories and Effective Practices*. Taylor & Francis.

10. *Longman Dictionary of Contemporary English(English-Chinese)*. (2003). Longman.

11. Makkai, A., Boatner, M.T., & Gates, J. E. (1995). *A Dictionary of American Idioms, 3rd. edition*. Barron's.

12. O'Dell, F. & McCarthy, M. (2008). *English Collocations in Use*. Cambridge University Press.

13. *Oxford American Wordpower Dictionary for Learners of English*. (2000). Oxford University Press.

14. *Oxford Collocations Dictionary for Students of English*. (2002). Oxford University Press.

15. *Oxford Dictionary of American English*. (2005). Oxford University Press.

16. *Oxford Phrasal Verbs*. (2001). Oxford University Press.

17. Peter, A. & Ehrlich, S. (1992). *Teaching American English Pronunciation*. Oxford UP.

18. Scragg, D. G. (2011). *A History of English Spelling*. Manchester University.

19. Swan, M. (2005). *Practical English Usage*. Oxford University Press.

20. Swick, E. (1999). *American Idioms and Some Phrases Just for Fun*. Barran's.

21. Terban, M. (1996). *Scholastic Dictionary of Idioms*. Scholastic Inc.

22. 伍毅强. 英语最常用词汇用法范例 [M]. 厦门：厦门大学出版社，2016.

23. 伍毅强，刘福英，任彤. 美国校园英语交流突破 [M]. 长沙：湖南师范大学出版社，2017.

24. Wu, Y. & Liaw, M. (2002). *How to Teach English to Chinese Effectively*. Asian Publisher.

25. Young, S. (1994). *Scholastic Rhyming Dictionary*. Scholastic Inc.

26. http://baby-names.familyeducation.com/popular-names/girls/#ixzz3TiP7mwFo.

27. http://colleges.usnews.rankingsandreviews.com/best-colleges.

28. http://en.wikipedia.org/wiki/American_and_British_English_spelling_differences.

29. http://en.wikipedia.org/wiki/Main_Page.

30. http://en.wikipedia.org/wiki/TV_Guide%27s_50_Greatest_TV_Shows_of_All_Time.

31. http://englishgenie.com/vocabulary/the-top-100-most-common-adjectives/.

32. http://grad-schools.usnews.rankingsandreviews.com/best-graduate-schools.

33. http://grammar.yourdictionary.com/spelling-and-word-lists/150more.html.

34. http://quizlet.com/14590452/popular-american-proverbs-flash-cards/.

35. http://quotesmin.com/American-proverb.php/.

36. http://travel.cnn.com/explorations/eat/best-usa-travel/top-50-american-foods-513946.

37. http://www.amtrak.com/home.

38. http://www.broadway.com/.

39. http://www.buzzfeed.com/alejandroalba/extreme-outdoor-activities-to-try-before-you-die#.uk6Jab9z9.

40. http://www.cbp.gov/travel/us-citizens/sample-declaration-form.

41. http://www.claremontmckenna.edu/pages/faculty/alee/extra/American_values.html.

42. http://www.fodors.com/news/photos/10-best-surfing-spots-in-the-us#!1-intro.

43. http://www.fun-with-words.com/palin_example.html.

44. http://www.goenglish.com/Index.asp.

45. http://www.iciba.com/.

46. http://www.movieinsider.com/.

47. http://www.nytimes.com/best-sellers-books/.

48. http://www.parks.ca.gov/?page_id=531.

49. http://www.phrases.org.uk/meanings/american-phrases-and-sayings.html.

50. http://www.ranker.com/list/the-best-museums-in-the-united-states/nychick.

51. http://www.realsimple.com/food-recipes/recipe-collections-favorites/american-recipes-00000000061159/.

52. http://www.smart-words.org/list-of-synonyms/.

53. http://www.TheFreeDictionary.com/.

54. http://www.timeanddate.com/holidays/us/2016.

55. http://www.urbandictionary.com/.

56. http://www.usingenglish.com/.

57. http://www.usnews.com/education/best-high-schools/rankings-overview.

58. https://en.wikipedia.org/wiki/Academic_regalia_in_the_United_States.

59. https://web.cn.edu/kwheeler/English_hard_2learn.html.

60. https://www.turtlediary.com/.

61. www.apastyle.apa.org/.

62. www.apastyle.org/learn/tutorials/basics-tutorial.aspx.

63. www.easybib.com/.

64. www.easybib.com/.

65. www2.lib.unc.edu/instruct/citations/index.html？section=aa&page=1>.

66. www.eazypaper.com/index.cfm/www.refpt.net/.

67. www.liu.edu/cwis/cwp/library/workshop/citapa.htm.

68. www.nick.com/games/.

69. www.nickjr.com/games/.

70. www.owl.english.purdue.edu/owl/resource/560/01/.

图书在版编目（CIP）数据

美国语言文化知识必备 / 伍毅强主编. --长沙：湖南师范大学出版社，2018.12
ISBN 978-7-5648-3419-7

Ⅰ.①美… Ⅱ.①伍… Ⅲ.①留学生－学生生活－美国 Ⅳ.①G649.712

中国版本图书馆CIP数据核字(2018)第245666号

Essentials of American English and Culture
美国语言文化知识必备

主　编：伍毅强
副主编：任　彤

责任编辑｜庄习文　廖小刚
责任校对｜皇孟孟　杨　洁

出版发行｜湖南师范大学出版社
　　　　　地址：长沙市岳麓山　邮编：410081
　　　　　电话：0731-88853867　88872751
　　　　　传真：0731-88872636
　　　　　网址：www. hunnu. edu. cn/ press
经　　销｜湖南省新华书店
印　　刷｜湖南天闻新华印务有限公司

开　　本｜787 mm×1092 mm　　1/16
印　　张｜18
字　　数｜456千字
版　　次｜2018年12月第1版第1次印刷
书　　号｜ISBN 978-7-5648-3419-7

定　　价｜58.00元

图书出现印装问题，请与经销商调换